PERFORMANCE MEASUREMENT AND MANAGEMENT CONTROL: A COMPENDIUM OF RESEARCH

STUDIES IN MANAGERIAL AND FINANCIAL ACCOUNTING

Series Editor: Marc J. Epstein

STUDIES IN MANAGERIAL AND FINANCIAL ACCOUNTING
VOLUME 12

PERFORMANCE MEASUREMENT AND MANAGEMENT CONTROL: A COMPENDIUM OF RESEARCH

EDITED BY

MARC J. EPSTEIN

*Jesse H. Jones Graduate School of Management,
Rice University, Texas, USA*

JEAN-FRANÇOIS MANZONI

INSEAD, Fontainebleau, France

2002

JAI
An Imprint of Elsevier Science

Amsterdam – Boston – London – New York – Oxford – Paris
San Diego – San Francisco – Singapore – Sydney – Tokyo

ELSEVIER SCIENCE Ltd
The Boulevard, Langford Lane
Kidlington, Oxford OX5 1GB, UK

First edition 2002

Library of Congress Cataloging in Publication Data
A catalog record from the Library of Congress has been applied for.

British Library Cataloguing in Publication Data
A catalogue record from the British Library has been applied for.

ISBN: 0-7623-0867-2

∞ The paper used in this publication meets the requirements of ANSI/NISO Z39.48-1992 (Permanence of Paper).
Printed in The Netherlands.

CONTENTS

LIST OF CONTRIBUTORS

Lars-Göran Aidemark	Växjö University, Växjö, Sweden
Stefano Baraldi	Università Cattolica di Milano, Milan, Italy
Lars Bengtsson	University of Gävle, Gävle, Sweden
J. Bilderbeek	University of Twente, Enschede, The Netherlands
Emilio Boulianne	John Molson School of Business, Concordia University, Montreal, Quebec, Canada
X. Q. Cao	University of Twente, Enschede, The Netherlands
Lai Hong Chung	Nanyang Technological University, Singapore
Martine Cools	UA University, Antwerp, Belgium
Mandar Dabhilakar	University of Gävle, Gävle, Sweden
Marc J. Epstein	Rice University, Houston, Texas, USA
Mark L. Frigo	DePaul University, Chicago, Illinois, USA

Ingmar Gehrke	ESSEC Business School, Cergy-Pontoise, France
Patrick T. Gibbons	University College, Dublin, Ireland
Péter Horváth	University of Stuttgart, Stuttgart, Germany
John Innes	University of Dundee, Dundee, UK
Paolo Maccarrone	Politecnico di Milano, Milano, Italy
Jean-François Manzoni	INSEAD, Fontainebleau, France
Carla Mendoza	ESCP-EAP, Paris, France
Belverd E. Needles, Jr.	DePaul University, Chicago, Illinois, USA
Gweneth Norris	Deakin University, Australia
Marian Powers	Northwestern University, Evanston, Illinois, USA
Gavin C. Reid	University of St. Andrews, Scotland, UK
Barbara Sainty	Brock University, St. Catharines, Ontario, Canada
Olivier Saulpic	ESCP-EAP, Paris, France

Herbert P. Schoch   Macquarie University,
                               New South Wales, Australia

Julia A. Smith   Cardiff Business School,
                               Cardiff, UK

INTRODUCTION

EDHEC Business School is deeply involved in management control research, and more specifically in the field of performance measurement and strategy implementation. So in October 4–5, 2001, we were particularly proud to host a *Workshop on performance measurement and management control* in our Nice Campus in France. This book is the result of the various presentations and discussions made during this conference, and we are also proud today for this realisation.

In participating in this kind of event and publication, along with the European Institute for Advanced Studies in Management (EIASM), whose quality and results in the area of international research are well-known, EDHEC Business School aims to contribute actively toward the production and development of the main principles of management for the benefits of business, and thereby to amply fulfil our role on research, which is, in my view, inseparable from our missions.

I would like to thank all those who have collaborated to assure the success of this event and the realisation of this book, particularly Professor Marc Epstein and Professor Jean-François Manzoni as editors of this book and invited speakers during the workshop. I would like also to thank Professor Eric Cauvin and Professor Pierre-Laurent Bescos for the organization of the workshop.

Olivier Oger
EDHEC Business School Dean
(Lille and Nice Campus, France – www.edhec.com)

PREFACE

The fields of performance measurement and management control have changed dramatically in recent years. Industry has recognized the importance of the implementation of strategy and the coordination of strategy with organizational structure, management systems, and managerial behavior. Companies are examining alternative ways to improve management and corporate performance. They are looking to various tools and strategic management systems to provide significant improvements. Stretch budgets and targets, along with various performance incentive systems, are being used to motivate performance, evaluate performance, and control behavior. Managers as well as researchers are attempting to find better ways to link performance metrics to strategy through systems like balanced scorecard and shareholder value analysis and to drive improved corporate performance.

There are, also, several unresolved issues. For example, we are still struggling with understanding the drivers of corporate performance, the linkages between them, and how to measure their impacts on profitability. We also need to better understand the conditions under which various performance measurement and management control systems are more or less effective, how they fit with alternative organizational structures and strategies, and the causes of their successes and failures.

This book contains a compendium of some of the excellent papers presented at a workshop on Performance Measurement and Management Control in October, 2001. Sponsored by the European Institute for the Advanced Study in Management (EIASM) and held in Nice, France on the campus of EDHEC School of Management, this workshop attracted leading scholars on management control and performance measurement from around the world. We were privileged to provide invited plenary addresses to the workshop and were involved in the selection of the papers that were presented at the conference. The call for papers drew a response far higher than anticipated and thus the competition to make a presentation at the conference was quite high. Further, given the space limitations in this book, another competitive selection was required. The contents of this book represent a collection of leading research in management control and performance measurement and provide a significant contribution to the growing literature in the area.

New frameworks for management control and the implementation of strategy in organizations have been developed in recent years and been widely adopted by managers. But, in many cases, the effect on performance of these new approaches is unclear. Research is necessary to determine how the use of various strategies, structures, and systems impact ultimate corporate performance.

The papers in this volume address this question using a variety of research methods. Experimental, analytical, empirical, and field studies are all used to explain how management control and performance measurement can aid in the implementation of strategy and the improvement of organizational performance. The approaches are used in both for-profit and not-for-profit organizations.

The answers are not yet clear. But it is hoped that the papers included in this volume contribute to this growing body of knowledge and lead us to an improved understanding of how to build better organizations and evaluate and understand their performance.

The workshop owes its success to numerous individuals and institutions. Their superb support and assistance is greatly appreciated. Among those who contributed significantly are Graciella Michelante, Katrin Stichtenoth, and Gerry Van Dyck at EIASM and Pierre-Laurent Bescos, Eric Cauvin, and Olivier Oger at EDHEC School of Management. Finally, we want to thank the speakers and participants in the workshop. Their attendance and enthusiastic participation made the workshop an enjoyable learning experience. We are hopeful that this book will continue the search for additional understanding and development in performance measurement and management control, and provide guidance for both academics and managers as they work toward improving organizational performance.

Marc J. Epstein and Jean-François Manzoni
Editors

PART I:
A NEW DIRECTION IN
MANAGEMENT CONTROL AND
PERFORMANCE EVALUATION

MEASURING THE PAYOFFS OF CORPORATE ACTIONS: THE USE OF FINANCIAL AND NON-FINANCIAL INDICATORS

Marc J. Epstein

ABSTRACT

With increased attention on the drivers of corporate profitability and new approaches to the measurement of organizational performance, managers and academics alike are beginning to focus on the causal relationships that are critical to improving performance. Though approaches such as balanced scorecard and shareholder value analysis do provide frameworks for analysis and management, increased specificity is necessary to model, measure, and manage the organizational links that operationalize these approaches. This paper provides a discussion of both the academic models and the managerial applications of the analysis and measurement of causal relationships and the measurement of payoffs of corporate actions, and provides suggestions for research needs in management control and performance measurement.

Performance Measurement and Management Control, Volume 12, pages 3–13.

INTRODUCTION

Management control researchers have long proposed that by aligning strategy, structure, and systems, organizational performance should improve. This proposition is at the heart of management control and performance measurement. But, though there has been substantial research, little conclusive evidence exists to guide managers in the implementation of strategy.

To adequately guide resource allocation decisions, managers need to know the likely payoffs of alternative corporate actions. Thus, the identification and measurement of the causal relationships in organizations is necessary to test the efficacy of management structure and system designs and the new approaches that have been developed for the implementation of strategy and the measurement of performance. This is critical both for improving the effectiveness of managerial practices and for academic research to test the most basic tenets of management control and performance measurement.

At this workshop on management control and performance measurement, a significant number of papers were presented on the balanced scorecard and value based management. Senior corporate managers have suggested that among their most important concerns are customer focus and shareholder value; they want to become more customer-focused and generate more shareholder value. But how does an organization become more customer- focused or drive the creation of shareholder value?

In principle, the field we call management control is centered on concentrating managers' attention to drive the corporate focus in some direction(s). But both academics and managers want to know what specific mechanisms can be used to improve performance. In this paper I want to examine the actions that managers can take to improve performance and how they can measure the success of those actions. To do this, we will examine:

(1) what some companies are trying to do to identify and measure the payoffs of various corporate actions using both financial and non-financial measures of performance;
(2) look at some theoretical models that have been developed and some limited corporate experience in the application and testing of those models; and
(3) provide some suggestions on research that is needed to further develop the academic disciplines of management control and performance measurement.

These questions are at the heart of management control and performance measurement. Both academic researchers and practicing managers need to better understand what structures and systems can be used to improve performance and when, if, and how they should be used and how much they pay off in improved corporate performance.

MODELING AND MEASURING CAUSAL RELATIONSHIPS AND PERFORMANCE

Let me first provide two short stories as background. Both occurred three years ago. First I was asked to give a presentation to about 100 R&D senior managers involved in new product development. As I was preparing for the presentation and examining both the academic and managerial literature, I realized there has been very little written on the subject of measuring performance in new product development. So I decided to discuss it with the specialists. Each of the participants managed R&D budgets in the billions of dollars and it seemed that they should and would have measures to assess how well they spend their money and the payoffs of their expenditures. Well, they don't! They can't predict success early on, nor can they predict how to adjust inputs to increase the likelihood of success. The input, process, output, and outcome measures were either poor or nonexistent. As academics in the field of management control and performance measurement, we have provided little guidance to these managers.

At about the same time I was asked to give a presentation in Italy on Balanced Scorecard and customer profitability. In preparation for the presentation I read the work of leading academics in customer satisfaction and employee satisfaction. This includes work in the marketing literature on the service profit chain suggesting that employee satisfaction leads to improved customer service, satisfaction, and retention which then leads to greater profitability (Heskett et al., 1994). Likewise, work by academics in human resources maintains that employee satisfaction does pay off in improved profitability. (See for example Pfeffer (1998). But, though there are numerous anecdotes to support these suggestions, there is little significant evidence and few measures that informs us if, when, or how employee satisfaction will improve customer satisfaction and ultimately lead to improved profitability. Further, management control researchers have yet to provide data as to the success of various management control tools and when and if they provide the promised benefits. Researchers tend to use relatively weak measures and as a result have an equally poor understanding of cause-effect relationships.

Similarly, a large number of articles have been written on the concept of Balanced Scorecard (BSC) (See for examples Kaplan & Norton, 1992, 1993, 1996; Epstein & Manzoni, 1998). The value of the BSC is predicated on the idea that better alignment between the firm's strategy and its performance measures leads to better performance. But do we really know this proposition to be true? We have some interesting cases, we have suggestive strategy maps, but we don't really have much conclusive scientific evidence.

Simons' (1995) excellent work on balancing empowerment and control suggests that coordinated usage of the right interactive, boundary, diagnostic, and belief systems should lead to improved performance. But here again, we have limited conclusive evidence supporting this proposition.

In *Counting What Counts: Turning Corporate Accountability to Competitive Advantage*, Epstein and Birchard (1999) propose that corporate performance can be enhanced through four elements of accountability. This includes improved corporate governance, a broader set of financial, operational, and social measures of performance, an integrated system of internal and external reporting, and an effective management control system to drive this through the organization. As with other approaches, they suggest that companies adopt a broader set of non-financial measures of performance and the use of more leading indicators of performance to supplement the historical measures currently used. But, again, there is limited scientific evidence that this indeed does produce higher levels of performance.

So, really, what actions should managers take to improve long term corporate profitability? This question is at the core of strategy implementation, management control, and managerial effectiveness. The BSC provides a framework to translate a strategy into operational terms and is based on four perspectives (financial, internal business process, customer, and learning) that are all linked to strategy. But, unless companies clearly understand the causal relationships underlying the primary drivers of value in their organization, the effectiveness of the balanced scorecard is limited. Thus, we need to identify and measure these linkages to improve the effectiveness of management decisions and to concretely understand the actions that managers should take to improve that effectiveness and the likely payoffs of those actions.

MANAGERIAL APPROACHES

Recently some companies have been trying to better identify and measure the causal links between actions (inputs and processes), outputs, and outcomes. Most of these efforts have occurred in selected business units and functions with partial models and were not necessarily driven throughout the organizations. Kaplan and Norton discuss numerous cases of balanced scorecard implementations that began in an organizational unit (such as Mobil Oil United States Marketing and Refining) rather than from corporate headquarters (Kaplan & Norton, 2001). The Swedish based global insurance company

Skandia developed a balanced scorecard type model that is focused on the management of intellectual capital (Edvinsson & Malone, 1997).

U.S. based retailer Sears Roebuck has developed a model that tries to focus on the causal linkages that are central to the concept of the balanced scorecard. Relying primarily on the service profit chain model, the company examined the link between employee satisfaction, customer satisfaction, and corporate profitability. Sears was facing a severe crisis and a critical piece of the recovery plan designed by top management involved making Sears a great place to work, shop, and invest. To support this process, the company developed an approach to carefully identify and measure the drivers of profitability and the links between employee attitudes, customer satisfaction, and store performance.

In a recently documented case (Datar, Epstein & Cott, 2001), Verizon Communications, the giant telecommunications company, developed a human resources balanced scorecard to help them identify and measure the causal relationships between actions in human resources and business units and functions throughout the company. Among other investments, the company was spending $75 million per year on training. Managers wanted to know how effective this investment was. Do staff members learn from this training? Does this learning translate into superior corporate performance? Overall, is the company receiving value for this investment? Does the current training provide the skills that are necessary for the company presently and likely to be needed in the future?

Most companies (and universities) have very poor data on the effectiveness of education and learning. Training may, or may not benefit employees. It could benefit employees but not the corporation. Further, which type of training provides the greatest benefits? Which employee training programs provide the greatest corporate benefits? Verizon was also interested in better understanding the value of other human resource activities. A better understanding of the causal relationships could aid other managers, for example, in making critical decisions and taking actions on items such as corporate downsizing. The cost of recruitment, retention, termination, retraining, etc are all critical to making decisions as to whether companies downsize or retain existing employees during difficult economic environments.

Shell Oil has also been working on understanding causal relationships. In this case, Shell created a model to better understand the payoffs from invest-ments in social and environmental responsibility. The company is now working on developing both the organizational structure and the management control and performance measurement systems that are necessary to implement this model and drive it throughout the organization. If a company wants to drive managerial sensitivity and actions aimed at increased social and environmental responsibility, the strategy and the various systems (including performance measurement and compensation systems) must be aligned.

ACADEMIC APPROACHES

In addition to the company experiments, there has been some academic and managerial literature aimed at modeling relationships and understanding the drivers of value. These academic approaches include: the Service Profit Chain model, the Return on Quality framework, the Balanced Scorecard, and Customer Profitability Analysis. These four approaches have all provided some guidance to the drivers of value in organizations but lack the specificity that is necessary to identify and measure the causal relationships that is necessary to make these models fully operational. In addition, though the models are valuable, these approaches have generally not been tested to determine where and when they do actually drive improved performance. (See Epstein & Westbrook, 2001; Epstein, Kumar & Westbrook, 2000) for discussions of each of these approaches and a review of related academic literature.)

The questions that academic researchers are asking are the same as both corporate managers and external financial analysts ask: (1) What are the drivers of value? (2) How can companies increase corporate value? (3) What are the specific actions that managers can take to improve value? (4) What are the payoffs of various corporate actions? It seems that if researchers in management control and performance measurement would focus more attention on these questions, both the academic and managerial literature would be significantly improved. Further, they would better understand the organizational structures and systems that could be used and managerial actions that could be taken to improve corporate performance.

From a research perspective, the question can be stated as: How do we get from strategy development to superior financial performance? In particular, does the alignment of strategy, structure, and systems improve organizational performance? Though some analysis has been completed, very little managerial or academic work goes all the way from strategy to the specific managerial actions to implement strategy to financial performance. Marketing researchers have focused on increasing customer satisfaction but have done little research on either the antecedents or consequences of customer satisfaction. Unless the customer satisfaction translates to increased corporate profitability, the value of the investment in that satisfaction is questionable. Researchers in human resources focus on improving employee satisfaction but we have limited scientific evidence that increasing employee satisfaction necessarily improves either employee productivity or organizational performance, and limited scientific basis on which to make decisions and investments on the various trade-offs and resource allocations that must be made.

ACTION-PROFIT-LINKAGE MODEL

It is these concerns that led us to develop the Action-Profit Linkage (APL) Model. The APL model provides guidance on the identification and measurement of causal relationships. It helps to provide additional specificity on the drivers and payoffs of actions. Finally, it provides a model for testing the success of individual managerial actions. From a research perspective it provides a model that can be tested to determine: (1) whether various managerial actions do lead to improved performance, and (2) whether specific strategies, structures or management control systems improve performance. Generally, the model provides an approach to identify and measure the drivers of performance and causal relationships going from corporate strategy to various corporate actions that can be taken throughout organizations. It then looks at the impact of those actions on the delivered product or service, customer actions, the economic impact of those actions, and ultimately customer and corporate profitability. This comprehensive approach can be used to help operationalize various other approaches including the balanced scorecard. (For more information about the Action-Profit-Linkage model see Epstein & Westbrook, 2001; Epstein, Kumar & Westbrook, 2000).

Epstein and Westbrook (2001) provide descriptions of two company approaches to identifying and measuring causal relationships. Browning Ferris Industries (BFI) (the large, global trash hauler) and Canadian Imperial Bank of Commerce have both seen significant increases in profitability through actions taken as a result of this better understanding of causal relationships and the application of these models. Other academic research into causal relationships also shows promise.

Building on the APL, Epstein and Roy (2001) have developed a model of the drivers of corporate sustainability and sustainability action measures that can be used to measure these variables and relationships. Bagozzi, Epstein, and Wisner (2001) developed a theoretical management control performance model and have tested it with a set of data of U.S. corporations. It examines the specific management control system mechanisms that can be used to improve both environmental and financial performance. There has not been much prior research on the links from management control systems to environmental performance (or the effect on performance generally). There has also been little previous scientific work on the links from environmental performance to financial performance. Without understanding these relationships, companies

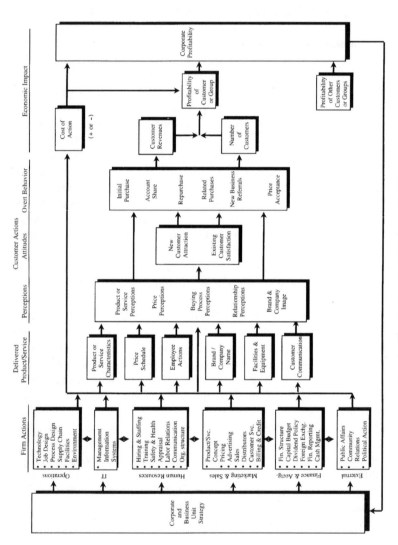

Fig. 1. The Action Profit-Linkage Model.

Source: Epstein, Kumar and Westbrook (2000).

cannot effectively make decisions about the effectiveness of environmental investments.

We are also looking to apply this model in other academic areas of research and managerial settings. To do this, we are currently working on better understanding the payoffs of managerial actions and the effectiveness of management control systems in areas such as new product development and innovation, information technology, supply chain management, corporate government affairs, and post merger integration. For example, what are the management control systems that can be used to drive increased innovation in organizations? Why is it that so many mergers fail to deliver on their promises? It is likely that management control has a central role to play in the conversion of potential value to improved performance.

Verizon managers needed to do a better job articulating and demonstrating the value they create. But, first they needed to be able to identify and measure how they create value. Similarly, information technology managers often complain that the organization sees them as cost centers rather than value creating centers. An approach to better measure these relationships can provide functional managers with the information to demonstrate their value to the organization. Researchers in management control should be able to provide better guidance to merger candidates as to the structures, systems, and actions that they need to put into place to successfully integrate two companies.

DIRECTIONS FOR FUTURE RESEARCH

There is a significant role for academics in improving organizational performance and improving our understanding of organizational relationships. There is substantial work that is needed to improve both the research and managerial practice in management control and performance measurement. Among these needs are:

(1) Further specification and testing of the model:

   (a) Specification of the model requires substantial examination of the drivers of value in organizations and the careful identification and measurement of the causal relationships that are critical to drive that value. Thus, further development of new models can be completed and further specification of existing models needs to done.
   (b) Testing of the various models is critical to the understanding of the success and potential for success of management control and performance measurement systems. Existing models must be tested to

determine if they produce improved results and, if so, when, how, under what conditions, how long does it take to produce results, etc. Among the research that could be conducted would be: I) cross sectional designs (types of companies and decision contexts where these models are more successful in producing improved performance), II) longitudinal designs (what are the lag times in producing results and how do the causal linkages evolve over time in organizations), and III) what is the profitability of various firm actions across decisions contexts. The development of empirical generalizations and the development of taxonomies would both be very useful in a research context.

(2) Development and testing of inter-disciplinary measures

  (a) There is a need for developing improved financial and non-financial measures of performance. Both academics and managers maintain that one of the primary impediments to understanding the drivers of value is the lack of good measures of performance and measures of these causal links. The development of reliable measures would be a significant advancement in this area.
  (b) The reliability of the measures can only be determined through substantial testing. Do these measures really describe the performance of these drivers and the significance of these relationships? Substantial empirical work is necessary to determine the reliability of these measures.
  (c) A standardized set of measures must then be developed. Then, measures can be mapped to various decision contexts.

(3) Improvement in the implementation of strategy

  (a) Testing the impact of adoption of APL or BSC models on management effectiveness;
  (b) Testing the effectiveness of APL models in improving the understanding and managing of drivers of costs in Activity-Based Costing;
  (c) Testing the impact of APL models on the effectiveness of Balanced Scorecard implementation(s);
  (d) Testing the impact of APL models on specification of the drivers, linkages, and perspectives in the Balanced Scorecard;
  (e) Testing the impact of APL models on the acceleration of organizational learning.

These research questions are aimed at determining: (1) The specific actions that managers can take to improve performance; (2) When specific strategies, structures, and management control systems work better than others, and (3) The payoffs of various managerial actions and clear measurements of those payoffs. It is only with significant increased research and implementations can we determine how management control and performance measurement systems can improve organizational performance.

REFERENCES

Bagozzi, R. P., Epstein, M. J., & Wisner, P. S. (2001). Evidence of the Influence of Management Control Systems on Environmental and Financial Performance (Working paper).

Datar, S., Epstein, M. J., & Cott, J. (2001). Verizon Communications, Inc.: Implementing a Human Resources Balanced Scorecard, *Harvard Business School Case, 9*, 101–102.

Edvinsson, L., & Malone, M. S. (1997). *Intellectual Capital: Realizing Your Company's True Value by Finding Its Hidden Roots.* New York, NY: HarperCollins.

Epstein, M. J., & Birchard, B. (1999). *Counting What Counts: Turning Corporate Accountability to Competitive Advantage.* Reading, MA: Perseus Books.

Epstein, M. J., Kumar, P., & Westbrook, R. (2000). The Drivers of Customer and Corporate Profitability: Modeling, Measuring, and Managing the Causal Relationships, *Advances in Management Accounting.*

Epstein, M. J., & Manzoni, J.-F. (1998). Implementing Corporate Strategy: From Tableaux de Bord to Balanced Scorecard, *European Management Journal.*

Epstein, M. J., & Roy, M.-J. (2001). Sustainability in Action: Identifying and Measuring the Key Performance Drivers. *LRP: Long Range Planning* (October).

Epstein, M. J., & Westbrook, R. (2001). Linking Action to Profits in Strategic Decision Making, *MIT Sloan Management Review*, 39–49.

Heskett, J. L., Jones, T. O., Loveman, G. W., Sasser Jr., W. E., & Schlesinger, L. A. (1994). Putting the service-profit chain to work. *Harvard Business Review* (March/April).

Kaplan, R. S., & Norton, D. P. (1992). The balanced scorecard – Measures that drive performances. *Harvard Business*, Review, 71–79.

Kaplan, R. S., & Norton, D. P. (1993). Putting the balanced scorecard to work. *Harvard Business Review*, 134–147.

Kaplan, R. S., & Norton, D. P. (1996). Using the balanced scorecard as a strategic management system. *Harvard Business Review, 74*(1), 75–85.

Kaplan, R. S., & Norton, D. P. (2001). *The Strategy-Focused Organization: How Balanced Scorecard Companies Thrive in the New Business Environment.* Boston, MA.: Harvard Business School Press.

Pfeffer, J. (1998). *The Human Equation: Building Profits by Putting People First.* Boston, MA: Harvard Business School Press.

Rucci, A. J., Kim, S. P., & Quinn, R. T. (1998). The Employee-Customer-Profit Chain at Sears. *Havard Business Review, 76*, 83–97.

Simons, R. (1995). *Levers of Control: How Managers Use Innovative Control Systems to Drive Strategic Renewal.* Boston: Harvard Business School Press.

MANAGEMENT CONTROL: TOWARD A NEW PARADIGM?

Jean-François Manzoni

ABSTRACT

This chapter gathers some humble thoughts from a researcher initially trained in Management Control, returning to this field after a few years working closely with managers on organizational (rather than accounting) issues. These humble remarks are divided into four sections: (1) Opaqueness by design, or "why most bosses really prefer not to have clear, transparent accounting systems". (2) Five reasons why the RAPM literature cannot succeed using the methods and approach that have prevailed over the last twenty years. (3) Two reasons why the Budgetary Slack literature is not finding as much slack as they would like. (4) Are we observing the development of a new Management Control paradigm in a few High Performance companies, which seem to have learned how to make subjectivity in performance evaluation and reward work for them?

INTRODUCTION

Articles proposing a new paradigm for a research domain usually do not start with a brief biographical detour. In this case, however, I feel I must impose that short detour on the reader because articles proposing a new paradigm are usually written by the most prolific and respected authors in the field, which I am clearly not. So what gives me the right, or any legitimacy, to suggest that

Performance Measurement and Management Control, Volume 12, pages 15–46.
© 2002 Published by Elsevier Science Ltd.
ISBN: 0-7623-0867-2

the Management Control research community may sometimes – not always, but sometimes – be studying the wrong issues, in suboptimal ways and in the wrong places?

The reader will have to assess whether what follows gives me any legitimacy, but here is where I am coming from. My doctoral dissertation ("Use of Quantitative Feedback by Superiors: Causes and Consequences"), completed eight years ago, received the second place award in the dissertation competition sponsored by the Accounting, Behavior and Organizations section of the American Accounting Association. From an academic discipline point of view, the dissertation had one foot in "Management Control" and the other in Organizational Behavior. My objective then was to publish a few components of this research project in accounting journals, before slowly moving the center of gravity of my research and teaching toward Organizational Behavior.

When I joined INSEAD, two things happened. First I was asked to teach Organizational Behavior subjects faster than I had anticipated. Secondly, I was asked to teach the bulk of a massive teaching load in executive programs. These teaching requirements forced me to speed up my transfer toward Organizational Behavior on the research front. They also influenced the type of subjects I was studying and the approach I was using to study them; teaching experienced managers requires more institutional knowledge and a more down to earth vocabulary than does teaching MBAs or Ph.D.s.

As a result, I have spent most of the 1990s doing applied research and a fair bit of consulting on Organizational Behavior and cross-disciplinary issues. Without it ever being a conscious choice, I evolved toward a Last In- First Out publishing strategy, which explains why I have published in many fields but Management Control!

Two years ago Marc Epstein proposed that we work on some papers together. This collaboration has led me to return to a literature that I had followed from a distance, this time armed with a very different mind set and experience base than I had as a doctoral student. That is the basis on which the remarks that follow were developed. I write this chapter not as an acknowledged authority on Management Control, but rather as a field researcher trained in Management Control returning to this field, after eight years of applied research and consulting work using a very different lens that the one I was using as a Management Control specialist.

I do not pretend that every aspect I comment on below is absolutely new and has never been mentioned in Management Control writings; In part because I know some papers that have touched on this or that aspect, in part also because I have not read every single article and book written in the field over the last ten years. Still, having done some catching up on the literature and attended research conferences over the last eighteen months, it is my sense that practice may have evolved in ways that make some aspects of the traditional management control paradigm somewhat obsolete. I prepared a first draft of these remarks to present a personal view aimed at stimulating debate at the Nice Conference and, through this chapter, beyond the conference itself. This chapter should be read in that spirit.

ON THE OPAQUENESS OF MANAGEMENT ACCOUNTING SYSTEMS

In his keynote speech at the Conference, Marc Epstein referred to a series of interactions he had with a group of very senior R&D managers. He recalled how, to his surprise, these senior managers seemed to make very significant decisions based on very limited, often rudimentary, accounting data. Coming at the issue from a rational angle, Marc asked: "Given the large amounts of money involved in these decisions, shouldn't we have a better model of cause and effects relationships?"

From a business rationale, shareholder value maximizing point of view, we should indeed. Yet I stopped being surprised a few years ago by the opaqueness of management accounting systems. While we too often persist at looking at this opaqueness as an error that top management should want to correct, I have come to see it as "opaqueness by design", with top managers often being the chief design officers of the opaqueness!

My first shock in this area came shortly after I joined my current institution and was immediately asked to join the Executive Education Committee. Graduating from HBS in the early nineties, after observing from very close the development of Activity-Based Costing by Robin Cooper and Bob Kaplan, I couldn't help noticing that the management reports we were receiving did not allow us to make intelligent business decisions. In short, our accounting system was completely opaque due a series of very arbitrary decisions regarding the allocation of indirect costs, the definition of the "products" and the decision to treat some of them as "marginal" and hence worthy of a different accounting treatment.

Armed with all the good will of a young "expert", I went to one of our co-deans, explained how and why the cost accounting system was dysfunctional and proposed to head a small task force to fix it. I waited for a reply for weeks, then decided I must have been unclear in my verbal communication and proceeded to send a memo reiterating my proposition. Again, no reply. A few months later the other co-dean invited me for lunch. I took this opportunity to expose the issue to him and renew my proposal to fix the problem. He appeared delighted with my idea and expressed a strong interest. "Let me get back to you", he said. That was 1993, I'm still waiting . . . .

About a year later, still frustrated by committee discussions too often stalled by bickering on the adequacy of the numbers, I informed the Associate Dean of executive education that I would spend a few days – just a few days – to make some rough cut re-calculations on our product profitability. I can't say he was thrilled by the idea, but he didn't stop me. I communicated my findings at the next committee meeting, suggesting on the basis of the calculations (which confirmed what most of us sensed) that one of our expanding products was in fact not profitable long term. (This was a "no brainer": The product met with expanding demand because it was priced too low and hence transferred all the value to the client! This was exactly like the competitors of Schrader Bellows, who used to buy spare parts from Schrader Bellows and resell them at a premium, rather than make the parts themselves!).[1] The Associate Dean's reaction was a non discussible assertion that I was "exaggerating" the point. I never managed to get a better discussion than this "you are exaggerating".

Frustrated by my inability to communicate, I went to a senior colleague in the department and explained my attempts at improving our cost accounting situation and their individual and collective failure to have any impact. My colleague sighed, paused for a second and then said: "You see, I, too, reached the same conclusion about fifteen years ago." So I, too, went to the Dean of the time and made the same proposal you made. To his credit, he answered quite honestly that this was a generous offer but he couldn't accept it because, he said, "you are right, our accounting system doesn't tell us much, but the great thing is it tells absolutely nothing to the Board! Now, we have other ways to get numbers, but they don't, so this is an excellent situation."

Much more recently, a few weeks ago, our new Dean stood in a Faculty Meeting and put an end to a strategic discussion on "which products should we push more actively" by an unambiguous statement that "we make money on our all products, all our products are profitable." While this would be a wonderful situation to be in, some of us believe that this statement can only be true if the cost accounting system is specifically designed to make it true.

One conclusion could of course be that Business Schools have notorious governance problems and that our colleagues in management positions should not be in those positions. Unfortunately, I have seen the very same situation in too many for-profit organizations to conclude that ours is an isolated problem. In too many companies, I have seen top managers espouse clarity and transparency in public, but nurture opaqueness in practice. They do so because opaqueness has significant advantages for bosses.

(1) It allows them to continue "shooting from the hip" when discussing strategy or operations. In the absence of reliable data, bosses can say whatever they want. That is convenient and economical on their time and energy.

(2) It helps them centralize decision rights. They would of course like to delegate these decisions but, unfortunately, they are the only ones who have an overview of all the parameters and hence they *must* make the decisions . . . .

(3) It helps them to avoid being challenged on current and past decisions. Again, in the absence of reliable data decision making enters the realm of "gut feelings". "My intuition tells me", "my gut tells me". And when boss and subordinates' guts tell different things, the boss' "gut" tends to carry more weight.

(4) Last but not least, opaqueness allows bosses to tweak or simply manage profitability data in ways that help them manage their political coalition. If I need the support of unit A, I can either tweak the system so that unit A appears profitable, or else explain that unit A's lack of profitability is due to the inadequacies of the accounting system but, really, they do alright.

The well-known Scovill Nutone case provides an excellent illustration of several of these motivations.[2] The company was using grossly inflated labor standards to estimate standard costs. As a result gross margins were largely underestimated by the system. Top management of the unit felt that, as some people set their watches a few minutes ahead to help them manage timeliness, depressing reported margins helped salespeople and management protect margins when negotiating with clients or bidding on contracts.

In practice, the system was used by the CEO to centralize decision rights from his subordinates and to shield himself from his bosses' potential intervention. Even when on vacation, he had to be consulted in numerous daily bids, as he was the only one who understood all the ramifications of the system (or, at least, felt that he did). Similarly, the CEO could argue whatever he wanted (and hence deny any challenge to his views) regarding product or sector profitability, arguing on his superior knowledge of "true profitability". The system also allowed the CEO to build enormous credibility with, and hence protect his autonomy from, Head Office. He did so by reversing part of the cumulative provision when needed to reach intermediate targets, and releasing the rest at the end of the year, i.e. when Headquarters are usually scrambling to find excess profit from some units in order to compensate for under-performing units.

Bosses hence have many incentives to maintain opaqueness by design. So do subordinates, of course. Functional heads can use such opaqueness to protect themselves from the unit boss's oversight and/or to accumulate power at the expense of other functions. In this respect, I have seen numerous instances of "new cost accounting systems" fail because one function (usually Marketing) did not want enhanced clarity on the cost and benefits of their decisions.

Using this lens, one comes to realize that in many companies, very few individuals *really* want a new, more transparent and accurate cost accounting system to appear! Similarly, I have met only one CEO who openly opposed the concept of Balanced Scorecard. All the other management teams with whom I have interacted openly supported the principle of agreeing on a clear strategy and then developing a set of indicators that would allow them to monitor and steer strategy implementation.

In practice, however, I have seen very few companies really use a Balanced Scorecard to guide their decision making! I have seen a lot more examples of the following outcomes:

- The management team is enthused about the BSC concept and leaves the program or meeting fully determined to start a development process. One year later, the process has not yet started.
- The management team does start a BSC development process, but the project loses momentum over time and the project team folds before reaching consensus on a strategy or a BSC.
- A BSC is developed and used in meetings for a short period of time. Then momentum weakens, often when the firm has difficulties meeting its financial objectives and takes short term measures to improve profitability, sometimes at the expense of other perspectives.
- A BSC is developed at the top level and starts getting used, but the process does not reach the next level down who continue to report the way they always have. The BSC slowly loses momentum as much of the data needed to support it should come from lower levels in the organization.

My point is obviously not that Activity-Based Costing systems or the BSC are bad tools in themselves. They can indeed be very helpful for a corporation. My point is that the *technical* difficulties in developing, implementing and using these tools are much *easier* to solve than the *organizational* dynamics their introduction triggers. When a reasonably large, well resourced organization lacks good data on their activities, I have come to see this situation not as an error due to ignorance, but rather as a "designed error". Opaqueness is more often than not designed. As a colleague of mine used to say: "When there's smoke somewhere, there's usually a guy with a smoke-making machine not far away"!

This view leads us not to look for the fire that creates the smoke, but rather try to identify the several individuals activating smoke-making machines throughout the organization. From there, we can start investigating what their motivations are, which will typically point to power and influence issues, as well as to serious issues related to the way data is used in the organization.

These may not be issues on which Management Control specialists have a competitive advantage, but they are nevertheless the more complex component of "getting the right kind of data to be effectively used by managers".

ON THE RAPM BODY OF RESEARCH

Research on the causes and effects of bosses' Reliance on Accounting Performance Measures (RAPM) was described by Brownell and Dunk (1991) as the only area of Management Control to have achieved some critical mass of research. Ten years later, "this critical mass" should be even richer. Yet, as four articles published in the May–July 2000 issue of *Accounting, Organizations and Society* show clearly, this body of research has produced very few consistent and reproducible findings.[3]

These four articles perform an exhaustive review of the research findings since Hopwood's (1972) seminal study and discuss several reasons why this body of research has not produced as many reliable findings as one would have expected at this stage. Rather than trying to replicate their work, I just want to highlight five issues that have become apparent to me through field research and consulting on leaders' use of performance measures in their interaction with subordinates.

Problem No. 1
The first dimension is: Why limit the study to Accounting Measures (AM) of performance? This made a lot of sense twenty to thirty years ago, when AMs were arguably the most prevalent measures of performance. More recently, however, managers have been increasingly using quantitative, non-accounting measures in their interactions with, and evaluation and reward of, subordinates. This trend is clearly supported and illustrated in the work by Ittner and Larcker (among others). Consider the two sets of measures and the four simplistic quadrants that companies and managers can occupy in terms of how they use quantitative performance measures (see Fig. 1).

By focusing only on the use of AMs, we are bundling together very different realities of organizations making different uses of non-accounting measures. Yet it is intuitively clear that, among subordinates whose bosses make low use

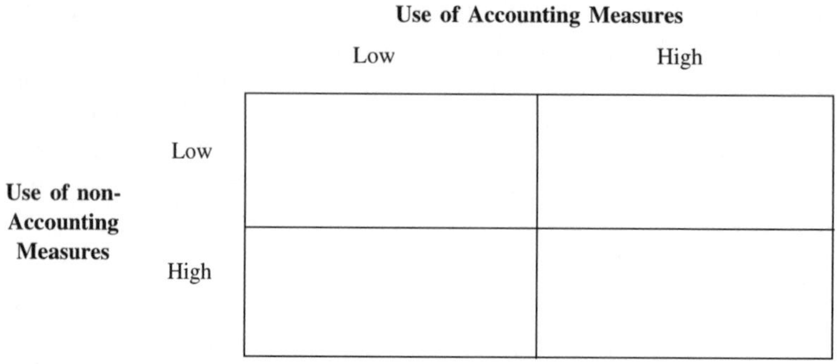

Use of Accounting Measures

Low   High

Use of non-
Accounting
Measures

Fig. 1.   Use of Accounting vs. non-Accounting Performance Measures.

of accounting measures, the attitudes and behavior of subordinates will vary a lot depending on how the boss uses other types of quantitative indicators.

Problem No. 2

The second dimension has to do with the *location of the variance* and the way we sample boss-subordinate dyads. Setting aside the first issue mentioned above and hence focusing only on the way bosses use accounting measures, we can find variance in boss use of accounting measures at three distinct levels:

• Across companies (some companies focus more than others on accounting measures),
• Across bosses (within a given company, some bosses focus more than others on accounting measures), and
• Within bosses – across subordinates (bosses tend to use performance measures more tightly with their perceived weaker performing subordinates).

When we use convenience samples of subordinates working in different organizations, we sample across all three of these levels. That is, we include in the same sample a perceived weaker performer of a boss making high use of accounting measures in an organization that puts a lot of emphasis on performance measures, and a high performer working for a boss who puts limited emphasis on AM in an organization that also tends to put limited emphasis on AM, with all the combinations located in between these two extremes.

Intuitively, however, the *legitimacy* of boss behavior, and hence the reaction of subordinates, is probably influenced by the context set by the various levels of analysis. Working for a boss that displays high RAPM in an organization that tends to display high RAPM is probably different than if the organization tends to be very loose on accounting measures. Similarly, "my boss displays high RAPM but does so fairly uniformly" may trigger different reactions than "my boss is usually low RAPM except with me".

Note that the initial studies by Hopwood (1972) and Otley (1978) focused on single organizations, and hence controlled for at least one cause of variance.

Problem No. 3

Setting aside the first two complexities ("accounting vs. non accounting measures" and "how many levels of analysis are we sampling across"), the third dimension is: what do we mean by "Reliance on Quantitative Performance Measures"? In particular, are we talking about managers' *day-to-day behavior* toward subordinates, or about the way subordinates' *performance is evaluated and rewarded* at the end of the year? These are two very distinct issues. Over the years I have seen organizations and managers in each of the four simplistic quadrants one can construct around these two dimensions (see Fig. 2).

For example, I have seen organizations and managers discuss quantitative performance measures very intensely during the year to guide discussions and decisions, but then prefer to introduce significant managerial judgment when evaluating and rewarding subordinates (the top right quadrant). I have also seen organizations where performance was managed on an exception basis throughout the year (and hence QPM were hardly discussed as long as performance was within agreed upon bounds), and was then evaluated and rewarded in very mechanical, numbers-driven ways (the bottom-left quadrant in Fig. 2). I have also seen organizations and managers in the low-low and high-high quadrants.

Use of Measures day-to-day

		Low	High
Use of measures for performance evaluation and reward	Low		
	High		

Fig. 2. Use of (Accounting) Performance Measures in Daily Interactions vs. For Performance Evaluation and Reward.

In this context, focusing on only one dimension of the problem means that we are sampling across quadrants on the second dimension, which is bound to introduce much noise in the system. The fact that RAPM studies do not systematically focus on the same dimension (day-to-day vs. end of year) does not help much either!

Notice again that Hopwood's and Otley's initial studies both commented heavily on both dimensions of boss use of performance measures.

Problem No. 4.

(Disregarding for now the first three issues and agreeing that we are going to focus on subordinates' reactions to RQPM for evaluation and reward purposes), how do we go about assessing the real impact of quantitative performance measures on subordinates' evaluation and reward(s)?

The first difficulty is: which reward? In my dissertation I asked subordinates to distinguish the impact of quantitative performance on various rewards, and they reported statistically significant differences with respect to the importance of performance vs. targets (with "reputation within the firm" being most, and "promotion prospects" being least, tightly linked to performance against targets).

But let's focus on year-end bonus, for a minute. I was recently teaching a group of very senior managers from a well-known global oil and gas company. (Note the *senior* managers; these people were very high up in their organization). The issue of bonuses came up, I took advantage of the opportunity to ask them how their bonus was set: Through application of a formula, they said. They could even articulate the formula in real time (which, in my experience, is pretty rare, at least among European managers). So I wrote down the formula and asked again: "So this is how your bonus is established?", and they said again "yes, it is".

Then one of the participants said "well, that's how the bonus is established *unless we miss our targets*". "Well, sure" said the others. I asked for more details, which came as follows: "It *is* true that our bonus is calculated this way as long as we are roughly in line with the targets. If we miss our targets badly, then management usually re-adjusts the targets downward in order to maintain our overall pay at the desired level on a global scale. Otherwise they'd run the risk of some of us leaving."

This is one of many examples that showed me how difficult it is to get an accurate description of the way managers are rewarded. And note again this is only referring to bonuses, i.e. to one of various rewards offered to managers.

Problem No. 5.

Last but not least by any means, and again notwithstanding the first four issues mentioned above, it is *very difficult* for subordinates to *untangle* the way their boss uses performance measures from the rest of the boss' behavior toward them, i.e. from the boss's *overall leadership style*. This point was driven home to me at a crucial moment of my dissertation research, i.e. as I was concluding the last interview of my pilot project.

As I was gathering pens and tapes, the last interviewee said: "It's been fun talking with you, and I've chatted with the others at the site they all enjoyed it. And if this is what you've got to study, that's fine, you know? But we just thought we should tell you: You're asking us all these questions on the way our boss uses performance measures, and we can answer them, but that's not really where the problem is! I mean, that's not what bugs us the most".

Notice one more time that the initial, seminal studies on RAPM all included a leadership style dimension. Since then, however, leadership style has often been disregarded or is sometimes used as a potential moderator. My interviewees' point was deeper: It had to do with "how do you separate the five minutes during which we discuss performance measures from the fifteen measures before and the ten minutes after, during which we did not discuss performance measures but did have an important interaction"?

On the basis of these five dimensions, I find it much less surprising that RAPM studies have produced such inconsistent results over the years. Use of quantitative performance measures by bosses is a complex phenomenon involving different levels of analysis, different types of performance measures (accounting and non-accounting) potentially used in different ways for different purposes (daily interaction vs. performance evaluation and reward), some of which are not easy for respondents to articulate (e.g. how is your bonus set?), and all of which is embedded in the manager's leadership style.

DESPERATELY SEEKING BUDGETARY SLACK

Budgetary slack has been studied less often than RAPM but has still been the object of much attention over the years. In their (1998) review of this literature, Dunk and Nouri conclude – as was the case for the RAPM studies – that research studies have produced limited consistent and reproduced findings. I want to highlight two factors that management control researchers have tended to disregard, yet become very clear when working with managers in practice.

(1) Budgets have other roles besides being yardsticks in performance evaluation and reward.
Dunk and Nouri (1998) review the inconsistent results obtained on three questions that, in principle, should be clear cut: Other things equal, we would

expect to observe more slack in environments where subordinates are evaluated more tightly based on performance vs. budgets. Similarly, we would expect to observe more slack when subordinates have more say in budget setting (higher budgetary participation) and/or when subordinates have an information asymmetry advantage over their boss.

After reviewing the conflicting results obtained in studies investigating these questions one at a time, Dunk and Nouri (1998) recall how Dunk (1993) made what seemed to be a very sensible suggestion: Like a crime, slack would require mean, motive and opportunity. The *motive* is given by the tightness of the link between rewards and performance against budget, which is captured by the superior's RAPM. Participation provides subordinates with the *opportunity* to make targets easier for themselves, but the boss knows what subordinates are up to and hence can fight this process (counter-bias). Subordinate then need information asymmetry to successfully negotiate for slack. Information asymmetry is the *mean* the subordinate uses to 'get away' with introducing slack.

In principle, budgetary slack should then be higher when budget emphasis is high (motive), participation is high (opportunity) and information asymmetry is high (mean). Dunk (1993) looked for such an effect and found its exact opposite. Slack was low under these conditions.

Dunk and Nouri (1998) propose 3 possible explanations for Dunk's (1993) findings.

(1) Managers' credibility in negotiation would be weakened if the bosses came to believe that the goals are too slack.
(2) Organizational performance norms may encourage managers to propose, and bosses to demand, less slack in budgets.
(3) Competition between managers may encourage them to propose less slack in budgets.

All three possible explanations are related to managers proposing 'difficult goals' (containing little slack) in order to signal around them (and particularly to their boss) that they are energetic, competent and self-driven players. That does not completely explain Dunk's result; in particular, it doesn't explain the role of information asymmetry. It is, nevertheless, a fact of organizational life that managers must manage not only their unit but also the impressions they give and the signals they send. Shooting for aggressive targets may be construed by bosses as a signal of energy and drive. A well-known "managerial aphorism" indeed encourages managers to submit difficult goals, "this way you will only be blamed once, when you fail to reach them. Otherwise you'll be blamed twice, during budget negotiation for failing to set ambitious enough targets and at the end of the year when you fail to achieve the ambitious targets they will set for you".

Signaling energy and drive is but one factor discouraging managers to bid for large amounts of slack. Two other factors can be mentioned.

The first is *competition for resources* across organisational units. Corporations tend to require a return on the investments they make. Hence managers vying for investment money must promise adequate returns on the investments they require. Budgets incorporating much slack may not feature high enough rates of return. Lukka (1988) called this objective the *"resource intention"*.

Another factor discouraging managers from trying to negotiate large amounts of slack is *the impact this (slack) budget will have on their own subordinates*. Accounting studies quote Locke and Latham's (1990) statement that performance tends to be enhanced by pursuing challenging targets, but always in the case of the budgeting superior wanting to extract a more difficult goal from the budgeted subordinate. In accounting laboratory experiments, *subordinates never have subordinates of their own*.

In real life, subordinates do have subordinates of their own. Managers negotiate a budget with their boss, then use that budget to manage their own units and inspire their own troops. Managers hence face contradictory incentives in terms of the impact of slack on their expected rewards. On one hand, negotiating slack decreases the target against which their unit's performance will be compared to evaluate and reward managerial performance. On the other hand this easy-to-reach target may lead to lower actual performance by the unit. Lukka (1988) called this incentive to shoot for higher targets the *"motivation intention"*.

Overall, accounting studies assume simple tasks and simple roles for subordinates and hence restrict their 'self-interest' to negotiating more slack in this year's budget. Reality is much more complex and can lead managers-subordinates to accept, even to *propose* very challenging budgets featuring little slack. No wonder, in this context, that accounting studies are not very successful at predicting the amount of budgetary slack.

(2) Ex ante slack is a meaningless notion; Slack only becomes clear ex post.

Appendix 1 presents several definitions of budgetary slack that have appeared in management control studies. Almost all these definitions refer to a kind of 'best estimate' on the part of the budgeting actor. Producing such a best estimate is probably doable for tasks where the only determinant of performance is effort. If actors understand well the production process (how effort translates into performance), the reward function (how performance translate into reward) and their preference functions (how they trade-off effort and reward), then they can make a "best estimate of their likely production". In a normal distribution the 'best estimate' would be the mean/median/mode of the distribution (see Fig. 3).

But what if the distribution of expected profit is not normal? For example, a company with which I worked recently is very dependent of the price of a metal on the LME (London Metals Exchange). Their profit distribution looks much more like the one in Fig. 4. Where, in this case, is the "best estimate"? Is it at Point A? Point B? Point C?

In real life managers face several sources of uncertainty, which can give rise to all sorts of funny looking distributions where the 'best estimate' becomes rather unclear! In all likelihood, managers hence don't select targets based on their 'best estimate' but rather based on 'probability of achievement', i.e. the area under the curve to the right of the best estimate. Depending on the probability of achievement they are aiming for, they will select point A, B or C (with decreasing probability of achievement).

One could argue that budget based on target A contains much slack because it has a high probability of achievement. But whether the extra resources are really slack resources or will end up being needed depends on the state of nature. If exogenous factors turn out to be very favorable, then indeed the budget will include much slack resources. If, however, nature turns out to be extremely unfavorable (e.g. the price of the company's metal goes down due to exceptionally low demand and excess supply), then the company may reach profitability level A only thanks to outstanding effort and performance.

In other words, budgetary slack ex ante is a fragile concept. Ex ante, the "slack resources" are really an insurance against an unfavorable environment.

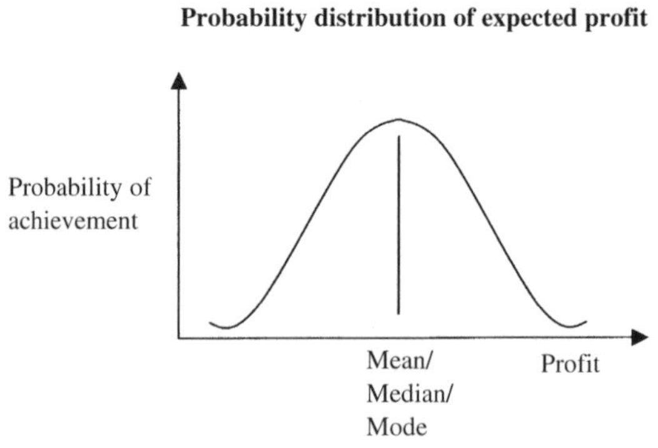

Probability distribution of expected profit

Fig. 3. Probability Distribution of Expected Profit.

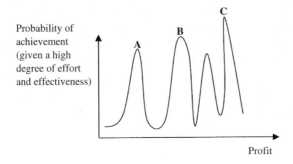

Probability of
achievement
(given a high
degree of effort
and effectiveness)

Profit

Fig. 4. More Complex Probability Distribution of Expected Profit.

Whether this insurance turns out to be real slack resources can only be determined as the state of nature unfolds during the year. This issue makes it more difficult for managers and researchers alike to assess the precise level of slack contained in budgets.

THE TRADITIONAL MANAGEMENT CONTROL PARADIGM

At the heart of the traditional management control paradigm is an acute awareness of the disadvantages of subjectivity, or managerial judgment, in subordinate performance evaluation and reward. Subjectivity raises the potential of personal bias by the boss and hence unfairness. It also encourages subordinates to expend energy trying to manage the boss's impressions, which can, at the extreme, lead to the development of an "excuse culture". Last but not least, subjectivity opens the door for a progressive slippage of standards of performance.

I have indeed seen corporations affected by these diseases. Some companies are affected by the extreme arbitrariness of their evaluation system, which leads most employees (who choose to continue working for the company) to disconnect mentally from the process and hence robs the system of any power to influence employee behavior. On the impression management and standard slippage front, the CEO of a client recently told me: "One of the things we are great at is explaining to one another why we did not reach the targets we had set for ourselves". This is the prototype of the excuse culture Merchant (1989, pp. 135–137) warned against.

This fear of the disadvantages of subjectivity leads to a search for employee accountability and for rewarding results. This is easy to do when employees' output is perfectly measurable and measured performance is perfectly controllable by employees. Unfortunately (or fortunately, depending how one looks at it), these are rare occurrences at the managerial level. More often than not, the performance of units headed by managers can be significantly influenced by factors that are out of the managers' control. From that observation evolved the controllability principle, which states that "one should only be evaluated based on what one controls".

The notion of "control" can quickly become problematic as CEOs themselves completely control precious little, but the controllability principle is generally understood in terms of "having administrative control" over the issue, i.e. being the one within the firm who can make the decision on that issue. Hence while I do not fully control market prices because my competitors can force me to set prices at level A rather than B, at least I make the decision within the firm of setting prices at level A or B.

Once the controllability principle is accepted, managers are quickly going to argue for a management-by-exception kind of supervision. "I don't mind being accountable for this performance target, but then I need to be allowed to make the major decisions – at least as long as my performance falls between acceptable boundaries."

In a system characterized by management-by-exception, managers clearly have incentives to set the acceptable performance boundaries as low as possible, in order to maximize their likely autonomy. In other words, managers are given an incentive to try to create budgetary slack for themselves. The notion of pay-for-numerical-performance has the same effect, hence a dual incentive to try to introduce slack (to increase expected rewards and to maximize autonomy).

Bosses are of course aware of the incentives they give to their subordinates and hence work hard at extracting slack, at least in some of their units. They will be more inclined to leave some budgetary slack in the units whose managers they trust not to under-perform, which is a convenient way to restrict the decision making autonomy of less trusted managers and to provide positive reinforcement to trusted managers.

This is, by and large, the environment Ken Merchant observed over ten years ago in a field study of 52 profit center managers and which was documented in Merchant (1989) and Merchant and Manzoni (1989). The picture was of course more subtle, bosses also managed the degree of risk they were exposing their subordinates to and tried to balance risk and return for the subordinates, but I think this is the basic paradigm we have been looking for as a community of researchers. (See Fig. 5 for a visual representation).

Hence the study of how much slack subordinates will want to, and will be able to, introduce in budgets. Hence the study of the effects of bosses' RAPM

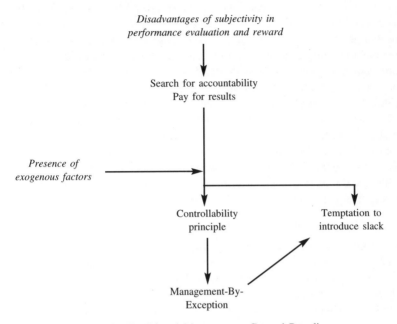

Fig. 5. The Traditional Management Control Paradigm.

on subordinates' attitudes and behavior, depending on: (a) how complete and controllable AMs are for the subordinates (which in turn depends on the variability and uncertainty of the task, environment, etc.), (b) the subordinates' psychological dispositions (e.g. locus of control, national culture), etc.

I believe this paradigm still exists in practice. I see it often. I also believe that some corporations, particularly corporations that are considered High Performance Organizations by many observers, no longer function on that basis.

TOWARD A NEW, HIGH PERFORMANCE, MANAGEMENT CONTROL PARADIGM?

Over the last few years I have had the good fortune of working closely, in training and/or consulting mandates, with companies like General Electric Capital, L'Oréal, Pfizer and several excellent but less international companies whose name would not ring a bell on the global scene. I have also studied other companies second hand, like Johnson & Johnson whose systems have been richly described and analyzed by Simons [(1987a) and (1987b)]. I am not claiming at this stage that this was systematic field research. It was opportunistic and non-systematic observation. Two colleagues and I are about to launch a formal research project designed to study 30 or so High Performance Organizations, in an attempt to study these issues more carefully and systematically. We intend to come back two years from now with reliable findings based on a solid research design and a carefully selected sample.

Still, I can't help but see a different pattern in some of these organizations. The pattern rests on two very different starting points from the "traditional paradigm". Rather than being overly concerned with the disadvantages of subjectivity in performance evaluations and reward, I see these companies more preoccupied with two other dimensions: The disadvantages of strict accountability and numbers-driven performance evaluation and reward, and the benefits of stretch targets. Let's examine these two pillars in turn.

(1) Disadvantages of strict accountability.

As documented in several management control studies, one of the downsides of strict accountability and numbers-driven performance evaluation and reward is that employees tend to produce what they are rewarded for, not more, and nothing else, a phenomenon often called *goal displacement*. Leaders in these High Performance firms tend to prefer *not* to specify and quantify all managerial performance parameters ex ante.

This preference follows, or at least fits with two key beliefs and associated practices in these firms.

(a) Assumption/belief No. 1:

"Overall firm performance is unlikely to be maximized by focusing managers' efforts on dimensions and measures that are controllable by them, for two reasons":

With respect to *exogenous* factors, managers may not be able to influence the state of nature but they should work as hard as necessary at anticipating and reacting to events, including by decreasing the firm's exposure to these events. If managers are fully insulated from the impact of these events (e.g. a firm that evaluates and rewards its managers based on operational income adjusted for movements in currency or raw material prices), they are unlikely to devote as much attention to these factors as they would if their measured performance included the impact of these factors.

Internally, overall firm performance depends enormously on issues that are managed at the interface of different functions and business units. Focusing each manager on what s/he strictly controls is likely to lead to insufficient focus on these intersections.

As a result, these firms tend to prefer to set targets in terms of performance measures that are *complete* measures of subordinates' performance, rather than *controllable* ones. Instead of the controllability principle, they tend to follow the "completeness principle", which can be defined as: "One's evaluation should take into account all the elements on which one has influence". For the same reasons, these firms also often make managers of different sub-units jointly accountable for results that depend on their combined performance.

By focusing on complete measures of performance and encouraging joint accountability, these firms introduce in managers' measured performance an "uncontrollable dimension" (through the impact of events that are partly uncontrollable by managers, and the impact of decisions over which managers must share administrative control with others). Making managers fully accountable for these measures, i.e. displaying an extreme RQPM in performance evaluation and reward, would make managers bear a lot of risk which: (a) they would need to be compensated for; and (b) may lead them to make sub-optimal decisions. One way to remove at least part of this risk is to allow the managers' bosses to introduce some personal judgment, and hence some subjectivity in the managers' performance evaluation and reward.

(b) Assumption/belief No. 2:

"We cannot specify ex ante the firm's "performance grading scheme" for the year, for two reasons: First, because how much the firm should achieve depends on exogenous factors, the state of which we will only know at the end of the year. Secondly, because business conditions evolve too fast to be frozen in a reward system one year at a time; we would rather be flexible and adjust priorities as the year progresses."

The first sub-point is very consistent with our discussion of budgetary slack in an earlier section: The degree of difficulty of business targets is hard to appreciate ex ante and becomes clearer as the state of nature unfolds. Rather than focusing managers' attention on exceeding targets set months ago based on hypothetical circumstances, these firms want to encourage managers to achieve as much as can be achieved under the circumstances. This approach avoids managers being tempted to give up (or renegotiate targets) when the state of nature turns out to be harder than expected, as well as managers being tempted to coast when the state of nature turns out to be significantly more favorable than had been anticipated in the plan.

The second sub-point follows from the first. As the state of nature (e.g. economic conditions, raw material prices, competitors' actions) unfolds, we may need to adjust objectives and priorities to reflect a different understanding of reality than the one that existed when the initial targets were set.

These two arguments both point to the same conclusion: Managers' performance can only be evaluated at the end of the year, once we know how exogenous factors unfolded and we can look back at what the key priorities should have been. This process is bound to involve some managerial judgment/subjectivity, as no firm possesses a perfect theory associating each possible event to its impact on the firm's results (e.g. how can one perfectly isolate the impact of September 11 2001's events on a firm's results).

Wrapping up this first pillar, these firms tend to refuse to specify ex ante controllable performance parameters for managers. As a result, the presence of managerial subjectivity in performance evaluation and reward becomes inevitable.

(2) The role of stretch targets.

The second major pillar of these firms' approach is their belief in the power of setting difficult goals and committing to exceed them. Senior managers in these companies believe that setting difficult goals, or stretch goals, leads employees to think outside the box and find creative ways to reach joint high performance on issues that have traditionally be seen as incompatible (e.g. cost and quality; efficiency, discipline and innovation; low cost and customer care, etc.).

In that vein I heard the CEO of Unilever Asia exhort his troops to set more ambitious objectives and commit their heart to them. He explained his point by saying: "When you are three hundred meters away from the top of Mount Everest, what does your brain tells you? It says "Go down NOW! This place is no good for you!". The energy that you need to climb the last three hundred meters does not come from your brain, it comes from the emotional commitment you made to an unreasonable goal." He then went on to explain that the region would keep growing at single digit rate as long as country managers would continue to set single digit growth objectives.

With respect to budgets, Novartis used stretch budgets to support the development of a High Performance Organization culture (Kroop & Datar, 1998). Diageo's CEO refers to Hairy, Audacious Targets and explains that "HATs are the way to focus managers on raising performance. Incrementalism is no longer good enough. We have set our people very aggressive targets that will force them to explore every possibility" (Willman, 1998, p. 31). In the same vein, Jack Welch characterized budgets as the "Bane of Corporate America", because "making a budget is an exercise in minimalization. You're always trying to get the lowest out of people, because everyone's negotiating to get a lower number" (Loeb, 1995, p. 73).

These leaders realize that if they systematically penalize failure to achieve stretch targets, subordinates will quickly refuse to accept such targets as motivational objectives. The target-related component of the moral contract in these firms could be summarized as follows: "We prefer you to set yourself a 20% growth objective and reach only 18% while containing competition to 10% growth, rather than grow 14% on a 12% objective while competition grew 15%." The overriding goal is to reach the best possible result and beat competition by as wide a margin as possible, even if we fall short of these stretch objectives, rather than beating our own outdated, conservative targets.

This emphasis on stretch goes in the same direction as the first pillar described above: We will only know at the end of the year how well we did vs. competition given the circumstances, hence we reserve the right to assess managerial performance at the end of the year taking into account all these parameters in a process that is bound to involve some managerial judgment/subjectivity.

Among many public statements of well-known CEOs that illustrate this position, here are two. First, Jack Welch:

> Our plastics business last year had an up year, something like 10 or 11%. But in my view they had a relatively poor year. They should have been up 30 to 40%. They got caught in a squeeze with prices; and they didn't react fast enough. So their bonuses were affected. Our aircraft engine business went down $50 million in earnings to $500 million. But we increased their bonus pool 17%. They had a drop but they knocked the hell out of the competition around the world. They lost $2 billion in sales as the military market and the airline business came down. But they responded to their environment better and faster than their competitors did (in Loeb, 1995).

Larry Bossidy's quote makes the same point but also illustrates the fact that managers must still strive for the goal, even if some forgiveness is likely. The journalist followed Bossidy at a plant and reported the following: "Bossidy lets his managers at the brake division know that they aren't growing profits fast enough for his taste. His managers insist they'll make the goals. Bossidy isn't convinced: "You better hardwire your hopes", he tells them, "or we'll have a discussion in a few months nobody will be comfortable with." As Bossidy's jet takes off from the South Bend brake plant, he admits that he's more pleased with his people than he let on. "Remember, these are tough stretch targets", he says. "You can't punish people managers for not getting 100%." Downing an inflight CD-size cookie, Bossidy even says that even if the braking business falls slightly short of the goal, its managers will still get fat bonuses." (Tully, 1995).

Bossidy allowed this quote to be printed, which suggests that he wanted his managers to be aware of its content. At the same time, he maintains enormous pressure on the need to beat the goals. This is a fine line that great leaders walk better than less effective ones. This fine line seems is also very salient at Johnson & Johnson, as described in Simons' (1987a) Codman and Shurtleff case.

With the two major pillars of these firms' approach both pointing to the use of more subjectivity in managerial performance evaluation and reward, the next question must obviously be: How do these firms manage to make subjectivity (in performance evaluation and reward) work? How do they bypass, or counteract the difficulties that have led so many firms to design a completely different approach in order to avoid this subjectivity?

A Short Digression on Budgets' Multiple Roles within the Firm

Before tackling this major issue, a short digression: I have so far emphasized how these firms encourage managers to stretch in their target setting process, including their budgeting process. But budgets have other functions besides their motivational one; in particular, budgets act as planning and coordinating mechanisms within companies. By setting goals at levels that are far from certain to be achieved, firms jeopardize their budget's usefulness as a planning and coordination device.

This issue of the conflicting roles of budgets received much attention in the 1970s but has been somewhat disregarded since, as most academic studies of the last twenty years have focused on identifying the degree of target difficulty that leads to highest motivation and performance. Marc Epstein and I have been taking another look at this issue and have documented four mechanisms that can help firms to reconcile this dilemma: Corporate/division reserves, contingency funds, dual budgets and the use of virtual divisions (see Epstein & Manzoni, 2002). We have collected preliminary evidence suggesting that the majority of large firms use one or more of these mechanisms (Epstein & Manzoni, 2001) and we are currently designing a large scale survey to substantiate these preliminary findings.

In the short run, Simons' (1987a) Codman and Shurtleff case provides an excellent illustration of how J&J uses a device called "contingency fund" to combine stretched budgets at the business unit level, with safe numbers for planning and coordination at the corporate level.

Avoiding the Dysfunctions of Subjectivity in Performance Evaluation and Reward

As shown in Fig. 6, which represents graphically this potential new paradigm, I believe that two major issues need to be tackled to make subjectivity work in managerial performance evaluation and reward: the fairness issue, and the stimulation and drive issue. I address each of them in turn.

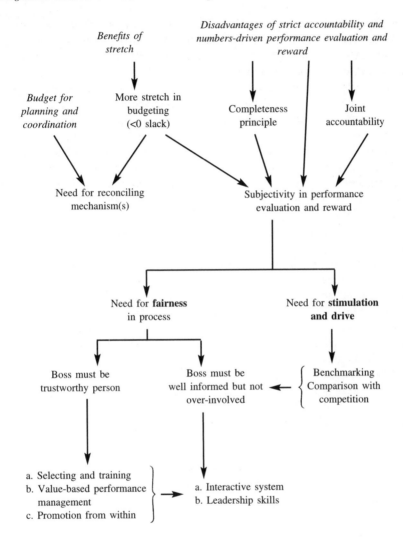

Fig. 6. The new, High Performance, Management Control Paradigm?

The Need for Fair Process

Procedural justice – that is, subordinates' perception that the *process* that led to the outcome was fair – is increasingly recognized as a major issue, as a rapidly growing number of studies establish a strong link between fairness perceptions and a host of desirable outcomes such as job satisfaction, enhanced commitment to the organization, intention to remain with the organization, greater trust and willingness to go beyond the call of duty, and, maybe most important, on the job performance.[4]

Intuitively, we would expect that a "subjective performance evaluation and reward system"[5] has more chances to be perceived as fair if the vast majority of bosses involved in the system are perceived by subordinates as having *two fundamental characteristics*: They must be *trustworthy* as individuals (e.g. being fact-driven as opposed to arbitrary, unbiased as opposed to prone to favoritism), and they must be *well informed* on subordinates' job, actions, and performance. Furthermore, they must be well informed about subordinates' jobs, actions etc. *without being over-involved* in subordinates' jobs and trying to repatriate decision rights.

On the first dimension, these firms simply work harder than most firms at having trustworthy (and, more generally, more effective) managers. The Johnson & Johnson *Credo* is a good illustration of this emphasis, specifying as it does that "We are responsible to our employees . . . We must provide competent management, and their actions must be just and ethical".[6] In the same vein, General Electric's 2000 Letter to shareholders includes an unambiguous discussion of Type IV managers – the managers who deliver the numbers but don't share GE's leadership values – and how "they must be found" and "they must leave the company".

More concretely, these companies' emphasis on developing trustworthy and effective leaders is visible through a number of actions:

- The care and concern these firms invest in the *recruiting* process;
- The greater amount of investment (in money as well as top management time and energy) they devote to *Leadership training*;
- Their strong commitment to a *performance management system* that makes "good leadership" (as defined by the company) and "adherence to company values" an essential component of managers' evaluation and reward, and "weak leadership" and non-conformance to company values a motive for dismissal;[7]
- Heavy (though not exclusive) *promotion* from within, in order to reinforce the firm's value system and leadership model.

Regarding the second dimension of fairness (the bosses must be well informed without infringing on their subordinates' autonomy), two different components seem to be involved. The first is the use of what Simons calls "interactive system", i.e. line managers using a particular system to trigger regular, systematic face-to-face meetings aimed less at reviewing numbers per se than at *discussing and debating managers' actions*, assumptions and intentions (see Simons (1995) or Simons (2000) for more on interactive systems and Simons's four levers of control). The traditional Management-by-Exception approach (which Simons calls "diagnostic" approach to control) has the disadvantage of positioning the boss's involvement as a punishment and hence something to be avoided. In an interactive system approach, meetings and discussions are systematic, regardless of whether the unit is on budget or not, which offers the potential for boss involvement to be perceived as much less evaluative and threatening than in an MBE context, where the boss becomes involved only when results fall outside of acceptable bounds.

This "potential for boss involvement to be perceived as much less evaluative and threatening" must then be realized through the second component of this dimension, the leaders' *skill* at being involved without usurping subordinates' autonomy. Simons's four levers of control provide a frame that is indeed very representative of what I see in High Performance companies, but leaders must then have the required *skills* to optimize the potential of this frame.[8] It is not easy for a leader to ask questions, to challenge subordinates' facts and reasoning, to encourage them to stretch their ambitions and fight the temptation to coast, without at the same time running the risk of pushing one's point of view hard on subordinates.

Numerous books have been written on this aspect of Leadership. I am currently writing one myself, tentatively called *Tightrope Walking: The Making of a Learning Leader* (Manzoni, 2003). The issue is too complex to be summarized here in a few words, but the point is that managers do need specific leadership skills to make this system work. Note that the companies' investment in developing trustworthy managers, discussed above, also pays dividends on this front.

The Need for Stimulation and Drive

For this paradigm to function, conditions must be in place for managers to be able to be perceived as subjective, but fair. That is a necessary, but not a sufficient condition, as fairness alone is not a sufficient protection against the dangers of complacency and of an excuse culture. To fight those evils companies must make sure that managers remain focused on where they stand vs. competition and, more generally, vs. best performers in class. The firm must set internal targets, financial as well as non financial ones, but one can go bankrupt meeting internal targets that have lost touch with today's competitive requirements!

When I work with Better Performing companies, I am struck by their constant search for new ideas and better ways of doing things. This intensity and drive usually starts at the top with a CEO obsessed with excellence, if not perfection. These companies are also very focused on one or two competitors and know exactly where they stand compared to them. They fight these competitors with a passion, an intensity that most other firms lack. This intensity usually starts at the top, but to permeate the organization it must be *nurtured* by a continuous flow of *performance* data. Some of these data must come from outside the organization, but a lot can also come from customers and employees – the two groups who generally know first and best how well an organization's processes are working and how well the firm's products/services compare to that of competitors.

As shown in Figure 6, this flow of data, particularly data comparing the firm's performance against competition, also pays dividends on the "fairness" front by helping bosses to be better informed on their subordinates' real performance.

CONCLUSION

Let me reiterate at this point the acknowledgement with which I started this chapter. This was not meant to be a definitive statement written by one of Management Control's gurus. These are simply a few reactions from a researcher initially trained in Management Control, who did some research in that field and then worked for a few years in other areas spending most of his time interacting with managers as an executive education instructor, a researcher or a consultant. While I would not recommend my career path to any doctoral student, it has forced me to outgrow my initial training, to get close to managers' preoccupations, dilemmas and constraints, and to become much more familiar with other research fields than I would have normally done.

From that perspective, it seems to me that we – the Management Control research community – should devote more attention to studying *organizational factors* that make new accounting methods and systems so hard to implement successfully in practice. While power and influence considerations do not explain everything, they are of overwhelming importance in real life.

Looking at RAPM research, it seems to me that this line of work is unlikely to produce many reliable findings over the coming years using the typical cross-sectional, survey approaches that have been prevalent over the last twenty years. These methods make it hard to study the use of all (financial and non-financial) quantitative performance indicators managers use in their interaction with subordinates; Samples often cut across levels of analysis that each contribute to the context, and hence probably also to subordinate reactions;

Studies may spend too much time examining the impact of the way performance measures are used for evaluation and reward (which, by the way, is in itself a very difficult exercise), while under-studying the use of performance indicators in daily boss-subordinate interactions, and how this use of performance indicators is embedded in the bosses' "leadership style".

As for budgetary slack, I think there is much less of it out there than there used to be, as the ever increasing intensity of competition and financial market expectations are creating strong incentives for managers to accept, and even set for themselves, more challenging goals than in the past. In addition, it is very difficult to specify ex ante what is true budgetary slack and what is protection against unfavorable states of nature.

Last, I tried to share my evolving views on what I perceive to be a new Management Control paradigm used in a few, High Performance firms. I think these firms start from a different point of view than our traditional "individual accountability – let's pay for results and avoid subjectivity" paradigm. These firms emphasize instead the difficulties and dangers of trying to specify and quantify ex ante, controllable performance targets for managers. They prefer to make managers feel responsible for more complete measures of performance with joint ownership of overlapping areas. They also prefer managers to focus on maximizing results given the state of nature, rather than beating targets based on outdated expectations of nature. They want to keep the freedom to modify priorities and objectives as the year unfolds, and they believe that setting challenging targets can help managers find new, innovative ways of doing business.

The counterpart of these choices is that while managers are expected to strive as hard as possible to reach these difficult targets, they are not systematically penalized for failing to achieve them in a given year. Performance evaluation and reward is understood to require some managerial judgment, it is understood to be a subjective process. Starting from that essential foundation, these companies work hard at creating an environment where subjectivity in performance evaluation and reward is effective, i.e. where it is associated with higher performance instead of perceptions of unfairness, temptations to manage the bosses' impressions and/or to develop an excuse culture.

At this point, I view the two major pillars of this environment as the need for (the immense majority of) managers to be perceived as fair in their subjective assessments, and the need for an intense performance culture to maintain a sharp performance drive. I see these companies working hard at using all the levers at their disposal to develop trustworthy and effective leaders, skilled at being informed without overstepping their role and thus at maximizing the potential offered by Simons' notion of interactive control. I also see these companies make sure they create a continuous flow of performance data, coming from both inside and outside the firm, to keep reinforcing the fact that the race has no finish line and to maintain a high degree of intensity and focus on severely beating competition.

At this stage, I regard these comments as educated impressions. I offer them here for discussion, to be tested and probably partially discomfirmed, partially enriched in the forthcoming field study of a solid sample of High Performance Organizations that Marc Epstein, another INSEAD colleague and I are starting this year. It is clear that many firms today still function on the basis of the "traditional" management control paradigm, but that should not restrict our research efforts. I think we need more efforts like these – trying to study excellent companies – to understand how we can re-produce and spread their successful ways, and maybe less studying average organizations to try to identify complex patterns of interactions among variables that, sometimes, produce pockets of higher performance in their midst.

NOTES

1. See Robin Cooper's case series on Schrader Bellows, HBS No. 9-186-272 and 273.

2. See the Scovill, Inc.: NuTone Housing Group HBS case (No. 9-186-136) and the accompanying Scovill, Inc.: NuTone Housing Group Video (No. 9-887-504). The video explains how years after the case was written, the "provision" became big enough to threaten the integrity of the *whole Group's* financial reporting and led to the Group's audit committee instructing the unit's general manager to correct the situation. The case is also discussed in Merchant and Shields (1993).

3. See in particular the articles by Hartmann (2000); Otley and Pollanen (2000); Otley and Fakiolas (2000); Vagneur and Peiperl (2000).

4. See Korine (1998) for an excellent study linking perceived fair process and on-the-job performance. For a more exhaustive review of the evidence and research issues, see Folger and Cropanzano (1998) and Gilliland et al. (2001). In the management accounting field, Lindquist's (1995) experimental results showed that subordinates attitudes toward difficult goals being assigned to them depend on how much involvement subordinates were given in the budget setting process. Subjects who expressed budget level preferences and were then budgeted at a higher level were *less* satisfied with budget and task than subjects offered less involvement in the first place. Similarly, Fisher et al. (2000) reported significantly lower performance for subjects that were imposed a (typically higher) target after their budget negotiations failed. In both cases subjects seemed to react against what they perceived as pseudo-participation.

5. A quick remark on the term "a subjective performance evaluation and reward system". I could have said a "*somewhat* subjective system" to highlight the fact that the system need not be (and generally is not in these firms) 100% subjective. We can still have goals and performance measures to guide the evaluation and reward process. I chose not to use the qualifier "somewhat" because subjectivity is to some extent like pregnancy: you're either pregnant or you're not, and a system features some subjectivity

or none. From the moment some subjectivity is allowed, the system becomes a subjective one.

6. See *www.jnj.com* for the full text of the company's Credo.

7. Simons would refer to this component as emphasizing the company's belief system and boundary control, two of his levers of control. See Simons (1995) or Simons (2000) for more details.

8. I did not specifically refer to Simons's other two levers of control (belief systems and boundary systems) till now, but notice how they are implicit in my characterization of a "value-based performance management system".

ACKNOWLEDGMENTS

I presented a first draft of these remarks as a keynote address during the Conference. This address was followed by a Q&A session, during which I received several helpful comments and reactions. Special thanks to Marc Epstein, for his encouragement before, and his helpful comments after, the intervention.

REFERENCES

Brownell. P., & Dunk, A. S. (1991). Task Uncertainty and its Interactions With Budgetary Participation and Budget Emphasis: Some Methodological Issues and Empirical Investigation. *Accounting, Organizations and Society, 16*, 693–703.

Cooper, R. (1986). Schrader Bellows Case Series, HBS No. 9-186-272 and 273.

Dunk, A. S. (1993). The Effects of Budget Emphasis and Information Asymmetry on the Relation Between Budget Participation and Slack. *The Accounting Review*, April, 400–410.

Dunk, A. S., & Nouri, H. (1998). Antecedents of Budgetary Slack: A Literature Review and Synthesis. *Journal of Accounting Literature, 17*, 72–96.

Epstein, M. J., & Manzoni, J.-F. (2001). Reconciling Conflicting Roles of Budgets: Review and Survey of Corporate Practices. Paper presented at the AAA Annual Meeting.

Epstein, M. J., & Manzoni, J.-F. (2002). Conflicting Roles of Budgets: Beyond Trade-off Toward Reconciliation. INSEAD Working Paper.

Fisher, J. G., Frederickson, J. R., & Peffer, S. A. (2000). Budgeting: An experimental investigation of the effects of negotiation. *The Accounting Review, 75*(1), 93–114.

Folger, R., & Cropanzano, R. (1998). *Organizational Justice and Human Resource Management.* Sage: Foundations for Organizational Science series.

Gilliland, S., Steiner, D., & Skarlicki, D. (2001). Editors, *Theoretical and Cultural Perspectives on Organizational Justice.* Greenwich, Connecticut: Information Age Publishing Inc.

Hartmann, F. G. H. (2000). The Appropriateness of RAPM: Toward the Further Development of Theory. *Accounting, Organizations and Society, 25*, 4–5, 451–482.

Hopwood, A. G. (1972). An Empirical Study of the Role of Accounting Data in Performance Evaluation. *Journal of Accounting Research*, Supplement, 156–182.

Korine, H. (1998). Strategic decision-making processes and performance: Multiple levels, reciprocal influences. (Working Paper, 40/1998), London Business School Strategic Leadership Research Programme.

Kroop, C.-I., & Datar, S. (1998). Novartis (A): Being a Global Leader. Harvard Business School Case No. 9-198-141.

Lindquist, T. M. (1995). Fairness as an Antecedent to Participative Budgeting: Examining the Effects of Distributive Justice, Procedural Justice and Referent Cognitions on Satisfaction and Performance. *Journal of Management Accounting Research*, 7, 122–147.

Locke, E. A., & Latham, G. P. (1990). *A Theory of Goal-Setting and Task Performance*. Prentice-Hall.

Loeb, M. (1995). Jack Welch lets it fly on budgets, bonuses, and buddy boards". *Fortune*, *131*, 10 (May 29), 145–146.

Lukka, K. (1988). Budgetary biasing in organizations: Theoretical framework and empirical evidence. *Accounting, Organizations and Society*, *13*(3), 281–301.

Manzoni. J.-F. (2003). *Tightrope Walking: The Making of a Learning Leader*. Boston, MA: Harvard Business School Press.

Merchant, K. A. (1989). *Rewarding results: Motivating profit center managers*. Boston, MA: Harvard Business School Press.

Merchant, K. A., & Ferreira, L. (1985). Scovill, Inc.: NuTone Housing Group. Harvard Business School case (No. 9-186-136)

Merchant, K. A., & Manzoni, J.-F. (1989). The Achievability of Budget Targets in Profit Centers: A Field Study. *The Accounting Review*, July, 539–558.

Merchant, K. A., & Shields, M. D. (1993). When and Why to Measure Costs Less Accurately to Improve Decision Making. *Accounting Horizons*, June.

Otley, D. (1978). Budget Use and Managerial Performance. *Journal of Accounting Research* (Spring), 122–149.

Otley, D., & Fakiolas, A. (2000). Reliance on Accounting Performance Measures: Dead End or New Beginning? *Accounting, Organizations and Society*, *25*, 4–5, 497–510.

Otley, D., & Pollanen, R. M. (2000). Budgetary Criteria in Performance Evaluation: A Critical Appraisal Using New Evidence. *Accounting, Organizations and Society*, *25*, 4–5, 483–496.

Simons, R. (1987a). Codman and Shurtleff, Inc.: Planning and Control System. Harvard Business School Case No. 9-187-081.

Simons, R. (1987b). Planning, Control and Uncertainty: A Process View. In: W. J. Bruns Jr. & R. S. Kaplan (Eds), *Accounting and Management: Field Study Perspectives*. Boston, MA: Harvard Business School Press.

Simons, R. (1995). Control in an Age of Empowerment. *Harvard Business Review*, *7*(2), 80–88.

Simons, R. (2000). *Performance Measurement & Control Systems for Implementing Strategy: Text and Cases*. Prentice Hall.

Tully, S. (1995). So, Mr. Bossidy, we know you can cut. Now show us how to grow. *Fortune*, *132*(4), 42–48.

Vagneur, K., & Peiperl, M. (2000). Reconsidering Performance Evaluative Style. *Accounting, Organizations and Society*, *25*, 4–5, 511–526.

Van der Stede, W. A. (2000), The Relationship Between Two Consequences of Budgetary Controls: Budgetary Slack Creation and Managerial Short-Term Orientation. *Accounting, Organizations and Society*, *25*(6) 609–622.

Willman, J. (1998). Don a Hat and Get Ahead to Meet Hairy Audacious Targets. *Financial Times*, *17*, 31.

APPENDIX 1

Some definitions of budgetary slack in the literature.

Merchant (1985a, p. 201) (cited in Dunk & Nouri, 1998)	Slack = "Excess of the amount budgeted in an area **over that which is necessary**".
Lukka (1988, pp. 282–283) (cited in D&N)	Slack budget = "one in which the figure has been **intentionally made easier** to achieve in relation to the forecast", where the forecast is the **budgeting actor's "best estimate"**.
Lukka (1988, pp. 282–283) (in Van DerStede, 2000, p. 615)	A budget contains slack if the business unit managers have intentionally set their budget targets lower **than their best guess** forecast about the future so that the budget becomes easier to achieve.
Young (1985) (in D&N)	Amount by which subordinates understate their productive capability when given the opportunity to select work standards against which their performance will be evaluated.
Waller (1988) (in D&N)	Excess of resources over and above **those required to complete a task**.
Dunk (1993) (in D&N)	Express incorporation of amounts in the budget to make it easier to attain.
Dunk and Nouri (1998, p. 73)	"Slack may be defined as the ***intentional underestimation*** of revenues and productive capabilities and/or overestimation of costs and resources **required to complete a budgeted task**".
Fisher, Frederickson and Peffer (2000, p. 96)	"Budgetary slack is the difference between subordinates' **best estimate** of performance and the budget".
March (1988, p. 4) in Van der Stede (2000, p. 611)	"Slack is generally defined as resources and efforts toward activities that cannot be justified easily in terms of their immediate contribution to organizational outcomes".

Van der Stede (2000, p. 615).	"There is slack in the budget if the business unit managers have been able to negotiate easy budget targets."
Note: VDS mentions 5 different definitions of slack.	Conversely, a budget has little slack if the probability that it will be met is low (Merchant & Manzoni, 1989) or if it requires serious effort and a high degree of efficiency in accomplishment (Simons, 1988).

PART II:
MANAGEMENT CONTROL IN
LARGE ORGANIZATIONS

LINKING STRATEGIC CHOICES AND MANAGEMENT ACCOUNTING SYSTEMS SCOPE: AN EMPIRICAL ANALYSIS

Emilio Boulianne

ABSTRACT

The present research aims at a better understanding of the relationship between strategic choices and the scope of management accounting systems in a Canadian context. A survey research was conducted using the strategy typology developed by Miles and Snow. Results suggest that the impact of broad scope information usage on performance will be more beneficial for managers operating in prospector-type firms than for managers operating in defender-type firms.

INTRODUCTION

Understanding the relationship between strategic choices and management accounting systems design has been considered a research priority over the last two decade. Simons (1987) identifies this relationship as a necessity to develop theories regarding relevant accounting systems. However, few studies have

Performance Measurement and Management Control, Volume 12, pages 49–60.
Copyright © 2002 by Elsevier Science Ltd.
ISBN: 0-7623-0867-2

investigated the fit between business strategy and management accounting systems scope. The present paper aims to improve our understanding in this area.

Our research motivations are the following. First, obtain in a Canadian context a better understanding of the relationship between strategic choices and accounting systems scope. Previous studies investigated this relationship with Australian firms (see Abernethy & Guthrie, 1994; Chong & Chong, 1997). This study will add to the cumulative knowledge in this research area. A second motivation is to take into account two different industries, manufacturing and service, to add external validity of the results, when Chong and Chong's study covered manufacturing firms only.

The paper is organized as follows. The next section addresses the hypothesis development. The research methodology is then explained followed by the results. The findings are then discussed along with directions for future research. The last section discussed limitations and conclusion.

HYPOTHESES DEVELOPMENT

This section describes the way we determine business strategy, information systems scope, and business performance constructs. This is followed by the research hypothesis.

Business Strategy

Although different strategic typologies have been developed to classify the strategy pursued by an organization, we chose the Miles and Snow (1978) typology for the following reasons.[1] First, Miles and Snow "are very clear in their statements that the control system of a firm should be congruent with its strategy" (Simons, 1987, p. 359). Second, this typology has been widely used in research, in different industries, and has shown reliability and validity (Shortell & Zajac, 1990; Doty, Glick & Huber, 1993). In accounting research, several studies have used Miles and Snow's typology.

Miles and Snow formulated three viable strategic types: defenders, prospectors and analyzers. Defenders deal with a stable environment and propose few products and services. They preserve their market share through cost leadership and efficiency. In contrast, prospectors deal with a hostile and dynamic environment, and offer many products and services. They are innovators and always seek new markets. Defenders and prospectors may be conceptualized as opposite ends of a products/services change continuum, where analyzers represent firms in a position located between these two extremes. Several accounting researchers used only the two extreme types of strategy (defenders vs. prospectors) in their studies (Simons, 1987, 1988, 1990; Abernethy & Guthrie, 1994; Ittner, Larcker & Rajan, 1997; Chong & Chong, 1997; Abernethy & Brownell, 1999).

Information System Scope

The information provided by an accounting information system can be characterized in many ways but accounting researchers have paid specific attention to three characteristics: focus, quantification and time horizon (Dermer, 1973; Larcker, 1981; Gordon & Narayanan, 1984; IMA, 1995). *Focus* refers to the extent to which information focuses internally i.e. on the organization, or has an external focus that relates to the organization's environment. *Quantification* refers to financial information or nonfinancial information, the latter being expressed in non-monetary terms (Mia, 1993). *Time horizon* refers to historical information (*ex post*), or future-oriented information (*ex ante*).

These three information characteristics define the Management Accounting System (MAS) scope construct (Chenhall & Morris, 1986). A narrow MAS scope consists of internal, financial and historical information. A typical accounting system corresponds to a narrow information system scope (Gordon & Narayanan, 1984). In addition to internal, financial and historical information, a broad MAS scope consists of external, nonfinancial and future-oriented information. The MAS scope construct has been used in previous accounting studies.

Business Unit Performance

We chose business unit performance as the criterion variable because our research interest is to examine the impact on performance of the fit between strategic choices and MAS scope. We only focus on the financial perspective due to the availability and reliability of multidimensional performance indicators. Financial performance indicators have been recognized as an acceptable surrogate for business unit performance, and we used in the present study return on assets and net profit margin indicators.

Hypothesis Formulation

The relationship between strategic choice, MAS scope and business unit's performance is based on a contingency approach. Miles and Snow (1978) provide the foundation of our framework.

As discussed earlier, defenders deal with a stable environment which may be compatible with reliance on historical information, as there is indication that typical accounting systems, which provide historical financial information, deal with stable production processes (Brownell & Merchant, 1990). Defenders propose few products and services, which may reduce the necessity to scan the external environment, and preserve their market share through cost leadership which tend to be congruent with financial information use (Simons, 1987). Consequently, historical, internal and financial information, which corresponds to a narrow MAS scope, may be considered more suitable for managers of defender-type businesses.

In contrast, prospectors deal with a dynamic environment, and offer many products and services through monitoring the organization's environment. Gordon and Miller (1976) suggest that in a hostile and dynamic business environment, accounting systems should include more non-financial information and more forecasts. Prospectors are innovators, seek new markets, and need nonfinancial information on events that may occur in the future (Simons, 1990). As a result, external, nonfinancial and future-oriented information, which corresponds to broad MAS scope, is considered more appropriate for managers of prospector-type businesses.

Two empirical studies support the above discussion on the relationship between business strategy using Miles and Snow's typology, MAS scope, and business unit performance. First, Abernethy and Guthrie (1994) found that broad MAS scope has a more positive impact on business unit performance for prospector firms than for defender firms. Therefore, it appears that performance is dependent on a match between information system scope and strategic type. This study suggests that prospector firms require traditional accounting information be supplemented with broad-based information i.e. that has an external focus, nonfinancial and future-oriented. Second, Chong and Chong (1997) found an indirect relationship between business strategy and business unit performance through the extent to which managers use broad scope MAS. Hence, MAS scope is considered an important antecedent of performance, which is consistent with Abernethy and Guthrie study. In short, it appears that managers operating in defender-type businesses should fit with narrow scope information, whereas managers operating in prospector-type businesses fit with broad scope information.

A core assumption in management accounting research is that an accounting system that provides relevant information to managers, in line with business strategy pursued, translates into higher performance (Merchant & Simons, 1986). Consequently, to achieve a higher business unit performance, a fit between information characteristics used for decision-making and business strategy pursued is suggested. We summarized the previous discussion with the following hypothesis:

The impact of broad scope information usage on business unit performance will be more beneficial for managers operating in prospector-type businesses than for managers operating in defender-type businesses.

The assumption is that broad information scope is less likely to be essential to managers operating in defender-type firms. Some authors argue that a broad information system scope, when provided in an inappropriate context, may have an adverse impact on performance (Gul & Chia, 1994; Chong, 1996).

RESEARCH METHODOLOGY

Sample

A survey research was employed to test our hypothesis. We used the directory of a professional accountants organization to pre-select a set of firms from manufacturing and service industries in order to reinforce generalization.[2] We chose that accountants' organization since we had developed relationship with it in a previous research project. To select the final sample, we contacted members by telephone and first asked if the firm was organized as a business unit. Second, we targeted only firms of 100 employees or more, since it is recognized that business units with fewer than 100 employees are unlikely to have clearly attributed fields of responsibilities (Brownell & Dunk, 1991). For those firms which fulfilled these criteria, we explained the nature of the study, and forwarded questionnaires to the firms that agreed to participate. The questionnaire was designed to collect an assessment on performance, to categorize strategy, and to estimate information scope level. This questionnaire had to be answered by the person who occupied the *highest management position* in the unit. Questionnaires were reviewed to be clear to respondents.

We sent questionnaires to 380 business units. Three telephone reminders at intervals of two weeks, four weeks, and six weeks were conducted after the first sending to reinforce the importance of participation. In total, we received questionnaires from 128 units, but as instruments from 38 units were not usable, they were only 90 usable instruments for a response rate of 24%. In regard to industry groups, we obtained 48 manufacturing firms and 42 service firms. Including all variables, a t-test indicates no significant differences between the two industries at the 0.05 level.

The *highest management position* respondent profile is a general manager who holds a bachelor's degree in commerce, and has an average age of 45 years. At the business-unit level, the average number of employees is 156 and average revenues of $22 million.

To estimate the non-response bias, we compared *late respondents* vs. *early respondents*, those that answered within six weeks and those that answered in more than six weeks. Including all variables, a t-test indicates no significant differences between the two groups at the 0.05 level. Consequently, the results tend to indicate that we do not have the presence of non-respondents bias.

Measures

Three variables were measured: MAS scope, business strategy, and business unit performance. Respondents were asked to answer the questionnaire for their business unit.

MAS Scope

To assess MAS scope we used the six-item instrument developed by Chenhall and Morris (1986). This instrument has been used in previous accounting research, but with adaptation regarding the question asked and items. In the present study, we asked the respondent to indicate the extent to which information items are used for decision-making in their unit. A seven-point Likert scale ranging from "very seldom use" to "very often use" was employed. The instrument is presented in Appendix A. The six items, two questions for each of the three information characteristics (focus, quantification and time horizon), were summed to assess the level of information scope. The higher the score, the broader is the MAS scope. The Cronbach coefficient alpha was 0.62, which is low compare with coefficients obtained in previous studies.

Business Strategy

Strategy was assessed with Miles and Snow's (1978) typology based on Snow and Hrebiniak's (1980) definitions. The respondents were presented with a short description of a defender, a prospector and an analyzer firm, and were asked to choose which description most closely fits their business units, compared to other firms in the industry. Accordingly, in the present study business strategy is a categorical variable. The 90 business units were classified as follows: 27 defenders, 24 prospectors, and 39 analyzers. Since our hypothesis does not included analyzers, this strategic-type is not examined. Accordingly, the sample size to explore is 51 observations, 27 defender and 24 prospector, which is comparable to studies that investigated the business strategy/MAS scope link i.e. Abernethy and Guthrie (1994) with n = 49 and Chong and Chong (1997) with n = 62. The sample of business unit to analyze consists of 31 manufacturing firms (60%), and 20 service firms (40%).

Business Unit Performance

The respondents were asked to classify their business unit performance, compared with their peers, using a 4-point scale on two indicators: return on assets and net profit margin. These financial indicators are commonly used as a key dimension of business unit performance. From the respondent, we obtained a subjective assessment ranging from 4 (the best) to 1 (the worst) for each indicator. The two indicators were summed to form the business unit performance variable. Previous studies showed that subjective assessments obtained from senior managers may be employed as acceptable operationalization since these assessments tend to strongly correlate with the secondary data (see notably Venkatraman & Ramanujam, 1987, for a discussion).

Table 1 provides descriptive statistics of variables measured, whereas Table 2 provides correlation matrix.

As anticipated, the two indicators that form the performance variable, Return on assets and Net profit margin, are positively and significantly correlated at the 0.01 level. Independent variables, MAS scope and business strategy, are positively correlated (0.22), but the correlation is not statistically significant at the 0.05 level.

RESULTS

To test our hypothesis on the fit between strategic choice and information scope, we used the following regression models:

$$Y = \beta_0 + \beta_1 X + \beta_2 Z + \varepsilon$$

and

$$Y = \beta_0 + \beta_1 X + \beta_2 Z + \beta_3 XZ + \varepsilon$$

Table 1. Descriptive Statistics of Variables.

	Mean	S.D.	Min	Max	Theoretical Range
MAS Scope	27.2	5.4	18	42	6–42
Business unit performance (Two indicators summed)	6.04	1.8	2	8	2–8

Business strategy (categorical variable):
Defender, n = 27 and Prospector, n = 24.

Table 2.   Correlation Matrix of Indicators and Variables.

	ROA	NPM	Performance	Scope	Strategy
ROA	1.00				
NPM	0.900**	1.00			
Performance	0.978**	0.971**	1.00		
Scope	0.292*	0.317*	0.311*	1.00	
Strategy	0.275	0.222	0.257	0.228	1.00

Pearson correlation is significant at the 0.01 level**, and at the 0.05 level *,
(2-tailed), n = 51. ROA = Return on assets; NPM = Net profit margin;
Performance = ROA + NPM.
In our study, Strategy has been measured as a dichotomous variable, so we performed a
Point-Biserial correlation for that variable.

where Y = Performance, X = MAS scope, Z = Business strategy (code 0 for
defender strategic-type, and 1 for prospector strategic-type), and XZ an
interaction term representing MAS scope by Business strategy. The hypothesis
is tested when we compare the variance explained by these two regression
models i.e. without and with the interaction term (β_3). An interaction effect is
corroborated by the additional variance explained with the interaction term
(Hartman & Moers, 1999).

   The results are presented in Table 3. Both regressions are statistically
significant, and the R^2 is slightly higher with the interaction term, supporting
weakly a joint effect of strategic choice and MAS scope on performance.[3] This
result suggests to support our hypothesis that the impact of broad information
scope usage on performance is more beneficial for managers operating in
prospector-type firms than for managers operating in defender-type firms.

DISCUSSION AND DIRECTIONS FOR
FUTURE RESEARCH

The aim of this paper was to improve our understanding of the relationship
between business strategy, MAS scope, and performance. Results suggest that
the impact of broad information scope usage on performance is more beneficial
for managers operating in prospector-type firms than for managers operating in
defender-type firms.

   The present study, conducted with Canadian firms, is in line with previous
findings conducted with Australian firms in regard to the importance of the
relationship between strategic choices and MAS scope (see Abernethy &

Table 3. Regressions Results.

	R^2	F	Sig.	Sum of Square	Mean Square	Estimate
Regression models:						
Without interaction term	0.120	3.380	0.042	39.254	19.627	2.41
With interaction term*	0.124	2.210	0.098	39.307	13.102	2.44

Two-tailed test, n = 51.

Guthrie, 1994). Our results may add to the cumulative knowledge in that research area. As well, in their study of strategic choice and MAS scope, Chong and Chong (1997) were concerned that their sample included only manufacturing firms, and stated that generalizing their results to service industry should be done with care. In the present study, we took into account manufacturing and service firms to add to external validity of our results. Our sample of business unit consists of 60% manufacturing firms and 40% service firms. As a t-test indicates no significant differences between the two industry groups, we ran data with both groups and obtained significant results, suggesting that the relationship between strategic choices and MAS scope may apply as well in the service sector.

We still need to improve our understanding of management accounting system design with a contingency approach. For the future, other constructs such as organizational structure should be include in research models.

LIMITATIONS AND CONCLUSION

The present study has several limitations, and we will only note the most pertinent. First, the sample used to test our hypothesis is small. A larger sample would increase confidence of our results. Second, even though the results with a broader range of firms could add to external validity, generalization should be done prudently. Third, organizational performance is a multidimensional construct and we only covered the financial perspective. Finally, even if we have designed the questionnaire to be concise and clear, some respondents may have misunderstood the instrument.

In spite of these limitations, we believe that the present study made a contribution to understanding the relationship between strategic choices and management accounting system scope in a Canadian context, with enhanced external validity made possible by a wider sample i.e. manufacturing and service firms.

ACKNOWLEDGMENTS

The author thanks participants's comments and suggestions made during presentation at the Workshop on Performance Measurement and Management Control, Nice, France, October, 2001. This paper is based on my dissertation, and I thank Suzanne Rivard, Michel Vezina, Claude Laurin and Michel Guindon from HEC Montreal, and Alain Pinsonneault from McGill University. Thanks also to the Lawrence Bloomberg Chair in Accountancy at Concordia University, and CGA-Canada and CGA-Quebec for financial support. The present paper is only reflective of the author's viewpoint.

NOTES

1. Different strategic typologies have been conceptualized, but Miles and Snow (1978) is one of the most widely used, including in the field of accounting research. Miles and Snow formulated three viable strategy types, Defender, Analyzer and Prospector. They also identified a dysfunctional type called Reactor.

2. This organization is CGA-Quebec, a professional accounting association located in the province of Quebec, Canada, and affiliated with CGA-Canada (Certified General Accountants' Association of Canada).

3. In regard to multicollinearity, Durbin-Watson index is 2.28. For VIF (variance inflation factor), indexes are below the suitable level of 10. Accordingly, these results tend to indicate that multicollinearity does not seem to pose a problem.

REFERENCES

Abernethy, M. A., & Brownell, P. (1999). The Role of Budgets in Organizations Facing Strategic Change: An Exploratory Study. *Accounting, Organization and Society, 24*, 189–204.

Abernethy, M. A., & Guthrie, C. H. (1994). An Empirical Assessment of the Fit Between Strategy and Management Information System Design. *Accounting and Finance, 34*(2), 49–66.

Brownell, P., & Dunk, A. S. (1991). Task Uncertainty and its Interaction with Budgetary Participation and Budget Emphasis: Some Methodological Issues and Empirical Investigation. *Accounting, Organization and Society, 16*(8), 693–703.

Brownell, P., & Merchant, K. A. (1990). The Budgetary and Performance Influences of Product Standardization and Manufacturing Process Automation. *Journal of Accounting Research, 28*(2), 388–397.

Chenhall, R. H., & Morris, D. (1986). The Impact of Structure, Environment, and Interdependence on the Perceived Usefulness of Management Accounting Systems. *The Accounting Review, 61*(January), 16–35.

Chong, V. K. (1996). Management Accounting Systems, Task Uncertainty and Managerial Performance: A Research Note. *Accounting, Organizations and Society, 21*(5), 415–421.

Chong, V. K., & Chong, K. M. (1997). Strategic Choices, Environmental Uncertainty and SBU Performance: A Note on the Intervening Role of Management Accounting Systems. *Accounting and Business Research, 27*(4), 268–276.

Dermer, J. (1973). Cognitive Characteristics and the Perceived Importance of Information. *The Accounting Review*, July, 511–519.

Directory members of CGA-Quebec (1997). Quebec, Canada: CGA-Quebec Ordre.

Doty, D. H., Glick, W. H., & Huber, G. P. (1993). Fit, Equifinality, and Organizational Effectiveness: A Test of Two Configurational Theories. *Academy of Management Journal, 36*(6), 1196–1250.

Gordon, L., & Miller, D. (1976). A Contingency Framework for the Design of Accounting Information Systems. *Accounting, Organization and Society*, 59–76.

Gordon, L. A., & Narayanan, V. K. (1984). Management Accounting Systems, Perceived Environmental Uncertainty and Organization Structure: An Empirical Investigation. *Accounting, Organization and Society, 9*(1), 33–47.

Gul, F. A., & Chia, Y. M. (1994). The Effects of Management Accounting Systems, Perceived Environmental Uncertainty and Decentralization on Managerial Performance: A Test of Three-way Interaction. *Accounting, Organizations and Society, 19*(4/5), 413–426.

Hartman, F. G. H., & Moers, F. (1999). Testing Contingency Hypothesis in Budgetary Research: An Evaluation of the Use of Moderated Regression Analysis. *Accounting, Organizations and Society, 24*, 291–315.

Institute of Management Accountants (1995). *Developing Comprehensive Performance Indicators.* Statement no. 4U, 57 pages.

Ittner, C. D., Larcker, D. F., & Rajan, M. V. (1997). The Choice of Performance Measures in Annual Bonus Contracts. *The Accounting Review, 72*(2), 231–255.

Larcker, D. F. (1981). The Perceived Importance of Selected Information Characteristics for Strategic Capital Budgeting. *The Accounting Review*, July, 519–528.

Merchant, K. A., & Simons, R. (1986). Research on Control in Complex Organizations: An Overview. *Journal of Accounting Literature*, 183–203.

Mia, L. (1993). The Role of MAS Information in Organizations: An Empirical Study. *British Accounting Review, 25*, 269–285.

Miles, R. E., & Snow, C. C. (1978). *Organizational Strategy, Structure and Process.* New York: McGraw Hill.

Shortell, S., & Zajac, E. (1990). Perceptual and Archival Measures of Miles and Snow's Strategic Types: A Comprehensive Assessment of Reliability and Validity. *Academy of Management Journal, 33*(4), 817–832.

Simons, R. (1987). Accounting, Control Systems and Business Strategy: An Empirical Analysis. *Accounting, Organization and Society, 12*(4), 357–374.

Simons, R. (1988). Analysis of the Organizational Characteristics related to Tight Budget Goals. *Contemporary Accounting Research, 5*(1), 267–283.

Simons, R. (1990). The Role of Management Control Systems in Creating Competitive Advantage: New Perspectives. *Accounting, Organization and Society, 15*(1/2), 127–143.

Snow, C. C., & Hrebiniak, L. G. (1980). Strategy, Distinctive Competence, and Organizational Performance. *Administrative Science Quarterly, 25*(June), 317–336.

Venkatraman, N., & Ramanujam, V. (1987). Measurement of Business Economic Performance: an Examination of Method Convergence. *Journal of Management*, 109–122.

APPENDIX A – MAS SCOPE INSTRUMENT

(7 point Likert scale ranging from "very seldom use" to "very often use")

In making decisions that affect your business, to what extent you use the following information items:

- Information on the likelihood of future events, for example, probability estimates of an investment project.
- Information of a non-financial nature such as work atmosphere, customer preferences, competitive threats, etc.
- Information on factors external to the business, for example, economic conditions, population growth, technological developments, etc.
- Information that relates to possible future events, for example, future government trade policies.
- Information of a non-financial nature related to operating activities such as output rates, employee absenteeism, etc.
- Information related to products /services market such as market size, growth in market share, etc.

THE ROLE OF TRANSFER PRICING FOR MANAGEMENT CONTROL IN MULTINATIONAL ENTERPRISES

Martine Cools

ABSTRACT

The management control function of transfer pricing is studied in an international context using in-depth case studies. Transaction costs economics provides some basic insights in the development of the transfer pricing policy. The role of the implemented policy for performance measurement and evaluation is however severely limited. The influence of transfer prices has been eliminated and, increasingly, non-financial performance measures are used. Exceptions to the formal transfer pricing policy are inevitable to overcome the restricted business flexibility, created by the fiscal compliance requirements. Future research should extend the analysis inside this multinational and compare the situation with other enterprises.

1. INTRODUCTION AND RESEARCH QUESTIONS

The domestic transfer pricing literature describes transfer pricing as a part of the management control system of the company with two main objectives: the promotion of goal congruence and the provision of a suitable system of performance measurement and evaluation (Grabski, 1985; Leitch & Barrett,

Performance Measurement and Management Control, Volume 12, pages 61–83.
ISBN: 0-7623-0867-2

1992). This study focuses on the management control aspects of transfer pricing in an international environment. The largest difference with domestic transfer pricing is that multinational enterprises (MNEs) in an international context have to cope with fiscal rules: national authorities impose transfer pricing regulations out of fear for tax abuse by MNEs. Worldwide, corporate income tax legislation has become remarkably more severe since 1994.

Since the introduction of international transfer pricing rules, 'arm's length' has been chosen as the international yardstick to reach correct fiscal transfer prices. The arm's length principle, incorporated in article 9 of the OECD Model Tax Convention, means that transfer prices between interrelated parties are acceptable for the tax authorities if the same prices would have been chosen for the same or a similar transaction between independent parties. While 'arm's length' continues to be the main principle, it cannot be denied that the fiscal regulations have become increasingly strict and detailed over the last years. The impetus was given by the U.S. Internal Revenue Service (IRS) whose 1994 regulations[1] still provide the most severe and detailed transfer pricing regulations in the world. The OECD reacted to this development by updating its OECD Transfer Pricing Guidelines in 1995. The 1995 Guidelines, although a lot more detailed than the earlier versions, do however not aim at being as strict as the IRS rules. More and more local tax authorities are incorporating the 1995 OECD Transfer Pricing Guidelines in their national regulation and an increasing number of countries are making their transfer pricing rules more severe than in the past.[2]

The main consequence of the current transfer pricing rules is that MNEs have to justify explicitly that their transfer pricing policy does not violate any fiscal rules, and that their policy is based on sound business grounds. This requirement led to a drastic increase in the administrative burden for the MNEs: extensive contemporaneous documentation needs to be provided. A functional analysis (an explicit study of the functions assumed by the two parties in the transaction, the risks incurred, and the assets involved) and comparables (prices and margins used by external parties, used to prove that the MNE is respecting the arm's length principle) have to be included. The better the documentation sustains the MNE's transfer pricing decision, the more the tax authorities are inclined to accept the policy. Practice is controlled by transfer pricing audits and potential penalties. Besides, more and more countries offer advanced pricing agreements (APAs) for the multinationals. These agreements imply that both parties nego-tiate to determine a mutually acceptable transfer pricing system before the transactions actually occur and that is valid for a limited number of years.

The recent changes in the regulations provide an opportunity to study and learn from possible changes in the management control system. Field research is used to investigate the influence of the fiscal transfer pricing rules on the management control function of transfer pricing in multinational enterprises. While the issues of tax planning and tax management are endogenous to the study, tax abuse is excluded as much as possible: the MNEs selected for the preliminary study and the MNE of the main study are companies that have traditionally complied well with the tax rules.

Transfer pricing has been studied from various angles in the literature. As described further, the different approaches highlight parts of the theme, but none of them seem to capture the research topic completely. Although also subject to a number of limitations, transaction cost economics is used as the broad underlying theoretical basis for this study. Transaction cost economics investigates the way transactions are coordinated, through market, hierarchy or a hybrid, by specifying a number of characteristics of the transactions. This study uses transaction cost economics to provide insights in the way in which MNEs handle the fiscal requirements related to the managerial role of transfer pricing. In line with practice, where transfer pricing guidelines are written in terms of transactions, transaction cost economics determines the unit of analysis as a transaction or a series of similar transactions. This choice enables the researcher to get hold of the research questions in the large amount of influencing factors in the field. The research questions are formulated as follows:

(1) What are the consequences of the tighter regulations for the design and use of transfer pricing as an instrument of management control?
(2) The possible opposite causal relationship is taken into account: 'does the use of transfer pricing as a management control instrument have an influence on the MNE's fiscal transfer pricing policy?'

Both aspects of the research question are represented in Fig. 1. Lobbying by the MNEs with the regulatory bodies to influence the official regulations (through approaching the OECD working party and national tax authorities) falls outside of the scope of this study.

The remainder of the text is structured as follows. Section 2 gives an overview of the contributions of the study. In Section 3, the theoretical basis is described. The Sections 4 and 5 present the research method and the analysis. In Section 6, the conclusions and suggestions for future research can be found.

2. CONTRIBUTIONS OF THE STUDY

This transfer pricing study contributes to the literature for a number of reasons. First, a meta-analysis (Borkowksi, 1996) on transfer pricing research reveals that existing empirical work does not fully explain the relationships between

lobbying

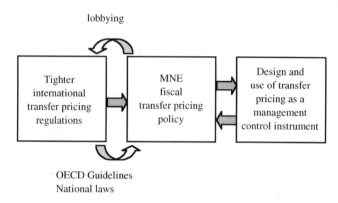

Fig. 1. The Management Control Function of Transfer Pricing in an International
Context.

environmental and organizational factors, and the transfer pricing method choice
by multinational corporations. This project aims at going beyond a mere enumer-
ation of transfer pricing methods and objectives (Shih, 1996) and tries to respond
to the call for stronger theoretical contributions that explain how transfer pricing
processes are actually managed (Colbert & Spicer, 1995).

Second, transfer pricing as an aspect of the management control system in
a company is considered in a fiscal context. The goal is to make a contribution
in narrowing the gap between 'management accounting' and 'tax' studies
of transfer pricing. Until now, empirical accounting studies have mainly
approached the regulatory environment as an incentive for international transfer
pricing manipulation and income shifting (e.g. Jensen, 1986; Halpirin &
Srinidhi, 1987, 1991; Grubert & Mutti, 1989; Harris et al., 1982; Klassen
et al., 1993; Harris, 1993; Jacob, 1996; Swenson, 2001). The purely fiscal studies
have often focused on the different regimes in different national jurisdictions,
or discussed the optimal fiscal approach towards the transfer pricing issue
(Picciotto, 1992). Since it is still not well understood in which way political
forces drive organizational change (Libby & Waterhouse, 1996), this study
investigates the influence of the change in fiscal rules on transfer pricing as an
internal instrument in the MNE.

Third and last, field research provides insights in the implications of the new
transfer pricing regulations. Do the new regulations decrease the distortions
between the fiscal and the managerial transfer price? In a number of countries
penalties have been imposed, which results in an increasing role of tax in the
decision making process. If the stricter regulations push MNEs to use fiscally

determined prices in their internal decision making, the reach of the arm's length principle is clearly overextended (Eden, 1998; Hamaekers, 1999).

3. THEORETICAL BASIS

A number of different literature streams provide the building blocks for this study. After a short overview of the transfer pricing literature, transaction cost economics as the basic underlying theory is discussed. In order to identify the a priori constructs, concepts from the transfer pricing literature are supplemented by specific elements from the management control literature. Table 2 provides an overview of the a priori constructs.

3.1. The Transfer Pricing Literature

In the domestic management control literature, the role of transfer pricing to promote goal congruence and to measure and evaluate performance is studied (Benke & Edwards, 1980). Goal congruence is related to decisions on the efficient allocation of resources, strategy and make-or-buy decisions. Performance measurement concerns managerial evaluation and reward (Leitch & Barrett, 1992). International approaches have often focused on how transfer pricing contributes to global profit maximization (Jensen, 1986; Halpirin & Srinidhi, 1987, 1991; and others). Attention to the role of transfer pricing within the management control system of the multinational company has so far been minor. Both in the domestic as in the international context, transfer pricing has been investigated from different theoretical and empirical angles. Table 1 incorporates the most important approaches that have been used.

Originally, domestic transfer pricing was studied. In the 1950s, micro-economic concepts (Hirschleifer, 1956) were used to determine the optimal internal transfer price. Later, mathematical programming approaches were applied. Only in the 1970s, the behavioral aspects of transfer pricing started to be studied. In the first place, the individual's reaction towards transfer pricing was taken into account. This approach has grown into a considerable stream of negotiated transfer pricing studies. Later the behavior of the organization started to gain attention. Transfer pricing studies of the 1980s and 1990s added insights from organizational theory (Swieringa & Waterhouse, 1982), agency theory (Harris et al., 1982; Wagenhofer, 1994), contingency theory (Borkowski, 1990), transaction cost economics (Spicer, 1988; Colbert & Spicer, 1995) and strategy (Eccles, 1985).

Table 1. A Broad Overview of the Transfer Pricing Literature.

	Theoretical approaches:	*Empirical approaches:*
d	micro economics	TP as dependent variable:
o	competitive advantage (strategy)	• TP method
m	organisational theory	• TP objectives
e	transaction cost economics	TP as independent variable:
s	contingency theory	• management of TP processes and
t	behavioural theory	outcome of TP policy
i	agency theory . . .	
c		
i	*Theoretical approaches:*	*Empirical approaches:*
n	micro economics	TP as dependent variable
t	competitive advantage (strategy)	• TP method
e	contingency theory	• TP objectives
r	theory of foreign direct investment	TP as indepenent variable
n	income shifting	• income shifting proofs
a		• management of TP processes and
t		outcome of TP policy

Articles on international transfer pricing are based on the theory of foreign direct investment (Rugman, 1981; Eden, 1998), income shifting (Samuelson, 1982; Conover & Nichols, 2000), micro economics (Jensen, 1986; Halpirin & Srinidhi, 1987; Prusa, 1990), competitive advantage (Cravens, 1997) and contingency theory (Borkowski, 1992). Empirical approaches have mainly focused on transfer pricing as the dependent variable: which method is chosen by the MNE and what are the objectives of the MNE's transfer pricing policy (Tang, 1979, 1992; Al-Eryani et al., 1990; Lin et al., 1993). The management of transfer pricing processes and the outcome of the transfer pricing policy are only addressed in a limited number of studies (e.g. Emmanuel & Mehafdi, 1994; Cravens & Shearon, 1996). Empirical income shifting studies on international transfer pricing focus on how the transfer pricing policy is chosen in order to decrease the tax burden by the MNE (Grubert & Mutti, 1991; Harris, 1993; Klassen et al., 1993; Swenson, 2001).

Contingency theory, competitive advantage theory and transaction cost economics provide some interesting ideas to approach the research questions in this study. The main reason is that the focus goes to individual transactions that need to be studied in the relevant context. Internal and external influencing variables, organizational strategy and structure are therefore of primary importance. As explained below, transaction cost economics has been selected as the most suitable approach.

3.1.1. Contingency Theory

Borkowski (1992) studied existing practice concerning international transfer pricing in a contingency framework. Survey data were used to identify organizational and environmental variables that affect the choice of the transfer pricing method (as in Borkowski, 1990). In contrast to Borkowski's study of transfer pricing decisions in a particular setting of specific circumstances, this study investigates changes in the role and use of transfer pricing in the international context. The focus is on the 'changes', since the processes of drawing up transfer prices and the related procedures and rules are considered to be at least as important as the prices, procedures and rules themselves (Swieringa & Waterhouse, 1982; Colbert & Spicer, 1995).

3.1.2. Competitive Advantage Theory

Eccles (1985) found that strategy and the administrative process are the most important determinants of domestic transfer pricing practices, while Cravens (1997) used surveys to focus on the strategic role of transfer pricing in an international context. Cravens (1997) stressed that management evaluation and performance are generally of major concern with respect to domestic transfer pricing. In the international context, transfer prices are still experienced as an important instrument of performance evaluation by multinational enterprises, although transfer pricing decisions have to be taken in an environment that is a lot more complicated. Taking into account the importance of strategy and the useful insights from a strategic point of view, the role of transfer pricing for management and control is the focus of the study presented here, since management control has been the main subject in the domestic transfer pricing accounting literature.

3.2. Transaction Cost Economics

By its focus on the advantages of the organizational form, transaction cost economics has tried to redefine the analysis of the dynamics of the firm (Picciotto, 1992). According to Williamson (1979, 1993), a transaction can possibly be governed by three coordination mechanisms: the market, the hierarchy, or a hybrid. The choice of the mechanism to govern a transaction depends on a comparative analysis of the transaction costs caused by one of the three alternatives. The transaction costs depend on a combination of the characteristics of the transaction taking place – asset specificity, uncertainty and frequency – and of certain human characteristics – bounded rationality and opportunism. The focus on bounded rationality emphasizes the rejection of the neo-classical paradigm based on the rational choice of the pure individual with perfect information

(Picciotto, 1992). Williamson (1979, 1993) predicted that the structure with the lowest transaction costs would be used to govern the transaction. The larger the transaction costs in a relationship are, the more hierarchical controls are used. Essentially, transaction cost economics tries to explain different ways of organizing transactions, although it does not study how the managers in the firms make their assessments of the transaction costs involved.

A number of studies have applied transaction cost theory to domestic transfer pricing. Spicer (1988) incorporated Eccles' ideas in an organizational theory on the transfer pricing process. He developed a number of hypotheses on the relationships among diversification strategy, intra-firm transactions, organizational structure and management accounting and control systems. In the case studies by Van der Meer-Kooistra (1993), the transaction cost theory was used to determine the factors influencing in which way internal domestic transactions were coordinated by means of transfer pricing systems. Similarly, Colbert and Spicer (1995) refined Spicer's model into a theory of the sourcing and transfer pricing process from a transaction cost perspective. Their case study research revealed that the management of internal transfers and internal prices are indeed determined by the reported degree of transaction-specific investment (asset-specificity) associated with each transfer. Besides, there was a clear link with the strategic importance of the transferred component and the nature of the component division's production capabilities.

In an international context, the nature of the internal transfer does not change: it still concerns a transaction involving goods, services or intangibles, where operational considerations are the basis for all other decisions. Williamson (1987) argued that the growth of the firm into the multidivisional corporation, the conglomerate and the transnational company results not so much from economies of scale in production (which could be realized through contracting) but from the advantages of the organizational form, both in controlling and applying technological innovation and in taking strategic capital investment decisions (Picciotto, 1992). The transaction cost theory is considered as a useful approach towards international transfer pricing if it is extended in a number of ways.

First, the theory ignores historical trends: the transfer pricing policy within a MNE evolves continuously over time (Boyns et al., 1999). This evolution is not only caused by internal factors, but also by external factors such as the increasing importance of fiscal rules. Second, the international aspects of transfer pricing need to be explicitly incorporated in transaction cost theory. In an international context transfer prices undergo a lot more influences than in a purely domestic context. The increased uncertainty concerning international transfers is partly incorporated in the 'uncertainty' aspect defined as a transactional characteristic. Besides, the stricter and more elaborated fiscal rules force MNEs to comply and to set up a formal transfer pricing policy. 'The issue of transfer pricing vividly demonstrates the political dimensions of forms of economic calculation, since it stands at the intersection of the firm and the state' (Piciotto, 1992, p. 793). The fiscal requirements can be incorporated in the transaction cost approach. The OECD Guidelines are basically directed to the level of the transaction in the MNE, so the 'transaction' can be used as the unit of analysis in an international context. The burden on MNEs to meet the fiscal requirements leads to an important cost of compliance that can be expressed as a transaction cost. The cost of compliance is different for every transaction, depending on the different national jurisdictions that are involved. It can be considered as an additional cost that influences management to organize the transaction through the organization or the market. If the cost of compliance becomes too high, it might be better to organize the transaction in a different way.

Third, transaction cost economics is rather static, in the sense that it ignores dynamic aspects as well as organizational and procedural mechanisms of governance (Ghoshal & Moran, 1996). This shortcoming is addressed by paying explicit attention to transfer pricing processes. The development, implementation and adaptation of the transfer pricing policy are studied. Moreover, the focus is on changes in order to increase insights into the dynamics. A fourth point is that management control systems form only a part of organizational forms or governance structures, and remain implicit in the original transaction cost framework. Management control instruments can be incorporated in the transaction cost approach as hierarchical control instruments (Gulati & Singh, 1998). Colbert and Spicer's (1995) multi-case investigation in a domestic context stresses that 'the transfer pricing process represents an important and pervasive problem in designing and implementing management information and control systems' (Colbert & Spicer, 1995, p. 423). Although Colbert and Spicer mention the importance of management control instruments, they do not study them explicitly, while these aspects are addressed by the research questions proposed here.

3.3. The Management Control Literature

A useful representation of the elements of a management control system was provided by Chow et al. (1999): they defined decentralization, structuring of activities, participative budgeting, standard tightness, performance evaluation, controllability filters, and performance contingent financial rewards. Based on this and other articles (Merchant & Manzoni, 1989; Ittner & Larcker, 1998; Otley, 1999; Merchant et al., 1995; Bushman et al., 1996; Dent, 1996), the management control constructs are defined.

3.4. The A Priori Constructs

Table 2 represents the constructs for the study, categorized as taxation-related aspects of transfer pricing, international and operational aspects, and internal management-oriented aspects (Abdallah, 1989; Leitch & Barrett, 1992). The 'transfer pricing system' or 'policy' is defined along the lines of Eccles (1985) and Leitch and Barrett (1992): it incorporates decisions on pricing and sourcing, including production, operation and location decisions. Given the focus on corporate income tax aspects, the fiscal rules prescribed by the OECD and the national tax authorities are the basis for the definition of the tax-related aspects. The most pronounced influence comes from the administrative requirements, to say the documents needed and involving an explicit functional analysis and the provision of comparables. The resulting costs of compliance are a major concern for the MNEs. Besides, the fear for audits and penalties, as well as possible advance pricing agreements are taken into account.

The field study is guided by the following working propositions:

Proposition 1a: In the context of the tighter regulations, management control systems are not influenced by international transfer pricing fiscal rules and MNE compliance.

Proposition 1b: If there is an influence of fiscal international transfer pricing rules on the management control systems, this influence can be explained in terms of transaction cost economics.

Proposition 2a: The MNE's international transfer pricing policy and compliance are not influenced by the management control systems.

Table 2. The A Priori Constructs Based on the Literature.

Fiscal rules	Transfer pricing literature	
Tax-related	Operational & International	Management control
Administrative requirements: Documents Comparables Functional analysis	Pricing decisions Sourcing decisions Routing of products, services, intangibles Make or buy	Goal congruence: Evaluation of business units and segments Performance measurement of individual managers
Compliance costs Audits/penalties APAs		

Proposition 2b: Any influence of the use of transfer pricing for management control on the fiscal transfer pricing policy and compliance can be explained in terms of transaction cost economics.

4. RESEARCH METHOD

While a preliminary study using four large MNEs provided the first insights, the main study is based on one MNE, selected from the four original companies. Within the largest product group of this MNE, an embedded case study (Yin, 1994) is undertaken, investigating several transactions (multiple cases) in-depth.

4.1. Case Studies

The aim is to refine the theory on international transfer pricing by 'inducting insights from field-based case data' (Brown & Eisenhardt, 1997). The context is highly pertinent to the phenomenon of study (Yin, 1994) since the design and implementation of transfer processes is studied in a specific organizational context. Another point is that transfer pricing is a sensitive topic: the data is not publicly available and the use of one-to-one interviews reduces response biases (Ferreira & Merchant, 1992). A longitudinal approach is used to focus on dynamics and processes (Van der Meer-Kooistra, 1994). 'Transfer pricing systems are in a permanent flux, not only because of changing circumstances, but also because the parties involved learn as they go along. Changes in the formal regulations need time. Therefore, research into the functioning of transfer pricing systems has to take full account of the processes of change and adaptation, or the dynamics of the phenomenon' (Van der Meer-Kooistra, 1994). To incorporate the dynamics, different phases i.e. development, implementation and adaptation of the transfer pricing policy are examined. In the tradition of Yin (1994) analytic generalization, as opposed to statistical generalization, is important in this study (Ferreira & Merchant, 1992).

4.2. The Choice of the Research Site

A preliminary study was undertaken to refine the ideas on the topic and to select a suitable site for the main study. The first study was also useful to gain experience in interviewing business people. Four large MNEs were chosen that did not have problems with the tax authorities, and that used one set of books for transfer pricing. Transfer pricing experts at corporate tax level were interviewed. All MNEs used centrally imposed transfer pricing policies within their product groups. In terms of tax compliance, 3 of the 4 companies were still working out how to correspond to the requirements of the OECD and local governments. Consequently, the MNE that complied in the most advanced way with the fiscal transfer pricing rules was selected for the in-depth study. The choice was therefore made by theoretical sampling (Yin, 1994). The chosen MNE is a large, highly divisionalized manufacturing company, operating both in the business-to-business market as in the final consumer market. The advantage of a field study in one MNE is that the specific situation of the company can be taken into account, and that other important factors, such as corporate culture and competitive strategy, are homogenized (Otley, 1999). Moreover, this multi-case study takes place in one product division, the most global one, characterized by the most elaborated transfer pricing policy and by the largest variety of transactions. The activities of the product division are focused on the industrial, business-to-business market. The study was limited to one product division in order to come to a deeper understanding. Differences in culture and strategy between major product groups are controlled in this way.

The unit of analysis is the cross-border transaction or a series of transactions, comparable to the transaction cost economics approach by Colbert and Spicer (1995). The cases consist of the study of three different transactions. The selection criteria for the transaction are represented in Table 3.

The three transactions under study have a number of aspects in common. All three transactions concern the transfer of goods. Since international transfer pricing is emphasized, every case investigates a cross-border transaction (or a series of transactions). As explained above, differences among product groups are controlled for by selecting transactions from the same product group. Moreover, the transactions have to be significant for the MNE and dynamic. This dynamism can be caused by factors like the introduction of comparables, reorganization of the transfer pricing policy or the activity's structure etc. At the same time, the transactions are chosen in order to maximize the difference

Table 3.   Selection of the Transactions.

Constant across transactions:	Cross-border
	Transfer of a good
	Same product group
	Significant to MNE
	Dynamic
Variation across transactions:	Technology
	Application
	Market

between them. The main selection criteria are the variation in technology, application and market.

4.3. Variables (Table 2)

The first two propositions investigate the relationship between the international transfer pricing policy (sourcing and pricing aspects) and the management control system. In order to come to a better hold on the management control system, the different aspects as identified by Chow et al. (1999) are basically investigated: structuring of the activities, participative budgeting, standard tightness, performance evaluation, controllability filters and performance contingent financial rewards. A number of control variables are identified: degree of decentralization (Chow et al., 1999), size, organizational and product group culture are controlled by investigating one product group in one MNE. Although the influence of national culture is expected to be minimized because the management control system is imposed by corporate headquarters (Merchant et al., 1995), the cases indicate that national culture has a major influence on performance evaluation. Other contingent variables, such as technology, national regulations and competitive strategy are explicitly taken into account in the choice of the transactions.

4.4. Research Process

The first transaction is studied in an exploratory way, while the next ones are used as explanatory case studies (Eisenhardt, 1989). The parties involved at both ends of the transaction are interviewed. Eighteen persons have been interviewed, with the interviews ranging from half an hour to two hours. At top level, the corporate fiscal director and his tax colleagues are involved. Moreover, interviews were made with the corporate quality manager, the product group corporate controller and the product group internal auditor. Further SBU controllers and human resources managers within the selected product group were addressed. At the levels below, subunit controllers and human resources managers, as well as accountants are interviewed.

The semi-structured interviews are based on open-ended questions. The questions are prepared in order to focus on the basic theme and a priori constructs (Table 2) while they are open enough for unexpected elements to come in (Eisenhardt, 1989). Triangulation is reached by complementing the in-depth interviews with official company data: the published financial statements, the official transfer pricing policy documents, the transfer pricing documents used by the SBU and subunit managers, and human resources documents. The raw interview transcripts are written up in order to come to one case per transaction. In order to increase the internal validity of the cases, the interviewees have been contacted for follow-up questions, and a number of interviewees were asked to verify the case concerning the transaction they are involved with.

The research process is highly iterative. In order to gather and analyze the data, the methodological recommendations by Eisenhardt (1989), Yin (1994) and Miles and Huberman (1998) are followed. Eisenhardt (1989) stresses the need of triangulation and suggests the use of within-case and cross-case analysis methods. Global measures need to be constructed to describe the data, and events should be transformed into variables. Yin (1994) focuses on the design of case study research and favors the replication logic when using multiple case studies. Miles and Huberman (1998) describe procedures to analyze, manage and present qualitative data. Their strategy is called visual mapping (Langley, 1999).

Apart from writing up the different cases, a document providing the general context of the cases has been prepared[3]. Following Miles and Huberman (1998), contact summary sheets have been made after each interview, and document summary forms are used to put each document in context. Coding (Miles & Huberman, 1998) has started a provisional 'start list' developed prior to the fieldwork, based on the a priori constructs and the research questions. This provisional list was tested out on the product group's official transfer pricing document, and also during the actual coding process, the provisional list has been revised a number of times.

5. ANALYSIS

The MNE is a large industrial multinational with production facilities and sales organizations all over the world. The MNE's customers are located both in the consumer as in the industrial market. The company has been selected since it complies in a very advanced and proactive way with the fiscal transfer pricing requirements. The product group under investigation is situated in the business-to-business market. On the one hand, the product group is structured on a product axis, divided into SBUs and subunits. On the other hand, it is organized on an organizational axis in a number of production facilities and sales organizations. Every SBU and its subunits can make use of the production facilities that provide the required technology and capacity, and markets and sells its products through the sales organizations.

The three cases – series of transactions – have been chosen from different SBUs. As indicated by the selection criteria, the cases have different character-istics. Case 1 involves a complicated, customer specific product. Case 2 concerns a simple commodity product, and case 3 focuses on a simple, customer specific product. The technology is different: the products involved in transaction 1 use a different, more advanced technology than the products of transactions 2 and 3. Besides, the goods transferred differ in the degree of customization. The transfer of customer specific products (transaction 1 and 3) is contrasted to the processes involved for customized, commodity goods (transaction 2). Consequently a different market strategy characterizes the different transactions.

The three cases pass through a number of countries at different stages in the value chain. Consequently, they are all confronted with different compliance requirements along the process. While at some stages external comparables have to be provided for fiscal compliance, at other stages in other countries, no fiscal comparables are asked for, and are therefore also not identified. In other words, the search for comparables is closely related to the geographical routing of the transfers: whether it involves heavily regulated countries (where the use of comparables to prove that the internal transaction does indeed respect the 'arm's length principle' is imposed) versus less heavily regulated countries.

In order to study processes and changes, the phases of development, implementation and adaptation of the transfer pricing policy are discussed.

5.1. Development of the Transfer Pricing Policy

The development of the international transfer pricing policy contains two aspects. The policy has to be set up and worked out, and moreover the official transfer pricing documentation, an important instrument towards the tax authorities, needs to be prepared. The MNE's headquarters leaves the initiative for installing an adequate and acceptable worldwide transfer pricing policy to the product group centers. The main reason for the decentralization is that the product group centers are better placed to optimize their transfer pricing policy in close consultation with their local business organizations. In this way, bounded rationality is taken into account. Consequently, a specific transfer pricing document is prepared and published by each product group. Within the MNE, the way in which the official document is determined, is considered as an important evidentiary proof towards the tax authorities: the policy is set up in advance, and in principle the transfer prices cannot change because of concrete circumstances. Only fundamental business changes could be a reason for updating the transfer pricing policy. Such changes are then carefully documented to justify the modification towards the local tax authorities.

An important evolution compared to the past is that after development by the product group, the transfer pricing policy is fed back to the corporate tax department. Especially since the new international transfer pricing regulations

(OECD Guidelines and their implementation in the different countries) came out, the MNE does not want to take any risk on the fiscal side. Therefore, the corporate fiscal department has to make sure that the transfer pricing policy, as proposed by the product groups, respects the international taxation rules. For large companies it is of primary importance to be on good terms with the national authorities, especially if these companies need the authority's goodwill for other (fiscal) questions.

Largely influenced by the stricter regulations, the corporate fiscal department together with the product group controller have made efforts to simplify the transfer pricing policy. Over the whole product group, a uniform transfer pricing method is used for all activities. The three cases have to follow the same pricing instructions, which are specific to each stage in the supply chain. The system intends to leave no discretion for adapting the prices or policy to particular national or international circumstances. The chosen policy is motivated in the fiscal documentation using explicit business arguments. A detailed functional analysis justifies the selection of the internal prices. Interviewees at all levels within the product group find that the installment of the uniform transfer pricing policy is a positive evolution, both towards the business as towards the national tax authorities.

The uniform pricing decisions in the product group can be explained using the logic of transaction cost economics. Possible confusion is minimized, so bounded rationality as well as potential opportunism seems to be handled by this simple system. Internal prices at different stages in the supply chain are higher or lower according to the degree of asset specificity involved. On the other hand, the uniform system does not leave room for the different product-related characteristics of the three cases under study. The technology used in case 1 is a lot more complicated than the technology in case 3, which in turn is more complicated than technology 2. Also differences in frequency are largely ignored by the uniform transfer pricing policy: the frequency of case 2 is a lot higher than of the customer specific cases 1 and 3. Still, transfer prices for the three cases are calculated in exactly the same way.

4.2. Implementation of the Transfer Pricing Policy

Transfer prices are based on budget information. This means that the prices are calculated once a year during the budgeting process. Only periodical changes are allowed if urgent external reasons come up. During the budgeting process, the budgets proposed by the different organizational levels are incorporated. The proposals by the subunits are gathered at the SBU level. The proposals by the SBUs come together at the product group center, and the product group's resulting proposal is then sent to the board of management. The product group management stresses that this way of setting up the budget has led to an improvement of management control.

Recent company reports stress that the creation of value should be the focal point of any decision made. The principles of value-based management are implemented by using EVA (economic value added) to measure the financial performance of all the businesses. A value-based management approach is going to be incorporated in the incentive compensation program to reward managers for creating shareholder value. The SBU managers are also accounted for at EBIT (earnings before interest and tax). Because of the organizational structure of the company, the performance of each unit is only determined by external elements: the costs of materials and other inputs at the beginning of the process, compared to the sales revenues at the end of the process. As explained above, each SBU makes use of the common production and sales organizations it needs. Therefore, all intermediate prices are neutralized against each other. The only place where taxation comes in is in the calculation of EVA. This measure is calculated by applying a number of corrections to EBIT, such as the correction for the perceived tax burden. This tax correction factor is imposed by the corporate tax department. However, at all levels management seems to realize that EVA contains a number of factors that the managers cannot influence. There is a general awareness that it would be unfair to account people for these factors going beyond their control. Over the last years, the balanced scorecard has been used, which involves the increasing role of non-financial performance measures.

While the influence of transfer pricing on the SBU managers seems to be neutral, the meaning of transfer pricing for the production facilities needs to be scrutinized. In that context, it seems that make-or-buy decisions are not taken based on transfer pricing information. Location and outsourcing decisions are based on strategy and the technology required in the process.

5.3. Adaptation of the Transfer Pricing Policy

Transfer prices are fixed once a year, and, as indicated above, adaptations are only possible in exceptional cases. During the interviews one example came up of a situation in which the transfer price needed to be adapted in order to make the product competitive on the final product market. This example indicates that some degree of flexibility for business reasons is inevitable. When the policy is not compatible with the market, the official pricing model is critically analyzed in order to come to a solution. In the case of required adaptation, the SBU controller acted as a mediator, while the product group controller was the person who actually officially allowed the deviation. Again, any form of adaptation, related to managerial and commercial flexibility, is thoroughly motivated in the fiscal transfer pricing documents.

5.4. The Cost of Compliance

A lot of people are involved when the transfer pricing policy has to be documented towards the tax authorities: the corporate fiscal department, the product group controllers, as well as divisional tax managers who gather information in the countries. Moreover, putting in place the documentation is a long process, starting from a thorough study of the regulations, gathering information from the businesses, discussions concerning the functional analysis, searching for comparables etc. Moreover, it is impossible to establish a general procedure for documentation, since the requirements differ according to the local legislations.

External costs are incurred in the sense that consultants' databases need to be used for the search for comparables. The costs of owning commercial databases are often too high for the corporate fiscal department, especially because these databases cannot be used in other departments within the MNE. A related cost is that the corporate tax department needs the help of consultants to learn how to search for the comparable data, required in the fiscal documents. An expensive pilot study has been undertaken by external consultants in order to search for comparables for a certain region. The cost of compliance also involves the difficulties of compliance itself: it is often not possible to find comparables for products or services and a lot of products or markets operate under different conditions. There is a regular need to update the comparables search. Moreover, the information provided should cover several years.

An important aspect of the cost of compliance is the significant simplification of the official transfer pricing policy. The aim of this development is to provide a transparent and simple system towards the tax authorities. This simple structure seems to be applied at the expense of commercial flexibility and the use of transfer pricing for performance evaluation and remuneration. Instead of using the transfer pricing system for performance measurement, the company is evolving towards other means of management evaluation, in which non-financial performance measures play an important role. It seems to be a large burden for the normal functioning of the business that the international transfer pricing policy has to be checked thoroughly by the corporate tax department to make sure that no official transfer pricing regulations are violated. Compared to the past where transfer pricing was purely determined by the product division, more time and effort needs to be spent for fiscal compliance.

6. CONCLUSIONS

Proposition 1 states that management control systems are not influenced by international transfer pricing fiscal rules and MNE compliance. However, the analysis indicates that the use of transfer pricing for management control does undergo a clear influence from the international fiscal rules. Applied to the cases, transaction cost economics provides a useful theoretical background for this study of international transfer pricing. The information gathered confirms the hypotheses of Spicer (1988) and the results of Colbert and Spicer (1995): the reported degree of transaction-specific investment, asset specificity, is a very important determinant of the transfer prices. It means that asset specificity has a direct influence on the way the prices are managed. The pricing methods are clearly motivated by the MNE's functional analysis, provided in the official transfer pricing document. On the other hand, the differences in transaction-specific characteristics among the three cases are not reflected in the official transfer pricing policy.

The influence of the international transfer pricing rules is noted especially in performance evaluation. Controllability plays an important role: the impact of transfer prices, which cannot be determined or influenced by the managers in the divisions, is minimized as much as possible. Besides, the system is made as transparent and simple as possible towards the tax authorities. The strategic possibilities are therefore limited, and sometimes the prices need to be adapted in order to increase commercial and managerial flexibility.

Proposition 2 is concerned with the impact of management control systems on the MNE's international transfer pricing policy and compliance. No evidence to refute this proposition has been found so far. This research can be extended in a number of ways. In the first place, hypothesis 2 should be investigated more profoundly. Moreover, the analysis in this paper focuses on three products in three different SBUs. The study of the production and sales units of the MNE could lead to additional insights in the management control role of international transfer pricing. Finally, the study needs to be repeated in other MNEs, so that the results found here can be compared and contrasted to other situations.

NOTES

1. These regulations are incorporated in sections 482 and 662(e) of the Internal Revenue Code and regulations thereunder.
2. A lot of countries did not have any specific transfer pricing legislation and did just refer to the OECD Guidelines.

3. The general document starts with a short description of the MNE as a whole (general background information, organizational structure, overall strategy and transfer pricing policy), followed by a detailed description of the selected product group (general aspects on the product and production process involved, the market, key activities, the business' organization, and the product group's transfer pricing policy).

ACKNOWLEDGMENTS

The author would like to thank Ann Jorissen, Clive Emmanuel and Regine Slagmulder for their comments on earlier draft versions of this work. Any shortcomings are of course the author's.

REFERENCES

Abdallah, W. M. (1989). *International Transfer Pricing Policies*. Westport, CT: Quorum Books.
Anderson, S. W. (1995). A framework for assessing cost management system changes: the case of activity based costing implementation at General Motors 1986–1993. *Journal of Management Accounting Research*, Fall, 1–51.
Al-Eryani, M. F., Alam P., & Akhter S. H. (1990). Transfer Pricing Determinants of U.S. Multinationals. *Journal of International Business Studies*, *21*(3), 409–425.
Benke, R. L., & Edwards, J. P. (1980). Transfer pricing, techniques and uses. *Management Accounting*, June, 44–46.
Birnberg, J. G., Shields, M. D., & Young, S. M. (1990). The case for multiple methods in empirical management accounting research (with an illustration from budget setting). *Journal of Management Accounting Research*, *2*(Fall), 32–66.
Borkowski, S. C. (1990). Environmental and Organizational Factors Affecting Transfer Pricing: A Survey. *Journal of Management Accounting Research*, Fall, 78–99.
Borkowski, S. C. (1992). Organizational and international factors affecting multinational transfer pricing. *Advances in International Accounting*, *5*, 173–192.
Borkowski, S. C. (1996). An Analysis (Meta- and Otherwise) of Multinational Transfer Pricing Research. *The International Journal of Accounting*, *31*(1), 39–53.
Boyns, T., Edwards, J. R., & Emmanuel, C. (1999). A longitudinal study of the determinants of transfer pricing change. *Management Accounting Research*, 85–108.
Brown, S. L., & Eisenhardt, K. M. (1997). The art of continuous change : linking complexity theory and time-spaced evolution in relentlessly shifting organizations. *Administrative Science Quarterly*, *24*, 1–34.
Bushman, R., Indjejikian, R., & Smith, A. (1996). Aggregate Performance Measures in Business Unit Manager Compensation: the Role of Intra-firm Interdependencies. *Journal of Accounting Research* supplement, 101–128.
Chow, C. W., Shields, M. D., & Wu, A. (1999). The importance of national culture in the design of and preference for management control for multinational organizations. *Accounting, Organizations and Society*, July/August, 441–461.
Colbert, G. J., & Spicer, B. H. (1995). A Multi-Case Investigation of a Theory of the Transfer Pricing Process. *Accounting, Organizations and Society*, *20*(6), 423–456.

Conover, T. L., & Nichols, N. B. (2000). A further examination of income shifting through transfer pricing considering firm size and/or distress. *The International Journal of Accounting, 35*(2), 189–211.

Covaleski, M. A., & Dirsmith, M. W. (1990). Dialectic tension, double reflexivity and the everyday accounting researcher: on using qualitative methods. *Accounting, Organizations and Society, 15*(6), 543–573.

Cravens, K. (1997). Examining the role of transfer pricing as a strategy for multinational firms. *International Business Review, 6*(2), 127–145.

Cravens, K., & Shearon, W. T. (1996). An outcome-based Assessment of International Transfer Pricing Policy. *The International Journal of Accounting, 31*(4), 419–443.

Demski, J. (1994). *Managerial Uses of Accounting Information.* Boston: Kluwer Academic Publishers.

Dent, J. (1996). Global competition: challenges for management accounting and control. *Management Accounting Research, 7,* 247–269.

Eccles, R. (1985). *The Transfer Pricing Problem: a Theory for Practice.* Lexington, MA: Lexington Books.

Eden, L. (1998). *Taxing multinationals: Transfer Pricing and Corporate Income Taxation in North America.* Toronto: University of Toronto Press.

Eisenhardt, K. M. (1989). Building Theories from Case Study Research. *Academy of Management Review, 14*(4), 532–550.

Emmanuel, C. R., & Mehafdi, M. (1994). *Transfer Pricing.* London: Academic Press Ltd.

Ferreira, L. D., & Merchant, K. A. (1992). Field Research in Management Accounting and Control: a Review and Evaluation. *Accounting, Auditing and Accountability Journal, 5*(4), 3–34.

Ghoshal, S., & Moran, P. (1996). Bad for practice: a critique of the transaction cost theory. *Academy of Management Review, 21,* 13–47.

Grubert, H., & Mutti, J. (1991). Taxes, tariffs and transfer pricing in multinational corporate decision making. *The Review of Economic and Statistics,* May, *73,* 285–293.

Gulati, R., & Singh, H. (1998). The architecture of cooperation: managing coordination costs and appropriation concerns in strategic alliances. *Administrative Science Quarterly, 43,* 781–814.

Hamaekers, H. (1999). Transfer pricing en het arm s length beginsel: historie, huidige situatie, toekomst. *Liberale Gift, Vriendenbundel Ferdinand Grapperhaus.* Deventer: Kluwer, 159–174.

Halpirin, R. M., & Srinidhi, B. (1987). The effect of the U.S. income tax regulations transfer pricing rules on allocative efficiency. *The Accounting Review,* October, 686–706.

Halpirin, R. M., & Srinidhi, B. (1991). U.S. Income Tax transfer pricing rules and resource allocation: the case of decentralized multinational firms. *The Accounting Review, 66*(1, January), 141–157.

Harris, D. G. (1993). The impact of U.S. tax law revision on multinational corporations, capital location and income shifting decisions. *Journal of Accounting Research, 31*(supplement), 111–140.

Harris, M., Kriebel, C. H., & Raviv, A. (1982). Asymmetric information, incentives and intrafirm allocation. *Management Science, 28*(6, June), 604–620.

Ittner, C. D., & Larcker, D. F. (1998). Innovations in Performance Measurement: Trends and Research Implications. *Journal of Management Accounting Research, 10,* 205–238.

Jacob, J. (1996). Taxes and Transfer Pricing: income shifting and the volume of intrafirm transfers. *Journal of Accounting Research, 34*(2, Autumn), 301–313.

Jensen, O. W. (1986). Transfer Pricing and output decisions: the dynamic interaction. *Decision Sciences, 17*(summer), 428–436.

Klassen, K., Lang, M., & Wolfson, M. (1993). Geographic income shifting by multinational corporations in response to tax rate changes. *Journal of Accounting Research, 31*(supplement), 141–173.

Langley, A. (1999). Strategies for theorizing from process data. *Academy of Management Review, 24*(4), 691–710.

Leitch, R. A., & Barrett, K. S. (1992). Multinational Transfer Pricing: Objectives and Constraints. *Journal of Accounting Literature, 11*, 47–92.

Libby, T., & Waterhouse, J. (1996). Predicting change in management accounting systems. *Journal of Management Accounting Research, 8*, 137–150.

Lin, L., Lefebvre, C., & Kantor, J. (1993). Economic determinants of international transfer pricing and the related accounting issues, with particular reference to Asian Pacific countries. *International Journal of Accounting, 28*, 49–70.

Merchant, K. A., Chow, C. W., & Wu, A. (1995). Measurement, evaluation and reward of profit center managers: a cross-cultural field study. *Accounting, Organizations and Society, 20*(7/8, October/November), 619–638.

Merchant, K. A., & Manzoni, J. (1989). The Achievability of Budget Target in Profit Centers: A field study. *The Accounting Review*, 539–558.

Miles, M. B., & Huberman, A. M. (1998). *Qualitative data analysis, an expanded sourcebook.* London: Sage Publications.

OECD (1995, 1996, 1997). *Transfer Pricing Guidelines for Multinational Enterprises and Tax Administrations.* France: Head of Publications Service OECD.

Otley, D. (1999). Performance management: a framework for management control systems research. *Management Accounting Research, 10*, 363–382.

Plasschaert, S. (1994). Transnational Corporations. Introduction: Transfer Pricing and Taxation. In: S. Plasschaert (Ed.), *U.N. Library on Transnational Corporations* (Vol. 14, pp. 1–21). Routledge.

Picciotto, S. (1992). International taxation and intrafirm pricing in transnational corporate groups. *Accounting, Organizations and Society, 17*(8), 759–792.

Prusa, R. J. (1990). An incentive compatible approach to the transfer pricing problem. *Journal of International Economics, 28*, 155–172.

Rugman, A. (1981). *Inside the Multinationals.* New York: Colombia University Press.

Rugman, A. (1986). New theories of the multinational enterprise: an assessment of internationalisation theory. *Bulletin of Economic Research, 38*(2), 101–118.

Samuelson, L. (1982). The multinational firm with arm s length transfer pricing limits. *Journal of International Economics, 13*, 365–374.

Scapens, R. W. (1990). Researching Management Accounting Practice: the Role of Case Study Methods. *British Accounting Review, 20*, 259–281.

Shih, M. S. H. (1996). Optimal Transfer Pricing Method and Fixed Cost Allocation. *Abacus, 32*(2), 178–195.

Slagmulder, R. (1997). Using management control systems to achieve alignment between strategic investment decisions and strategy. *Management Accounting Review, 8*(1), 103–139.

Spicer, B. H. (1988). Towards an Organizational Theory of the Transfer Pricing Process. *Accounting, Organizations and Society, 13*(3), 303–322.

Swenson, D. (2001). Tax Reforms and Evidence of Transfer Pricing. *National Tax Journal*, March, 7–25.

Swieringa, R. J., & Waterhouse, J. H. (1982). Organizational Views of Transfer Pricing. *Accounting, Organizations and Society, 7*(2), 149–165.

Tang, R. Y. W. (1992). Transfer Pricing in the 1990s – The Emphasis on multinational and tax issues. *Management Accounting*, February, 22–26.

Tang, R. Y. W., & Chan, K. H. (1979). Environmental Variables of International Transfer Pricing: A Japan-United States Comparison. *Abacus*, June, 3–12.

Van der Meer-Kooistra, J. (1994). The Coordination of International Transactions: the Functioning of Transfer Pricing Systems in the Organizational Context. *Management Accounting Research*, 5, 123–152.

Wagenhofer, A. (1994). Transfer Pricing under asymmetric information, an evaluation of alternative methods. *The European Accounting Review*, 3(1), 71–106.

Williamson, O. E. (1979). Transaction cost economics: the governance of transactional relations. *Journal of Law and Economics*, 22, 3–61.

Williamson, O. E. (1987). *The economic institutions of capitalism: firms, markets, relational contracting.* New York: The Free Press.

Williamson, O. E. (1993). Transaction cost economics and organizational theory. *Industrial and Corporate Change*, 2, 107–156.

Yin, R. K. (1994). *Case Study Research: Design and Methods.* Applied Social Research Methods Series, Vol. 5 (2nd ed.). London: Sage Publications.

THE ROLE OF ACCOUNTING WHEN EMPLOYEES PARTICIPATE IN DECISION-MAKING

Barbara Sainty

ABSTRACT

Accounting information is made available to managers and employees to facilitate their participation in decision-making. However, both research and management experience have demonstrated that employee participation is useful under limited circumstances. Therefore a study using accounting information that examines employee participation in a controlled environment is warranted.

Laboratory experiments demonstrate the ability to increase productivity by sharing accounting information with players in a prisoner's dilemma. Explicit information in the form of a report (much like accounting information) is successful in achieving greater productivity. However, implicit information does not achieve the same results. Interestingly, the two mechanisms together offer the highest level of productivity.

INTRODUCTION

Employees are becoming more and more involved in decision-making procedures at all levels of organizations. A variety of accounting information is made available to managers and employees to facilitate decision-making.

Performance Measurement and Management Control, Volume 12, pages 85–108.
Copyright © 2002 by Elsevier Science Ltd.
All rights of reproduction in any form reserved.
ISBN: 0-7623-0867-2

Some organizations call this practice open-book management (OBM). Others use the terms business literacy, employee empowerment, employee participation or employee involvement. Whatever the name, the practice of sharing information has become increasingly popular in recent years (Cotton, 1993; Lawler, 1993). Surveys of *Fortune 1000* firms have shown that the vast majority of large organizations use some form of employee involvement (EI) and that this trend is increasing (Lawler, Mohrman & Ledford, 1992). Many disciplines, such as economics, psychology, sociology and communication, among others, have studied employee involvement in the workplace, although few studies focus on the accounting function, itself.

The results of these studies are mixed. For example, Wagner (1994, p. 325) defines participation as a process in which influence is shared among individuals who are otherwise hierarchical unequals. He concludes that although participation is positively related to both employees' performance and satisfaction, the magnitude of its effects is small enough to raise questions regarding the practical benefits of such programs. Several major reviews of the literature on EI and worker participation define participation and involvement from a variety of perspectives. The findings suggest that any positive relationship between employee participation and enhanced work attitudes and behaviours is relatively small (Locke & Schweiger, 1979; Schweiger & Leana, 1986; Wagner, 1994).

However, most of these studies do not isolate or manipulate the effect of specific variables. Rather, they conduct field studies or use survey instruments to analyze participation's effect on performance and job satisfaction. Two meta-analyses of the participation literature (Wagner & Gooding, 1987a, b) indicate that significantly different conclusions can be reached concerning the effects of participation on both performance and attitudes, depending on the ways in which participation and outcomes are operationalized and measured. Essentially, they argue that studies that rely on percept-percept methods (data on both participation and outcomes are measured using a single questionnaire at a single point in time from the same group of respondents) artificially inflate the relationships between participation and outcomes. Therefore, both scientific literature and management experience have demonstrated that participation is useful only under certain circumstances. The concept of employee involvement clearly warrants further study.

Employee involvement and participation can be facilitated in a variety of ways. One possibility is through the dissemination of relevant accounting information to employees in an effort to reduce informational asymmetry and increase employee productivity. This study explicitly examines the sharing of accounting information with employees. Using experimental economics techniques, I directly manipulate variables and isolate the effect of accounting information and determine whether it leads to greater productivity.

I examine the effectiveness of two mechanisms to increase productivity in a prisoner's dilemma. One mechanism provides information directly to participants as to the effort choice of their partner. This explicit mechanism is much like an accounting system as it allows participants to observe numerical outcomes. The other mechanism is endogenous through correlation of the two environments. It is much like environmental factors having a similar effect in different divisions of a firm. This creates an implicit mechanism. Both mechanisms reduce noise in a prisoner's dilemma setting.

The results of the laboratory experiments demonstrate the importance of accounting in increasing productivity by sharing accounting information with players. In addition, the form of information is critical in increasing productivity. Explicit information in the form of a report (much like accounting information) is successful in achieving greater productivity. However, implicit information does not achieve the same results. Interestingly, the two mechanisms together offer the highest level of productivity.

The rest of the paper is organized as follows. The next section outlines the theoretical and practical development of employee involvement. I then outline the experimental hypotheses, followed by a description of the experimental procedure. The results are discussed in the next section. Finally, I develop conclusions and identify future research opportunities.

BACKGROUND LITERATURE

Many disciplines, such as economics, psychology, sociology and communication have studied employee involvement in the workplace, although few studies focus on the accounting function, itself. In economics, for example, from an agency perspective, the subordinate (agent) acts on behalf of another (principal), creating informational asymmetry. A subordinate knows more about his or her task and task environment than does his or her superior, thus necessitating the need for employees to be involved. Employee involvement is used by the superior to gain information – reduce uncertainty – about the subordinate's task and task environment (Christensen, 1982; Baiman & Evans, 1983; Penno, 1984; Kirby et al., 1991). A consequence of this information sharing is that the superior is able to design and offer the subordinate a more efficient, goal-congruent incentive contract that increases subordinate motivation to achieve the organization's goals. The agent exerts effort and uses his or her information to improve outcomes. Employee goals and actions are more closely aligned with those of owners, greatly reducing the agency problem (inadequate goal congruence) between employees and the owners.[1]

Besides modeling how uncertainty and vertical information asymmetry are mitigated by EI, economic researchers have modeled how EI can be used to reduce horizontal information asymmetries by enabling the superior to gain information about subordinates' interdependent tasks and thus co-ordinate their information (Kanodia, 1993). Most of this research is done from a theoretical perspective.

Much EI research has been based on psychological theories (Becker & Green, 1962; Ronen & Livingstone, 1975; Hopwood, 1976; Brownell, 1982; Young, 1988; Murray, 1990). Locke and Schweiger (1979) and Locke and Latham (1990) consider mechanisms by which EI between a superior and a subordinate can affect decision-making. One mechanism, value attainment arises from giving the employee the opportunity to express his or her values. This action is theo- rized to affect satisfaction and morale because the process (act) of participation allows a subordinate to experience self-respect and feelings of equality thereby increasing performance.

Two other mechanisms, motivation and cognition, also are theorized to affect performance. The motivational mechanism increases a subordinate's trust, sense of control, and ego-involvement with the organization through his or her involvement in the decision-making process. These characteristics may cause less resistance to change and more acceptance of, and commitment to, the orga- nizational decisions, in turn causing improved performance. The cognitive mechanism assumes that the process of participation improves subordinate performance by increasing the quality of decisions as a result of the subordi- nate sharing information with the superior.

Sociological theories have been used to model how organizational context (e.g. environmental uncertainty) and structure (e.g. decentralization, functional differentiation) are antecedents to EI. The theoretical underpinning of this research has been the contingency theory of organizations (Hopwood, 1976; Brownell, 1982; Otley & Wilkinson, 1988; Fisher, 1995). This theory predicts that as an organization's external environment becomes more uncertain, the organization responds by increasing its differentiation (e.g. number and type of subunits). Consequently, the organization requires an increase in the use of inte- grating mechanisms, such as participative budgeting to co-ordinate the actions of its subunits (Lawernce & Lorsch, 1967; Brownell, 1982). Thus, EI is assumed to be a reaction to environmental uncertainty. Greater EI reduces environmental uncertainty and increases productivity in a result similar to economic theory.

Research in communications considers the role of trust and communications when uncertainty and complexity grow, and as market conditions shift and change without warning. The time available to act and react grows shorter and mutual cooperation among employees working under these conditions is achieved through increased communication and mutual trust. In fact, trust can influence coordination and control at both institutional and interpersonal levels of the organization (Pettit, Vaught & Pulley, 1990; Daft & Huber, 1987; Shapiro, 1987; Zucker, 1986; Granovetter, 1985; Pennings & Woiceshyn, 1987).

Communication researchers identify three factors that affect perceptions of trustworthiness: (1) accurate information, (2) explanations for decisions, and (3) openness. Employees see managers as trustworthy when communication between the parties is accurate and forthcoming. In addition, adequate and timely explanations on decisions lead to higher levels of trust (Folger & Konovsky, 1989; Konovsky & Cropanzano, 1991; Sapienza & Korsgaard, 1996). Open communication, in which managers exchange thoughts and ideas freely with employees, enhances perceptions of trust (Butler, 1991; Farris, Senner & Butterfield, 1973; Gabarro, 1978; Hart, Capps, Cangemi & Caillouet, 1986).

Managerial sharing and delegation of control may promote trust because of the interplay between economic and social factors. When managers involve employees in decision-making, employees have greater control over decisions that affect them and, therefore, can protect their own interests. In agency terms, this control by employees reduces the risk of opportunism and increases the likelihood of favourable outcomes for the firm.

Kim (1975) and Clampitt & Downs (1993) examine the relationship between productivity and communication. Kim (1975) finds that higher productivity is associated with more effective feedback about performance. Clampitt and Downs (1993) find that communication is perceived to have an effect on productivity. The effect varies in both kind and magnitude; however, the link between communication and productivity is more complex than previously assumed.

Academics, government officials, management, and labour practitioners continue to encourage organizations to increase employee input into decision making to enhance organizational performance (Applebaum & Batt, 1994; Commission on the Future of Worker-Management Relations, 1994; Levine, 1995). Evidence exists, however, that raises questions about the efficacy of employee participation programs (Locke & Schweiger, 1979; Schweiger & Leana, 1986; Wagner & Gooding 1987a, b; Wagner, 1994). For example, Wagner (1994, p. 325) concludes that although participation is positively related to both employees' performance and satisfaction, the magnitude of its effects on firm performance is small enough to raise questions regarding the practical benefits of such programs. Several major reviews of the literature on EI and worker participation suggest that any positive relationship between employee participation and enhanced work attitudes and behaviours is relatively small (Locke & Schweiger, 1979; Schweiger & Leana, 1986; Wagner, 1994). Employee participation has, at best, consistent but small positive effects on performance and satisfaction.

Schwochau et al. (1997) argue that benefits of participation will be realized only when certain individuals at particular levels of the organization provide input and then only under specific circumstances and in certain types of organizations. Despite only moderate empirical support for the specific hypotheses tested thus far (Wagner & Gooding, 1987b), researchers continue to argue that participation programs are likely to yield expected gains only under certain circumstances, and that additional research is necessary to identify and understand the influences on mediating variables (Pasmore & Fagans, 1992).

With these conflicting results, it is clear that additional work is needed in the area.

EXPERIMENTAL HYPOTHESES

As stated by Pasmore and Fagans (1992), in order to advance the study of employee involvement, researchers need to examine and manipulate specific variables in a controlled setting to determine their effect. Therefore, the methodology of experimental economics is ideal for testing specific variables. Should results obtain, work can be extended beyond the laboratory. Results are best demonstrated with a simple process of interaction where benefits can be obtained (production can be increased) by utilizing information. Players should benefit from mutual cooperation and have the opportunity to develop trust with each other. A repeated prisoner's dilemma fits these requirements.

Based on previous work (Axelrod, 1984; Bendor, Kramer & Stout, 1991; Roth & Murnighan, 1978; Murnighan & Roth, 1983; Andreoni & Miller, 1993) noise reduction in a prisoner's dilemma setting can increase productivity. However, few previous studies examine the form of noise reduction to determine if it influences productivity. Noise reduction in a prisoner's dilemma is parallel to employee involvement in that both employees and players receive additional information that they can use to evaluate their decisions. It is important for managers to understand how best to communicate information to their employees in order to increase productivity, if, indeed, EI can increase productivity. This study examines two different mechanisms, one explicit and one implicit, to determine if either has an effect on productivity. That is, does the form of communicating information to employees affect decisions?

Previous studies by both Kahn and Murnighan (KM) (1993) and Miller (1996) introduce various types of noise into the environment. KM (1993) introduce noise through two different mechanisms. The first is through manipulations in the expectation of an opponent's potential strategy and the second is through uncertainty about each other's payoffs. The impact of payoff uncertainty increases the incidence of cooperation (production) only in relatively restricted situations. Overall, KM (1993) finds that players cooperate much more than predicted, and that they are more likely to cooperate when they are certain of each other's payoffs.

Miller (1996) considers imperfect reporting of the opponent's actual moves. He introduces a probability (a percentage) that indicates the percentage of time an opponent's move is reported to be the opposite of what the opponent actually did, while the remainder of the time, the move is perfectly transmitted. Three levels of informational accuracy are explored: perfect information, one percent noise and five percent noise. He studies the strategies that emerge, and finds that the average payoff paths of the three environments quickly trifurcates and each remains significantly different from the others. He finds that cooperation (increased production) emerges in all three systems, although to varying degrees. Cooperative strategies tend to proliferate in low noise conditions, although even with no noise, cooperation is not perfect.

A natural progression from these previous studies is an examination of the type of noise manipulations that are most effective in encouraging greater productivity (increased cooperation). We can think of the players as a partnership in which each player supplies an unobservable input (q_j) to a production process as in Radner (1986). The output depends stochastically on the quantities of both inputs and is divided among the partners in a prearranged way. This is the model of double-sided moral hazard.

Model description

At the beginning of each period, each player selects between two effort levels: low effort (e_l^i) or high effort (e_h^i) (where $i \in \{1,2\}$). Low effort is costless; high effort has a cost of τ. By selecting low effort, the player receives a high quality (low quality) asset with probability π_0 $(1-\pi_0)$. The asset quality is denoted q_j^i ($i \in \{1,2\}$, $j \in \{l,h\}$, where $q_h^i > q_l^i$). If the player selects high effort, the probability that the high (low) quality asset is generated is π_1 $(1-\pi_1)$. High effort gives a higher probability of a high quality asset ($\pi_1 > \pi_0$). The outputs are combined to produce joint earnings according to the joint production function, defined below. The expected earnings of the partnership, shared equally by both players, depend on the joint output obtained from the combined inputs of both players.

The joint production process takes the asset obtained from each player and generates an output that produces earnings. Earnings are a function of the two assets received and a synergistic parameter obtained from the combining of resources. This synergy factor (λ) is a constant such that $1 < \lambda < 2$. The synergy factor is selected so that benefits are obtained from joint production ($\lambda > 1$), but the dominant, single period strategy is to select low effort ($\lambda < 2$). This parameterization produces a prisoner's dilemma and captures the synergies from repeated interaction within the firm (Alchian & Demsetz, 1972). Therefore, total partnership earnings in any period are $\theta = l\,(q_j^l + q_j^2)$ ($j \in \{\lambda, h\}$). The expected value of earnings generated from the joint production function if both players select high effort is: $E\,[\theta \mid e_h^l, e_h^2] = 2\lambda\,[q_h\,\pi_1^2 + (q_h + q_l)\pi_1(1 - \pi_1) + q_l(1 - \pi_1)^2]$. The increase in expected earnings from both players selecting e_h over e_l is $2\lambda(q_h - q_l)(\pi_1 - \pi_0) > 0$. The benefits obtained from selecting high effort must exceed the cost of effort (i.e. $2\lambda(q_h - q_l)(\pi_1 - \pi_0) > 2\tau$) in order for the principal to prefer high effort.

This model creates benefits from selecting high effort but does not map directly into effort choice. The rationale is that the economic environment may not be perfectly correlated with effort choice and may introduce variations not controlled by the effort choices of individuals. In many situations, the payoffs obtained may reflect exogenous shocks from the economy, the behavior of customers, suppliers, the workforce, etc. that may not be perfectly known by their colleagues. As a result of these disturbances that are external to the organization's dyadic relationship, decision makers may occasionally draw incorrect inferences about their peers' actions. Therefore, this experiment utilizes a stochastic nature of asset. Individual effort choices are not observable, but the joint outcome provides some information on individual inputs.

Experimental design

Two different approaches are taken to reduce noise in the environment. The first is through explicit feedback that eliminates the first order uncertainty about probability distributions of individual outcomes. This is achieved by providing players with the asset value generated from their effort choice ($q_j, j \in \{l,h\}$) based on the appropriate probabilities of π_i and $1 - \pi_i$ ($i \in \{0,1\}$ for $0 = $ low effort; $1 = $ high effort). This allows each player to perfectly determine the other player's q by observing total earnings (θ) and to better infer the other player's effort choice in order to evaluate his own appropriate strategy. However, joint outcomes still contain second order uncertainty as the outcome of the other participant does not map directly into his effort choice.[2] This information is much like interdivisional information shared amongst managers in firm. It is a form of accounting information.

The second approach to noise reduction is through correlation in the environment creating an implicit feedback mechanism. Correlation is a measure of association between attributes and is operationalized using the same technique as in Arya, Glover, and Young (1996).[3] Higher output correlation levels provide the ability to make more precise inferences of effort choices. The expected payoffs to the players are invariant to whether or not correlation is present. However, the probability of receiving a high type asset, given that the other player also receives a high type asset, is different. In general, the reduction of noise in this experiment is consistent with the idea of Holmström's informativeness (Holmström, 1979) that states that any informative signal, regardless of how noisy it is, will have positive value if costless.

The concept of noise reduction is tested using four experimental cells in a 2×2 design that contrasts the presence/absence of an explicit feedback mechanism with and without an implicit feedback mechanism. Figure 1 illustrates the experimental design. Experimental parameters are defined in Table 1. The hypothesis is that noise reduction leads to greater productivity.

A high quality asset (q_h) generates an asset value of 50 points. A low quality asset (q_l) generates an asset value of 30 points. In each market period, each player has two choices regarding effort. When low effort is selected, a low quality asset (q_l) obtains 75% of the time; a high quality asset (q_h) obtains 25% of the time. Selecting high effort returns a high quality asset (q_h) 75% of the time and a low quality asset (q_l) 25% of the time. Low effort can be selected without cost whereas the cost for high effort is 10 points. The expected benefits from both players selecting high effort versus both selecting low effort increases earnings by 30 points $[(0.75 - 0.25)(150 - 90)]$[4].

	No Explicit Mechanism	*Explicit Mechanism*
No Implicit Mechanism	**B**	**EMO**
Implicit Mechanism	**IMO**	**EIM**

Key: B = Baseline; EMO = Explicit Mechanism Only; IMO = Implicit Mechanism Only; EIM = Both Explicit and Implicit Mechanisms.

Fig. 1.   Experimental Design.

Table 1.   Experimental Parameters.

Variable	Description	Experimental Value
e_l	Low Effort	0
e_h	High Effort	10
q_l	Low Quality Asset	30
q_h	High Quality Asset	50
τ	Cost of Effort	10
π_0	Prob (q_h / e_l)	0.25
$1 - \pi_0$	Prob (q_l / e_l)	0.75
π_1	Prob (q_h / e_h)	0.75
$1 - \pi_1$	Prob (q_l / e_h)	0.25
λ	Synergy Factor	1.5

Example of Noise Reduction

Noise in a prisoner's dilemma occurs when the observed outcome does not perfectly indicate the player's effort choice in the immediately preceding round. Reducing noise increases the probability that the observed outcome can be explained by the effort choice of the player. In this study, both explicit and implicit mechanisms reduce noise allowing for more accurate belief revisions about the other player's effort choice. A general proof is available from the author. However, an example will serve to illustrate.

With no mechanisms available to reduce noise, the joint production output is the only ex post observable. The inputs are obtained independently from each player. In comparison, when the explicit mechanism is present, individual asset qualities are also observable. This new observable allows for more accurate belief revisions. Second, when environments are correlated through the implicit mechanism, the new probability structure leads to less noise when compared to no mechanism being available. Third, when both the explicit and implicit mechanisms are available, there is less noise when compared with either mechanism alone. These mechanisms allow players to more accurately revise their beliefs toward that of the actual effort choice made by their partners, on average. Expectations are used to calculate posterior beliefs in order to facilitate comparisons between cells. A numerical example is detailed in Appendix B.

Experimental Hypotheses

Hypotheses are developed by building on theories from several disciplines, especially previous work regarding prisoner's dilemmas. I expect that reducing noise in the environment will significantly increase production. Therefore, both the explicit and implicit mechanisms are expected to lead to higher productivity. There is no explicit interaction effect predicted.

EXPERIMENTAL PROCEDURE

Subjects were recruited from undergraduate business classes. Twelve subjects (six pairs) were used for each cell. The average amount of cash earned by each subject was $17.76. A "best case" scenario (always cooperate) was set such that expected earnings were approximately $19 for each subject participating in the experiment at an expected length of 30 periods.

Each experimental cell had an unknown time horizon of at least 25 periods. On period 25, and each period thereafter, the experimenter rolled a pair of dice in the presence of subjects. If the two dice matched (a "pair") the experiment ended. Otherwise, the experiment proceeded to the next period.[5] Subjects were informed of a maximum time limit for each experimental session. They were asked to return to complete the experiment should it be necessary.[6]

Players were randomly paired with the same partner for the training rounds and then randomly paired with another partner throughout the experiment. Repeated play allowed players to respond to each other's actions and use prior information to develop cooperation and trust. As Miller (1996) found, cooperation may be an evolving process. Also Andreoni and Miller (1993) found evidence that partners (repeated play) helped sustain cooperation. Thus, the experiment was designed to capitalize on this by providing an ability to build a reputation.

Each experimental session consisted of the same sequence of events: instruction and training, market periods, and the post-experimental phase. Upon arrival at the computer lab, subjects were given written instructions that were also read aloud. Following the instructions, the players were randomly paired and the training phase began. Training consisted of two example periods in which subjects were given the selection information to enter where applicable followed by four training periods in which subjects made their own decisions with respect to effort selection. The purpose of the example and training periods was to familiarize the subjects with the computer terminal and the experiment's structure. The example periods were used to demonstrate the possible outcomes that could obtain from different effort choices. Training periods allowed subjects to become familiar with the experimental structure when different decisions were entered. Points earned in the training phase had no value.[7]

Players were randomly paired again for the market periods that proceeded in the following sequence:

(1) Participants selected an effort choice. (Bin selection)
(2) *Cells EMO and EIM only*: Participants received a report of the input gener-
    ated by the effort choice made in step 1 (q_h or q_l). This was the
    operationalization of the explicit feedback mechanism.
(3) Reports were received with respect to the joint output (earnings) for the
    period.
(4) Individual payments were calculated according to the 50 : 50 sharing rule.
(5) Points were updated.

At the end of all market periods, the subjects' screens informed them that
the experiment was complete and displayed their cash earnings. Subjects
received 1¢ for each point in their ending point balances. Prior to payment,
subjects completed a post-experimental questionnaire in an effort to elicit
supplemental information on strategy choices. Sessions lasted approximately
one hour.

RESULTS

Measuring Results

Effort choices can be measured in a variety of ways. The dependent variable
is the mean effort choice for each pair of participants.[8] For analysis, effort is
categorized 0 (both select low effort), $1/2$ (one selects high effort, one selects
low effort), or 1 (both select high effort).[9] The average effort choice of each
pair is calculated over all periods' observations.[10] This creates six observations
per cell (one per subject pair). Due to the 0,1 dependent variable and the limited
sample size, non-parametric methods are used to analyze the data.[11] This
suggests the stochastic mechanism used to decide when the experiment would
terminate was successful in reducing end-gaming.

In cell B, participant pairs both chose high effort 44.4% of the time.
The average effort choice for all participants was 0.654 and the standard
deviation was 0.204. (Average effort choice represents the average number
of times a participant selected high effort.) For cell IMO, both participants
chose high effort 44.1% of the time and the average effort choice was 0.651.
The standard deviation for the cell was 0.139. In cell EMO, both participants
chose high effort 49.3% of the time. The average effort choice for participants was 0.717 and the standard deviation was 0.144. In cell EIM, both
participants chose high effort 68.4% of the time. The average effort choice
for all participants was 0.822 and the standard deviation was 0.123. Data are
summarized in Fig. 2.

	Baseline	Implicit Mechanism Only	Explicit Mechanism Only	Explicit and Implicit Mechanisms
Pair No. 1	0.742	0.694	0.760	0.607
Pair No. 2	0.576	0.855	0.620	0.839
Pair No. 3	0.667	0.597	0.920	0.911
Pair No. 4	0.303	0.548	0.720	0.804
Pair No. 5	0.727	0.710	0.500	0.804
Pair No. 6	0.909	0.500	0.780	0.964
Average Effort	**0.654**	**0.651**	**0.717**	**0.822**

Fig. 2. Average Effort Choices.

Analyzing Results

This study focuses on the production levels achieved by an explicit or implicit reporting mechanism. The effect of an explicit mechanism on production choices is tested by comparing the average effort levels of cells B and IMO (where the system is not available) to the average effort levels of cells EMO and EIM (where the system is available) in a Wilcoxon signed rank test. The hypothesis that reduced noise increases production is supported at p=0.03, with higher effort choices in cells with an explicit feedback mechanism.[12]

The effect of an implicit mechanism on production is tested by comparing the average effort levels of cells B and EMO to both cells with the implicit mechanism (cells IMO and EIM). Results are not significant at conventional levels. Second, cell IMO (only) is compared to cell B (only). Again, results are not significant.

A possible reason for the failure of the implicit mechanism is that the Bayesian updating required of individuals to update prior beliefs is complex when correlation alone is present. Participants must first infer an asset quality and then infer the effort choice of the other player in order to find an expected posterior probability. Heuristically, these calculations may be difficult to perform. Problems with subjects' calculations using Bayes formula are found by Tversky and Kahnemann (1973); Bar-Hillel (1973 and 1980); Cohen (1981); and de Dombal (1988). Bar-Hillel (1973) finds that as complexities increase, the ability to correctly update prior beliefs deteriorates. Therefore, the additional calculations required in the correlation cells may be beyond the limits of the participants. With an explicit mechanism, by contrast, the calculation is more intuitive.[13]

Finally, both mechanisms together are tested to determine their effect on production. This is tested by comparing results in cell EIM with those obtained in cell EMO. This comparison is significant at a p value of less than 0.05. There also is a significant difference between cells IMO and EIM (p value < 0.03), illustrating that the two mechanisms together achieve the greatest level of production and that the explicit mechanism is superior to the implicit mechanism.

Both results are consistent with the theory that noise reduction can influence effort choices and the fact that Bayesian updating only requires inference of an effort choice in cell EIM in order to find an expected posterior probability for the actual effort choice made by the other player. When the two mechanisms work together, benefits are even greater.[14] Results are summarized in Fig. 3.

CONCLUSION

The results of this study suggest that the method selected to communicate information to employees has an effect on its ability to achieve greater production.

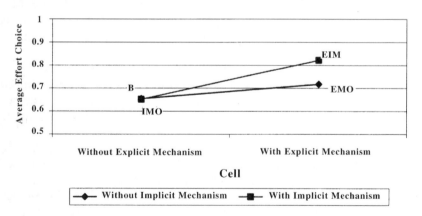

Key:
B = Baseline; IMO = Implicit Mechanism Only; EMO = Explicit Mechanism Only; EIM = Explicit and Implicit Mechanisms.

Fig. 3.   Effect of Noise Mechanisms.

These results support the use of accounting information as a means of communicating with employees to increase production. The study addresses concerns raised by Pasmore and Fagans (1992) by identifying at least one specific variable, accounting information, which can have a positive effect on employee involvement and productivity. It also provides evidence that EI can have a significant positive effect on productivity.

The controlled setting and abstract nature of the accounting information limit, to some extent, the generalizability of the study. The next step will be to move from a theoretical and analytical examination of EI to direct discussion with managers. If accounting information is to be used effectively to increase productivity, a concrete definition of what accounting information should be shared is necessary.

NOTES

1. For details on agency theory and implications for financial management, see Jensen and Meckling (1976).

2. Because both asset types may obtain with either effort choice, any joint output combination $[(q_i^1 + q_j^2); i \in \{l,h\}, j \in \{l,h\}]$ is available with any combination of effort choices.

3. Correlation is operationalized using a correlation coefficient that affects the marginal probability of receiving an asset type, given the other player's asset type. The correlation coefficients are chosen such that the joint probability of both players receiving a certain asset type are different depending on the effort level selected by each player. The correlation coefficients available when both players select the same effort can range from $-1/3$ to 1. However, the range available when participants select different effort levels is from $-1/3$ to $1/3$. A correlation coefficient of $2/3$ is used when both players select the same effort level. The correlation coefficient is $1/3$ when one player selects low and the other player selects high effort. A higher correlation level, when both players make the same effort choice, is used to increase the benefits obtained from correlation. This reduces the noise for any combination of effort choices without eliminating all noisy observations. Positive correlations are used because they relate to correlated divisions within a firm. See Appendix A for contingency tables and numerical details using the experimental parameters.

4. $150 = (50 + 50) * 1.5$; $90 = (30 + 30) * 1.5$. Earnings are calculated based on the asset types both players obtain. Both players will obtain the same asset type depending on the experimental probabilities and correlation levels between environments.

5. Thus, there was a one-sixth chance of the experiment ending any period after period 24. This essentially produced a discount factor of 16.67% (p = 1/6) for the subjects. The expected number of experimental periods was 30 periods per session.

6. The time allotment for each cell was sufficient to complete each session. Cell B ran for 33 periods; Cell EMO ran for 25 periods; Cell IMO ran for 31 periods; Cell EIM ran for 28 periods.

7. There is no evidence of carryover effects from the training periods to the actual experiment.

8. Individuals are paired together for the entire experiment. Therefore, each pair is considered a single observation for each period. This is because pairs can be thought of as forming strategies together and observations of individuals are not independent.

9. These three categories are chosen to represent high effort by neither player (0), high effort by one player ($^1/_2$), and high effort by both players (1). Analysis was also done with paired observations categorized as 0 (both do not select high effort) or 1 (both select high effort). Results are similar to those reported here. Analysis of individual observations was also conducted; results are similar to those reported for most results.

10. Sensitivity analysis was done using all periods and various groups of periods to determine if choices were significantly different in early rounds as compared with later rounds. This was done to mitigate concerns about learning of the experimental process, sometimes considered a factor in experimental economics. Results were not statistically significant.

11. Since these comparisons are based on expected values, they assume risk neutrality. Experimental subjects might not be risk neutral, limiting the predictive value of the equations in an experimental setting. However, the primary objective is not to test if the equations/model hold, but determine whether sharing information with employees leads to increased production, for which the only confound would be systematically different risk preferences across cells. Randomization in the assignment of participants to experimental cells should control for this risk. Also, the experiment is constructed such that the expected payments across all four cells are the same, given the same effort choices. Therefore, the cell manipulations alone should explain any variations.

12. The data was tested for robustness due to outliers by removing all observations from the sample that are more than 3 standard errors from the mean. (This consisted of the following observations: Baseline cell – Pair No. 4; IMO – Pair No. 2; EMO – Pair No. 3 and No. 5; EIM – Pair No. 1.) The results of tests conducted with this reduced sample are substantially similar to those reported. Therefore results are reported using the complete data set.

13. A reviewer pointed out another problem that may explain the lack of results: the probability diagrams may be confusing to participants who read the instructions. The subject is told that if both participants choose high effort, a high outcome for the subject will be combined with a high outcome for his partner 91.67% of the time. Yet, if the subject chooses low effort, while his partner chooses high effort, a high outcome for the subject will be combined with a high outcome for the counterpart 100% of the time. This information might actually lead some subjects to (mistakenly) infer that the most preferred outcome (high/high) is actually improved by a choice of the default bin (low effort). However, this does not take into account that a high outcome occurs only 25% of the time when selecting from the default bin. This point had been clarified when the instructions were read to the participants. Examination of responses to the post-experimental questionnaire also indicated that participants understood the probabilities correctly. Moreover, there did not seem to be a problem in understanding correlation when there was also an accounting system. Therefore, it does not appear that this biased the results.

14. A reviewer suggested that it might not be the nature of the mechanism (either implicit or explicit) that accounts for the observed results. He suggests an alternative and plausible hypothesis that there exists a threshold level of noise above which a noise reduction mechanism would not be effective. Thus, the implicit mechanism did not work because it did not reduce the level of noise enough to reach a threshold level.

The level of noise reduction between the two mechanisms in the model depends first on the parameters chosen for the experiments and second on the prior probabilities players assign to their partners as outlined in Appendix B. Therefore, one mechanism could be designed to be more effective in reducing noise with certain experimental parameters. However, with the parameters used in the experiment, either mechanism could be more effective in reducing noise, depending on the prior probabilities inferred by the players. Therefore, I concluded that it is the nature of the mechanism (either explicit or implicit) that accounts for the observed result and not a threshold level of noise. This also implies that the findings should be robust to changes in the parameters.

ACKNOWLEDGMENTS

This paper has benefited from the discussions with Gail Cook, Gary Taylor and Dave Williams as well as feedback from anonymous reviewers. Participants at the Workshop on Performance Measurement and Management Control also contributed to its development.

REFERENCES

Alchian, A., & H. Demsetz. (1972). Production, Information Costs, and Economic Organization. *American Economic Review, 62,* 777–795.

Andreoni, J., & Miller, J. H. (1993). Rational Co-operation in the Finitely Repeated Prisoners' Dilemma: Experimental Evidence. *The Economic Journal, 103* (May), 570–585.

Applebaum, E., & Batt, R. (1994). *The New American Workplace.* Ithaca, N. Y. ILR Press.

Arya, A., Glover, J., & Young, R. (1996). Capital Budgeting in a Multidivisional Firm. *Journal of Accounting, Auditing, and Finance,* Fall.

Axelrod, R. (1984). *The Evolution of Cooperation.* New York, NY: Basic Books.

Baiman, S., & Evans, H. (1983). Pre-decision information and participative management control systems. *Journal of Accounting Research, 21,* 371–395.

Bar-Hillel, M. (1973). On the Subjective Probability of Compounded Events. *Organizational Behavior and Human Performance, 9,* 396–406.

Bar-Hillel, M. (1980). The Base-rate Fallacy in Probability Judgments. *Acta Psychologica, 44,* 211–233.

Becker, S., & Green, D. (1962). Budgeting and employee behavior. *Journal of Business, 35,* 392–402.

Bendor, J., Kramer, R. M., & Stout, S. (1991). When in doubt . . . cooperation in a noisy prisoner's dilemma. *Journal of Conflict Resolution, 35,* 691–719.

Brownell, P. (1982). Participation in the budgeting process: when it works and when it doesn't. *Journal of Accounting Literature, 1,* 124–150.

Butler, Jr., J. K., (1991). Towards understanding and measuring conditions of trust: Evolution of a conditions of trust inventory. *Journal of Management, 17,* 643–663.

Christensen, J. (1982). The determination of performance standards and participation. *Journal of Accounting Research Supplement, 11,* 225–253.

Clampitt, P. G., & Downs, C. W. (1993). Employee perceptions of the relationship between communication and productivity: A field study. *Journal of Business Communication, 30*(1), 5–28.
Cohen, L. J. (1981). Can Human Irrationality be Experimentally Demonstrated? *Behavioral and Brain Science, 4*, 317–370.
Commission of the Future of Worker-Management Relations (1994). *Fact-finding report.* Washington, D.C.: Department of Labor.
Cotton, J. L. (1993). *Employee involvement: Methods for improving performance and work attitudes.* Newbury Park, CA: Sage.
Daft, R. L., & Huber, G. P. (1987). How organizations learn: A communications framework. In: N. DiTomaso & S. B. Bacharach (Eds), *Research in the Sociology of Organizations:* (Vol. 5, pp. 1–36). Greenwich, CT: JAI.
de Dombal, F. T. (1988). Computer Aided Diagnosis of Acute Abdominal Pain: The British Experience. In: J. Dowie & A. Elstein (Eds), *Professional Judgement,* (pp. 190–199). Cambridge: Cambridge University Press.
Farris, G., Senner, E., & Butterfield, D. (1973). Trust, culture and organizational behavior. *Industrial Relations, 12*, 144–157.
Fisher, J. (1995). Contingency-based research on management control systems: categorization by a level of complexity approach. *Journal of Accounting Literature, 14*, 24–53.
Folger, R., & Konovsky, M. A. (1989). Effects of procedural distributive justice on reactions to pay raise decisions. *Academy of Management Review, 14*, 57–74.
Gabarro, J. J. (1978). The development of trust influence and expectations. In: A. D. Athos & J. J. Gabarro (Eds), *Research in Organizational Behavior,* (Vol. 14, pp. 129–177). Greenwich, CT: JAI.
Granovetter, M. (1985). Economic action and social structure: The problem of embeddedness. *American Journal of Sociology, 91*(3), 481–510.
Hart, K. M., Capps, H. R., Cangami, J. P., & Caillouet, L. M. (1986). Exploring organizational trust and its multiple dimensions: A case study of General Motors. *Organization Development Journal, 4*(2), 31–39.
Holmström, B. (1979). Moral hazard and observability. *The Bell Journal of Economics, 10*(1), 74–91.
Hopwood, A. (1976). *Accounting and Human Behavior,* Englewood Cliffs, NJ: Prentice Hall.
Jensen, M., & Meckling, W. (1976). Theory of the firm: Managerial behavior, agency costs and ownership structure. *Journal of Financial Economics, 3*, 305–360.
Kahn, L. M., & Murnighan, J. K. (1993). Conjecture, uncertainty, and cooperation in prisoner's dilemma games: Some experimental evidence. *Journal of Economic Behavior and Organization, 22*, 91–117.
Kanodia, C. (1993). Participative budgets as coordination and motivation devices. *Journal of Accounting Research, 31*, 172–189.
Kim, J. S. (1975). Effect of feedback on performance and job satisfaction in an organizational setting. Doctoral dissertation, Michigan State University.
Kirby, A., Reichelstein, S., Sen, P., & Palk, T. (1991). Participation, slack, and budget-based performance evaluation. *Journal of Accounting Research, 29*, 109–128.
Konovsky, M. A., & Cropanzaon, R. (1991). Perceived fairness of employee drug testing as a predictor of employee attitudes and job performance. *Journal of Applied Psychology, 78*, 698–707.
Lawler, III, E. E., Mohrman, S. A., & Ledford, G. E. (1992). *Employee involvement and total quality management: Practices and results in Fortune 1000 companies.* San Francisco, CA: Jossey-Bass.

Lawler, III, E. E. (1993). Creating the high-involvement organization. In: J. Galbraith, E. Lawler & Associates (Eds), *Organization for the Future: The New Logic for Managing Organizations* (pp. 172–193). San Francisco, CA: Jossey-Bass.

Lawrence, P., & Lorsch, J. (1967). *Organization and Environment.* Homewood, IL: Irwin.

Levine, D. I. (1995). *Reinventing the Workplace: How Business and Employees Can Both Win.* Washington, D.C. Brookings Institution.

Locke, E. A., & Latham, G. (1990). *A Theory of Goal Setting & Task Performance.* Englewood Cliffs, NJ.: Prentice-Hall.

Locke, E. A., & Schweiger, D. M. (1979). Participation in decision making: One more look. In: Staw, B. M. (Ed.), *Research in Organizational Behavior* (Vol. 1, pp. 265–339). Greenwich, CT.: JAI.

Miller, J. H. (1996). The coevolution of automata in the repeated prisoner's dilemma. *Journal of Economic Behavior and Organization, 29,* 87–112.

Murnighan, J., & Roth, A. (1983). Expected continued play in prisoner's dilemma games. *Journal of Conflict Resolution, 27* (June), 279–300.

Murray, D. (1990). The performance effects of participative budgeting: an integration if intervening and moderating variables. *Behavioral Research in Accounting, 2,* 104–123.

Otley, D., & Wilkinson, C. (1988). Organization behavior: strategy, structure, environment, and technology. In: K. Ferris (Ed.), *Behavioral Accounting Research. A Critical Analysis* (pp. 147–170). Columbus, OH. Century VII Publishing Company.

Pasmore, W. A., & Fagans, M. R. (1992). Participation, individual development, and organizational change: A review and synthesis. *Journal of Management, 18* (June), 375–397.

Pennings, J., & Woiceshyn, J. (1987). A typology of organizational control and its metaphors. In: S. Bacharach & S. Mitchell (Eds), *Research in the Sociology of Organizations: Vol. 5* (pp. 75–104). Greenwich, CT.: JAI.

Penno, M. (1984). Asymmetry of pre-decision information and managerial accounting. *The Accounting Review, 59,* 177–191.

Pettit, Jr. J., Vaught, B., & Pulley, K. (1990). The role of communication in organizations: Ethical considerations. *The Journal of Business Communication, 27*(3), 233–249.

Radner, R. (1986). Monitoring Cooperative Agreements with Imperfect Monitoring and No Discounting, *Review of Economic Studies, 53,* 43–58.

Ronen, J., & Livingstone, J. (1975). An expectancy theory approach to the motivational impact of budgets. *The Accounting Review, 50,* 671–685.

Roth, A., & Murnighan, J. (1978). Equilibrium behavior and repeated play of the prisoner's dilemma. *Journal of Mathematical Psychology, 17* (April), 189–198.

Sapienza, H. J., & Korsgaard, M. A. (1996). Managing investor relations: The impact of procedural justice in establishing and sustaining investor support. *Academy of Management Journal, 39,* 544–574.

Schweiger, D. M., & Leana, C. R. (1986). Participation in decision making. In: E. A. Locke (Ed.), *Generalizing from Laboratory to Field Settings* (pp. 147–166). Lexington, MA. Lexington Books.

Schwochau, S., Delaney, J., Jarley, P., & Fiorito, J. (1997). Employee participation and assessments of support for organizational policy change. *Journal of Labor Research, XVIII*(3), 379–401.

Shapiro, S. (1987). The social control of interpersonal trust. *American Journal of Sociology, 93,* 623–658.

Tversky, A., & Kahnemann, D. (1973). Availability: A Heuristic for Judging Frequency and Probability. *Cognitive Psychology, 5,*(2), 207–232.

Wagner, III, J. A. (1994). Participation's effect on performance and satisfaction: A reconsideration of research evidence. *Academy of Management Review, 19*, 312–330.

Wagner, III, J. A., & Gooding, R. Z. (1987a). Effects of societal trends on participation research. *Administrative Science Quarterly, 32* (June), 241–262.

Wagner, III, J. A., & Gooding, R. Z. (1987b). Shared influence and organizational behavior: A meta-analysis of situational variables expected to moderate participation-outcome relationships. *Academy of Management Journal, 30* (September), 524–541.

Young, S. M. (1988). Individual behavior: performance, motivation, and control. In: K. Ferris (Ed.) *Behavioral Accounting Research: A Critical Analysis* (pp. 229–246). Columbus, OH.: Century VII Publishing Company.

Zucker, L. (1986). The production of trust: Institutional sources of economic structure, 1840–1920. In: B. Staw & L. Cummings (Eds), *Research in Organizational Behavior: Vol. 8* (pp. 55–111). Greenwich, CT.: JAI Press.

APPENDIX A

Contingency Tables illustrate the joint probabilities of events occurring.
No Correlation (Events are Independent)

Table 1A.   Both Select High Effort.

		Asset Quality Received Low	High	*Marginal Probabilities*
Asset Quality Received	Low	0.0625	0.1875	0.25
	High	0.1875	0.5625	0.75
Marginal Probabilities		0.25	0.75	1.00

Table 2A.   Column Selects Low Effort and Row Selects High Effort.

		Asset Quality Received Low	High	*Marginal Probabilities*
Asset Quality Received	Low	0.1875	0.0625	0.25
	High	0.5625	0.1875	0.75
Marginal Probabilities		0.75	0.25	1.00

Table 3A.   Both Select Low Effort.

		Asset Quality Received Low	High	*Marginal Probabilities*
Asset Quality Received	Low	0.5625	0.1875	0.75
	High	0.1875	0.0625	0.25
Marginal Probabilities		0.75	0.25	1.00

Table 4A.   Both Select High Effort.

		Asset Quality Received		*Marginal Probabilities*
		Low	High	
Asset Quality Received	Low	0.1875	0.0625	0.25
	High	0.0625	0.6875	0.75
Marginal Probabilities		0.25	0.75	1.00

Table 5A.   Column Selects Low Effort and Row Selects High Effort.

		Asset Quality Received		*Marginal Probabilities*
		Low	High	
Asset Quality Received	Low	0.25	0	0.25
	High	0.50	0.25	0.75
Marginal Probabilities		0.75	0.25	1.00

Table 6A.   Both Select Low Effort.

		Asset Quality Received		*Marginal Probabilities*
		Low	High	
Asset Quality Received	Low	0.6875	0.0625	0.75
	High	0.0625	0.1875	0.25
Marginal Probabilities		0.75	0.25	1.00

Labeling the joint probabilities in the contingency table in the following manner:

a	b
c	d

The measure of correlation is calculated with the following formula:

$$\frac{ab-bc}{\sqrt{(a+b)\,(c+d)\,(a+c)\,(b+d)}}$$

Therefore, the measure of correlation for the independent Contingency Tables (**1A**, **2A**, and **3A**) is zero; the measure of correlation for Contingency Tables **4A** and **6A** is 2/3 and for Table **5A** is 1/3.

APPENDIX B

Example of Noise Reduction

E[pr(High|High)]:
{This is the expected posterior probability that Player 2 chose a high effort level after seeing the outcome and given that Player 1 chose high effort. Since the probabilities are symmetric, the same technique can be used to calculate E[pr(Low|Low)].}

No Mechanism to Reduce Noise (Baseline):
Expected posterior:

$$P\,(ll \mid e_h^1, e_h^2)*P\,(e_h^2 \mid e_h^1,\,ll) + P\,(lh,hl \mid e_h^1, e_h^2)*P\,(e_h^2 \mid e_h^1,\,lh,hl)$$
$$+\,P\,(hh \mid e_h^1, e_h^2)*P\,(e_h^2 \mid e_h^1,\,hh)$$

Explicit Mechanism Only (EMO):
Expected posterior:

$$P\,(ll \mid e_h^1, e_h^2)*P\,(e_h^2 \mid e_h^1,\,ll) + P\,(lh \mid e_h^1, e_h^2)*P\,(e_h^{2c} \mid e_h^1,\,lh)$$
$$+\,P\,(hl \mid e_h^1, e_h^2)*P\,(e_h^2 \mid e_h^1,\,hl) + P\,(hh \mid e_h^1, e_h^2)*P\,(e_h^2 \mid e_h^1,\,hh)$$

Implicit Mechanism Only (IMO):
Expected posterior:

$$P\,^c(ll \mid e_h^1, e_h^2)*P\,(e_h^{2c} \mid e_h^1,\,ll\,^c) + P\,^c(lh,\,hl \mid e_h^1, e_h^2)*P\,(e_h^{2c} \mid e_h^1,\,lh\,^c,hl\,^c)$$
$$+\,P\,^c(hh \mid e_h^1, e_h^2)*P\,(e_h^{2c} \mid e_h^1,\,hh\,^c)$$

Both Mechanisms (EIM):
Expected posterior:

$$P\,^c(ll \mid e_h^1, e_h^2)*P\,(e_h^{2c} \mid e_h^1,\,ll\,^c) + P\,^c(lh \mid e_h^1, e_h^2)*P\,(e_h^{2c} \mid e_h^1,\,lh\,^c)$$
$$+\,P\,^c(hl \mid e_h^1, e_h^2)*P\,(e_h^{2c} \mid e_h^1,\,hl\,^c) + P\,^c(hh \mid e_h^1, e_h^2)*P\,(e_h^{2c} \mid e_h^1,\,hh\,^c)$$

Where:

$P^c(jk|e^1_h, e^2_h) =$ Joint probability of obtaining jk (for j,k $\in$ {l,h}) given both players selected high effort; c=correlated environments

$P(e^{2c}_m | e^1_n, jk) =$ Probability that Player 2 selected effort level m (for m $\in$ {l,h}) given that Player 1 selected effort level n (for n $\in$ {l,h}) and the joint output obtained was jk (for j,k $\in$ {l,h}) c = correlated environments

$P(e^2_m | e^1_n, jk)$ is calculated using Bayes' formula in the following manner:

$$P(e^2_m | e^1_h, jk) = \frac{P(jk|e^1_h, e^2_h) * P(e^2_h)}{P(jk|e^1_h, e^2_h) * P(e^2_h) + P(jk| e^1_h, e^2_l) * P(e^2_h)}$$

Where:

$P(jk|e^1_h, e^2_h) =$ Joint probability of obtaining jk (for j,k $\in$ {l,h}) given Player 1 selected high effort and Player 2 selected effort level m (for m $\in$ {1,h}).

$P(e^2_m) =$ Prior probability that Player 2 selected effort level m (for m $\in$ {l,h}).

Similar calculations are used for correlated environments. Also, similar calculations are used to determine E[pr(Low|Low)]. An example follows.
For $P(e^2_h) = 60\%$ (and $P(e^2_b) = 40\%$), and using the probabilities from the contingency tables in Appendix A, the expected posterior probabilities that player 2 selected high (low) effort are shown below.

	Actual Effort Choice	
	E[pr(High High)]	E[pr(Low Low)]
No Mechanism to Reduce Noise	0.659	0.488
Explicit Mechanism Only	0.697	0.545
Implicit Mechanism Only	0.687	0.530
Both Mechanisms	0.725	0.587

Fig. 1B. Example of Noise Reduction.

No Mechanism to Reduce Noise < Explicit Mechanism Only and Implicit Mechanism Only < Both Mechanisms.

INTRODUCTION

Over the past 25 years or so, researchers in strategy, control systems and accounting, among others, have focused on exploring the role, evolution and management practices of multinational corporations (MNCs), to gain a better understanding of this major phenomenon in world trade and direct foreign investments. Traditional theory suggests that one of the main motivators for multinational expansion is the ability to exploit knowledge assets. Correctly linking the structure and control process to strategy is critical today given the importance of knowledge creation and transfer across subsidiaries of MNCs (Bartlett & Ghoshal, 1989; Hedlund, 1993). Control is defined by Child (1973) as a concern with regulating activities within an organisation so that they are in accordance with expectations. Increasingly MNCs are required to co-ordinate activities along product lines, geographical lines and functional lines (Hedlund, 1993). Controls used by MNCs extend from the reliance on formal reporting systems to informal mechanisms (Marschan et al., 1996). Given the complex nature of this coordination problem, this study addresses the control choices made by MNCs as they seek to ensure that different national subsidiaries contribute to the MNC's specific mission.

It is evident from prior research that organisational structures, management processes and control practices are differentiated to match the specific context of different national subsidiaries (Ghoshal & Nohria, 1989). Contextual factors addressed in the control literature include environmental uncertainties (Brownell, 1987), subsidiary location (Schweikart, 1986; Daley et al., 1985), nationality of the parent company (Egelhoff, 1984; Kriger & Solomon, 1992; Ulgado et al., 1994; Chow et al., 1999), and level of foreign subsidiary development (Muralidharan & Hamilton, 1999). More recently, studies have investigated the relationship between the mandates of MNC subsidiaries and controls (Gupta & Govindarajan, 1994; Birkinshaw, 1997).

While this study focuses on the performance metrics and socialisation practices employed in the sample of MNC subsidiaries, it does not investigate the structural arrangements of the MNC in totality, as the unit of analysis is the MNC subsidiary. The authors felt that the respondents (from MNC subsidiaries) would have greater insight into the performance metrics used and the socialisation practices employed as they are actively involved in or subject to those practices. Thus, corporate headquarters creates value by designing suitable systems of planning and control, as reflected in its "parenting style" (Goold et al., 1994). We investigate the key performance metrics utilised by the parent to evaluate subsidiary performance. With respect to socialisation, two themes were investigated. The first was the extent to which the MNC emphasised corporate acculturation and the second was the reliance on managerial transfers to form a cadre of senior managers to control foreign subsidiaries.

There is an abundance of literature (Coates et al., 1992; Carr & Tomkins, 1992; Teoh et al., 1998) that suggests that nationality is a key influence on the management processes and control practices of organisations. Given that our sample covers MNCs from different countries, we expect that the administrative mechanisms and socialisation practices employed will be influenced by the MNC nationality.

Therefore, this study makes a contribution to our understanding of control choices made by MNCs by studying the effects of parenting style and MNC nationality on performance metrics and socialisation practices used in subsidiaries across four host countries. This framework is shown in Fig. 1.

LITERATURE REVIEW

Parenting Style

The whole notion of parenting style is predicated on assessing how headquarters in a multi-divisional organisation "adds value". Goold and Campbell (1989) and Goold et al. (1994) identified three main parenting styles that are particularly successful, namely, strategic planning, financial control and strategic control. The parenting style reflects how the parent chooses to influence strategic

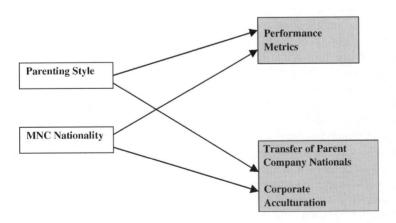

Fig. 1.   Framework of Study.

planning and follow-up within the business unit. Headquarters with a strategic planning style is highly involved in and influences the development of business unit strategy by establishing a planning process and contributing to strategic thinking. Less emphasis is placed on financial controls and performance budgets are set flexibly, and reviewed within the context of long term progress against strategic objectives. In contrast, headquarters using a financial control style limits its role to approving investments and budgets and monitoring performance and has little influence in developing strategies and does not formally review long term plans. Instead, it emphasises strict adherence to financial targets. The strategic control style combines some of the characteristics of the other two parenting styles. Firms that employ a strategic control style believe in the autonomy of unit managers, although they are still concerned with the plans of their units. Plans are reviewed in a formal planning process but headquarters does not advocate strategies or interfere with major decisions. Control is maintained by the use of financial targets and strategic objectives that are agreed with headquarters.

Nilsson (2000) showed through case studies that a successful parenting style balances the parent company's need for coordinated control systems against the need of subsidiaries for situation-specific control systems. Hence, the use of performance metrics as a control mechanism should reflect the different parenting styles that contribute to value creation.

Performance Metrics

The successful implementation of a chosen strategy is possible only if management has access to relevant information when making decisions and evaluating performance. While performance evaluation has always been a difficult issue, it is made even more complex when the focus of evaluation is a foreign subsidiary. In addition to external contextual variables, parent companies of MNCs may impose decisions and constraints on subsidiaries in order to maximise efficiency and global profit. These actions unfortunately create additional distortions in performance measurements (Noerreklit & Schoenfeld, 2000). As a result, there is a need to incorporate qualitative and non-financial data into the control process to prevent misinterpretation of subsidiary performance. One implication of this finding is that MNCs need to create an evaluation system for subsidiary managers that reduces the emphasis on local financial performance and increases the role of other performance criteria, for example, the subsidiary's contribution to regional and global strategy. One method of doing so is by using a balanced scorecard which puts the strategy of the business at the centre, and designs measures that allows management to evaluate performance relative to the strategic objectives (Kaplan & Norton, 1992, 1996).

The balanced scorecard complements and extends traditional financial performance measures with operational and managerial measures that are the drivers of shareholder value. The scorecard includes customer, internal business process, learning and innovation and ultimately, financial performance measures. The customer perspective requires managers to measure factors that matter to customers as well as overall customer satisfaction. Typically, these metrics involve time, quality, performance and cost. The internal process perspective focuses on what the firm needs to do internally in order to meet customers' expectations efficiently. Metrics might include items such as cycle time, cost and productivity. In addition, the core competencies which the organisation has, and the ones it needs to develop must be identified. A company's ability to survive in the face of global competition hinges critically on its ability to innovate and learn continually. Thus, performance measures of the extent to which learning and knowledge acquisition is occurring are required. These could for example include R&D spending and hours of employee training. Finally, the financial performance measures indicate whether the company's strategy and operations are contributing to the improvement of profitability and shareholder value. Typical measures are profits, sales growth, return on equity and shareholder value added.

A survey of balanced scorecard implementers by the consulting firm Towers Perrin in 1996 revealed that the majority of weight is still placed on financial measures (56%), followed by customer measures (19%), internal business (12%), learning and innovation (5%) and others (8%) (Ittner & Larcker, 1998). Such a profile is hardly surprising, given the long history of using financial measures, the relative ease of measuring financial outcomes, the primary objective of creating shareholder value and the need to consistently meet stock market expectations.

In another study which focused only on non-financial measures, using U.S. *Fortune 500* and Canadian *Post 300* firms, Stivers et al. (1998) reported that 93% of the respondents rate customer service measures as the most important. Factors in the innovation category were perceived as the least important.

Therefore, we expect that financial metrics will receive the most emphasis, followed by customer metrics. Moreover, we propose that the parenting style would also have an effect on the performance metrics used. Since parenting style focuses on the systems of strategic planning and follow-up used by the parent in creating value, these must be linked to the information for controlling operations, such as the performance metrics. For instance, MNCs with the financial control style may place more emphasis on financial metrics compared with those with the other two styles. In contrast, with the strategic planning style, value is created through the parent's involvement in the strategic planning process of the business unit. Thus, for control, the parent may rely more on internal business and customer metrics derived from the strategy of the business unit.

Socialisation Practices

Socialisation practices are effective means of controlling the behaviours of organisational members. When organisational members become socialised with a similar world-view, one can expect that they will behave in a similar manner under similar circumstances. Socialisation, therefore, reduces the need for management to measure performance or directly monitor behaviour (Hennart, 1991).

Socialisation is an informal and subtle mechanism that can be added to the structural and formal mechanisms to help MNCs cope with their complex environments (Martinez & Jarillo, 1989; Nohria & Ghoshal, 1994). Socialisation practices incorporate two control mechanisms: corporate acculturation and the transfer of parent company nationals to foreign subsidiaries. Kuin (1972) and Gupta and Govindarajan (1991), for example, refer to socialisation or corporate acculturation as a control mechanism whereby the subsidiary objectives and corporate goals are aligned, and as a means through which subsidiary managers' values become closely aligned with those of the parent. Through corporate acculturation, managers internalise norms of behaviour that are consistent with, and create a commitment to the organisation.

The assignment of parent company nationals to upper and middle management positions in foreign subsidiaries is a means to monitor and evaluate the activities and behaviour within the subsidiary. The use of parent company nationals allows headquarters to maintain informal linkages with subsidiaries by means of corporate culture transmitted through these managers who have been "socialised" while working in the home office of the parent company (Egelhoff, 1984).

MNC Nationality

In outlining the key influences on the choice of performance metrics and socialisation practices, an important factor is the nationality of the parent company. According to Mooraj et al. (1999), the national culture of international organisations affects the balanced scorecard primarily in terms of the approach towards financial performance (e.g. U.S. organisations may consider shareholder wealth maximisation as their overriding objective), and secondarily in the definition of performance indicators by MNCs (e.g. U.S. and Japanese organisations may define "customer satisfaction" differently). The different cultural paradigms will influence the development as well as the acceptance of the balanced scorecard.

Coates et al. (1992) investigated the strategic management styles and key performance indicators used by headquarters in a small sample of German, U.S. and U.K. companies. They found little difference among the nationalities, except that U.S. and U.K. firms used strategic planning, strategic control and financial control styles, whereas German companies used only the former two. In terms of key performance indicators, U.K. and U.S. companies placed greater emphasis on financial than on other performance indicators. The differential importance placed upon capital markets and different capital market pressures were invoked by the authors to explain their findings. These results were corroborated in a more recent study by Carr and Tomkins (1998) which reported the findings of case studies of strategic decisions taken by vehicle component manufacturers in Germany, Japan, U.K. and U.S. They found that when making strategic investment decisions, U.K. and U.S. companies placed more than three times as much emphasis on financial calculus than German and Japanese companies. Not surprisingly, more of the U.K. and U.S. companies were characterised as using the financial control style, in contrast with the German and Japanese companies. Carr and Tomkins (1998) suggest that differences in strategic approaches are shaped by context and culture. For example, they compared the contextual factors such as differences in institutions, interest groups, nature of firms and nature of the labour market across German, Japanese and U.S. companies. German and Japanese companies have a closer relationship with financial institutions, thus rendering them less subject to stock market pressure, and under less pressure to maximise short-term profits, allowing them to focus more on investments for the longer term.

The nationality of the MNC is expected to be associated with the use of the transfer of parent company nationals as a means of control. A number of studies have found that Japanese firms tend to use large numbers of parent company nationals in management positions in the subsidiaries (e.g. Tung, 1988; Torbiorn, 1994; Liebau & Wahnschaffe, 1992; Chang & Taylor, 1999). In a study of Japanese, European and U.S. firms operating in Malaysia, Liebau and Wahnschaffe (1992) found a marked difference in the use of parent company nationals in top management positions. The Japanese employed few administrative control instruments; instead, they relied on a large number of Japanese managers. This number was far greater than that in U.S. or European firms. On the other hand, U.S. and European MNCs relied more on formal administrative control mechanisms: top management continuously scrutinise foreign operations through a narrow set of rules regarding financial, budgeting and market variables. Given these strict formal control parameters, U.S. and European MNCs are able to give local managers autonomy in many functional areas and fill important management positions with local nationals.

While the reliance on organisational norms as a means of control has long been associated with Japanese firms (Jaeger & Baliga, 1985; Bartlett & Ghoshal, 1989), it is not clear whether Japanese MNCs will emphasise corporate acculturation as a control mechanism for their foreign subsidiaries.

RESEARCH METHODOLOGY

Sample and Administration

The subsidiaries included in our sample are based in Australia, Ireland, Malaysia and Singapore. These countries were selected because of their high dependence on foreign investment. In Australia, the revenues brought in by foreign companies have increased over the years. In 1994, the 500 largest foreign-owned companies in Australia accounted for 11.8% of its total revenue. By 1999, the combined revenue of the top 500 has increased 72% and represented 16% of the nation's revenues (Ruthven, 2000).

Ireland, Malaysia and Singapore advertise their attractiveness to MNCs through low corporate taxes, a supportive policy infrastructure and highly productive and skilled workforce. The government investment agencies in these countries aggressively promote their countries as the ideal location for multinational businesses. In total, there are more than 6,000 foreign companies based in Singapore, a country that attracted S$9.2 billion in fixed asset investments in 1999, with U.S. as the biggest investor, accounting for 40% of the total investments, followed by European and Japanese investments (Singapore Economic Development Board, 2001).

Similarly, MNCs from more than 40 countries have invested in over 3,000 projects in Malaysia's manufacturing sector (Malaysia Industrial Development Authority, 2000). In the first part of 2001, for example, 64.4% (RM4.7 billion) of investment in Malaysia's manufacturing sector came from foreign investments (New Straits Times, 2001).

Ireland has as a tradition since the 1950s of inviting MNCs. The country's economic success has also been attributed to a large extent to foreign direct investment. In 1996 Ireland was host to over 1000 foreign firms, up from 650 in 1986, and the 16% growth in manufacturing output in 1997 was attributed primarily to foreign-owned, high-technology sectors, who have found Ireland as a very profitable production site for exports to the EU market (Aust, 1999). In particular, Ireland has benefited disproportionately from a large share of U.S. investment.

Samples of MNC subsidiaries were drawn from various lists of the largest corporations in the four countries[1]. In total, 1479 MNC subsidiaries were selected as the sample. Out of this, 359 subsidiaries provided responses to the questionnaire, giving an overall response rate of 24%. As it was not possible to compare respondents with non-respondents directly, and since late respondents have been found to be similar to non-respondents, comparisons are made between the early respondents (the first ten) and the late respondents (the last ten) in terms of the size of the subsidiary (measured by annual sales), the relative importance of the subsidiary to the parent company and the designation of the respondent. None of these comparisons revealed a significant difference between the early and late respondents, thus alleviating the concern of a response bias. This check for response bias is in line with the general approach suggested by Oppenheim (1992).

The MNCs represented in our sample are headquartered in Australia, Japan, U.K., U.S. and various other Asian and European countries. In order to analyse the effects of MNC nationality, we focused on a subset of MNC subsidiaries with headquarters in the Japan, U.S. and Western Europe.[2] The number of responses from MNCs of other nationalities (e.g. Hong Kong and Malaysia) was too small for inclusion in the analyses. This reduced the useable responses to 308 (122 from U.S., 76 from Japan and 110 from W. Europe). Further, 6 of the responses had missing data on parenting style, giving us a final useable total of 302 responses. The frequency distribution of parenting style across MNC nationality is presented in Table 1.

A letter explaining the nature and objective of the study and requesting participation was addressed to the Chief Executive Officer (or other appropriate title such as Managing Director) in each subsidiary. It is expected that the CEO is the most knowledgeable individual in the subsidiary about its strategic context

Table 1. Frequency Distribution of Parenting Style by MNC Nationality.

	Japan	U.S.	W. Europe	Total (%)
Strategic Planning	23	17	19	59 (19.5%)
Strategic Control	46	90	78	214 (71%)
Financial Control	5	12	12	29 (9.5%)
Total	74	119	109	302

(Huber & Power, 1985). A questionnaire, together with a self-addressed, stamped envelope were enclosed. Over 70% of the respondents were either CEOs or Managing Directors. The other respondents are senior managers with functional or operational responsibilities. More than 50% of the respondents have been with their current organisations for more than 10 years.

Measurement of Variables

The questionnaire was designed to measure the parenting style employed by headquarters, and the performance metrics employed, as measured by the balanced scorecard and the extent to which the two socialisation practices were used to control the subsidiaries. We also identified the *MNC nationality* by the country in which the company is headquartered.

Parenting style was measured using a nominal scale with paragraph descriptions of each approach, and the respondent ticking whichever one best described the approach in use.

Performance metrics were measured by asking respondents to allocate 100 points across the four elements of the balanced scorecard, with the weightage reflecting the relative emphasis by headquarters on each of the four components. Examples of measures employed in each of the components of the balanced scorecard were provided.

Both socialisation practices were measured. *Corporate acculturation* was measured by asking the respondent to identify on a 7-point scale (1: little effort; 7: greatest effort) the emphasis placed by the MNC on developing a strong organisational culture to ensure that all subsidiaries know and share the main goals of the firm and values of top management[3]. The *transfer of parent company nationals* was measured by the number of the top five management positions in the subsidiary that are held by nationals from the MNC's home country.

RESULTS

Subsidiary size was treated as a control variable. Subsidiary size was measured using annual sales revenue as provided by respondents in the questionnaire. Using a one-way analysis of variance (ANOVA), we found that the size of the subsidiary does not differ significantly across the three parenting styles ($p = 0.84$).

To explore whether parenting style and MNC nationality affect the key performance metrics and socialisation practices used for control, the data were analysed using multivariate analysis of variance (MANOVA). The independent

Table 2. Summary of Results of MANOVA.

	Parenting Style F value (significance level)	MNC Nationality F value (significance level)
MANOVA*	3.055 (0.000)	14.028 (0.000)
ANOVA		
Financial	6.451 (0.002)	7.820 (0.000)
Internal Business	1.881 (0.154)	5.016 (0.007)
Customer	4.224 (0.016)	3.239 (0.041)
Innovation & Learning	4.131 (0.017)	2.209 (0.112)
Transfer of Parent Company Nationals	4.378 (0.013)	69.070 (0.000)
Corporate Acculturation	6.903 (0.001)	12.678 (0.000)

* Results shown here were obtained using Pillai's Trace. Results from Wilks' Lambda and Hotelling's Trace also provided a significance level of $p = 0.000$.

variables were parenting style and MNC nationality while the dependent variables were the four categories of the performance metrics, transfer of parent company nationals and corporate acculturation. Pillai's Trace is used in this analysis as it is most robust to possible violations of assumptions necessary for MANOVA (Tabachnick & Fidell, 1989). The results are summarised in Table 2. The results are significant for both independent variables ($p = 0.0000$). The significant results indicate that the six dependent variables taken together varied due to the parenting style and MNC nationality. The ANOVA results for each dependent variable are also presented in Table 2.

Factors affecting Performance Metrics

With regards to the dependent variables associated with the performance metrics, the ANOVA results show significant parenting style effects for all performance metrics except internal business while significant MNC nationality effects occur for all performance metrics except innovation and learning.

To further explore the nature of the relationships for the significant parenting style effects, post-hoc comparisons of means were conducted using Tukey comparisons. The means of the relative emphasis on the four categories of performance metrics (out of a total of 100%) by the parenting style of the MNC are presented in Table 3. The comparisons that are significant at the 0.05 level are discussed below.

Table 3.   Means of Performance Metrics Emphasis by Parenting Style.

Parenting Style	Financial	Internal Business	Customer	Innovation & Learning
Strategic Planning	39.8	18.6	28.8	12.8
Strategic Control	43.7	14.4	29.2	12.7
Financial Control	57.6	14.5	19.7	8
Total	44.1	15.3	28.3	12.3

Most of the significant comparisons involve the financial control style, which differs significantly from the other two styles in several aspects. MNCs using the financial control style emphasised financial measures to a greater extent than the strategic planning ($p = 0.000$) and strategic control styles ($p = 0.002$). At the same time, they placed less emphasis on customer and innovation and learning measures than those using the strategic planning ($p = 0.037$; 0.033) and the strategic control styles ($p = 0.011$; 0.015).

Similarly, to further analyse the MNC nationality effects on the financial, internal business and customer performance metrics, post-hoc comparisons of means were made. The means of the relative emphasis on the four categories of performance metrics are presented in Table 4.

The significant comparisons result from the Japanese MNCs which differ from the U.S. and European MNCs in terms of their reliance on performance metrics. The Japanese MNCs placed less emphasis on financial metrics than the U.S. ($p = 0.001$) and European MNCs ($p = 0.000$). At the same time, they placed more emphasis on the internal business and customer performance metrics than their U.S. ($p = 0.002$; 0.051) and European ($p = 0.009$; 0.031) counterparts.

Table 4.   Means of Performance Metrics Emphasis by MNC Nationality.

MNC Nationality	Financial	Internal Business	Customer	Innovation & Learning
U.S.	46.1	13.6	27.1	13.1
Japan	35.2	19.6	32.7	12.7
W. Europe	47.9	14.3	26.6	11.1
Total	44.1	15.3	28.3	12.3

Factors affecting Socialisation Practices

The socialisation practices used by MNCs include the transfer of parent company nationals to the subsidiary and the efforts at corporate acculturation in order to exercise control over the subsidiaries. The ANOVA results show significant effects for both socialisation practices.

Further interpretation of the effects on the transfer of parent company nationals is made by performing post-hoc comparisons to determine the nature of the effects. The means are presented in Table 5. In terms of parenting style, the results show that MNCs with the strategic planning style transferred more of their parent company nationals to the subsidiaries than the strategic control style ($p = 0.000$) and financial control style ($p = 0.007$). Again, the significant MNC nationality effect arises from the Japanese MNCs who transferred more parent company nationals to their subsidiaries than U.S. ($p = 0.000$) and European ($p = 0.000$) MNCs.

Similarly, to understand the effects on corporate acculturation better, post-hoc comparisons are made. The means are also shown in Table 5. The significant parenting style effect is due to the financial control style which relied less on corporate acculturation for control than either the strategic planning ($p = 0.004$) or the strategic control ($p = 0.003$) styles. The significant nationality effect arises because Japanese MNCs relied less on corporate acculturation as a means of control compared with the U.S. ($p = 0.000$) and European ($p = 0.007$) MNCs. There is also a marginally significant difference between the U.S. and European MNCs ($p = 0.093$), with the U.S. relying more on corporate acculturation for control.

Table 5. Means of Socialisation Practices.

Factors	Transfer of Parent Company Nationals	Corporate Acculturation
Parenting Style		
Strategic Planning	2.00	5.11
Strategic Control	1.10	4.98
Financial Control	1.14	3.93
MNC Nationality		
U.S.	0.76	5.36
Japan	2.96	4.16
Europe	0.73	4.91

DISCUSSION

This study presents strong evidence that both the parenting style and nationality of the MNC influence the performance metrics used to evaluate the performance of subsidiaries and the socialisation practices used for control.

The financial control style relies heavily on financial measures, while paying less attention to customer and innovation and learning metrics of the balanced scorecard. This finding is consistent with the value creation mandate associated with such a parenting style. The subsidiaries are charged with the responsibility of achieving financial targets, which are typically short-term in nature. Hence, the performance metrics that attempt to capture the longer term effects of subsidiary actions are not as critical. In terms of the socialisation practices utilised, it is not surprising that those employing a financial control style put much less effort on corporate acculturation to align subsidiary and corporate goals, as the benefits of such efforts are not likely to accrue in the short term.

The strategic planning style reflects the interest of the parent in developing the strategy of the subsidiary and in influencing its business model of value creation. Our results indicate that this is achieved through transferring more parent company nationals to the subsidiary to influence the planning process as compared to the other two parenting styles.

In assessing the impact of different nationalities of parent companies, it is found that the Japanese MNCs differ from the others in terms of the socialisation mechanisms employed and the performance metrics they choose to rely on. First, the Japanese rely heavily on the transfer of Japanese managers to the foreign subsidiaries. This could be the result of the language barriers and cultural differences that make the integration of non-Japanese into the senior management team somewhat difficult due to potential communication problems with headquarters (Teoh et al., 1998). Secondly, the evidence suggests that Japanese MNCs rely less on financial metrics and corporate acculturation for control. This is not surprising given the heavy reliance on a cadre of Japanese managers who have been socialised to the corporate culture of the parent company. Hence, channelling efforts to build the corporate culture at the subsidiary is less of a priority. These Japanese managers are able to influence the operational activities of the subsidiary and performance can be evaluated using customer and internal business measures, instead of relying on lag financial measures. Conversely, the U.S. and European MNCs, who have fewer of their managers transferred to the overseas site must rely more on other mechanisms of control, namely, building a strong corporate culture and relying on financial metrics for accountability and control.

Despite the demonstrated differences due to MNC nationality and parenting style, distinct similarities exist across all MNCs in our sample. In terms of performance metrics, the pre-eminence of financial metrics is evident. All MNCs, regardless of nationality and parenting style, place the highest emphasis on financial measures (44.1%). Moreover, the relative emphasis on the other metrics is also common across nationalities and parenting style. After financials, the second most emphasised category is customer (28.3%), followed by internal business (15.3%), and finally innovation and learning (12.3%). This pattern is consistent with other surveys conducted mainly in the U.S. (for example, Stivers et al., 1998 and Ittner & Larcker, 1998). The low emphasis on innovation and learning metrics is troubling, as many have argued that the source of sustainable competitive advantage lies in intangibles and knowledge-based assets. One possible reason for this low emphasis may be due to the inability to satisfactorily measure these factors. Kloot and Martin (2000) noted that while innovation and learning are recognised as important, there are few measurement processes in place to manage performance in this area. Similarly, Stivers et al. (1998) found a substantial "importance-measurement" gap: many companies that view non-financial measures as important are not capturing the data on these factors. This gap is greatest for factors of innovation and employee involvement that are perceived to be difficult to measure. While various researchers and consultants have proposed new measures of intangibles and knowledge assets such as intellectual capital, economic value added (EVA) and cash flow return on investment (CFROI), there is still no consensus on a valid measure. Instead, organisations may resort to other forms of control in such situations. In our earlier study of Australian firms (Chung et al., 2000), we found evidence that as knowledge inflows into the subsidiary increases, the reliance on socialisation control increases while reliance on output measures decreases. This suggests that formal performance measurement systems, however, sophisticated, may not be sufficient, and other forms of control, such as socialisation mechanisms may be needed.

In terms of parenting style, strategic control predominates: 71% of the sampled organisations use this style. Such a style requires senior managers to balance the need to allow the subsidiary sufficient autonomy while taking advantage of the synergies with the entire organisation. Either of the other two styles, which lie on one extreme or the other, would be less effective in managing this tension. In linking styles with performance metrics, it is also evident that the strategic control style reflects the balance of measures included

124 LAI HONG CHUNG, PATRICK T. GIBBONS AND HERBERT P. SCHOCH

in the balanced scorecard. While financial metrics are important, the other performance metrics are also used in this popular parenting style. Moreover, the prevalence of the strategic control style displays the changing expectations on MNC subsidiary managers. Recent research suggests that subsidiary initiative contributes to building firm-specific advantages. Furthermore, subsidiary initiative is strongly associated with the leadership and entrepreneurial culture in a subsidiary (Birkinshaw et al., 1998). Rather than merely "implementing" policies and strategies that are formulated elsewhere, the strategic control style encourages more entrepreneurial and direction-setting activities from the subsidiary general manager.

IMPLICATIONS

Our study describes the performance metrics and socialisation practices employed in MNC subsidiaries, while noting the potential influence of the parenting style and MNC nationality. We recognise that while our survey methodology has allowed us to describe and summarise the "what" (in a functional, technical sense) and test some of the expected relationships, it has limitations in addressing other equally important issues. One such issue is how performance measures are used by organisations in the wider organisational context that would include behavioural, motivational and organisational aspects of performance measurement. The choice and use of a specific performance measure affect the motivation of managers, influence behaviours, and thus shape organisational reality. One potential way of understanding the differing use of controls is by using the dichotomy provided by Simons (1994). He distinguishes between diagnostic and interactive measures. A case study could be designed to gain a better understanding of the processes involved in the diagnostic and interactive uses of various performance metrics. In fact the MNC headquarters-subsidiary linkage would provide an important extension to this work as different subsidiaries face different strategic uncertainties which drive the interactive/diagnostic use of specific controls.

Our study was basically static and thus reveals little on why or how changes take place and their impact on the variables under consideration. Longitudinal and holistic approaches, through in depth case studies, could more effectively explore these issues (Wickramasinghe & Hopper, 2001). Such an approach could be used to provide richer descriptions and insights into the emergence and development of non-financial measures using an organisational perspective. Vaivo (1999), for example, provided an exploratory case study of the emergence of non-financial measures of a British chemicals company, guided by the institutional framework. In conducting future research, different methodological approaches and theoretical lenses could be utilised to deepen our understanding of the important management and control issues facing MNCs. Interpretative perspectives, such as institutional theory, may provide different insights not available through the contingency lens. The theory of "diffusion of innovation" (Rogers, 1962; Rogers & Shoemaker, 1971) offers potential to explore the process of diffusion of the balanced scorecard (as the innovation) from headquarters to subsidiaries, or between subsidiaries.

The study did not address some key factors that could influence the results. One such factor is the effect of specific host country characteristics, including cultural differences. Horng (1993) proposed that as the cultural distance between headquarters and subsidiaries increases, the use of financial controls would increase and reliance on strategic controls would decrease. As MNCs compete globally in more culturally diverse countries, the task of defining appropriate performance criteria and subsequently designing MNC control systems appropriate to both parent company and local subsidiary will be most challenging (Hamilton & Kashlak, 1999). Future studies could include in depth analysis of cultural factors in the host country and their impact on one or more of the variables considered in our study.

Further work would need to be done to overcome other weaknesses in this paper. Reliance on multi-item as opposed to single-item scales would be an important improvement. In addition, designing a study within a limited number of MNCs might provide important access to headquarters-subsidiary relationships, holding the headquarters variable "constant" and elaborating the relationships between headquarters and subsidiaries.

For a richer understanding of the complex social issues surrounding MNCs, paradigmatic pluralism is warranted (Covaleski et al., 1996; Hopper, 1999). The triangulation of research theories and methods of inquiry will further enrich our understanding of the organisational complexities of the modern MNC as it continues to grapple with the difficult issue of designing the appropriate control mechanisms for subsidiaries operating in increasingly diverse contexts (Chung et al., 2000).

NOTES

1. *BRW Top 1000 Corporations* in Australia, *Business and Finance Top 1000* in Ireland, *Singapore 1000* and *Dun's Key Business Directory* in Malaysia.

2. U.K., France, Germany and Ireland were grouped into this category because the individual sample sizes were too small for analysis.

3. This operationalisation was used by Martinez and Jarillo (1991) to measure the degree of socialisation in their sample of MNCs in Spain.

ACKNOWLEDGMENTS

We are grateful for the contributions made by the participants of the *Department of Accounting and Finance Seminar, Macquarie University, Sydney*, May 2001 and the *Workshop on Performance Measurement and Management Control*, Nice, Oct 2001.

REFERENCES

Aust, A. (1999). The 'Celtic Tiger' and Its Beneficiaries: Competitive Corporatisation in Ireland. Paper presented at Mannheim Joint Session, Workshop 19, 1–22, http://www.essex.ac.uk/ecpr.

Bartlett, C., & Ghoshal, S. (1989). *Managing Across Borders: The Transnational Solution*. Boston: Harvard Business School Press.

Birkinshaw, J. M. (1997). Entrepreneurship in Multinational Corporations: The Characteristics of Subsidiary Initiatives. *Strategic Management Journal, 18*(3), 207–229.

Birkinshaw, J., Hood, N., & Jonsson, S. (1998). Building Firm-specific Advantages in Multinational Corporations: The Role of Subsidiary Initiative. *Strategic Management Journal, 19*, 221–241.

Brownell, P. (1987). The Role of Accounting Information, Environment and Management Control in Multi-national Organizations. *Accounting and Finance, May*, 1–16.

Carr, C., & Tomkins, C. (1998). Context, Culture and the Role of the Finance Function in Strategic Decisions: A Comparative Analysis of Britain, Germany, the U.S.A. and Japan. *Management Accounting Research, 9*, 213–239.

Chang, E., & Taylor, S. (1999). Control in Multinational Corporations (MNCs): The Case of Korean Manufacturing Subsidiaries. *Journal of Management, 25*(4), 541–565.

Child, J. (1973). Strategies of Control and Organizational Behavior. *Administrative Science Quarterly, 18*, 1–17.

Chow, C., Shields, M., & Wu, A. (1999). The Importance of National Culture in the Design of and Preference for Management Controls for Multi-National Operations. *Accounting, Organizations and Society, 24*, 441–461.

Chung, L., Gibbons, P., & Schoch, H. (2000). The Influence of Subsidiary Context and Head Office Strategic Management Style on Control of MNCs: The Experience in Australia. *Accounting, Auditing and Accountability Journal, 13*(5), 647–666.

Coates, J, Davis, E., Emmanuel, C., Longdon, S., & Stacey, R. (1992). Multinational Companies Performance Measurement Systems: International Perspectives. *Management Accounting Research, 3*, 133–150.

Covaleski, M., Dirsmith, M., & Samuel, S. (1996). Managerial Accounting Research: The Contributions of Organizational and Sociological Theories. *Journal of Management Accounting Research, 8*, 1–35.

Daley, L., Jiambalvo, J., Sundem, G., & Kondo, Y. (1985). Attitudes Toward Financial Control Systems in the United States and Japan. *Journal of International Business Studies, Fall*, 91–109.

Egelhoff, W. G. (1984). Patterns of Control in U.S., U.K., and European Multinational Corporations. *Journal of International Business Studies, Fall*, 73–83.

Ghoshal, S., & Nohria, N. (1989). Internal Differentiation Within Multinational Corporations. *Strategic Management Journal, 10*, 323–337.

Goold, M., & Campbell, A. (1989). *Strategies and Styles: The Role of the Centre in Managing the Diversified Corporation*. Oxford: Basil Blackwell.

Goold, M., Campbell, A., & Alexander, M. (1994). *Corporate-level Strategy: Creating Value in the Multibusiness Company*. John Wiley.

Gupta, A., & Govindarajan, V. (1991). Knowledge Flows and the Structure of Control Within Multinational Corporations. *Academy of Management Review, 16*(4), 768–792.

Gupta, A., & V. Govindarajan (1994). Alternative Value Chain Configurations for Foreign Subsidiaries: Implications for Coordination and Control within MNCs. In: H. Thomas, D. O'Neal, R. White & D. Hurst (Eds), *Building the Strategically Responsive Organization*. New York: Wiley.

Hamilton, R., & Kashlak, R. (1999). National Influences on Multinational Corporate Control System Selection. *Management International Review, 39*, 167–189.

Hedlund, G. (1993). Assumptions of Hierarchy and Heterarchy, with Applications to the Management of the Multinational Corporation. In: S. Ghoshal & D. E. Westney (Eds), *Organization Theory and the Multinational Corporation*. London: St. Martin's Press.

Hennart, J. F. (1991). Control in Multinational Firms: The Role of Price and Hierarchy. *Management International Review, 31*, Special Issue, 71–96.

Hopper, T. (1999). Postcard from Japan: A Management Accounting View. *Accounting, Auditing and Accountability Journal, 12*(1), 58–68.

Horng, C. (1993). Cultural Differences, Trust, and Their Relationships to Business Strategy and Control. In: S. B. Prasad & R. B. Peterson (Eds), *Advances in International Comparative Management, 8*, 175–197.

Huber, G. P., & Power, D. J. (1985). Retrospective Reports of Strategic Level Managers: Guidelines for Increasing Their Accuracy. *Strategic Management Journal, 6*, 171–180.

Ittner, C., & Larcker, D. (1998). Innovations in Performance Measurement: Trends and Research Implications. *Journal of Management Accounting Research, 10*, 205–238.

Jaeger, A., & Baliga, B. (1985). Control Systems and Strategic Adaptation: Lessons from the Japanese Experience. *Strategic Management Journal, 6*, 115–134.

Kaplan, R., & Norton, D. (1992). The Balanced Scorecard: Measures that Drive Performance. *Harvard Business Review*, Jan-Feb, 71–79.

Kaplan, R., & Norton, D. (1996). Linking the Balanced Scorecard to Strategy. *California Management Review, 39*(1), 53–79.

Kloot, L., & Martin, J. (2000). Strategic Performance Management: A Balanced Approach to Performance Management Issues in Local Government. *Management Accounting Research, 11*, 231–251.

Kriger, M., & Solomon, E. (1992). Strategic Mindsets and Decision-making Autonomy in U.S. and Japanese MNCs. *Management International Review, 32*, 327–343.

Kuin, P. (1972). The Magic of Multinational Management. *Harvard Business Review Nov-Dec*, 89–97.

Liebau, E., & Wahnschaffe, P. (1992). Management Strategies of Multinationals in Developing Countries. *Intereconomics, July-August*, 190–198.

Martinez, J., & Jarillo, J. (1989). The Evolution of Research on Coordination Mechanisms in Multinational Corporations. *Journal of International Business Studies, Fall*, 489–514.

Marschan, R., Welch, D., & Welch, L. (1996). Control in Less-hierarchical Multinationals: The Role of Personal Networks and Informal Communication. *International Business Review, 5*(2), 137–150.

Ministry of International Trade and Industry (2000). Seminar on 'Business Opportunities in Malaysia'. 26 May, Irvine, USA, www.miti.gov.my/press24.htm

Mooraj, S., Oyon, D., & Hostettler, D. (1999). The Balanced Scorecard: A Necessary Good or an Unnecessary Evil? *European Management Journal, 17*(5), 481–491.

Muralidharan, R., & Hamilton, R. (1999). Aligning Multinational Control Systems. *Long Range Planning, 32*(3), 352–361.

New Straits Times (2001). Foreigners Continue to Invest in Manufacturing. *www.miti.gov.my/ news-30mac01.htm*, March 30.

Nilsson, F. (2000). Parenting Styles and Value Creation: A Management Control Approach. *Management Accounting Research, 11*, 89–112.

Noerreklit, H., & Schoenfeld, H. (2000). Controlling Multinational Companies: An Attempt to Analyze Some Unresolved Issues. *The International Journal of Accounting, 35*(3), 415–430.

Oppenheim, A. (1992). *Questionnaire Design, Interviewing and Attitude Measurement.* London: Pinter Publishers.

Rogers, E. (1962). *The Diffusion of Innovation.* New York: Free Press.

Rogers, E., & Shoemaker, F. (1971). *Communication of Innovations.* New York: Free Press.

Ruthven, P. (2000). Top 500 Foreign Companies, Big Earners, Small Hirers. *BRW, October 13*, 114–115.

Schweikart, J. (1986). The Relevance of Managerial Accounting Information: A Multinational Analysis. *Accounting, Organizations and Society, 11*(6), 541–554.

Simons, R. (1994). How Top Managers Use Control Systems as Levers of Strategic Renewal. *Strategic Management Journal, 15*, 169–189.

Singapore Economic Development Board (2001). Singapore Investment News. *www.sedb.com.sg*, April 3.

Stivers, B., Covin, T., Hall, W., & Smalt, S. (1998). How Nonfinancial Performance Measures are Used. *Management Accounting (U.S.), Feb*, 45–49.

Tabachnick, B. G., & Fidell, L. S. (1989). *Using Multivariate Statistics.* New York: Harper Collins Publisher.

Teoh, H. Y., Schoch, H., & Lee, M. H. (1998). Control Systems in Multinational Companies: A Multi-Case Analysis from an Organisational Context Perspective. *The International Journal of Business Studies, 6*(1), 82–96.

Torbiorn, I. (1994). Operative and Strategic Use of Expatriates in New Organizations and Market Structures. *International Studies of Management and Organization, 24*(3), 5–17.

Tung, R. (1988). *The New Expatriates.* Cambridge, MA: Ballinger.

Ulgado, F., Yu, C., & Negandhi, A. (1994). Multinational Enterprises from Asian Developing Countries: Management and Organizational Characteristics. *International Business Review, 3*(2),123–133.

Vavio, J. (1999). Exploring a 'Non-Financial' Management Accounting Change. *Management Accounting Research, 10*, 409–437.

Wickramasinghe, D., & Hopper, T. (2001). Political Economy and Culture: Ownership, Modes of Production and Management Accounting Controls in a Factory in a Traditional Sinhalese Village. Paper presented at the Department of Accounting and Finance Seminar Series, Macquarie University, Sydney, March 30, 1–67.

PART III:
BALANCED SCORECARD AND
PERFORMANCE MEASUREMENT

STRATEGIC MANAGEMENT AND MANAGEMENT CONTROL: DESIGNING A NEW THEORETICAL FRAMEWORK

Carla Mendoza and Olivier Saulpic

ABSTRACT

How can a firm design a management control system that fits the strategy it wishes to pursue? Although this issue would appear to be a relatively crucial one, few research projects have attempted to explore the links between management control and strategy. The present paper analyses three firms that have decided to implement a balanced scorecard (or its French version, a "tableau de bord" instrument panel). To understand the interrelationships between these tools and the strategic issues facing the companies that make up these examples, we have had to design a theoretical framework. This framework distinguishes between the concepts of strategic intent and strategic process. It also identifies three paradigms for this type of process: strategic analysis; and cultural and organizational learning paradigms. In addition to furthering our understanding of the situations being studied, the framework is also intended to help practitioners devise solutions to the aforementioned question. Its theoretical and practical implications are examined within that perspective.

Performance Measurement and Management Control, Volume 12, pages 131–158.

1. INTRODUCTION

In recent years, strategy has come to occupy an increasingly important position in management and organisational literature. Over this time, a variety of research avenues have been pursued, with different analytical frameworks for defining and appraising alternative strategical stances (Hofer & Schendel, 1978; Porter, 1980, 1985). Researchers have discussed the implications of alternative strategical stances for organisational design (Chandler, 1962; Miles & Snow, 1978). However, Langfield-Smith (1997) considers that we are just beginning to understand the links between strategy and management control tools. Numerous authors[1] have shown that the operational issue of choosing a management control system that fits a specific strategy is an important one and if the management control system does not fit the strategy, there is the risk that a company's strategic plan may be cut off from its day-to-day activities. Then, there may be a gap between the strategy as it is expressed and the strategy that actually results from the patterns of actions which are effectively being undertaken. This gap can result in the failure of strategy implementation.

Over the past decade, and in order to reduce this gap, more attention has been paid to the ties that exist between organisational strategy and management accounting (Lorino, 1991; Teller, 1999). Some of the research initiatives have involved the building of a system of strategy-related financial and non-financial measures (Kaplan & Norton, 1992; Maisel, 1992; Euske et al., 1993; Kaplan & Norton, 1996). One new management control tool that has appeared in the United States is called the "Balanced Scorecard" (BSC). It translates a company or business unit's strategy into objectives and indicators, covering four different areas (finance; customers; internal business processes; and learning and growth). Balanced Scorecards also establish bridges between the different indicators that a firm chooses. In France, a similar tool has been developed, called the "tableau de bord" (N. T., translated for the purposes of the present article as "Management Performance Indicators [system]"). The French approach emphasises the actual implementation of whatever strategy a firm has chosen (Guerny (de) et al., 1989; Cerruti & Gattino, 1992; Epstein & Manzoni, 1997; Löning & Pesqueux, 1998; Mendoza et al., 1999).

But Balanced Scorecards and Tableaux de Bord are designed to fit any strategy and any strategic context. It therefore remains difficult to provide an answer for the following operational question: How can a firm design a management control system that fits the strategy it wishes to pursue? However, inasmuch as these new tools constitute an attempt to enhance strategy implementation, their introduction in firms constitutes a great opportunity for researchers to gain insight into the interrelationship between management accounting and strategy.

From a more academic point of view, a few research projects have attempted to explore the links that exist between accounting practices and organisational strategy. Following the example of Gordon and Miller (1976), some researchers have advanced what are known as contingency arguments in an effort to encapsulate the relationships that exist between firms' strategies and the design of their control systems. Towards this end, they have made use of well-known strategy typologies, such as cost vs. differentiation (Porter, 1980, 1985), growth vs. harvest (Govindarajan & Gupta, 1984) or prospector vs. defender (Miles & Snow, 1978). Noteworthy studies in this field include Govindarajan and Gupta (1985), Merchant (1985) and Simons (1987)[2]. Such studies constitute a first step towards answering the question of how to choose a management control system that is adapted to a strategy. However, the typologies they use remain very simplistic; and recent developments in strategic management have moved towards more complex characterizations of strategies, for instance, by introducing the concept of rapid moves back and forth between cost and differentiation (Wallin & Ekholm, 2001). Moreover, such studies are rooted in the idea that strategy is first defined and then implemented. This idea is much questioned, as demonstrated by the introduction of concepts such as emergent strategy or strategic process (Mintzberg, 1994).

In our opinion, more research is needed to understand the choice of management control techniques that fit a specific strategy. The objective of this paper is to contribute to the research and, following Langfield-Smith's advice, we have carried out a field study project, based on an in-depth analysis of various case studies.

The findings are surprising. It became apparent that, in each case, BSC (or Management Performance Indicators System) implementation was strongly linked with strategic issues – but in very contrasting ways. To understand these findings, we went back to the corpus of literature on strategic management. This led us to the design of a theoretical framework that includes the concept of strategic process (Mintzberg, Ahlstrand & Lampel, 1998) and the recognition of three alternative paradigms fitting this process: the strategic analysis paradigm; the cultural paradigm; and the organisational learning paradigm. The framework enhanced our understanding of the situations observed on the field studies, but it is also intended to explain the choice of certain management control systems for a defined strategy.

The present paper is structured as follows. In the first section, we present our methodology. In the second section, we introduce the three case studies and analyse each of them in light of the three aforementioned paradigms. In the third section, we compare the case studies and, building on that comparison, design a theoretical framework that allows for a better comprehension of

the relationships that exist between management accounting techniques
and strategic management. In the final section, we explore the practical and
theoretical implications of the proposed model.

2. METHODOLOGY

Our work is based on 3 companies which implemented new performance
indicator systems. The suitability of developing theory on the basis of
particular examples has been highlighted by Yin (1984), Eisenhardt (1989), and
more recently by Langley (1999).

The companies, based in France, have been assigned the names of Alphacom,
Hybrid and Construction Materials Company and the nature of our involvement
varied in each case. In the Alphacom case, we carried out, over three months
a process-audit on the company's management performance indicator system.
In the Hybrid Company case, we conducted monthly interviews over a period
of three years within the framework of a research project on change processes.
During the three years period, all members of the Board of Directors were
interviewed, but more time was spent with the Financial and Human Resources
directors. In the CMC case, one of us was called on to advise the company
regarding the design of a new performance indicator system. The contact with
the firm lasted two years from the conception of the project to the beginning
of its implementation.

Though we studied these cases in depth by following a longitudinal approach,
this paper describes them without excessive detail. By so doing, we are trying
to overcome the risk of creating theories that are too elaborate and hence
difficult to use, a risk that Eisenhardt (1989) associates with research projects
which are based on specific case studies. That is why we have tried to
highlight only those ideas that are crucial for theoretical thinking.

As such, our analysis contains an intuitive component. But, as Weick (1989)
or Langley (1999) advocate, intuition cannot be completely overlooked and
must be integrated in theory building.

For each case, we analyse why the firm in question decided to implement a
Management Performance Indicators system – and we describe the actual process
that has been pursued towards this end. We then analyse the relationship between
this choice and the strategic issues that the company was dealing with at the time.

To explain our observations, we considered it necessary to design a new
theoretical framework. This framework could constitute a new analytical matrix
that might help to find answers to the aforementioned operational question. In
this sense, our methodology might be related to the "thought-action" cycle
defined by Kaplan (1998).

3. BUILDING AND IMPLEMENTING NEW INDICATORS: THE THREE CASE STUDIES

The three cases will each be examined in turn. For each case, we present the objectives that the company in question had been pursuing in implementing the new indicators. We also study the process that each company adopted and how the process and the chosen indicators of performance were related to the companies'strategic concerns.

3.1. Alphacom Company: Explicit Strategic Deployment

(a) Objectives
The Alphacom Company is a major telephone equipment supplier. Its activity consists of purchasing and installing equipment (PABX, ACD, telephones, phonecards, etc.) on behalf of its customers, mainly corporations and governmental entities.

In early 1999, Alphacom was facing profitability problems, and was finding it difficult to finance further growth. A diagnosis yielded several interesting conclusions. First of all, it became apparent that the firm had had the tendency to propose software solutions that were too sophisticated for its customers' needs. This resulted in higher prices than the original price quotes it had given. Secondly, because of a lack of co-ordination, each department had been pursuing its own activities. In addition, financial matters were being left to the CFO, who was relying on a standard budgeting and planning system that frontline managers scarcely understood and seldom used. To solve these problems, the CEO decided to pursue a Management Performance Indicator approach. He started by holding a meeting with the 5 members of his executive team. The purpose was to define the company's objectives – and to specify how they could be achieved.

A formalised strategic analysis was carried out, focusing on: opportunities (rapid growth and technological innovation); threats (increased competition, manufacturers' strong negotiating position); strengths (a young and dynamic team, internal control over software development, knowledge of the latest technological innovations, good brand image) and weaknesses (mainly the lack of financial resources). This analysis caused the executive team to develop a formal strategy in which it was to seek "to continue increasing sales by consolidating current customer loyalty and by gaining new customers – whilst maintaining sufficient profitability to fund further growth".
To enact this strategy, 3 objectives had to be met:

- Sales had to increase;
- Profitability had to exceed a certain threshold;
- Working capital needs had to be brought back under control.

It was decided to follow an approach that revolved around the design of a Management Performance Indicator system. The hope was that this system would help organise the deployment of the firm's 3 strategic objectives within each of its departments.

(b) The Development Process
After identifying the strategic objectives, the executive committee defined the key action variables that the firm needed to master in order to achieve them. This thinking process lead to the development of an objectives/action variables matrix, and subsequently to the selection of managers who were to have specific responsibility for each action variable.

To illustrate this, we applied the approach to the firm's 20 regional agencies. In each agency, the management team included a Sales Director as well as a Technical Director. The Sales Director is responsible for a team of commercial engineers and business managers. These managers visit customers – and working together with the Agency's Technical Department, they quote prices. The Technical Director supervises installations, maintenance and repairs. The chart presented in Table 1 shows the relationship between the strategic objectives and the action variables that need to be controlled at the agency level.

The next step consisted of identifying the key indicators that had to be incorporated in each manager's Performance Indicators system. The process was the following: Whenever managers were involved in controlling a key variable, they had to identify their action plans, as well as all of the corresponding indicators. Several indicators would track how well the action plans were being implemented, whereas others measured how much progress had been made with respect to key variables. The key variables represented the objectives that each manager had to meet – and they helped him/her to identify specific action variables and the corresponding indicators.
For the Technical Director, the outcome is described in Table 2.

Over a two-month period, and working in close collaboration with the management controller, managers called meetings with their teams in order to:

- define the objectives and key success factors for their own department;
- devise the corresponding action plans;
- determine those indicators that would enable them to achieve their objectives, control key factors and follow the action plans.

Table 1. Cartography of Responsibilities.

Action variables	Objectives			Managers concerned		
	Turnover	Contribution	Control of Working Capital	Agency Director	Sales Director	Technical Director
Commercial dynamism	X			X	X	
Customer Satisfaction	X	X	X	X	X	X
Staying within price estimate		X			X	X
Changes in product-mix	X	X		X	X	
Control over capacities		X		X		
Control over Agency expenditures		X		X	X	
Control over the collection of accounts receivable			X		X	

Table 2.   Management Performance Indicators for
Agency-level Technical Director.

Objectives	Action variables	Action plan indicators	Outcome indicators
Customer Satisfaction			
• Total installation within alloted time	Appropriate work organisation and efficient team supervision		Number of sites behind schedule/ total number of sites
• Quality of on-site interventions	Use of competent and motivated personnel	Number of Technical Department staff training days	• Number of customer complaints during warranty period • Number of breakdowns/ number of maintenance contracts • Number of sites where the customer refuses to pay for all outlays
• Rapidity of on-site actions	Having the necessary spare parts available	Stocks compared to minimum stock levels	
	Having the necessary number of employees available	Workdays in order book/ calendar days	
	Minimisation of down time		Time elapsed between call out and intervention
Control of Installation site costs	Avoiding the wastage of small supplies		Difference between actual and budgeted costing of small supplies
	Minimisation of the number of days on-site		Actual days spent on-site/number of days projected in original quotation

This stage required additional time and work insofar as it created qualitative indicators that were specific to each department, thus raising issues with data collection and definition. The information's reliability had to be assessed. It was also necessary to establish common indicators, approved by everyone, in order to control the co-responsibilities that had been previously identified.

(c) Effects on (and links to) the Firm's Strategic Concerns
In this attempt to solve Alphacom's problems the process allowed each responsibility centre to participate in strategy implementation by translating strategy into action variables and indicators. The responsibility cartography played a crucial role in the deployment process as it enabled each manager to know the framework in which he/she would have to situate the department's development.

Moreover, this was also an interactive process, inasmuch as each responsibility centre Manager was in a position where they could personally fulfil the pre-established cartography of objectives and action variables. As such, managers participated actively in the strategy's implementation. The corporate strategy was effectively being carried out at the operational level.

A first assessment took place in late 1999. In using a Management Performance Indicator system, each department had become involved in the implementation of strategy, and in the monitoring of outcomes. Previously, quarterly budget control meetings had been the sole embodiment of the dialogue between CEO and CFO – now, all of the managers were involved. They no longer hesitated to offer their diagnosis, or to propose solutions. The indicators, even though they reflected only part of the overall picture, constituted a starting point for discussions that could be very beneficial. Furthermore, inter-departmental relationships improved considerably.

This case is illustrative of a paradigm that is dominant in the field of strategic management. According to this paradigm, strategy results from a rational approach: Companies are encouraged to scan their environments, analysing their own strengths and weaknesses and positioning themselves in such a way as to minimise threats and maximise their ability to take advantage of opportunities (Learned, Christensen, Andrews & Guth, 1965). Strategy is viewed as something that is proactive, consciously formulated prior to decision and action.

A number of basic premises underlie this school of strategic management:

- Strategic formation should be a deliberate process of self-aware reflection: Action must flow from reason. Strategies derive from a controlled process of human thinking.

- Responsibility for designing corporate strategy lies at the apex of the organisational pyramid (Andrews, 1980).
- The design process is complete when strategies appear to be complete and are ready to be implemented. This is the viewpoint that normative literature on strategy (Hofer & Schendel, 1978; Porter, 1980; Porter, 1985) usually espouses.
- Central to this strategic analysis paradigm is the associated premise which holds that structure follows strategy: Every time a new strategy is formulated, the state of the structure and the indicators which have been selected must be considered anew.

These premises have been challenged by other approaches to strategic management. In the next case, indicators may once again have been devised in such a way as to be in tune with the strategic change that has taken place – but the process corresponds to a different type of strategic paradigm.

3.2. The Hybrids Company: Allowing for a Cultural Change

(a) Objectives

The Hybrids Company is a subsidiary of a large French electronics group. This company manufactures and sells hybrid circuits, electronic components that were originally used in various military applications. These circuits were developed in the late 1970s by a small team of researchers working for the group.

Thanks to an active relational strategy, the firm has experienced rapid growth in relatively protected markets, with certain clients being other group subsidiaries. Moreover, the firm was a supplier to the French army. However, lower military spending has lead to a drop in the firm's activity levels. It must find new clients to offset the predicted weakening of its current markets – but the new clients it now seeks operate on markets that are much more competitive. In this sort of environment, the company's senior management has defined two main strategic orientations:

- Cost control
  To fund its move into new sectors, the existing product profitability had to be maximised by cost-cutting actions. Until now, the company's personnel had adhered to the credo that "our products' technical performances constitute a (sufficient) guarantee of our success". This widely held belief can be explained by the firm's origins, and by its history. On one hand, the firm had been founded by researchers. On the other hand, its success had

been mainly based on its ability to improve its products. Cost-cutting therefore had never been a priority.

• Internationalisation and diversification
Weaker domestic markets had forced the company to seek new opportunities in the international markets, both in civil (i.e. automotive) and in military applications. As a result, it began to deal with customers for whom a product's technical qualities were not the decisive factor.

Alongside the definition of these objectives, the new senior management team carried out internal diagnosis, with help from an outside consultant. These revealed the existence of tensions and conflicts. In fact, two separate entities were being pitched against each other. On one side, there was the Headquarters; and on the other the Puiseaux factory, run at the time by a Head of Operations who was in disagreement with the then current CEO. This factory had in fact become a veritable citadel.

The analysis made the new management team aware of the gravity of the situation, with the CEO even declaring that his firm's *"very survival was at stake."* The company then embarked upon a process of overall change – and in the management team's opinion, strategic reorientation could only develop through a thorough change in culture. Everyone had to share in the desire to control costs and to enhance customer satisfaction. It was in this context that a Management Performance Indicators system was developed.

(b) The Development Process
Before initiating its Management Performance Indicators development process, the company's directors decided to redefine its management structure to promote an increasingly decentralised decision-making framework as well as greater overall responsiveness.

The former management structure featured about a dozen centres of responsibility. It was replaced by a structure which featured somewhere around 50 centres, comprised of small groups of 10 to 12 persons apiece. Each group leader was asked to fulfil a truly motivational role. For example, the foreman in charge of a 10-person workshop was given responsibility for achieving a certain number of objectives.

Two types of Management Performance Indicators were then developed, one alongside the other: Performance indicators at the level of each responsibility centre Manager; and performance indicators at a company-wide level.

After receiving training, managers were asked to develop their own set of indicators, proceeding on a step-by-step basis. First, they were to define their department's mission; its key management factors (KMF); and subsequently the indicators that best encapsulate any changes in these KMF's. The choice of indicators basically depended on the manager. At no time were any indicators to be forced on anyone.

All of the managers were equipped with computers enabling them to edit themselves their own department's performance indicators. Little by little, departmental Management Performance Indicators became an instrument of internal competition amongst the various teams. They were openly displayed within each department, and people were proud of whatever progress they made.

The company-wide Management Performance Indicators focused on that which was necessary for the control of key factors of success. The main elements were customer satisfaction (return rates, complaints), the ability to work to deadlines (deadlines for developing new references, the time needed to process an order), the ability to control costs (variances between budgeted and actual costs) and penetration rates on the new target markets. These indicators were therefore tied very closely into the firm' s strategic orientations.

The company-wide Management Performance Indicators were widely diffused. They were regularly communicated in a newsletter that was sent out to all personnel. In addition, they were broadcast on television screens throughout the firm's premises (i.e. in the canteen where staff would queue). During general staff meetings, organised by senior management at regular intervals, key indicators often served as a way of formulating that which had been achieved.

(c) Effects on (and links to) the Firm's Strategic Concerns
For the Hybrids Company, Management Performance Indicators were a vehicle for cultural change:

- On one hand, the very fact that each manager was given the chance to develop his/her own guidance indicators encouraged a participatory dynamic that broke with earlier compartmentalisation. The surveys we carried out two years after the system had been set up showed that managers (particularly workshop managers) felt that they were much more involved in the management of their particular entity, than had previously been the case.
- On the other hand, the company-wide Management Performance Indicators enabled a diffusion of the new "values" that were born out of the new strategic priorities. Customer satisfaction and the need for cost control both became themes that staff members increasingly incorporated into their own concerns, as we were able to observe during our investigation. This change in values and in shared representations cannot only be attributed to the Management Performance Indicators systems. However, it is undeniable that these systems

constituted a central element in the mechanisms underlying the cultural change.

In this firm, senior management thought of strategic development as a process that was rooted in the social dynamism of a given culture. To be competitive in markets that were less protected than its traditional ones, the firm had to enact a cultural reorientation.

This conception of strategy differs from Alphacom's, and corresponds to another paradigm in strategic management: The cultural paradigm. This paradigm emphasises the influence of organisational culture on strategy formation. Organisational culture represents the shared beliefs that are reflected in traditions and habits, and in more concrete manifestations such as anecdotes and symbols (Schein, 1985; Pettigrew, 1985). The main premises of this paradigm are that:

- Strategy formation is a process of social interaction, based on the beliefs and understandings that are shared by the members of the organisation.
- An individual acquires these beliefs via a process of acculturation that is partly tacit and which can be reinforced by more formal systems and procedures (like management control systems).
- Culture influences the style of thinking that is favored in an organisation and thereby influences the strategy formation process. It acts as a perceptual filter which in turn establishes people's decisional premises (Snodgrass, 1984).
- A strategic reorientation generally represents a cultural revolution.
  More than the strategic analysis paradigm, it is the cultural paradigm that provides an explanation for what we observed in this particular case.

We introduce below a third case, where the link between guidance indicators and strategic issues is again a different one. To interpret the CMC case, a third paradigm was required.

3.3. Construction Materials Company:
Building a Strategic Performance Model

(a) Objectives
The Construction Materials Company (CMC) is a major international cement group. The cement sector is at a stage of maturity. Its actors are groups that maintain a presence throughout the world. The competitive environment is characterised by local oligopolies and by new potential entrants.

The objectives which this firm is pursuing involves devising a system of indicators that can be shared by all of its cement units throughout the world (more than 20 business units). The project leader's mission statement specifies that these Management Performance Indicators should *"enable the business unit managers and the organisation's different levels to possess those key indicators that will allow them to measure their performance and better guide their activities."*

As such, at the project's origin lay the desire that all of the business units should possess certain shared management tools. This wish for standardisation was based on a preoccupation with internal benchmarking. More generally, behind the defined objectives one detects a desire to strengthen the common culture (particularly in order to facilitate the integration of new business units) and to capitalise on existing knowledge. The project therefore did not stem from any desire to modify or reverse existing strategic orientations.

(b) The Development Process
The project took two years to be implemented. Two operational business units were chosen to participate in its design phase. The project's initial phase involved all the frontline managers agreeing on one shared performance indicator model. In the factories, this step was facilitated by the existence of a set of shared technical indicators that had already been established by the functional management team in charge of financial performance monitoring. Whereas in the sales department, operational indicators were less developed. Consequently, senior management were more involved in defining and selecting the performance indicators that were to be applied.

The necessity of bringing both the operational and the financial indicators into a single document soon became apparent. In fact, the model had to satisfy both the headquarters' as well as the frontline operatives' needs, and it also had to replace other existing tools.

Performance indicators were defined for the Operational Business unit's executive team, the Industrial Department, the Logistics Department and the Sales Department. They were then deployed at the lower hierarchical levels. For example, in the Industrial Department, performance indicators were defined for the factory managers and for the different workshop managers.

The overall Management Performance system included cost indicators, performance indicators (volumes, yields, utilisation rates, etc.), quality indicators, indicators that were specific to a given business unit, and charts that showed any changes in key indicators.

This Management Performance system was designed to provide annual, monthly and daily indicators, depending on the hierarchical level.

The project's second phase consisted of defining the procedures relating to the way in which the new Management Performance Indicators could be used.

Table 3. One Sheet of the Management Performance System at CMC.

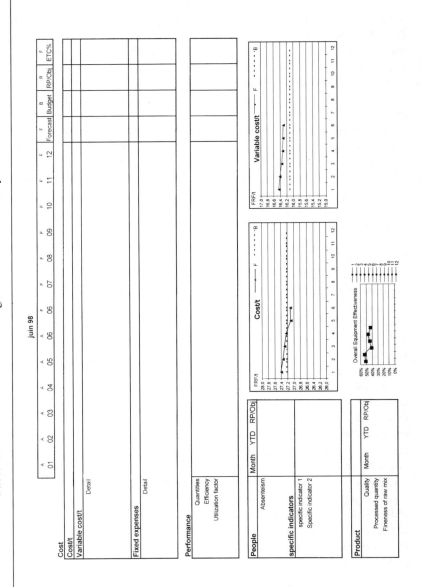

To head-off the usual criticisms of budget monitoring practices (attaching too much significance to the past, to the detriment of future decisions), a reforecasting column was included. This column was filled in on the basis of the information that was provided during the monthly steering meetings – whenever something happened that led people to believe that a given indicator would be very different at year-end from the original budget objective.

Although the project was not portrayed as a BSC-type of strategy implementation – reference to it became a useful way of conceptualising the project (notably during internal presentations). On one hand, the BSC aspects became all the more apparent since elements that had previously been analysed independently, or simply neglected (tracking of physical indicators, budget control, monitoring of safety and environmental issues, follow-up on investments, etc.) were being simultaneously incorporated into the performance indicators. On the other hand, the establishment of a reforecasting procedure led to references being made to the BSC model.

In actual fact, the novelty of this exercise (with respect to traditional systems) resided in the need for a simultaneous reforecasting of operational parameters *and* of their financial effects. This required the ability to make rapid evaluations of the financial impact resulting from the variances or operational decisions. Gradually the idea of the strategic-economic model on which the BSC is based, and which establishes a link between operational parameters and financial results was adopted. Nevertheless, in the customary portrayal of a BSC, the model is designed at a senior management level and is an *a priori* postulate.

In the case under study, we were seeking to focus on what was taking place at the lower hierarchical levels. The model was not necessarily discussed explicitly, nor was it seen as an *a priori* postulate. The challenge instead was to establish a procedure that would encourage the emergence of a shared representation of the conditions in which a targeted performance could be achieved. The need for an explicit modeling cropped up, ex post facto, in certain business units, indicating the need to facilitate the work of the front-line operatives or the management controller during the reforecasting phases. This involved carrying out automatic reforecasts for certain "easy" jobs and modeling some of the technical interactions between parameters. The models that were envisaged, therefore, remained incomplete (unlike the BSC model). At CMC, the core of the system remained the exchange of opinions that arised from the regular reforecasting meetings.

At the end of this phase, training was organised for future users to show them the positive effects that could be expected from the system's implementation.

(c) Effects on (and links to) the Firm's Strategic Concerns
The first effect was straightforward and constituted the main objective of the project – the creation of a common language based on identical indicators that will allow different business units to carry out joint benchmarking exercises.

The second effect was probably more subtle and did not correspond to the project's initial objectives in that the new performance indicators, and their related procedures, became a trampoline for collective thinking about the performance that is supposed to be achieved. This effect was the result of combining both the financial and non-financial indicators during the reforecasting exercise that encouraged a collective view on performance improvement.

The reforecasting exercise is an opportunity for managers to discuss new solutions for performance improvement. Moreover, in having to reforecast both the operational and financial elements, front-line operators were led to ask for decision-making tools that could formalize those techno-economic relationships considered as important. The procedures thus make it possible to create a basis for collective learning about the conditions in which a given performance can be achieved.

These effects, whether or not they were explicitly looked for, would seem to imply that the advent of the new procedure is part of a "learning paradigm" implementation strategy. This paradigm derives from an important question: Is it appropriate to separate strategy formulation and implementation? This question was raised in Lindblom's pioneering work on policy-making in government (1959). It led to the incrementalism theory (Lindblom, 1968), which states that policy-making is a serial and fragmented process in which decisions are taken to solve given problems – and that this process is not co-ordinated. A variant called logical incrementalism (Quinn, 1980) adds that "managers proactively guide [the] stream of actions and events incrementally toward conscious strategy" (p. 15).

The premises of this paradigm could be summarised as follows:

- Knowledge exists at a frontline operative level (Mintzberg et al., 1998, p. 214). Senior managers are not the only strategists who are working in a firm at a given moment in time (Mintzberg et al., 1998, p. 208).
- Over time, strategy making must transmogrify into process learning – with formulation and implementation ultimately becoming indistinguishable.
- Strategy emerges from interactions between actors involved in "routines" (Nelson & Winter, 1982) – and senior management should establish mechanisms for capturing and leveraging the learning that results from the experiments in which individuals, acting at the organisation's operational and middle levels, take part (Burgelman, 1988).

- The role of leadership is to manage the strategic learning process, thereby enabling novel strategies to emerge (see above).

These premises are a good fit with the procedures that CMC were enacting; the company operates in a mature industry, therefore, the pace of change is not very rapid. This is consistent with the conditions that are usually considered to be favorable for learning.

4. ARTICULATING MANAGEMENT CONTROL INDICATORS AND STRATEGY: DESIGNING A THEORETICAL FRAMEWORK

4.1. A Comparative Analysis of the Cases Being Studied

The comparative analysis of the three aforementioned cases reveals certain elements of differentiation. They are summarised in the table below.

When we compare the Hybrids Company's situation with Alphacom's, significant differences crop up. Alphacom has ended up with a complete Management Performance Indicators system, with each sub-system being clearly linked to all of the others, and perfectly in tune with the strategic priorities that have been defined by the executive committee. The approach that has been adopted stems from a top-down logic. At the Hybrids Company, on the other hand, each manager has been encouraged to think about his/her indicators in a relatively autonomous fashion. The indicators that are selected should simply reflect the values the firm is trying to emphasise. The result has been a group of performance indicators that are much more independent from one another than is the case at Alphacom. In addition, certain indicators have been purposefully

Table 4.   The Three Cases: A Comparative Analysis.

Criteria	Alphacom	The Hybrids Company	CMC
Strategic environment	Need for a more clearly defined strategy	Strategic reorientation	Continuance of current strategic choices
Objectives pursued	Organisation of the strategy's deployment throughout the entire organisation	Getting members to adhere to new values that are more in tune with the new strategic priorities	Development of a shared performance model revolving around the use of a common language

stressed, and are being used as means of communicating the emphasis that will henceforth be placed on certain main priorities, such as customer satisfaction, staff motivation, working to deadlines, etc.

In our third example, the starting point was the desire to install indicators that are shared by all of the entities in order to enable internal benchmarking. There has not been, as had been the case in the two other examples, any preparatory strategy definition work. Like the Hybrids Company, the indicators' determination has been mainly left up to the frontline operatives (a bottom-up approach). However as the objective is to organise a benchmarking system, the outcome of the thinking process has been a set of Management Performance Indicators that are identical for all of the entities in the group. Moreover, a new element has been injected into the approach, based on the reforecasting of objectives.

4.2. The Links Between Strategy and Management Control

Several research projects have explored the relationships between organisations' strategic stances and their control systems (Govindarajan & Gupta, 1985; Simons, 1987; Govindarajan, 1988). They have led to the conclusion that management control systems can be seen as part of the organisational arrangements that are associated with given strategies.

For instance, Simons (1987) uses Miles and Snow's descriptions of "pure strategic types" (Miles & Snow, 1978) (*defender, prospector, analyser* and *reactor*) to explain the attributes of financial control systems. He split his sample into "defenders" and "prospectors", and reported a correlation between control systems' attributes and financial performance.

Shank, Govindarajan and Spiegel's study offers another example; showing how the strategic stance a given Strategic Business Unit adopts influences the management control indicators it uses at any point in time. SBU's that have chosen a cost leadership strategy are implementing indicators that emphasise cost control and thus which track variances between real and standard costs. SBU's engaged in a differentiation strategy develop other types of indicators, focusing for example on product quality, the efficiency of promotional operations, etc.

All of these studies correspond to the strategic analysis paradigm. If we had remained within this framework, we would have tried to focus on the strategies' dissimilarities as a means of explaining the differences between the various Management Performance Indicator systems' development processes. Indeed, for each of the aforementioned case studies, the indicators definition and implementation process was clearly related to strategic issues.

However, a closer examination reveals major differences in the way in which firms link the indicators they choose to their strategic intent. We therefore feel that other paradigms may be useful in explaining the relationships between strategy and management accounting tools.

Several strategic management research projects have challenged the empirical validity and relevance of the strategic analysis paradigm. These works describe strategic decision-making as a messy, disorderly, disjointed activity that creates conflicts between a number of business units and sub-groups that often have conflicting interests (Braybrooke & Lindblom, 1963; Bower, 1970; Cohen et al., 1972; Pettigrew, 1973; Quinn, 1980). Strategic change is often difficult to achieve, since structural and cultural factors create inertia. Individuals working in an organisation develop shared meanings, interpretations and explanations for events.

This observation leads strategy research into at least two other paradigms: The cultural paradigm; and the organisational learning paradigm (Mintzberg, Ahlstrand & Lampel, 1998).

Lastly, each case study exemplifies a particular conception of the strategic process. The Alphacom case relates to the strategic analysis paradigm. According to this paradigm, a Management Performance Indicator system (and management accounting tools in general) must be considered as strategy deployment tools. They play a crucial role in the implementation phase. For instance, indicators help managers to realise that they are expected to contribute to the implementation of the strategy that has been formulated.

To analyse our second case study (the Hybrids Company case), another paradigm is clearly needed: The cultural paradigm. This paradigm highlights the importance of shared values that reflect deeply ingrained structures of meaning, by means of which individuals working in organisations interpret their worlds. This cultural paradigm of strategic change has significant implications for accounting and information systems. Management accounting systems select, sort and order bits of data. They are an important vehicle for shaping participants' perceptions of the organisation's relationship with its environment. According to the cultural paradigm, management accounting tools play a key role in accompanying the cultural change process. In this paradigm, indicators orient actors' perceptions of the organisation's priorities. As such, the definition of new indicators helps strategic change. Indicators have the potential to foster a sense of insecurity and to promote new values. This paradigm helps explain the observations we made regarding the second case study.

However, few management accounting research projects have positioned themselves within the framework of this paradigm. Ansari and Euske's study

(1987) shows how management accounting systems can be used for symbolic purposes. Boland and Pondy's (1983, 1986) work is also illustrative of this paradigm, with one of their conclusions being that management accounting can be seen as a way of formulating the categories that filter individuals' ordering and interpretation of the problems they face. Dent's research (1987) documents how embryonic management concepts can become manifest through new systems of planning, accountability and management measurement, and how in turn this can enable organisational change and the emergence of new strategies.

Our third case study relates to another paradigm: The organisational learning paradigm. In this example, the development and utilisation of performance indicators is part of a collective process leading to the progressive development of a company-wide performance model. According to this paradigm, a strategy cannot be defined once and for all. Its development infers a permanent learning process. Management control tools and procedures are likely to play a major role on several levels:

- Through the way in which the performance model is made explicit. The effect of following a given approach when devising a Management Performance Indicator system is to structure thinking around the key levers that will allow the firm to achieve its objectives. The product of this thinking process will be a set of indicators, yet it is also true that the process which has been followed helps to inform a performance model that will link the firm's objectives with certain action variables.
- Through the realisation of a common language and of shared experiences. Developing indicators that different organisational entities can share helps create a common language and allows for an exchange of experiences. Using Nonaka and Takeuchi's terms (1995), these indicators participate in an externalisation process, which is to say that thanks to them, tacit knowledge can be converted into explicit knowledge. They make it possible to transform a perception and/or an impression into a "fact" that can be measured – something that is more objective, and which can therefore more readily be transmitted. From that point onwards, the knowledge that these indicators convey can be transferred from one section of the firm to another, thus enabling a diffusion of the knowledge that has been acquired and encouraging strategic learning. Management accounting tools should therefore be compared to a language, that is a vehicle for the sharing of experiences and for the organisation of confrontations between diverging points of view.
- Through the implementation of procedures that encourage collective learning. The periodic reforecasting of operational and financial objectives is intended

to encourage group discussions on the conditions in which a certain performance level can be achieved, whilst leaving open the possibility of major incentives being offered towards the achievement of objectives (Ponssard & Saulpic, 1999).

4.3. The Model

In sum, we believe that it is important, when conducting research on the interfaces that exist between management control tools and strategic issues, to elucidate the strategic paradigm within which one is operating. The still dominant paradigm in the field of strategic management stipulates that all companies must possess a clearly and rationally defined strategy that will (at a later juncture) be implemented. As we have seen, rival paradigms have emerged, and they state that the concept of a *clearly formulated strategy* should be thoroughly questioned. In the cultural paradigm, strategy is deeply ingrained in the organisation's legends, and is a product of its history. All strategic reorientations are painful and imply changes in the beliefs and values that are held by the firm's members. According to the learning paradigm, strategy does not stem from a deliberate approach – instead, it results from a permanent and collective learning process.

We therefore feel that is necessary to distinguish between firms' *strategic intent* and the *type of strategic process* that they emphasise. We will admit that all firms follow, at a given point in time, a particular strategic intent. However, the strategic process that a firm will select depends on the paradigm within which it situates itself. In the three case studies presented in this paper, we saw three different strategic processes. We have seen how the articulation between management control tools and the firm's strategic intent depends upon the strategic process that is being emphasised. These considerations have lead us to propose a theoretical model that is presented in Fig. 1.

The traditional theoretical framework tries to analyse the link between the strategy's conception and the tools of its implementation, with a view towards designing tools that are consistent with the strategy. We would like to add to this the strategic process that the firm has chosen, and identify the three processes that are associated with three strategic paradigms. More specifically, our framework includes strategic intent, strategic process (as related to a specific paradigm) as well as the tools of strategic implementation.

In the following section, we will examine the practical and theoretical implications of the aforementioned model.

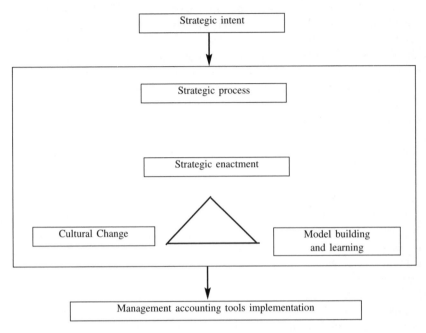

Fig. 1. A Theoretical Framework for Assessing the Articulation Between Strategic
Management and Management Control.

5. PRACTICAL AND THEORETICAL IMPLICATIONS

According to the tenets of this model, management tools must be adapted to a
tandem that is comprised of strategic intent and strategic process – instead of
to one particular strategy per se. For example, in a mature environment where
firms emphasise the optimisation of their production processes, a company can
choose to pursue a strategic intent that is based on improving its profitability
by increasing the extent to which its customers' interests are taken into account.
Depending on the firm's situation, the implementation of this strategic intent
will require either a cultural change process, a strategic deployment process,
or else a learning process. For one and the same strategic intent, different
management control systems will have to be adopted.

As such, each strategic process is associated with a specific management
control approach, particularly in terms of the system of indicators that are being

selected. This model has two types of consequences. On the one hand, this model should be taken into account when evaluating a given management control system or when comparing the respective merits of different tools on offer in Management Control literature (5.1). On the other hand, the model makes it possible to highlight potential contradictions between different management control tools. By so doing, it raises a serious point: How can one successfully implement a strategic intent whilst relying at the same time on all three types of strategic process (5.2).

5.1. Complementary Views on Management Control

A management control system, and more specifically a Management Performance Indicator system, can only be evaluated in light of the strategic process that has been chosen. For example, it is tempting to automatically criticise a budget control system that is focused on nothing more than a strict respect of financial objectives. However, if the firm is seeking to promote a cultural change whose ultimate aim is to increase actors' sense of responsibility with respect to the achievement of financial objectives, this system may well be a very suitable one.

Similarly, in France, many people accept the idea that Management Performance Indicators must be specific to each responsibility centre if they are to truly help managers with their decision-making. Yet if the strategic process stresses learning, a homogenisation of these performance indicators will be a welcomed outcome, since this can encourage the emergence of a shared language.

In addition, the model that we are proposing makes it possible to compare the different management control tools that one finds in literature. Above all, it sheds light on the debate that has been taking place concerning the differences between Management Performance Indicators and Balanced Scorecards (Epstein & Manzoni, 1997; Mendoza & Zrihen, 1998, 2001). Both have been defined as systems that measure performance and strategic deployment. The model that we are proposing explains the systems' differences on the basis of the strategic process underlying the design of each. Indeed, literature on Management Performance Indicators systems situates this tool within the strategic deployment paradigm (de Guerny et al., 1989; Cerrutti & Gattino, 1992; Löning & Pesqueux, 1998; Mendoza et al., 1999). The first work on Balanced Scorecards, on the other hand, showed how this system facilitated the devising of an organisational performance model. The Balanced Scorecard was therefore to be analysed within the context of the learning paradigm. However, experiences in implementing a Balanced

Scorecard have shown that one of the tool's contributions lies in its elucidation and communication of strategy (Kaplan & Norton, 2000). Designed with a view towards learning, the Balanced Scorecard may ultimately turn out to be an instrument of cultural change. It is therefore no longer relevant to evaluate BSC on its ability to support a strategic deployment process. Similarly, EVA can be analysed as an instrument of cultural change. Indeed, the main effect of EVA's introduction into companies has been to emphasise the creation of shareholder value and to incorporate the cost of invested capital into evaluations of frontline managers' performance.

All in all, our model contributes to the debate on management tools, and makes it possible to transcend the somewhat sterile quest for the "right" tool.

5.2. Potential Contradictions Between the Systems

The different management systems are not necessarily compatible with one another. It may be difficult for a firm which is seeking to encourage its managers to respect company objectives (i.e. via a standard budget control process) to try, at the same time, to promote a learning process (i.e. via procedures such as those that are described in Section 3.3. of the present paper, c.f., Ponssard & Saulpic, 2000).

Similarly, if a cultural change process has been engaged, it is necessary to set up a simple yet eloquent system of indicators, as the Hybrids Company was able to do. The firm was subsequently able to have at its disposal a measurement system that contained a few simple but highly symbolic indicators. However, a system of this sort could turn out to be too rudimentary to support a learning process. In addition, this analysis might explain why firms seldom undertake accounting re-calculations to calculate their EVA as an attempt to maintain the indicator's simplicity. Their primary aim is to introduce cultural change rather than precise measures of value creation.

The model that we have built thus has certain implications for the design of a Management Performance Indicator system. It is necessary to choose the strategic process that one wants to emphasise, and then (and only then) design a system that is adapted to this process. Of course, strategic processes are not necessarily contradictory. As Mintzberg et al. (1998, p. 115) state, "all real strategic behavior has to combine deliberate control with emergent learning." In the conclusion to their book "Strategy Safari", Mintzberg and his co-authors stress the potential usefulness of integrating these various processes (Mintzberg et al., 1998, p. 372). Nevertheless, the management techniques issue must still be resolved. As we have seen, the different tools that support these processes contain contradictions. For example, how can a management technique simultaneously support a learning dynamic and participate in a structured, top-down, completion of a set of indicators? How can the need to have detailed information, enabling an in-depth situational analysis, be reconciled with the need for succinct, action-oriented information? Is it possible to design a system that can ensure the vertical coherency of objectives, as well as an overall, horizontal, coherency (i.e. inter-departmental operational coordination)? It is in exploring these paradoxes, and in developing solutions to transcend them, that we will be able to make progress towards the implementation of mixed strategic processes that are capable of integrating strategic deployment, emergent learning and cultural change.

NOTES

1. Mintzberg (1994), Simons (1995), Berry (1983).
2. For a complete review of the litterature on that subject, see Langfield-Smith (1997).

REFERENCES

Andrews, K. R. (1980). Directors' Responsibility for Corporate Strategy. *Harvard Business Review*, *58*(6), 28–43.
Ansari, S., & Euske, K. J. (1987). Rational, Rationalizing, and Reifying uses of accounting data in Organisations. *Accounting, Organisations and Society*, *12*(6), 549–570.
Bjorkman, I. (1989). Factors Influencing Processes of Radical Change in Organisational Belief Systems. *Scandinavian Journal of Management*, *5*(4), 251–271.
Boland, R. J., & Pondy, L. R. (1983). Accounting in Organisations: A Union of Natural and Rational Perspectives. *Accounting, Organisations and Society*, *8*(3), 223–234.
Boland, R. J., & Pondy, L. R. (1986). The Micro-Dynamics of a Budget Cutting Process: Modes, Models and Structure. *Accounting, Organisations and Society*, *11*(4–5), 403–422.
Bower, J. L. (1970). *Managing the Resource Allocation Process*. Cambridge: Harvard University press.
Braybrooke, D., & Lindblom, C. E. (1963). *A Strategy of Decision*. New York: Free Press.
Burgelman, R. A. (1988). Strategy Making as a Social Learning Process: The Case of Internal Corporate Venturing. *Interfaces*, *18*(3), 74–85.
Cerruti, O., & Gattino, B. (1992). *Indicateurs et tableaux de bord*. Paris la Défense: AFNOR.
Chandler, A. D. (1962). *Strategy and Structure*. Cambridge MA: M.I.T. Press.
Cohen, M. D., March, J. G., & Olsen, J. P. (1972). A garbage can model of organisational choice. *Administrative Science Quarterly*, *117*, 1–25.
Dent, J. F. (1987). Tension in the design of formal control systems: A field study in a computer company. In: W. J. Bruns & R. S. Kaplan (Eds), *Accounting and Management: Field Study Perspectives* (pp. 119–145). Boston MA: Harvard Business School Press.
Eisenhardt, K. (1989). Building Theories from Case Study Research. *Academy of Management Review*, *14*(4), 532–550.

Epstein, M. J., & Manzoni, J. F. (1997). Translating strategy into action. *Management Accounting* (August), 28–36.

Gordon, L. A., & Miller, D. (1976). A contingency Framework for the Design of Accounting Informations Systems. *Accounting, Organisations and Society, 1*(1), 59–70.

Govindarajan, V. J. (1988). A contingency Approach to Strategy Implementation at the Business Level: Integrating Administrative Mechanisms with Strategy. *Academy of Management Journal, 10*(1), 828–853.

Govindarajan, V. J., & Gupta, A. K. (1985). Linking Control Systems to Business Unit Strategy: Impact on Performance. *Accounting, Organisations and Society, 10*(1), 51–66.

Guerny (de), J., Guiriec, J. C., Guyon, C., & Lavergne, J. (1989). *Comptabilité et contrôle de gestion.* Paris: Masson.

Gupta, A. K., & Govindarajan, V. J. (1984). Business Unit Strategy, Managerial Characteristics, and Business Unit Effectiveness at Strategy Implementation. *Academy of Management Journal, 27*(1), 25–41.

Hofer, C. W., & Schendel, D. E. (1978). *Strategy Formulation: Analytical Concepts.* New York: West.

Kaplan, R. S. (1998). Innovation Action Research: Creating New Management Theory and Practice. *Journal of Management Accounting Research, 10*, 89–118.

Kaplan, R. S., & Norton, D. P. (1992). The balanced scorecard-Measures that drive performance. *Harvard Business Review, 70*(1), 71–79.

Kaplan, R. S., & Norton, D. P. (1996). *The Balanced Scorecard: Translating strategy into action.* Boston: Harvard Business School Press.

Kaplan, R. S., & Norton, D. P. (2001). *The Strategy Focused Organisation.* Boston: Harvard Business School Press.

Langfield-Smith, K. (1997). Management control systems and strategy: A critical review. *Accounting Organizations and Society, 22*(2), 207–232.

Langley, A. (1999). Strategies for theorizing from process data. *Academy of Management Review, 24*(4), 691–710.

Learned, E. P., Christensen, C. R., Andrews, K. R., & Guth, W. D. (1965). *Business Policy, Text and Cases.* Homewood ILL: Richard D. Irwin.

Lindblom, C. E. (1959). The Science of Muddling Through. *Public Administration Review, 19*(2), 79–88.

Lindblom, C. E (1968). *The Policy Making Process.* Englewood Cliffs NJ: Prentice Hall.

Loning, H., & Pesqueux Y. (1998). *Contrôle de Gestion.* Paris: Dunod.

Lorino, P. (1991). *Le contrôle de gestion stratégique.* Paris: Dunod.

Lorsch, J. W. (1986). Managing Culture: The Invisible Barrier to Strategic Change. *California Management Journal, 28*(2), 95–109.

Mendoza, C., Delmond, M. H., Giraud, F., & Löning, H. (1999). *Tableaux de Bord pour managers.* Paris: Editions Revue Fiduciaire.

Mendoza, C., & Zrihen, R. (1999). *Le tableau de bord : en V. O. ou en version américaine? Comparaison entre le tableau de bord et le Balanced Scorecard.* Revue Française de Comptabilité, *309* (March), 60–67.

Mendoza, C., & Zrihen, R. (2001). *Balanced Scorecard: Measuring up.* Financial Management, April, 26–29.

Merchant, K. A. (1985). Organisational Controls and Discretionary Program Decision Making: A Field Study. *Accounting, Organisations and Society, 10*(1), 67–86.

Miles, R. E., & Snow, C. C. (1978). *Organisational Strategy, Structure and Process.* New York: McGraw-Hill.

Miller, D., & Friesen, P. H. (1978). Archetypes of Strategy Formulation, *Management Science, 24* (9), 921–933.

Miller, D., & Friesen, P. H. (1984). *Organisations: A Quantum View.* Englewood Cliffs NJ: Prentice-Hall.

Mintzberg, H. (1994). *The Rise and Fall of Strategic Planning.* New York: Prentice Hall.

Mintzberg, H., Ahlstrand, B., & Lampel, J. (1998). *Strategy Safari.* New York: The Free Press.

Mintzberg, H., Raisinghani, D., & Théorêt, A. (1976). The Structure of "Unstructured" Decision Process. *Administrative Science Quarterly, 21,* 611–622.

Nelson, R. R., & Winter, S. G. (1982). *An Evolutionary Theory of Economic Change.* Boston: Harvard University Press.

Nonaka, I., & Takeuchi, H. (1995). *The Knowledge Creating Company.* Oxford: University Press, Inc.

Pettigrew, A. (1973). *The Politics of Organisational Decision Making.* London: Tavistock.

Pettigrew, A. (1985). *The Awakening Giant. Continuity and Change in ICI,* Blackwell.

Ponssard, J. P., & Saulpic, O. (2000). Une reformulation de l'approche dite du "Balanced Scorecard". *Comptabilité, Contrôle, Audit,* 6(1), 7–25.

Porter, M. E. (1980). *Competitive Strategy: Techniques for Analysing Industries and Competitors.* New York: Free Press.

Porter, M. E. (1985). *Competitive Advantage: Creating and Sustaining Superior Performance.* New York: Free Press.

Quinn, J. B. (1980). *Strategies for Change: Logical Incrementalism.* Homewood ILL: Irwin.

Schein, E. (1985). *Organisational culture and leadership.* San Francisco: Jossey BASS.

Shank, J. K., Govindarajan, V., & Spiegel, E. (1989). *Strategic Cost Analysis: A case study.* Homewood ILL: Irwin.

Simons, R. (1987). Accounting Control Systems and Business Strategy. *Accounting, Organisations and Society, 12*(4), 357–374.

Simons, R. (1995). *Levers of Control: How Managers Use Innovative Control Systems to Drive Strategic Renewal.* Boston: Harvard Business School Press.

Snodgrass, C. R. (1984). Cultural Influences on Strategic Control System Requirements. Ph.D. dissertation, Graduate School of Business, University of Pittsburgh.

Teller, R. (1999). *Le contrôle de gestion: pour un pilotage intégrant stratégie et finance.* (Collection Les Essentiels de la gestion). Caen: Editions Management et Société.

Weick, K. (1989). Theory construction as disciplined imagination. *Academy of Management Review, 14,* 516–531.

Wallin, J., & Ekholm, B. G. (2001). Strategic priorities, company performance and management accounting: a cross-cultural study. Proceedings of the *European Accounting Association 24th annual congress* (Athenes, 18–21 April).

Yin, R. (1984). *Case Study Research.* Beverly Hills CA: Sage Publications.

1. INTRODUCTION

Considerable change in managerial accounting has occurred during the last two decades, both in theory and practice. According to Ittner and Larcker (2001, p. 350), managerial accounting practice in the U.S. moved from its "traditional emphasis on financially oriented decision analysis and budgetary control to a more strategic approach that emphasizes the identification, measurement and management of the key financial and operational drivers of shareholder value" and "a similar evolution has occurred in managerial accounting research" . . . "giving way to research on a variety of new techniques such as activity-based costing, the balanced scorecard, strategic accounting and control systems, and 'economic value' performance measures". The objective of this paper is twofold: first it provides cross national empirical data about the diffusion and adoption of Balanced Scorecard (BSC) as one part of these "new" techniques in French and German organizations, especially compared to use of the "old" French technique Tableau de Bord (TdB). Second it critically discusses the survey results based on two research perspectives: the cultural and the diffusion theory perspective. Thus we aim at discussing underlying conditions for change in measurement practices and thus understanding the rationales behind adoption and the extent to which performance measurement practices become more alike ("converge") over time in European organizations.

TdB and BSC are similar performance measurement systems from a conceptual point of view and both have been developed in a specific cultural and societal environment. The TdB, that had been theorized ex post, emerged "spontaneously from the need of manufacturing engineers and managers" evolved mainly since the early 60s "from a loosely defined tool into a formally structured instrument with well-defined purpose, content and form" (Lebas, 1994, p. 471). For example one standard management control textbook in France defines TdB as "a measurement system (dashboard) consisting of a few indicators (5–10), defined to allow managers to know the actual state as well as the evolution of the systems they are monitoring, and to identify the trends that are influencing those systems within a time horizon, in line with the nature of their functions" (Bouquin, 1991, p. 299).

The BSC was initially introduced by Kaplan and Norton (1992) and then refined in later publications (Kaplan & Norton, 1996a, b). The BSC has also been also developed on the basis of measurement practices (12 U.S. companies, Kaplan & Norton, 1996a, p. VII), but in the contrary to TdB concept, the BSC had not been really theorized yet (see also, for the German context, Weber & Schäffer, 1998, p. 342). The BSC translates a company's strategic objectives into a set of interlinked performance measures in four different perspectives (learning and growth, internal business process perspective, customer, and financial). Typically, each perspective should not exceed three to five measures. Implementation experiences with BSC in (U.S.) organizations have contributed to its evolution from a redefined performance measurement system to a "strategic management system" (Kaplan & Norton, 1996a, b). Thus the purpose of BSC goes far beyond TdB, which mainly remains a diagnostic tool for information purposes (Lebas, 1994, p. 482).

Numerous conceptual comparisons between TdB and BSC have been published for an international audience (Chiapello & Lebas, 1996; Epstein & Manzoni, 1997, 1998; Bourgignon, Malleret & Nørreklit, 2001) as well as for a French audience (Mendoza & Zrihen, 1999a, b; Ponssard & Saulpic, 2000; Lorino, 2001). Conceptual differences and similarities are studied by French academics from an essentially literary and theoretical point of view. However, as far as we know, the issue of comparative practices and implementation patterns of performance measurement systems such as TdB and BSC in European organizations has not been addressed so far. We therefore wanted to complete existing comparative research that in the past were more based on discourses than on implementation patterns. We will first present the results of our exploratory analysis on performance measurement practices, especially in France and Germany.

2. EXPLORATORY EMPIRICAL ANALYSIS ON PERFORMANCE MEASUREMENT SYSTEMS

The empirical results on the adoption and implementation of BSC presented hereafter are based on a broader European research project on SVM and BSC implementation (Horváth et al., 2001) conducted in the four largest economies in Western Europe (France, Germany, U.K. and Italy) between June and October 2000 by four local research institutions (respectively ESSEC and the Universities of Stuttgart, Bristol and Bocconi), The research concept of the study was an exploratory empirical cross-section analysis by means of a mail/e-mail/telephone survey with a standardized questionnaire identical for each country. The aim of this exploratory study was to analyse the current distribution and importance of Shareholder Value Management and BSC implementation in traditional large companies and young new market/pre-IPO companies. Therefore the original sample for each country (200 companies) was divided into three sub-samples with the following sizes: 125 largest companies; 50 companies of the new market; and 25 pre-IPO companies.

The selection of the 125 biggest companies was based on 1999 turnover in the U.K. ("FAME" index), Germany ("Die Welt" index) and Italy ("Le

Table 1. Overall Survey Response Patterns.

	Germany	Great Britain	France	Italy	Total
Sample size	200	200	309	200	909
Respondents	50	30	32	34	146
Questionnaires to be analysed	49	30	32	34	145
Overall response rate	24.5%	15.0%	10.4%	17.0%	16.0%
Biggest companies	31	18	26	24	99
New market/Pre IPO	18	12	6	10	46

principali società italiane" index, published by Mediobanca Research Department), In France, market capitalization was chosen as a suitable indicator to define the size of the largest companies. The selection of these companies was initially based on the SBF 120 index in which the CAC 40 index is embedded. Due to the weak response rate, the initial French sample for largest companies SBF 120 was extended to SBF 250. The selection of the new market companies was based in France, Italy and Germany on the respective "New Market". In the U.K., companies listed on the Alternative Investment Market (AIM) were selected. Pre-IPO companies were selected from the following websites: www.newissues-ipo.com (U.K.), (http://www.ilsole24ore.com, (Italy); www.boursedeparis.fr (France), Because there is no comprehensive listing of companies planning to seek funds from the stock market in Germany, the companies to be included in the third sub-sample were chosen by taking into account the planned date of their listing (after 31 July). Thus, the surveyed companies in both countries constitute a fairly representative cross-section. A pre-test was done in Germany (n = 8) and France (n = 3) to ensure consistency and comprehension of the questionnaire. The following table briefly summarizes the overall survey response patterns (cf. Table 1),

2.1. Comparative Diffusion and Adoption Pattern

The BSC is known by almost all (98%) of the German companies, and 24% of German companies have witnessed concrete BSC implementation. By contrast, the majority of the French firms interviewed (59%) do not know the BSC, and to date only one has adopted it.[1] Given the fact that the initial French survey sample (SBF 120) had to be extended (SBF 250) due to the weak response rate, real acquaintance with the BSC in France is likely to be even

Table 2.   Comparative Diffusion Pattern.

	Tableaux de Bord		Balanced Scorecard	
	Know	adopt	know	adopt
Germany (n = 49)	4	1	48	12
	8%	2%	98%	24%
France (n = 32)	32	32	13	1
	100%	100%	41%	3%
Great Britain (n = 30)	0	0	25	9
	0%	0%	83%	30%
Italy (n = 34)	21	14	21	9
	62%	41%	62%	26%

lower. Not surprisingly, use of the Tableaux de Bord seems to be institution-alized in French companies (100% adopters). Strong cultural peculiarities seem to be rooted in the past for French performance measurement concepts: not only is diffusion of the BSC low in France, but inversely, diffusion of TdB in other European countries is also low, especially in Germany and the U.K.

2.2. Comparative Implementation Patterns

BSC adopters and TdB adopters in the different countries were asked to answer a set of identical questions regarding their way of implementing performance measurement systems (cf. Table 3). Answers on objective-setting suggest that BSC is used for managerial performance evaluation at lower management level as well as at the operational level. Furthermore, BSC tends to promote individual compensation for the achievement of common organizational goals at levels other than the top. BSC seems to be a strategic control tool with a typical top-down "translation of strategy into action".[2] Companies seem to implement a holistic multidimensional performance measurement system with many non-financial perspectives by still maintaining a strong emphasis on financial indicators. Cross-functional performance measures such as internal business processes and learning and growth are also important (85% defined measures for the process perspective and 38% defined measures for learning and growth) giving an indication of conformance to the initial measurement concept of Kaplan and Norton (1992). Accordingly different measures in one scorecard are mostly interlinked in cause-effect relationships and different BSCs within an organization are interlinked nearly to the same extent. IT (constraints) are

Table 3. Comparative Implementation Pattern.

Questions	Answers	TdB	BSC-adopters			
		France (F) %	Germany (G) %	U.K. (U) %	Italy (I) %	Total (G,U,I) %
How did you implement your Scorecard(s)? (F)n = 22; (G)n = 13; (U)n = 5; (I)n = 10	Top down	32	77	60	80	75
	Bottom up	45	15	0	10	11
	Local (related several measures to perspectives)	23	8	40	10	14
How many scorecards have been deployed within your organization? (F)n = 32; (G)n = 11; (U)n = 7; (I)n = 10	One	6	27	43	30	32
	More	94	73	57	70	68
Are the scorecards interlinked, or do they stand alone within specific units? (F)n = 28; (G)n = 10; (U)n = 5; (I)n = 7	Interlinked	54	60	60	86	68
	Independent	46	40	40	14	32
Which perspectives did you implement in your Scorecard(s)? (F)n = 31; (G)n = 13; (U)n = 9; (I)n = 11	Financial	94	100	89	91	94
	Customer	55	92	100	82	91
	Internal Process	19	85	67	55	70
	Learning and Growth	13	38	56	45	45
	Quality	39	15	56	55	40
	Risk	32	15	33	1	15
	Other	13	38	33	27	33
Are the measures of the different perspectives interlinked in a cause-effect relationship? (F)n = 31; (G)n = 12; (U)n = 8; (I)n = 7	Yes	48	75	75	71	74
	No	52	25	25	29	26
Are there individual targets for employees derived from the Scorecard(s) and if so, at what level? (F)n = 31; (G)n = 9; (U)n = 9; (I)n = 10	No	41	15	11	0	9
	1st management level	18	0	0	10	3
	2nd management level	9	15	44	50	34
	3rd management level	5	46	22	0	25
	operational level	27	23	22	40	28
Is compensation linked to the Scorecard(s) and if so to what level? (F)n = 22; (G)n = 11; (U)n = 9; (I)n = 10	No	52	9	11	40	20
	1st management level	13	0	0	10	3
	2nd management level	10	27	44	30	33
	3rd management level	6	55	22	0	27
	operational level	19	9	22	20	17

assessed as important for BSC implementation (+1.16 on a scale of –3 to +3), although 16% of companies do not use IT at all, 42% use simple spreadsheet solutions and 42% use comprehensive software solutions.

The implementation pattern of BSC adopters tends to converge in the three countries, which is not surprising since there was a prior lack of implementation of such performance measurement systems. So, quite naturally, in an early adoption stage companies follow theoretical concepts, since little internal or external information on implementation experiences is available. It is therefore not surprising that adopters mostly stick to the implementation guidelines of Kaplan and Norton (e.g. cause-effect relationships, measure perspectives, top-down implementation).

When it came to the TdB implementation, we found both converging and diverging elements compared to the implementation of BSC adopters. TdB is more likely to be used for economic performance evaluation on the unit level than for individual managerial performance evaluation (41% of TdB adopters do not derive any individual targets from TdB and 52% do not link TdB to compensation, although 27% derive individual targets at operational level). TdB tends to promote individual compensation for achievement of unit specific/ individual performance (if individual objectives are derived from TdB and compensation is linked to TdB, mainly the top management and operational unit levels are concerned). TdB also tends to be a more operational than strategic control tool (94% use more than one TdB in the organization, 45% use the bottom-up approach, and 22% the unit-specific approach). Companies seem to focus more on operational measures such as risk, quality, customer/market, than more strategic cross-functional performance measures such as internal business processes and learning and growth, by still keeping a strong emphasis on financial indicators (only 20% of the companies defined measures for the process perspective and 12% defined measures for learning and growth). Cause-effect relationships between indicators in one TdB are not central to practice (only 48%). Causal relationships between the non-financial and financial measures of different perspectives seem to be less prescriptive in TdB than in BSC. Thus, French TdB adopters have a more "open" perception of cause-effect relationships. IT (constraints) is perceived as relatively important for TdB implementation and the use of spreadsheet solutions is widespread (67%).

2.3. The Implementation of the One French "BSC Adopter"

To gain more insights into the adoption pattern of French companies we held a follow-up interview with the only French company that reported BSC adoption in our empirical survey.[3] We briefly summarize the context of that company and the cornerstones of its existing control system, and then discuss adoption rationales of that company.

The French Bank is one of the big French players in the traditional banking sector. This bank is well known in the banking industry for its service focus on private households. Regional offices have operational responsibility for several branches in that region providing financial services to local customers. In addition to these regional offices, several hierarchically separated IT-centres develop host and support applications for branches to provide operational financial services to private customers. During the late 1990s intense pressure on commercial conditions came from other French banks present in the local area in the private sector since interest rates were at an historically low level and loan demands were high. Banks used this context to attract new customers by sometimes offering loans even at refinancing conditions. Although well established in the French market, the bank is also increasingly threatened by profound changes in the financial service value chain due to e-banking, widespread consolidation with important mergers of commercial and private sector banks as well as deregulation (companies outside the banking sector diversified their portfolio with financial services, ex. retail companies offering short-term loans and credit cards to their customers), Electronic banking came up with new competitors that focus on specific financial transactions (e-brokering, e-billing etc.), Therefore, most traditional banks recently added new electronic distribution channels, that in turn required a rethinking and a restructuring of the traditional branch structure (closure and part-time models for opening hours, etc.), Mergers and acquisitions in the banking sector (ex. the merger of BNP-Paribas in May 2000), initiated to increase profits through greater economies of scale, led to increased pressure for cost reduction.

As one of the consequences of an increasingly competitive environment, central management reinforced financial control of regional office performance by means of stretched budget targets in a three-year time horizon. Return on equity-targets doubled for this time frame and the so-called "operating ratio" objective ("coéfficient d'exploitation") defined as total overhead divided by "net banking margin" ("produit net bancaire": mainly revenue based on financing/refinancing margin) went down to a 10% decreased target. Finally, regional offices were challenged by the objective to double their actual net operating result in a three-year time horizon. Clearly, such an ambitious management culture was not in the tradition of that bank in the past and local employees were not yet ready to cope with the changes induced at their workplaces.

The existing controlling system of the adopting regional entity (920 employees) of the French bank was very traditional:

- strategy deployment within a three-year rolling planning system (3-year basis);
- budgetary control by functions, branches and services;
- monthly P&L at the aggregated regional level;
- Tableau de Bord for products and branches to monitor sales objectives;
- Tableau de Bord for each of the three major functions of the regional entity (HR, Sales/Marketing and Finance), in total 150 measures (1/3 financial and 2/3 non financial), 40–50 measures to be reported on a monthly basis within each function.

As to the concerns of existing TdB that prompted the organization to start thinking of changing the TdB system, the chief controller of the regional entity mentioned the following elements:

- Lack of cross-functional view in traditional TdB where information was reported and aggregated within each of the three major functions in the management board of the regional office (Sales/Marketing, HR and Finance), more precisely lack of cross-functional performance indicators in the corporate TdB;
- overflow of information in the existing TdB;
- no explicit link of information available in the TdB, to strategy, and therefore no consistent communication to employees regarding the degree of strategy implementation;
- local action plans (in branches) disconnected from regional strategy.

This bank started thinking of adopting BSC at a highly institutionalized stage of TdB implementation (decades of experience). One of the major concerns of the regional bank seemed to have been addressed by the BSC and not by the TdB: the shared view of strategy implementation within the organization ("courroie de transmission"). The scope of the BSC project was limited to the management board level. Sharing information about strategy implementation at the board level was seen as the most appropriate way to improve existing TdB. At an early implementation stage a very surprising comment on the BSC was that action-plans could not easily be defined even after having defined (result) measures for the different strategic objectives. The bank failed in overcoming the limitations of TdB with BSC, since the perspectives defined in their BSC (thus also the objectives within each measure) reflected their functional organization (customer = sales department, innovation = development department, learning = Human Resource department). Since processes and process responsibilities were not defined prior to the TdB improvement, the process perspective in the BSC reflected only secondary activities such as information systems, infrastructure and project management. The BSC therefore implicitly reflected the budgeting structure by departments/functions in that bank. Basically, even if new (result) measures were added compared to the existing "Tableau de Bord", especially in the innovation/learning perspective, none of the initial objectives to improve TdB could have been reached at that stage (especially shared view and track of strategy implementation, reduction of the number of measures and action focus).

2.4. Summary: Differences and Similarities

We found different practices regarding adoption and diffusion patterns in France and Germany. French companies strongly resisted adopting BSC and even the concept of BSC itself did not spread on a large scale. In Germany only a minority of surveyed companies had adopted the concept although it had spread nation-wide. Regarding implementation patterns, we found both different and similar practices in France and Germany. The most important differences between BSC and TdB that we found in our study can be seen in BSC's focus on strategic control (hierarchical top-down deployment) and managerial performance evaluation as compared to TdB's operational control at the sub-unit and top-management levels and its focus on economic performance evaluation (instead of compensation). The link to compensation seems to be a major concern for BSC implementation (91% of companies) whereas for TdB adopters it is less important. We also found similarities between the two concepts. Both try to avoid the pitfalls of predominance of financial performance measures by defining a set of multidimensional non-financial measures. Regarding the various types of perspective reported in the survey, TdB and BSC adopters seem to understand both concepts more as an "open" framework than as a normative template for performance measurement.

2.5. Comparison of Results to Previously Observed BSC and TdB Implementation Patterns

Unfortunately French academics in Management Accounting place little research emphasis on implementation issues. This has apparently led to a quasi-absence of empirical field data of performance measurement practices not only on BSC but also on TdB in French companies over the last decade. As far as we know, only Epstein and Manzoni (1998) have made some case studies and -anecdotal evidence on TdB practices as compared to BSC practices, although without providing any insights whatsoever in their empirical methodology. Compared to their observations on TdB implementation (Epstein & Manzoni, 1998, p. 197), French practices seem to have changed in the meantime. Surveyed

French companies using TdB did not "tend to over-emphasize financial measures and to contain much less non-financial measures than books on TdB recommend" but rather tend to focus on operational (non-financial) perspectives such as quality and risk and to neglect cross-functional perspectives. The TdB does not "tend to be significantly longer than the ideal BSC as recommended in textbooks". Rather, BSC tends to be significantly longer (in practice and compared to recommendations in textbooks) than TdB in terms of average number of indicators reported. Also, to a far lesser extent, French companies "tend to collect and disseminate existing performance indicators, rather than starting from the unit's vision and strategy and deducing which indicators should be collected and reported", since the top-down approach and the unit-specific approach to implementing TdB are nearly equally as important as the bottom-up approach. The significant number of companies reporting that TdB helped in communicating with financial communities also indicates that it is not "fair to say that at least at the top management level, the content and style of use of TdB in French companies often fell short of theory on the subject".

A recent survey in German DAX 100 companies conducted in 1999 came up with similar results concerning BSC adoption in German organizations (Speckbacher & Bischof, 2000), All 93 surveyed companies knew the BSC concept, but only 19% reported to have experimented with BSC implementation in the past. An updated version of that empirical survey conducted one year later revealed that the adoption rate increased over that time period from 19% to 27% (Bischof, 2001, p. 34), but also revealed that "most German companies did not accord the importance to BSC that recent publications lead us to believe" (Bischof, 2001, p. 35), Implementation patterns in the present study are to a large extent similar: 70% of surveyed companies reported using BSC for managerial performance evaluation, and two-thirds of these linked the BSC to compensation.

3. DISCUSSION OF OBSERVED PERFORMANCE MEASUREMENT PRACTICES

What drives German organizations to their readiness to "absorb" U.S. innovations in managerial accounting and what drives French organizations to resist them? We do not claim here to give a total picture of potential rationales behind these observed practices, since we are aware of the weak response rate, especially in France. Rather we aim to explain potential rationales for BSC adoption in German companies and for non-adoption in French companies. Moreover, we try to explain the observed different implementation pattern for performance measurement systems in the two countries.

3.1. The Culturalist Perspective

The results of our comparative study of performance measurement practices are suggestive of the existence of distinct nationally-rooted cultural differences in performance measurement thus giving indication for a "cultural contingency of management control systems" (Bhimani, 1999, p. 417). Thus the resistance of French organizations to link performance measurement systems to compensation accounts for one of these differences, and resistance to top-down implementation and deployment of performance measures observed within TdB practices are further examples of observed differences between French and German measurement culture. Also systematic differences in diffusion and adoption rate support the cultural argument in explaining different solutions to problems of management control design. If "we can expect accounting systems to vary along national cultural line" since "the technical imperatives are weak" (Hofstede, 1987, p. 8), performance measurement practices in general and the choice of adoption of specific measurement tools such as BSC in particular are even more likely to be ruled by social values and thus influenced by cultural differences.

The results of a recent field study of 11 major French firms on the satisfaction of 120 managers with management accounting information for decision making are suggestive of the ongoing importance of the cultural contingency of management accounting systems (Mendoza & Bescos, 2001, p. 279): "For cultural reasons and considering the significant role that the French state plays in economic matters, France is not specially advanced regarding the implementation of new tools or new approaches in management accounting". The problems behind the observed reasons for dissatisfaction of French managers with management accounting information for decision making are addressed by the "new ABC/ABM approaches" and that the "data provided by these (ABC/ABM) systems should be supplemented by non-financial external indicators, as recommended by the balanced scorecard approach". However prior fundamental conceptual considerations (Lebas, 1994) show that information management based on the "method of sections homogènes" combined with "Tableau de bord" are compatible with the approach of ABC and ABM, thus indicating that the French measurement system is not lagging behind U.S. innovations regarding technical concerns.

The cultural perspective "assumes that individuals affect and are influenced by control structures in similar ways because they have internalised core cultural values which are shared by virtue of their membership in a wider national society" (Bhimani, 1999, p. 417). BSC emerged from the U.S. national context in a same way that TdB had been developed earlier in a French national context. Major results of D'Iribarne's (1989) comparative field research suggest specific mindsets underlying the social ideologies behind the two measurement tools: thus "american life is ruled by contracts" (D'Iribarne, 1989, p. 257) and French life is ruled by "honour" and social ranks (D'Iribarne, 1989, p. 258). Measurement tools will play different roles in organizations whose members believe in these social values. This may partly explain that TdB is used more as a local performance tool in line with the local responsibility without link to compensation since "honour" forces to excel first in somebody's own domain without needing extrinsic monetary rewards.

Bourguignon, Malleret and Nørreklit (2001) are trying to shape different local management ideologies based on a collection of rather independent dimensions of culture specifically concerning performance measurement. Their research results are suggestive of further cultural rationales for our observed measurement practices in three ways. First the limited overall diffusion of BSC in France can be explained by the fact that management and management techniques enjoy a relatively low social status in France with its engineer-dominated management culture, so that "innovations" in administrative technologies do not attract the same attention as in countries with a higher status which may lead to the observed low diffusion rate. Also overall distrust but not ignorance of U.S. ideas such as BSC, for historical reasons, contribute to its limited diffusion. Second the non adoption of BSC by French companies can be explained by the fact that BSC is a tool for strategic planning and control, and planning is a way to reduce risk. In an intensely "risk-averse" culture like in France, "security is too important to be left to management systems; it is inscribed in the social structures". Furthermore BSC is based on a template idea and therefore offers the benefit of pragmatism, while TdB relies on a "very logical and systematic, but more abstract, methodology, which is consistent with the French intellectual and engineering tradition (*"esprit cartésien"*) and therefore offers the benefit of theoretical foundations valued more in France than implementation issues. Third particularities of observed performance measurement patterns may be explained by culture, since BSC reinforces hierarchy by means of a top-down control system. Top-down deployment cannot be the exclusive approach in French organizations, where "hierarchy and a local sense of obedience are kinds of facts of nature", and TdB "gives place to local initiative, the absence of which makes French strategic involvement impossible".

Even if national differences in implementation patterns can be better understood with the culturalist perspective, the theoretical explanatory power solely based on this approach remains limited. Beside general arguments (see for example a summary criticism of Bhimani, 1999, pp. 418–420), we think that prior research results on diffusion and adoption patterns of shareholder value management (SVM) in France and Germany (Gehrke & Zarlowski, 2002) are suggestive of the need to rely on further perspectives to understand cross national changes in performance measurement. Thus in the contrary to BSC, SVM diffusion and adoption tend to converge in France and Germany. This convergence can be characterized by increased adoption of SVM measures, particular EVA, for both external purposes (as a part of communication to financial markets) and internal purposes (as a part of planning and control systems) over the last five years in both countries. Also an increasing number of German and French companies change their corporate governance principles to a more shareholder-oriented model where shareholder objectives are given priority (Gehrke, 2002). This increasing diffusion and adoption in France occurred in spite of the very limited innovational character of shareholder value measures such as EVA regarding technical imperatives in the French financial measurement tradition (see for example the EVA criticism of Ponssard & Zarlowski, 1999; Lordon, 2000). The diffusion of SVM and the recent move to a more shareholder-oriented governance model in the French and Germany companies studied can be compared to recent trends in the institutional environment in these two countries. In France and Germany, the growing proportion of British and U.S. institutional investors in the capital of major listed firms is a recent phenomenon likely to profoundly modify the corporate environment and to legitimize the adoption of practices and discourses focused on shareholder value creation.

A further perspective that emerges out of the observed SVM implementation pattern to explain cross national performance measurement is the new institutional theory framework (Dimaggio & Powell, 1991) that suggests change in administrative technologies is more likely to occur in settings where practices become institutionalized and therefore offer the benefit of legitimacy. This new institutionalism perspective is suggesting the existence of specific conditions in the institutional environment of organizations that impact diffusion and adoption on a national level. In the following we try to discuss some of these conditions in both countries to understand observed diffusion and adoption especially related to diffusion theory.

3.1. A Diffusion Theory Perspective

Information economics has been used as a dominant theoretical framework to explain management accounting changes in organizations, suggesting that new tools (e.g. information from a Balanced Scorecard) are adopted in so far as they are expected to provide technical benefits that exceed the cost of their implementation. This framework suggests change in management accounting when internal decision makers require different and more appropriate information.

Information economics rely on rationality to explain adoption. Thus, the observed adoption rate and increasing diffusion of SVM in both countries over the last five years can be interpreted in terms of rational choice from the point of view of the firm since the evolution of the institutional environment (composition of shareholding with an increasing importance of foreign investment funds, corporate governance and legislative context) has helped to grant more importance to the objective of shareholder value creation and to highlight performance gaps in both countries (Gehrke & Zarlowski, 2002), SVM tools can then be analysed as an administrative technology likely to help firms reduce their value gaps which, in turn, reduces the risk of becoming the target of a hostile take-over bid[4] or being starved of the external capital needed to survive.

However, in the case of BSC-practices, the observed non-adoption in France as compared to adoption in Germany is an indicator that rationality – assumed to exist – may not be sufficient to explain diffusion of "new" accounting techniques in different settings. It calls for adoption motivation in organizations outside rationality. Abrahamson first included the "supply side" to explain organizational adoption decisions in a "diffusion and rejection of administrative technologies" framework[5] (1991, p. 591). In Abrahamson's framework especially fashion seems for us to be an interesting perspective beside rationality to explain diffusion and adoption in the two countries.

- "efficient choice perspective" that builds on the notion of performance gaps defined as discrepancies between an organizational goal and what it can attain: innovations are diffused when they help organizations to reduce performance gaps created by environmental changes;
- "forced selection perspective" that builds on influence and power of governmental bodies to dictate which innovations are diffused, so that organizations face a situation to adopt with no choice;
- "fashion perspective" that builds on the assumption that non-adopting organizations (consulting firms, business schools and mass media) have an impact on diffusion; under conditions of uncertainty, organizations tend to imitate other "fashion setting" organizations.
- "fad perspective" that builds on the assumption that adopting organizations have an impact on diffusion; organizations imitate other organizations to appear legitimate or to avoid the risk of competitors gaining a competitive advantage.

In the following we draw on this framework to highlight the perspectives that best fits into our perception of rationales behind country specific diffusion and adoption.

3.1.1. Diffusion and Adoption in Germany

Academic proponents of BSC in Germany tend to build on major rationales traditionally used to argue for non-financial measures in general (Ittner & Larcker, 1998, p. 217) and the BSC (Kaplan & Norton, 1996a) in particular. Thus, Speckbacher and Bischof (2000, p. 796) view BSC as an "answer to five key steering problems of the firm": limitations in relevance of traditional accounting-based measures, inability of financial measures to evaluate intangible assets, absence of a "stakeholder management concept" for strategic planning, insufficient communication and implementation of strategy and directing behaviour. However, their survey on DAX 100 companies (cf. point 2.4) revealed (Speckbacher & Bischof, 2000, p. 806) that early adopters of BSC in Germany (between 1996 and 1998) – supposed to be rational adopters, following findings by Malmi (1999) on adoption patterns of Management Accounting "innovations" – view a BSC neither as a stakeholder management tool nor as a measurement problem of intangible assets but primarily as a tool to "link strategic corporate objectives with operational action plans", to "better integrate non-financial value drivers", to "support the value-based steering system (SVM)", and to "improve company financial results in the long run". Thus, early (rational) adoption of BSC in German companies seems to be motivated by dissatisfaction with existing performance measurement and strategic planning systems. What may be drivers behind this (rational) motivation to change existing systems in German organizations?

The main effort of Management Control in German companies has been shifted significantly during the last 10 to 15 years: long-term and strategic aspects have moved into the focus of attention. The empirical study by Al-Laham on strategic planning in German companies is a good example for this shift of focus (Al-Laham, 1996), In Al-Laham's study the core problem of strategic management control in German organizations has become evident: How can the corporate strategy be translated into operational control at all corporate levels? At this point, in most German companies there is still a need for this question to be answered. Three aspects even increase the problem occurring at the interface between formulating and implementing a strategy:

- A company-wide implementation of value-based management systems has led to the question of how DCF, EVA or CFROI can be combined with value drivers.
- The increase of "clock-speed" in all industries has led to the demand for strategic flexibility (cf. Fine, 1999), Strategies currently have to be aligned with changing needs. The same applies to operational performance measures for implementing the strategy.

- In Germany, the staff needs more "empowerment" in order to be motivated, i.e. a better involvement in the process of generating and implementing the strategy. The strategy has to be unequivocally specified and communicated. Success depends on the process of implementation at the base.

The performance management systems prevailing in Germany, that only in exceptional cases are linked to non-financial measures and that originated in the Dupont-System with ROI as a key ratio (cf. Gleich, 2001), were not able to solve these problems. Thus, diffusion of BSC in Germany can be explained by the "efficient choice perspective": there is a problem – an interface problem – between strategy and operational control, which is reinforced by environmental changes outside the company (Shareholder Value-orientation, necessity of strategic flexibility, personnel empowerment), and existing systems used so far are perceived as being unable to provide answers to these problems.

Academic reaction to BSC in Germany was partly critical (cf. for example Weber & Schäffer, 1998), arguing that the theoretical foundation of the BSC is too weak and that the innovative character of BSC is very limited since non-financial measures introduced into quality management and strategic control systems included early warning signals based on financial and non-financial indicators. Thus fashion best explains BSC adoption in German organizations. This academic reaction may lead to the conclusion that perception of innovation is biased in organizations. However, a thorough and comprehensive discussion on the controversy over the novelty and the theoretical foundations of BSC is beyond the scope of this paper. We intend here to discuss diffusion patterns primarily based on the perception of "innovation" within practice although this in no way reflects any "judgement" by the authors.

In Germany it cannot be disregarded that consulting companies have a strong marketing effect: 14 out of 20 Top-Management consulting firms in that country (cf. the so-called Lünendonk list in: *FAZ*, 2001, p. 27) do offer the Balanced Scorecard in their product spectrum. In addition to that, the orientation towards the U.S. is very distinct in Germany, where "Balanced Scorecard Collaborative" consultancy initiated by Kaplan and Norton has become very active. The new book by Kaplan and Norton, *The Strategy-focused Organization* (2000b) has furthermore enhanced interest in the subject, and the German translation will be published as early as September 2001. Publication of the first article by Kaplan and Norton on the Balanced Scorecard (in the *Harvard Business Review*, 1992) immediately led to numerous articles in German management magazines, and their book on the subject (Kaplan & Norton, 1996) was immediately translated into German (1997) owing to keen interest in German companies. Strategic consultants have become able to offer a very successful consulting product contributing to a push on the supply side of BSC.

3.1.2. Diffusion and adoption in France

Whereas the BSC concept spread to German organizations, in France this has not been the case and adoption has been extremely limited. Thus, the question of rational choice turns out to be "rational rejection" in France. The obvious and intuitive reason for rejection is that in many French firms the similar TdB concept is in an institutionalized stage of maturity with refined and interrelated metrics that managers seem to have been using with total confidence (100% adoption rate of TdB in France) for quite a long time (cf. point 1). This evidence of institutionalized practices and a resulting advanced stage of conceptual maturity of TdB (feedback from practical use to theory) in France may have led French academics to state that the BSC concept originates in the TdB ideology (Chiapello & Lebas, 1996; Mendoza & Zrihen, 1999a). The title "TdB in original version or in American version" (Mendoza & Zrihen, 1999a) of a recent publication in a French accounting journal is an example of dominant academic perception of the "innovative" character of BSC in France and calls for differentiated discussion of diffusion, especially regarding the "socio-economic context" in which an approach originated. Moreover, the legacy of the ROI Dupont scheme for performance measurement practices in German organizations (cf. above) apparently does not apply to French management tradition where operational process information was traditionally very important along with financial information (Lebas, 1994). Thus, the "rational" problem of inadequate existing performance measurement systems that seems to be witnessed by German organizations cannot be relevant in France.

More technical rationales for "rational rejection" of the concept are given by Lorino (2001, p. 161) who states that the call for an ultimate link of all measures on a scorecard to financial objectives by causal paths (a cornerstone of Kaplan & Norton's BSC) is:

- "condradictory", since the concept itself leads to a control philosophy after the facts (*"après la bataille"*),
- "superficial", since the formal link between non-financial and financial indicators can lead to inconsistency in the relationship of long term and short term objectives,
- "unrealistic", since isolation of the impact of non-financial performance improvements on financial results is not possible.

Lorino gives a further even more powerful rationale for non-adoption in France: "elimination of managerial risk (assumed by the manager when evaluating a situation) by means of an automatic control device is an illusion. Steering priorities are based on a strategic choice and strategy is a human and risky judgement. That is why managerial risk exists and that is why managers are good or bad". Clearly, the idea of "mapping the strategy" (Kaplan & Norton, 2000a) is not in line with the dominant perception of strategy in France.

The BSC implementation case of the French bank (see 2.3) shows the drivers of change of existing TdB systems, originating both outside the organization (competitive pressure) and inside the organization (stretched target and high performance culture), rather than rational adoption of BSC. BSC seems to address concerns of TdB but also to be more a promising concept at a glance[6] that cannot really solve the problems reported for the TdB. Therefore, the case tends to confirm the hypothesis of "rational rejection" as the main reason for non-adoption.

The "fashion perspective" turns out to be a "fashion rejection perspective" with the assumption that business schools (cf. the discussion of French academics above) and mass media (cf. for example Mendoza & Zrihen, 1999b) have rather a negative or at best a "neutral" impact on diffusion. The assumption that adopting organizations have an impact on diffusion ("fad perspective") will presumably not become relevant, for obvious reasons. In the contrary to Germany, the conditions for BSC fashion to occur are not favorable in France.

4. CONCLUSION

The observed patterns of performance measurement concepts and the discourse accompanying it are very different in France and Germany and the rationales behind diffusion and adoption may be best explained only based on a combination of different research perspectives that impact organizations in a specific way to react on appearance performance measurement "innovations".

The "efficient choice perspective" may explain early adoption in Germany, especially regarding external influence factors: the dynamics of competition tend to require a stronger focus on strategy and a higher strategic flexibility. Implementation of "new" management approaches pushed by the supply side ("fashion") seems here to positively affect legitimization, even given the lack of rigour in the BSC concept itself. Moreover, the cooperative leadership culture as well as an "open-minded" and constructive position as regards U.S. ideas, prevailing in Germany, speed up the diffusion of the BSC.

In France, the traditional focus on non-financial measures and a highly institutionalized TdB-based steering culture, combined with an overall expectation of strong intellectual concept contributions, may explain the "rational rejection" of BSC.

Globalization and EU-integration may lead here to a stronger uniformity of performance measurement systems in the future, especially for European Management Practices. M&A-causesd integration processes and increasing capital market pressure will presumably be a driver of convergence in management control and performance measurement systems.

NOTES

1. In fact this company did not adopt the BSC "from scratch", but rather adapted their TdB performance measurement system based on conceptual elements of the BSC. Further insights in this case are provided in this paper.
2. This is also the subtitle of the German publication of Kaplan and Norton (1997).
3. The interview was conducted by I. Gehrke on 2 November 2000.
4. In this respect, in 1998 and 2000 Germany experienced two hostile take-over bids: take-over of Thyssen by Krupp-Hoesch and that of Mannesmann by the British group Vodafone, which largely helped to legitimize this type of restructuring in Germany ("Mannesmann syndrome"), This approach had been impossible until then due to the traditional type of "stakeholder" corporate governance. Similar examples exist recently in France: BNP's take-over bid for Société Générale and Paribas, and Elf's for Total.
5. Recently Abrahamson's framework (Abrahamson, 1991) has consistently been used to explain the diffusion of management accounting innovation across Finnish firms, based on the example of activity-based costing (Malmi, 1999), The study indicated that the initial ABC adopters implemented the system for efficient choice reasons and later adopters tended to implement ABC for "fashion" and "fad" reasons. Thus, changes in managerial accounting practices are pushed by consultants, business schools and mass-media publications as "supply-side" accounting innovations.
6. The controller read the French version of Kaplan & Norton (1996a).

REFERENCES

Abrahamson, E. (1991). Managerial fads and fashions: the diffusion and rejection of innovations. *Acadamy of Management Review, 16*, 586–612.

Al-Laham, A. (1996). *Strategieprozesse in deutschen Unternehmungen*. Wiesbaden.

Bhimani, A. (1999). Mapping methodological frontiers in cross-national management control research. *Accounting, Organizations and Society, 24*, 413–440.

Bischof, J. (2001). Balanced Scorecard in der Unternehmenspraxis – Ergebnisse einer aktualisierten Befragung und Empfehlungen für den Einsatz. *Bilanzbuchhalter und Controller, 25*(2), 34–37.

Bouquin, H. (1991). *Le contrôle de gestion*. Paris.

Bourguignon, A., Malleret, V., & Nørreklit, H. (2001). Balanced Scorecard versus French tableau de bord: beyond dispute, a cultural and ideological perspective, working paper DR 01005, ESSEC Research Center, March.

Chiapello, E., & Lebas, M. (1996). The Tableau de bord, a French Approach to Management Information. Communication presented at the 19th Annual Meeting of the European Accounting Association, Bergen (Norway), 2–4th May.

D'Iribarne, P. (1989). La logique de l'honneur. Gestion des entreprises et traditions nationales. Ed. du Seuil, Paris.

DiMaggio, P. J., & Powell, W. W. (1991). *The new institutionalism in organizational analysis.* Chicago: University of Chicago Press.

Epstein, M. J., & Manzoni, J. F. (1997), The balanced scorecard and tableau de bord: translating strategy into action, *Management Accounting (U.S.), 79*(2), 28–36.

Epstein, M. J., & Manzoni, J. F. (1998). Implementing Corporate Strategy: From Tableaux de bord to Balanced Scorecards. *European Management Journal, 16*(2), 190–203.

Fine, Ch. (1999). *Clockspeed: Wie Unternehmen schnell auf Marktveränderungen reagieren können.* Hamburg.

Gehrke, I. (2002). Valeur actionnariale: Le "rattrapage" de l'Allemagne, Les fonds d'investisse-ment étrangers en France. Enjeux pour les entreprises, Séries Etudes, La Documentation Française, Paris, 147–162.

Gehrke, I., & Zarlowski, P. (2002). Shareholder Value Management Diffusion Across Organisations: A Comparative Analysis of Large French and German Companies. In: H. Gammelsaeter & F. Mueller (Eds), *The Institutionalisation of Management Ideas: A European Perspective.* Routledge Press, Best Paper Proceedings, forthcoming.

Gleich, R. (2001). *Das System des Performance Measurement.* München.

Hofstede, G. (1987). The cultural context of accounting. In: B. E. Cushing (Ed.), *Accounting and Culture* (pp. 1–11). American Accounting Association.

Horváth, P., Minning, F., Lyne, S., Gehrke, I., Hinterhuber, H., Genovese, G., & Pechlaner, H. (2001). Value Based Management and Balanced Scorecard in European Companies – An international Comparison between Germany, France, Great Britain and Italy, Controlling Research Paper No. 67. Chair of Controlling, University of Stuttgart, August 2001.

Ittner, C. D., & Larcker, D. F. (1998). Innovations in Performance Measurement: Trends and Research Implications. *Journal of Management and Accounting Research, 10,* 205–238.

Ittner, C. D., & Larcker, D. F. (2001). Assessing empirical research in managerial acccounting: a value based management perspective. *Journal of Accounting and Economics, 32,* 349–410.

Kaplan, R. S., & Norton, D. P. (1992). The Balanced Scorecard – Measures that drive performance. *Harvard Business Review, 70*(1), 71–79.

Kaplan, R. S., & Norton, D. P. (1996a). The Balanced Scorecard – Translating strategy into action. Boston, MA.: Harvard Business School Press (deutsche Version (1997), Balanced Scorecard: Strategien erfolgreich umsetzen, Stuttgart 1997, (traduction française (1998): Le tableau de bord prospectif, Editions d'Organisation, Paris).

Kaplan, R. S., & Norton, D. P. (1996b). Using the balanced scorecard as a strategic management system. *Harvard Business Review, Jan–Feb,* 75–85.

Kaplan, R. S., & Norton, D. P. (2000a). Having Trouble with your strategy? Then map it. *Harvard Business Review, Sept–Oct.,* 167–179.

Kaplan, R. S., & Norton, D. P. (2000b). *The Strategy-focused Organisation.* Boston, MA.

Lebas, M. (1994). Managerial Accounting in France. Overview of Past Tradition and Current Practice. *European Accounting Review, 3*(3), 471–487.

Lordon, F. (2000). La "création de valeur" comme rhetorique et comme pratique. Généalogie et sociologie de la "valeur actionnariale". *L'année de la régulation, 4,* 115–167.

Lorino, P. (2001). *Méthodes et pratiques de la performance. Le pilotage par les processus et les compétences.* Paris: Editions d'Organisation (2nd ed.).

Malmi, T. (1999). Activity based costing diffusion across organizations: an exploratory empirical analysis of Finnish Firms. *Accounting, Organizations and Society, 24,* 649–672.

Mendoza, C., & Zrihen, R. (1999a). Le tableau de bord, en VO ou en version américaine? *Revue Française de Comptabilité, janvier,* 60–66.

Mendoza, C., & Zrihen, R. (1999b), Du balanced scorecard au tableau de pilotage. *L'Expansion Management Review, 95,* 102–110.

Mendoza, C., & Bescos, P. L. (2001). An explanatory model of managers' information needs: Implications for management accounting. *The European Accounting Review, 10*(2), 257–289.

FAZ (2001). Unternehmen denken immer kurzfristiger – Rangliste der großen Consulting-gesellschaften. *Frankfurter Allgemeine Zeitung, 23*(Mai), 27.

Ponssard, J. P., & Saulpic, O. (2000). Une reformulation de l'approche dite du "balanced scorecard". *Comptabilité, Contrôle, Audit, 6*(1), 7–25.

Ponssard, J.-P., & Zarlowski, P. (1999). Nouveaux indicateurs de création de valeur: des outils satisfaisants pour l'évaluation interne des activités des entreprises? *Revue Française de Gestion, January-February,* 91–98.

Speckbacher, G., & Bischof, J. (2000). Die Balanced Scorecard als innovatives Managementsystem. *Die Betriebswirtschaft, 60*(6), 795–810.

Weber, J., & Schäffer, U. (1998). Balanced Scorecard – Gedanken zur Einordnung des Konzepts in das bisherige Controlling-Instrumentarium. *Zeitschrift für Planung, 9*(4), 341–365.

THE ROLE OF BALANCED SCORECARD IN MANUFACTURING: A TOOL FOR STRATEGICALLY ALIGNED WORK ON CONTINUOUS IMPROVEMENTS IN PRODUCTION TEAMS?

Mandar Dabhilakar and Lars Bengtsson

ABSTRACT

In this paper we analyze the role of balanced scorecard in strategically aligned work on continuous improvements in production teams. The analysis is based on survey responses from 51 engineering industry companies and data from three case studies. Two continuous improvement strategies are identified with the use of cluster analysis, namely, the expert task force strategy and the wide focus strategy. These strategies were found to be closely related to specific features of the local work organization. The case studies shows that there is a clear connection between local work on continuous improvements in teams and implementation and use of the balanced scorecard. A common role of balanced scorecard is to facilitate focus, resource allocation, prioritization and comprehensive coordination of continuous improvement activities, which implies a potential for exploiting the local and operational knowledge base. The balanced

Performance Measurement and Management Control, Volume 12, pages 181–208.

scorecard applications, however, are adapted to each strategy for contin-
uous improvements as well as the features of the work organization by a
unique emphasis on control of content, process and goals.

1. INTRODUCTION

The balanced scorecard (BSC) management control method is now entering the
scene in Sweden at quite a high rate (Ernst & Young Management Consulting,
1998; Kald & Nilsson, 2000). Our own research estimates the use of BSC within
the Swedish engineering industry in general at 28% in 1999, and an even higher
diffusion rate in large companies (Bengtsson et al., 2000a). BSC has, however,
so far mainly been implemented at the top management level. There are
very few empirical studies exploring and illustrating in detail how BSC is
implemented and used in manufacturing (Ewing & Samuelson, 1998; Bengtsson
et al., 2000b). In particular, cases where the concept is implemented at top
management level as well as at the frontline within manufacturing are hard to
find. This is also interesting since previous research shows that the need for
information and management control systems differs for the management level
compared with the production team level (Jönsson & Grönlund, 1988; Meyer,
1994). There is thus a need for further research to analyze how the concept
could be designed and applied, and furthermore, to explore the effects and
potential of BSC when implemented in manufacturing that is organized in teams.

In this article we primarily focus our analysis on the interface between BSC
and the work on continuous improvements (CI) carried out by production teams.
There are two rationales for this focus. Firstly, one main idea behind BSC is
to enhance CI and learning (Kaplan & Norton, 1996b). The outcome of the
strategic measurements should constantly be reviewed and analyzed in order to
adjust the chosen strategy. This is in accordance with the concept of Total
Quality Management (Bergman & Klefsjö, 1994), which stresses the need to
engage all personnel at all levels in the CI work. This indicates a great
potential for CI work carried out by production teams, since the incidence of
team-based organizations is significant in the Swedish engineering industry
(Dabhilakar & Niss, 2000).

Secondly, research conducted by the Swedish National Institute for Working
Life states that in order to develop good working conditions and simultaneously improve the competitiveness of the Swedish engineering industry,
the companies have to align CI in production teams to the overall strategic
planning of the company. Unfortunately, this is not the case in general and
results in a lack of support and resources for the teams. Another aspect of the
problem is that top management does not exploit the local and operational

knowledge base in order to further improve the competitiveness of the company (Nilsson, 1999).

Our overall purpose in this paper is to analyze if and how the BSC approach may contribute to solving the problem of not exploiting the local knowledge base by linking local CI activities to the strategic objectives of the company

2. ANALYSIS MODEL, SPECIFIED PURPOSE AND HYPOTHESIS

How can the role of BSC in strategically aligning CI work in production teams be understood and analyzed?

The first issue concerns how to describe team-based CI work. Production teams, which have become more and more common in industrial companies, have successively increased their scope of work. In our previous research we have described and analyzed the development of production teams by discerning four different areas of responsibility (Bengtsson, 1998). These areas concern direct operational work, administrative and planning work, CI and finally process & business development. This trend towards a more integrated work organization is inherent in the trend towards process-oriented organizations, in which the role of operative teams has become even more important (Rentzhog, 1996). This applies also to changed roles for white-collar workers close to production who tend to become an integral part of the production teams (Berglund, 1998). An important contribution to the understanding of team-based CI work has been made by Berger (1997) and Lindberg and Berger (1997), who have distinguished among three different team-based strategies for designing, organizing and managing systems for CI in Sweden. These are the expert task force, the organic and the wide focus CI strategy. In companies that adopt the expert task force strategy, CI tasks are mainly performed by project staff or consultants. Production team members participate, but only to a limited extent. Management defines by whom and when (process) and what (content) activities should take place. In the organic strategy, it is the production teams that carry out the CI work and management controls by setting business-related targets (targets here mean specified and measurable goals). The wide focus strategy is a combination of the previous two. Both experts and production teams carry out the CI work, and process, content and goals are predefined. The authors notice that the CI strategies relate to different work organizations, but they do not elaborate this further. Other researchers have more explicitly discussed and stressed the intimate relationship between CI and learning in teams on the one hand and work content, responsibility and powers of the teams on the other hand (Hart et al., 1996; Ellström & Kock, 1999). Briefly put, multi-skilled teams with extensive work content are more capable of performing development-oriented learning (double-loop) as a basis for more fundamental improvements than teams with more restricted responsibility and competence.

The second issue concerns how to understand the meaning of strategically aligned CI work. Basically we interpret and define this as follows: The CI work carried out by the production teams should explicitly be linked to the strategies and targets valid for the entire organization. In our understanding it is an expression for the vertical/hierarchical and the integrative dimension of the organization. This does not, however, preclude the existence of or the need for local strategies based on local and process-oriented logic. The question is rather how to align the central and local strategies. Bessant and Francis (1999) claim that in developing a strategic CI capability, organizations need to develop a capability in which strategic goals are communicated and deployed to all levels and where local improvement activities are guided by a process of monitoring and measuring against these strategic objectives. The authors suggest a need for further research on generic enabling mechanisms for policy development and deployment and the adaptation of these enabling mechanisms to specific circumstances. In this paper we ask if and how BSC could be such an enabling mechanism. Furthermore, the specific circumstances are the contingent nature of the design and organization of CI processes, especially with respect to the local work organization and the work design in production teams.

The third issue concerns the role of BSC in strategically aligning CI work in production teams. Basically, the BSC is a model that integrates financial and non-financial strategic measures. It is different from other strategic management systems in that it specifies performance measurements as well as the drivers of outcomes in cause and effect relationships. Furthermore, it is important to note that there has been a progression in the concept. When it was first launched in 1992 it was mainly measurement oriented (Kaplan & Norton, 1992). In recent versions of the BSC, there is a greater emphasis on using the concept as a strategic management model in order to more effectively develop a strategy and then communicate the strategic direction of the company to everyone (Kaplan & Norton, 1996a, b, 2001). This implies that strategy development comes first and measurement becomes a secondary issue. The concept of BSC is furthermore strongly linked to the idea of strategic management as a cyclic learning process, including principal phases such as clarifying visions and strategies, implementation and target setting and feedback and learning.

In order to understand the role of BSC for the CI work carried out by production teams, we have to analyze the organizational aspect of BSC. In its original version BSC is mainly a tool for top management. Due to this BSC has been described as centralized and top-down oriented (Nörreklit, 2000; Bengtsson et al., 2000b). It is a method for communicating centrally formulated visions and strategies down through the organizational hierarchy. However, case studies show that the concept can also be implemented in a more decentralized way (Lundahl & Ewing, 1997; Ewing & Samuelson, 1998; Bengtsson et al., 2000b). ABB Sweden's approach to implementing the BSC is significantly different from Kaplan and Norton's original ideas in some aspects. The most evident is that ABB intended BSC to provide production teams with a development tool that permitted the teams to formulate their own strategies and objectives, which were formalized in a team scorecard. These scorecards were not strictly tied (aggregated) to other scorecards but related to the overall company scorecard and strategic planning. This design was chosen in order to support frontline teams in their daily work as their role changed and ABB became more process-oriented, thereby emphasizing the horizontal dimensions of control to a greater extent. The various forms of implementation of scorecards that this case illustrates are in line with the previous findings of Jönsson and Grönlund (1988) who showed that the management level and local level have different needs when it comes to information and management control systems.

To sum up, our concluding analysis model contains three corners, as illustrated in Fig. 1. Our main focus is on the relationship between team-based CI strategies and activities and the way BSC has been implemented. These CI strategies are affected by the work organization, and especially the

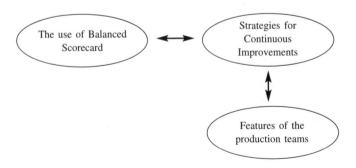

Fig. 1. Model to Analyze the Role of BSC in Strategically Aligned Work on CI in Production Teams.

characteristics of the production teams in terms of work content and skills, target-orientation and whether the teams include white-collar workers or not.

The analysis model presented gives us a basis for specifying our overall purpose of analyzing if and how the BSC approach contributes to exploiting the local knowledge base by linking local CI activities to the strategic objectives of the company. According to our analysis model, this question presupposes a deeper understanding of how CI are carried out and whether this varies in correlation with the local work organization. The purpose of this paper is therefore be specified in three objectives:

(1) Identify and analyze strategies in midsize and large Swedish engineering industry companies for carrying out local work on CI.
(2) Describe the features of the local work organization, the content of the local CI work as well as the uses of BSC that are linked to each strategy for carrying out the local work on CI.
(3) Analyze the role of BSC in strategically aligned work on CI in production teams by illustrating the interface between how the local CI work is carried out and how the BSC is used.

We expect the BSC to serve as an enabling mechanism for policy deployment. In order to respond to the work of Bessant and Francis (1999), we focus in this paper on the adaptation of the use of BSC in the companies to their chosen strategy for carrying out the local work on continuous improvement. From our point of view, the enabling mechanism (i.e. the use of BSC) ought to emphasize different aspects depending on which strategy for CI is undertaken by the company. The primary reason is that in our opinion the chosen CI strategy, defined by process, content and goals, is related to specific features of the work organization. Thus our hypothesis is that if there are different strategies for carrying out the local work on CI and if these strategies are related to specific features of the work organization, then the interface between CI and BSC should have a unique emphasis (in terms of controlling content, processes and goals, respectively) for each of the identified CI strategies.

3. METHOD

This study uses two main empirical sources: 51 responses from a mailed survey study of production teams and management control methods and a multiple case study at three engineering industry companies that have implemented BSC in production. The survey is mainly used for the two first objectives, while the third objective requires a case study approach. There are two motives for choosing a case study approach. Firstly, few of the companies in the survey have implemented BSC at the shop-floor level. Secondly, we regard each company as a set of subsystems. A case study approach allows us to acquire a deeper understanding of complex interrelations between the subsystems, as well as thoroughly describing each company. The combination of quantitative and qualitative data has implications for the generalization of findings. The results from the cluster analysis (i.e. strategies for CI) could be statistically generalized to the population of midsize and large Swedish engineering industry companies. This is also the case for the features of the work organization that are related to each of the identified strategies. The analysis of the role of BSC in manufacturing for strategically aligned work on CI relies mainly on the three cases. The issue must thus be generalized to theory. The cases may also serve as illustrations of how the BSC is being used. The multiple case study, furthermore, serves a validating purpose in favor of the survey study by illustrating the existence of the identified CI strategies, as well as features of the work organization that are related to them.

3.1. The Survey

The survey study was carried out during 1999. The population (N = 2297) consisted of engineering industry companies in Sweden that employed more than twenty persons. The sample (n_{total} = 200) was stratified in two size categories (n_{20-199} = 100; $n_{>199}$ = 100) within seven industry codes (SNI codes 28-32; 34-35). These industries were chosen to gain a representative distribution of engineering industry companies in Sweden.

After two remainders, 80 usable responses were received. The survey was mailed to company production managers and the response rate was 55% after removing companies that did not have production or production teams. The definition of production team used in the survey was: "*A team is a stable group of people that works together and has a common responsibility for certain production tasks.*" A telephone survey of 83 non-respondents was conducted. These non-respondents were asked to answer the first 9 constructs. No significant response bias was detected.

The survey included 30 constructs that covered eight different areas and were formulated after a comprehensive literature review. The first 9 constructs concerned company data and production teams. The subsequent questions covered team tasks, internal organization and wage systems, target orientation, CI, process management, BSC, change strategies and performance. Each question considered the situation in 1999 and the expected situation in 2001. Two different types of scales were mainly used; nominal and ordinal.

The questionnaire was pilot tested on two manufacturing companies in Sweden for readability, completeness and clarity. The figures on distribution have to some extent been validated by comparisons with other studies. Further details of the survey method and the profile of the involved companies are given in Dabhilakar and Niss (2000).

3.1.1. Data Analysis

The first step in the data analysis was to prepare the data set by selecting the engineering industry companies that had more than 199 employees. The reason for focusing on midsize and large engineering industry companies is to obtain a more homogeneous sample due to differences in management attention and control between small and large companies. Fifty-one of the 80 usable responses were selected. Secondly, the multivariate technique of cluster analysis was used in order to identify the CI strategies. Finally cross tabulations were conducted, where the identified clusters were tabulated against other categorical variables that describe the features of the local work organization, the content of the local CI work and the BSC implementation approach.

3.1.2. Cluster Analysis

Cluster analysis was chosen in order to classify the companies into mutually exclusive groups based on the similarities among the companies with respect to strategies for carrying out CI. The groups were not predefined. Instead, the method was used to identify the groups. However, most distance measures are sensitive to differences in standard deviation, etc., so the data were standardized by conversion into z-scores. The transformation eliminates this and other kinds of bias.

A combination of both a hierarchical and a non-hierarchical method was used in order to gain the benefits from each. The hierarchical approach was used by the furthest neighbor method to establish the number of clusters, since we expected the clusters to take a cylindrical shape, but to differ in variance and size (Aronsson, 1999). The stopping rule used identified the largest relative increases in the agglomeration coefficient by going from two clusters to one (Hair et al., 1998). Thus, two clusters were selected.

The non-hierarchical K means approach was used to fine-tune the two clusters. Table 1 presents the final cluster centers and the total number of cases in each cluster. When using z-scores, differences in distance become evident.

The disadvantage however, is that information about the average nominal value in each cluster for each variable is lost. This average nominal value was calculated separately and is also presented in Table 1 in order to gain a deeper understanding of the clusters. Thus, it becomes easier to compare our findings with previous research.

In accordance with the analysis model used, the variables of CI were entered into the cluster analysis. Constructs and variables are presented in detail in Appendix A. The results are given in Table 1.

3.1.3. Cross Tabulations

The cluster membership was saved for each case in order to interpret and understand the meaning of the clusters. The value of the cluster membership variable was tabulated against the following categorical variables in the data set in accordance with the analysis model used (Fig. 1): the organization of production teams, content of CI and the use of BSC. These variables are presented in Appendix A as well. The results are given in Tables 2–4.

3.2. The Case Studies

We chose to conduct a multiple case study that replicated the cases theoretically, in order to discern the different patterns stated in our hypothesis (Yin, 1994). The three Swedish engineering industry companies that we studied manufacture heat transfers, radio base stations and spherical roller bearings, respectively. In order to be able to test the hypothesis, the selection criteria for the companies were that they had: (1) different strategies for carrying out the local work on CI; (2) different features of the local work organization; (3) implemented BSC.

The main source of data was based on interviews with open-ended questions that reflected the analysis model used. The interviews took place during late fall 2000 and early spring 2001 and were recorded. Each company was visited at least twice. An average of six persons were interviewed separately for approximately 1.5 hours at every company in order to get a clear and balanced picture, as well as to allow triangulation of data. In addition to production managers, white-collar workers close to production, operators and union representatives were interviewed. In order to strengthen validity, other sources of data were used, such as documents (annual reports, information brochures, manuals and internal reports) and observations of the shop floor. Furthermore, our descriptions of the companies, which were used as basic data for abstraction, were discussed with representatives of the companies.

4. RESULTS

4.1. The Survey Study

4.1.1. Strategies for Carrying Out CI

These empirically induced clusters represent two different strategies for carrying out the local work on CI in the studied midsize and large Swedish engineering industry companies. The 30 companies that relate to Cluster 1 are character-ized by a management control approach that mostly predetermines the CI process and content by defining what, how, when and by whom the CI work should be carried out and expert task forces that carry out most of the local CI work. Cluster 2 consists of 21 companies that are characterized by a manage-ment control approach that mostly controls the local CI efforts by setting and communicating business-related goals. Both expert task forces and production teams carry out the local CI work. It is important to note that the variable measuring the management control approach (predetermined CI process and content or control by setting business-related goals) is the most significant of the two, when separating the clusters from each other ($F = 99,630$).

In the subsequent sections of the paper, Cluster 1 and Cluster 2 are named the expert task force strategy and the wide focus strategy respectively, in accordance with the typology developed by Lindberg and Berger (1997). A more thorough discussion of why the hierarchical cluster analysis suggested two clusters, as well as why these two names were taken, can be found in the analysis section.

Table 1.   Final Cluster Centres and the Total Number of Cases of the Identified Clusters.

	Cluster 1	Cluster 2	F	p
Control by predetermined CI process and content (1) or by business-related goals (5)	1.9 (−0.7)	4.0 (1.0)	100	0.000
Expert task forces (1) or production teams that carry out the CI work (5)	2.1 (−0.6)	3.1 (0.7)	49	0.000
Number of cases in each cluster	30	21		

Note: The figures represent the average nominal value. The figures in parenthesis are the Euclidean distance measures. The F-test scores are presented for descriptive purposes only.

4.1.2. Features of the local work organization related to each cluster
The next step is to further develop the strategies by characterizing the features of the work organization that are related to each strategy for carrying out the local work on CI. The result is presented in Table 2.

Table 2 shows a rather clear pattern. The companies that have chosen the wide focus CI strategy have, to a significantly higher extent, multi-skilled and enriched production teams, white-collar workers close to production integrated in the production teams, target-oriented production teams and team members who participate in formulating the targets.

4.1.3. The Content of the Local CI Work in Each Cluster
A correspondence analysis of the content of the local work on CI shows that the main pattern is the same across the two clusters. However, companies practicing the wide focus CI strategy seem, to a higher extent, to emphasize supplier relations, shop-floor working environment and customer relations. The companies that follow the expert task force strategy seem, on the other hand, to emphasize shop-floor layout, manufacturing methods and planning routines.

An additional finding concerning the variable on characteristics of implemented change indicates that companies that belong to the wide focus strategy seem to emphasize Kaizen to a greater extent than Business Process Reengineering (BPR). 91% of the wide focus companies as compared to 50% of the expert task force CI companies can be classified as Kaizen oriented (p = 0.003). These findings were in line with our expectations but serve a validating purpose.

Table 2. Features of the local work organization related to each of the identified strategies for carrying out the local work on CI in the Swedish industry.

Variable	Expert task force CI	*n*	Wide Focus CI	*n*	*p*
Multi-skilled and work-enriched production teams*	37%	30	62%	21	0.08
White-collar workers in production teams*	17%	29	40%	20	0.08
Target-oriented production teams**	62%	29	91%	21	0.02
Broad participation in formulation team targets*	25%	24	65%	20	0.06

Note: Percentages are based on the number of respondents in each cluster.
($p < 0.1 = $ *, $p < 0.05 = $ **)

Table 3.   The Five Most Important Features of the Content of the Local CI Work in Each Company.

CI field	Expert task force CI	Wide focus CI	Difference
Supplier relations	3%	19%	16%
Shop-floor working environment	66%	81%	15%
Customer relations	10%	24%	14%
Competence	41%	48%	7%
Cooperation and team spirit	41%	48%	7%
CI methods	38%	38%	0%
Relations to other teams on the shop floor	31%	29%	−2%
Planning routines	28%	14%	−14%
Manufacturing methods	93%	76%	−17%
Shop-floor layout	52%	33%	−19%
Number of valid cases	**29**	**21**	

Note: Percentages are based on the number of respondents in each cluster. There were 50 valid and 1 missing case.

4.1.4. The use of BSC in each cluster

Table 4 presents data on the implementation rate of BSC. The wide focus CI companies have implemented the concept to a slightly higher extent than the companies in the other cluster. The data on implementation level does not point

Table 4.   Number of Companies that had Implemented BSC or Similar Concept, Level of Implementation and if the Production Teams Constructed their own Scorecards.

	Expert task force CI	n	Wide Focus CI	n	p
Implemented BSC or similar concept at the company	31%	26	55%	20	0.1
Implemented BSC or similar concept at top management level	100%	7	91%	11	X
Implemented BSC or similar concept at middle mangement level	86%	7	55%	11	X
Implemented BSC or similar concept at production team level	43%	7	36%	11	X
Production teams that formulate their own scorecards	0%	7	57%	7	X

Note: Percentages are based on number of companies in each cluster (n). X = Expected count less than 5 therefore no level of significance calculated.

at any differences across the two clusters. However, on the issue of teams that formulate their own scorecards, all of the 4 cases can be related to the wide focus CI strategy. The expected count though, when cross tabulating the variable against each CI strategy, is less than 5, and thus no strong conclusions should be drawn.

As the different strategies for carrying out the local work on CI in midsize and large Swedish engineering industry companies are clarified, the issue of strategic alignment is still an open question. The case studies, however, provide for a deeper understanding of this matter and clarify the interface between each strategy for carrying out CI and how BSC is implemented and used.

4.2. The Case Studies

4.2.1. The Heat Transfer Manufacturer

The studied company (which is a part of an international industrial group) develops, produces and markets aluminum strips and sheets for radiators, air-conditioning systems and other heat exchangers for heat transfer applications. The company has 480 employees, of which 360 are blue-collar workers. The company is process organized and the manufacturing is divided into three sub-processes: manufacturing of ingots, refining heavy ingots and refining thin ingots. Both refining departments have their own slits. The unit of analysis was the thin ingot department, in which the products are refined in succeeding machine operations (mainly rolling mills). Mostly a single skilled operator mans each machine. Operators from several shifts form some kind of team, even though these teams are less developed in terms of cooperation or administrative work. However, the operators in these teams have common goals and they meet regularly. The team is controlled by the planned number of aluminum sheets per week, formulated by the logistics department.

The company implemented BSC in 1998 on three levels: the company level, the sub-process level and the workshop level (hot rolling mills, cold rolling or slits). The scorecards are based on barrier-breaking targets set up according to the annual business plan. The scorecards are revised every year. The scorecard at the company level, developed by the management team, comprises five measurements, which explicitly could be linked to four different perspectives (financial, customer, employee and process). The scorecard of the studied unit, developed by the sub-unit manager in cooperation with the line managers, comprises eight measurements. The scorecard is intimately related to the company scorecard. The measurements are almost identical, and it is explicitly formulated how much a target met on the lower level will contribute to the target set up on the company level. The scorecards on the workshop level are developed by the line managers and concern all the operations that the manager is in charge of. These scorecards are also linked to the above scorecard in the same fashion. Performance is measured once a month. The company has chosen not to implement scorecards at the team level, mainly because of their five shifts. Moreover, the operator that carries out a specific operation is not systematically involved in formulating strategies or targets for the operation. Furthermore, the targets in the scorecards do not seem to control the daily work in the production teams. The operators interviewed state they do not pay much attention to the scorecard. Their daily work is instead controlled by the planned production volume. Moreover, the wage system is not related to BSC performance.

The unit has a well-established system for working on CI that is explicitly linked to the BSC. One target in the scorecards is to increase the number of suggestions from operators. The individual suggestion system is frequently used. The elapsed time for processing employee suggestions has been reduced and a first response is usually given within less than three weeks. The character of the suggestions is both incremental and radical and operators are rewarded financially.

The systematic CI work however, is carried out in projects that are either cross-functional or functional. The cross-functional projects are explicitly linked to the company's overall scorecard and are usually quite extensive, which implies a greater impact on productivity and efficiency. The majority of the project members are white-collar workers, but operators participate too. The participating operators are appointed by the project leader. There is a project steering committee which usually consists of members of the management team; they hold the financial as well as the personnel resources. The intra-functional projects are linked to the functional scorecards and are usually less extensive and thus more Kaizen oriented. The division of white- and blue-collar workers is the same as in the large projects. In these projects the operators are appointed by the project leader as well. The process of solving problems during the projects is predetermined and specified in accordance with the company's quality system (QS-9000).

4.2.2. The Telecom Company
The telecom company, which is a production unit within a global corporation, has about 1600 employees, out of which 750 are blue-collar workers. The main products are radio base stations. The manufacturing department, employing about 1000 persons, is organized in product-oriented workshops, each one with complete resources for processing customer orders. The level of technology in

the workshops varies from automated machine assembly of components to testing and manual assembly of end products. The studied workshop consists of 175 employees organized in 14 production teams (two shifts with about ten persons in each team). The engineering, planning and quality staff is organized in functional support teams. The studied production team is responsible for manual assembly, several steps of testing and finally packaging of one kind of radio base station. Each team member is competent to handle at least two of the operations. There are four specialists in the team responsible for personnel (team leader), ordering of material, technology and quality respectively. The team is controlled according to the following three measurements: planned volume, productivity and product quality, which are reflected in the wage system.

During 1999 the company implemented BSC to control and follow up on strategic actions and performance. The main purpose was to strengthen the control along the organizational structure. Scorecards and measurements on four levels built up the BSC concept: plant level, department level, workshop level and production team level. The measurements and targets are vertically integrated, meaning that the same measurements occur on all levels and that the performance is aggregated. The scorecards on the team level are based on the three measurements mentioned above. The performance is measured every day. The employees at the shop-floor level have successively become less committed to BSC. The operators in production teams feel that they have no influence over the targets set up and that the scorecard is not a tool that facilitates their own planning and control of daily work. Furthermore, performance outcomes are not reported regularly. One supervisor said: "The BSC is purely a control tool for our plant manager." All scorecards were initially developed by a central group and the production teams were not involved in the processes of formulating strategies and measurements.

The company has implemented a specific methodology for carrying out CI, called Result Oriented Management (ROM), in which teams identify problems, change elements and formulate action plans based on the targets set up in the BSC. The ROM structure is project oriented, and ordinary teams, like management teams and production teams, as well as cross-functional improvement teams, participate. The targets set up in the BSC, which indicate strategic alignment, trigger the improvements. The teams are authorized to identify the problems, make their own improvement plans and to coordinate the improvement work with other teams and departments/workshops. The production teams are responsible for improvements in their own process. One of the production team members is also a member of a cross-functional improvement team that includes representatives from the support teams of white-collar production engineers. The improvement structure thus partly works in line with and partly across the organizational structure.

4.2.3 The Manufacturer of Spherical Roller Bearings

The company, which is part of a global corporation, manufactures standardized spherical roller bearings for the world market. The studied unit is one of five product-oriented production lines (called channels) within the company. The company has about 150 employees, of which 120 are blue-collar workers. Within the company there are also departments responsible for logistics, quality, personnel, procurement, business control and engineering. Based on stock orders, the studied production line produces up to 1600 roller bearings per week, divided into numerous variants. The manufacturing flow starts with several operations of milling and turning in automated machine systems and ends with the assembly and packaging of products ready for warehousing. Quality control is carried out after each operation. Each production line is run by a target-oriented production team (one per shift, four shifts) of about six persons, supported by one or two engineers (white-collar workers). The team is responsible for its internal work scheduling, planning and ordering of material, manufacturing and quality assurance. Most team members know all the manufacturing operations. Each team also has four appointed specialists responsible for personnel, technology, quality and logistics, respectively. The people that have these roles cooperate with staff at the corresponding department within the company. The team is controlled by targets on planned volume, machine utilization, product quality and on-time delivery.

Since 1998, the company has used BSC as a way of formulating and communicating strategic targets. BSC is implemented on three levels: the company level, the production line level and the level of improvement teams (CI team level). The scorecards are based on barrier-breaking targets set up every third year, which also reflect the annual business plan. The scorecards are revised every year. The scorecard at the company level, developed by the management team, comprises seven measurements, which implicitly could be linked to three different perspectives (financial, customer and process). The scorecard of the studied production line, developed by the production line manager, is based on the company scorecard and comprises nine measurements. The two levels are intimately related. Six of the measurements are identical, and it is explicitly formulated how much a target met on the lower level will contribute to the target set up on the company level. The scorecards on the third level concern the improvement teams, as described below. The company has chosen not to implement scorecards at the production team level, mainly because of the dependency between the four shifts. The teams are to a minor extent involved in the process of target setting. When the production line manager presents an outline of the measurements and targets for the next year, the teams are invited to discuss them. The targets in the scorecards do not control the daily work in the production teams. It is controlled by the production plans. The results of the BSC are presented once a month. A minor part of wages depends on the results of the production line scorecard. There seems to be a lack of commitment to the scorecard among production team members. One operator express this lack of influence by stating: "When the government proposes the national budget, you don't have a say!"

The improvement teams meet once every second week for two hours and consist of members from different production teams that are from the same production line. All operators participate and those operators that carry out the same kind of operations form an improvement team. A white-collar worker close to production chairs the meeting and takes the role as catalyst. He or she also forms an improvement team with other white-collar workers in order to share best practices. The explicit link of CI activities in the improvement teams to the production line scorecard is done very much in a target-oriented fashion.

The problems that the CI teams work on are identified by the operators themselves. The problems, initiatives and actions, however, have to be approved by the production line manager. As long as the team can link the activities in the CI team to the production line scorecard, the work can continue. The reason, according to the production line manager, is twofold. Firstly, when the CI teams have their meetings production is stopped, which affects productivity. Secondly, the solutions often entail investments and in order to invest financial resources, the solution must contribute to the overall strategic planning of the company. An example of one current problem that a team identified is spiral marks on bearing surfaces. It is clearly defined how the targets set up will contribute to the measurements on the production line level. The problems are handled as projects, which could last from one month up till one year. All the other departments within the company also form improvement teams that meet two hours every second week. All production lines and departments within the company are coordinated by a central improvement group, mainly consisting of company managers. The described CI work mostly concerns incremental changes and problems that could be handled by the production teams. More complex improvements or renewal of the production processes as well as investments are handled by separate projects manned by selected functions. Members of the production teams participate, too.

5. ANALYSIS

5.1. Strategies for Carrying Out Local Work on CI in Midsize and Large Companies

In order to analyze the role of BSC in strategically aligned work on CI, a first step was to identify how midsize and large Swedish engineering industry companies carry out their CI. With the multivariate technique used, our empirical finding clearly suggests two different strategies for carrying out local work on CI in midsize and large manufacturing companies. Either the companies chose a management control approach that mostly predetermines the CI process and content in detail, where expert task forces mostly carry out the CI work, or they chose an approach that mostly controls the local CI efforts by setting and communicating business-related goals. In the latter strategy, expert task forces and the production teams carry out the local CI work equally.

We have chosen to name these clusters of companies in accordance with the typology developed by Lindberg and Berger (1997), even though there is one difference between our findings and theirs. In the description of the wide focus strategy, the control emphasizes process, content and business-related goals to the same extent (ibid.). In the cluster group of companies that we call "wide focus" the emphasis is mainly on business-related goals. Thus, the findings partly verify previous research but also further contribute to our understanding of the wide focus CI strategy. We would like to suggest that among the wide focus companies, process and content are controlled but not to the same extent as business-related goals are communicated.

The 'organic' CI strategy does not appear in our data. A further analysis of the histogram (not shown here) of the variable that measured whether experts or the ordinary production teams carried out the CI work discloses that in very few companies do production teams alone carry out all CI work. There are at least two possible explanations for this. Firstly, in previous research the organic CI strategy has been found among companies with few employees and low turnover (Hart et al., 1996), which is the opposite of our target sample of midsize and large engineering industry companies with more than 200 employees. Thus, finding a pure organic CI strategy in our sample, where the production teams carry out all of the CI work and the control emphasizes goals only, would have been most unlikely. Secondly, the case studies presented in this paper, together with our previous experience, point at a need for coordination and cooperation across the entire shop floor in order to develop and share best practices, which makes it almost impossible to avoid cross-functional teams, especially in larger companies. Hence, the organic strategy may be interpreted as an extreme pole that is rare to find in reality.

5.2. CI Strategies and the Features of the Local Work Organization

Our second contribution is that we have to some extent clarified the features of the local work organization that are associated with each CI strategy. With the significant differences as a point of departure, it is fair to state that those companies that have implemented the wide focus approach seem to a greater extent to have multi-skilled and work-enriched teams, target-oriented teams, white-collar workers integrated in the teams and a broad participation among team members in formulating the targets, compared with companies that can be related to the expert task force strategy.

These significant differences not only contribute to our understanding of each of the identified CI strategies, they also strengthen the results of the performed cluster analysis by showing that the CI groups are mutually exclusive. Moreover, these findings indicate a need for change in the CI strategies towards a more decentralized, integrated and participatory approach when implementing a team-based production organization in midsize and large engineering industry companies.

The multiple-response construct on the content of the local CI work also showed interesting and interpretable differences across the two CI strategies, although the main focus in both was the same. The differences might have been greater if the respondents were asked to mark fewer alternatives than five out of ten. However, it seems like the teams that can be related to the wide focus strategy emphasize "softer" areas like supplier and customer relations as well as shop-floor working environment to a greater extent, while the other cluster group of companies emphasizes "harder" improvement areas such as shop-floor layout, manufacturing methods and planning routines. We interpret these differences as a result of the selected CI strategy, which in turn varies in correlation with the features of the work organization, which is clearly more integrated among the wide focus companies. In decentralized and integrated work organizations with multi-skilled production teams, it seems quite natural that horizontal relations towards suppliers and customers become more important for the teams. Furthermore, we interpret the focus on more engineering-based CI areas such as shop-floor layout and manufacturing methods to be a result of the greater dependence on expert-dominated task forces among the other companies.

5.3. The Role of BSC in Manufacturing for Strategically Aligned Work on CI in Production Teams

The survey shows a large diffusion of the BSC concept or similar approaches to measuring both financial and non-financial performance at the top management level. The diffusion seems to be greater among the wide focus cluster of companies. There are also a number of companies among these that have production teams that formulates their own scorecards. This result is, however, of less value, since so few of the companies have implemented the concept further out in their organizations. The qualitative case studies, though, have contributed to deepening our understanding of strategically aligned work on CI by illustrating the potential inherent in implementing BSC. We have summarized the characteristics of the case studies in Table 1.

The cases illustrate that a common role of BSC is to facilitate focus, resource allocation, prioritization and comprehensive coordination of CI activities in the studied companies. Operators either participate or initiate and carry out these

Table 5. Summary of Case Studies.

	The heat-transfer manufacturer	The base-station manufacturer	The bearing manufacturer
Continuous Improvements			
CI Strategy	Expert task force	Wide focus	Wide focus
Team-based CI work	Centrally initiated activities identified management	Both centrally and locally initiated activities	Locally initiated activities identified by the teams
Balanced Scorecard			
BSC Implementation approach	Centralized	Centralized	Centralized
BSC control emphasis	Content and process	Process and goals	Process and goals
Features of the work organization			
Multi-skilled and enriched production teams	No	Yes	Yes
White-collar workers in production teams	No	No	Yes
Target-oriented production teams	No	Yes	Yes
Participation in formulating team targets	Low	Low	Broad

CI activities and thus the local knowledge base are being exploited in order to improve company competitiveness. These finding are in line with Kaplan and Norton's later work, where they state that the role of BSC is to answer the question what should be done, whereas the role of Total Quality Management is to explain how things should be done (Kaplan & Norton, 2001). Our contribution is to deepen our understanding by illustrating and clarifying the interface between how the CI work is carried out and how the BSC is used within manufacturing.

Furthermore, it is clear that BSC is used to control different dimensions of the CI work, i.e. to control content, process and/or goals, respectively.

In the heat transfer manufacturer case; the BSC is principally a tool to control the content of as well as the process of the local CI work. This work on CI is mostly carried out by white-collar workers. The frontline operators do participate, but that is only when they are appointed to participate in a project by sharing their experience and competence. Since management formulates the actions in the scorecards (content) as well as selects participants for the BSC-linked CI projects (process), it seems reasonable to relate the company to the identified expert task force strategy. The teams at the company are furthermore less developed, not target-oriented and do not consist of white-collar worker close to production. The CI activities carried out mainly reflect areas from management's point of view.

In the telecom company case there is a clear connection between BSC and the methodology used for CI, called ROM. The production teams are very active in performing CI activities, both when it comes to the identification of the problem and in finding the way to solve it. These CI activities are not restricted to their own processes, but processes concerning the entire workshop via participation in cross-functional improvement teams. The targets in the BSCs trigger the local CI activities, thus making these strategically aligned. So BSC mainly facilitates focus. The fact that the CI methodology (ROM) predefines by whom and how the CI work should be carried out and that targets in the BSC trigger the local CI activities illustrate that there is an emphasis on controlling process and business-related goals, which relate the telecom company to the wide focus strategy. The production teams have a rather enriched work content and are target-oriented. However, there is not broad participation in formulating the targets. The CI activities in the production teams are locally initiated, whereas the activities in the cross-functional teams are both centrally and locally initiated. There are no white-collar workers integrated in the teams.

In the roller bearing manufacturer case, the BSC is mainly a tool to prioritize among, allocate resources to and coordinate the local efforts in CI. The production teams mostly carry out the CI work, though they are divided into project groups. A production team's CI initiatives and activities are developed in an organic fashion and later on matched with the targets in the production line scorecard. If it is not possible to relate the team's proposed CI initiative to these targets, the initiative is rejected by the production line manager. The latter illustrates that the CI work that is carried out by the production teams is strategically aligned, that the production teams are involved and have an important and recognized role in the execution of CI and that the control emphasizes business-related goals. The fact that the teams are divided into project-groups with a leader and also that their initiatives have to be matched to BSC targets illustrates that process and business-related goals are emphasized in the control of the CI work. The rather multi-skilled and qualified teams are responsible for the entire production flow, which makes it easier to understand and recognize problems as well as finding solutions. The integrated white-collar workers have an important role here as well. The company has taken many steps in line with process management and the channel-concept can serve as one illustration of this. The content and direction of the CI work can be characterized as "horizontal," when satisfying needs of the local and operational processes.

The three cases clearly illustrate the use of the BSC as a mechanism for policy deployment and furthermore the adaptation of these mechanisms to the expert task force and the wide focus CI strategy, respectively. The mechanisms emphasize detailed specification of *content* and *process* in the expert task force strategy and *process* and *business-related goals* in the wide focus strategy. The differences can be understood in broad terms as a product of the specific CI strategy implemented by the companies, which in turn are related to some features of the local work organization. More specifically, the mechanisms relate to how developed the teams are, whether white-collar workers are part of the production teams and whether the teams are target-oriented or not.

5.4. Additional Findings: A Note on Team Commitment to the BSC

Our main focus in this paper has been on CI. However, when analyzing the role of BSC the case studies reveal some issues that concern team commitment to the scorecards in their daily work.

To our understanding, BSC seems to have had a minor impact on the daily work in the production teams at the studied units. The teams are mainly focused on meeting the targets on planned production volume, rather than targets in the BSC, such as various quality measures. This expresses a lack of commitment to the use of scorecards as a management control system for the daily team work.

An analysis of the cases presents two tentative explanations for this: (1) The teams are involved to a limited extent in formulating strategies, measures or targets in the scorecards. (2) The BSC, as it has been implemented, is not a tool that supports the teams' planning and control of daily work. The main idea in the companies has been to support top management and their need for performance information. These explanations take into account critics of BSC, who have discussed difficulties in getting the method rooted in the employees due to its hierarchical and top-down approach. Nörreklit (2000) and Mouritsen et al. (1995/1996) state that the BSC approach as defined by Kaplan and Norton disregards any implementation problems. Furthermore, they state that winning support for the system is considered unproblematic, because local conditions are being defined by top management, local units can not act on their own and they are supposed to react rather than act. Nörreklit (2000) suggest that a method is needed that shows which actions will enable employees to attain the results envisaged. The control process should, according to her, be more interactive through a strategic dialogue in order to achieve goal congruence between different hierarchical levels at the company. These findings are in line with Nilsson and Rapp (1999) who have analyzed the role of management control systems at management as well as operational levels when implementing business unit strategies. Their concluding point is that management control systems should be highly adaptable, which is a question of using a frame of reference that is only partially common to the two organizational levels (management and operational) in order to create a meaningful dialogue between them. This finding could be regarded as a development of the work of Jönsson and Grönlund (1988) who have provided substantial evidence for a need to design control systems on different logics at management and operational levels. The reason for this is that the task, information needs and the learning processes at the two levels are all different.

This leads us to the interpretation that the scorecards for the shop floor at the three studied units could serve as common frames of references. However, the lack of strategic dialogue or "accounting talk" could serve as an explanation for the low commitment to the scorecards in the daily work. Furthermore, the "logic" of the implementation approach at the studied units clearly satisfies the needs of management. The missing part seems to be a control system at the shop-floor level, designed on the logic of learning processes among frontline operators in the production teams. If this system could support the team's planning and control of daily work and at the same time corresponded to the common frame of reference, it is likely that team commitment to the scorecards would be enhanced. We believe that this is an interesting area for further research and shall return to the issue in due time.

6. CONCLUSIONS

The purpose of this paper has been to analyze if and how the balanced scorecard (BSC) contributes to exploiting the local knowledge base in manufacturing by linking local work on continuous improvements (CI) to the strategic objectives of the company. In order to do this the analysis needed to start with an identification of strategies in midsize and large Swedish engineering industry companies for carrying out their work on CI and, furthermore, how these CI strategies relate to the work organization.

Two CI strategies in midsize and large Swedish engineering industry companies are identified with the use of cluster analysis. The expert task force strategy is characterized by a management control approach that mostly predetermines the process and the content of CI in detail. Expert task forces mostly carry out the CI work in these companies. The other strategy, namely the wide focus strategy, is characterized by a management control approach that mostly controls the local CI efforts by setting and communicating business-related goals. In the companies that have adopted this strategy, expert task forces and production teams carry out local CI work to the same extent.

With the use of cross tabulations, these strategies were found to be closely related to specific features of the local work organization. The production teams within the wide focus cluster of companies have a more enriched work content, are target-oriented, participate in formulating team targets and have integrated white-collar workers in the teams to a higher extent.

The cases illustrate that the BSC has affected local work on CI to a great extent. This applies particularly to aspects such as focus and resource allocation. The latter implies that with respect to strengthening the competitiveness of engineering industry companies, the initial stated problem of not exploiting the local and operational knowledge base may be solved.

Our main point, however, is that each strategy is accompanied by specific features of the work organization as well as a unique emphasis on the use of BSC in terms of different focus on the control of content, process and goals of CI. Thus, our quantitative as well as qualitative findings are line with our initially stated hypothesis. This implies a need for parallel changes in control methods as well as a consistent design of the overall control system in the management of local work on CI. One implication is that if companies strive for engaging all personnel in the work on CI, thus applying a wide focus CI strategy, the BSC has to be implemented to fulfil the needs of both central and local levels. A remaining challenge is to further develop mechanisms, of which strategic dialogue could be one, that balance the needs of these two levels.

REFERENCES

Aronsson, Å. (1999). *SPSS – En introduktion till basmodulen*. Lund: Studentlitteratur. (*In Swedish*).

Bengtsson, L. (1998). The Sensible Work Shop. Working paper, University of Gävle, Gävle.

Bengtsson, L., Dabhilakar, M., & Niss, C. (2000a). Production teams, control methods and performance – Results of a survey. In: T. Marek & W. Karwowski (Eds), *Proceedings of the 7th International Conference on Human Aspects of Advanced Manufacturing: Agility and Hybrid Automation – III* (pp. 354–357). Krakow: Jagiellonian University.

Bengtsson, L., Lind, J., & Samuelson, L. A. (Eds) (2000b). *Styrning av team och processer – Teoretiska perspektiv och fallstudier*. Stockholm: EFI: (*In Swedish*).

Berger, A. (1997). Continuous improvement and Kaizen: Standardization and organizational designs. *Integrated Manufacturing Systems*, *8*(2), 110–117.

Berglund, M. (1998). On White-Collar Work Close to Production. Unpublished licentiate dissertation, Linköping University, Linköping.

Bergman, B., & Klefsjö, B. (1994). Quality *From Customer Needs to Quality Satisfaction*. Lund: Studentlitteratur.

Bessant, J., & Francis, D. (1999). Developing a strategic continuous improvement capability. *International Journal of Operations and Production Management*, *19*(11), 1106–1119.

Dabhilakar, M., & Niss, C. (2000). Spridning av team och förändrade styrformer. In: L. Bengtsson, J. Lind & L. A. Samuelson (Eds), *Styrning av Team Och Processer – Teoretiska Perspektiv och Fallstudier*. Stockholm: EFI. (*In Swedish*).

Ellström, P.-E., & Kock, H. (1999). Ständiga förbättringar som lärandeprocess. In: T. Nilsson (Ed.), *Ständig Förbättring – Om Utveckling av Arbete och Kvalitet* (pp. 171–198). Solna: National Institute for Working Life. (*In Swedish*).

Ernst & Young Management Consulting. (1998). *Strategier för tillväxt*. Stockholm: Ernst & Young Management Consulting AB. (*In Swedish*).

Ewing, P., & Samuelson, L. A. (1998). *Styrning med balans och fokus*. Malmö: Liber ekonomi. (*In Swedish*).

Hair, J., Anderson, R., Tatham, R., & Black, W. (1998). *Multivariate Data Analysis*. New Jersey: Prentice-Hall.

Hart, H., Berger, A., & Lindberg, P. (1996). *Ständiga förbättringar – Ännu ett verktyg eller en del av arbetet i målstyrda grupper*. Solna: National Institute for Working Life. (*In Swedish*).

Jönsson, S., & Grönlund, A. (1988). Life with a subcontractor: New technology and management accounting. *Accounting, Organizations and Society*, *13*, 512–532.

Kald, M., & Nilsson, F. (2000). Performance measurement at Nordic companies. *European Management Journal*, *18*(1), 113–127.

Kaplan, R. S., & Norton, D. P. (1992). The Balanced Scorecard – Measures that drive performance. *Harvard Business Review, Jan–Feb.*

Kaplan, R. S., & Norton, D. P. (1996a). Using the Balanced Scorecard as strategic management system. *Harvard Business Review, Jan–Feb.*

Kaplan, R. S., & Norton, D. P. (1996b). *The balanced scorecard – Translating strategy into action.* Boston, MA: Harvard Business School Press.

Kaplan, R. S., & Norton, D. P. (2001). *The strategy focused organization – How balanced scorecard companies thrive in the new business environment.* Cambridge, MA: Harvard Business School Press.

Lindberg, A., & Berger, A. (1997). Continuous improvement: design, organization and management. *International Journal of Technology Management*, *14*(1), 86–101.

206 MANDAR DABHILAKAR AND LARS BENGTSSON

Lundahl, L., & Ewing, P. (1997). ABB's Evita puts customer-focused control center stage. *Measuring Business Excellence, 1*(3), 24–29.

Meyer, C. (1994). How the right measures help teams excel. *Harvard Business Review, May–June.*

Mouritsen, J., Hoholt, J., & Jorgensen, A. A. V. (1995/96). De nye og de gamle ikke-finansielle nogletal. *Okonomistyrning og informatik,* 387–409. (*In Danish*).

Nilsson, T. (Ed.). (1999). *Ständig förbättring – om utveckling av arbete och kvalitet.* Solna: National Institute for Working Life. (*In Swedish*).

Nilsson, F., & Rapp, B. (1999). Implementing business unit strategies: The role of management control systems. *Scandinavian Journal of Management, 15,* 65–88.

Nörreklit, H. (2000). The balance on the balanced scorecard – A critical analysis of some of its assumptions. *Management Accounting Research, 11,* 65–88.

Rentzhog, O. (1996). Core Process Management. Unpublished licentiate dissertation, University of Linköping, Linköping. (*In Swedish*).

Yin, R. K. (1994). *Case Study Research – Design and methods.* London: Sage Publications Inc.

APPENDIX A

Variables Entered into the Cluster Analysis

In accordance with the analysis model used (see Fig. 1) the following variables were entered into the cluster analysis:

- Variable 21 measured the organization of carrying out the local work on CI by pointing out whether expert task forces carried out most of the CI work, the ordinary production teams carried out most of the CI work or if there was a combination of the two strategies. A five-graded ordinal scale was used where (1) represented expert task forces, (5) ordinary production teams and (3) the combination. The construct is based on the work of Lindberg and Berger (1997).

- Variable 23 measured management control aspects of the local CI work by pointing out whether management governs the CI process and content in terms of what, how, by who and when the local CI should be carried out, if management sets business-related goals only or if there is a combination of strategies. A five-graded ordinal scale was used where (1) represented management control of process and content, (5) management setting business-related goals and (3) the combination. The construct is based on the work of Lindberg and Berger (1997).

Variables on Work Organization

- Variable 10 measured how advanced the production teams were with respect to the number of work tasks that were integrated into their daily work. The respondent could choose from 13 different administrative tasks, such as carry out internal division of labor, scheduling, coordination with other teams, CI, engineering work, formulation of strategies and targets, and so forth. The construct is based on the work of Bengtsson (1998). Teams that are responsible for 7 or more of the 13 tasks are denoted multi-skilled and enriched.
- Variable 15 measured whether white-collar workers were integrated in the production teams or not. The construct is based on the work of Berglund (1998).
- Variable 17 measured whether the production teams were target-oriented or not.
- Variable 18 measured the degree of participation among team members in formulating targets on a four-graded ordinal scale. (1) The teams do not participate at all. (2) A team representative participates. (3) Some of the members participate. (4) Almost all members participate.

The significant levels of differences among the clusters for these categorical variables were measured via a Pearson chi-square test.

Variables on the Content of the CI

The construct on the content of the local CI work was based on 10 different variables. The respondents were to indicate the five items that best described the content of the CI work carried out by the members of the production teams. A multiple-response construct was used and that is why no Pearson chi-square test was made. The variables were as follows:

- Competence
- Relations to other teams on the shop floor
- Supplier relations
- Customer relations
- Shop-floor working environment
- Cooperation and team spirit
- CI methods
- Manufacturing methods
- Planning routines
- Shop-floor layout

Variable on Kind of Change/Innovation

- Variable 29 measured if the implemented change could be mostly characterized by radical process innovations, such as 50% improvement within two
years (BPR) or incremental innovations, such as 3% per year (Kaizen). A
five-graded ordinal scale was used where (1) represented BPR, (5) represented Kaizen and (3) both approaches equally. While preparing the data set,
this variable was clustered by the k-means approach in order to obtain two
poles of companies.

The significance level of difference among the clusters for the final variable
were measured via a Pearson chi-square test.

Variables on BSC Inclination and Implementation Approach

- Variable 26 measured whether the BSC or a similar concept was implemented
or not at the company.
- Variable 27 measured on which hierarchical levels the BSC was implemented
(top management, middle management and production team).
- Variable 28 measured whether the production teams participated in formulating their own scorecards or not.

The significant level of differences among the clusters for these categorical variables was measured via a Pearson chi-square test.

THE BALANCED SCORECARD IN HOSPITALS: PERFORMANCE MEASUREMENT AS A DRIVER OF CHANGE: A CASE STUDY

Stefano Baraldi

ABSTRACT

Performance Measurement (PM) in health care is not an easy task but, at the same time, is a very topical subject. How should typical performance management problems be tackled in a hospital setting? What kind of "philosophy" and tools should lead and support an effective PM in hospitals? Could PM actually represent the missing link between the administrative and the clinical side of corporate culture? Could PM actually drive change in hospitals? Trying to shed some light on these questions, this paper analyses the experience of one of the biggest public hospitals of Milan. In this case, PM has been heavily affected by the implementation of the Balanced Scorecard.

Performance Measurement and Management Control, Volume 12, pages 209–233.
ISBN: 0-7623-0867-2

1. INTRODUCTION

For several industries, as for the Italian health-care system, the end of the millenium has been full of changes and innovations. The need to contain, or at least, to rationalize health expenditure has triggered a process to reform the structure of the Italian health-care system. A "business" logic is being introduced in health care organizations (HCOs) emphasizing the need to do *better with less*. For these reasons Italian HCOs have had to acquire rapidly (and not effortlessly) some of the most elementary measurement instruments (financial accounting, cost accounting, budgeting, responsibility accounting, etc.).

A quick glimpse into the future seems to suggest that today's efforts, aiming at measuring and making HCO performances "visible", should needs increase in the future. Various factors require health-care organizations to improve their performance in an increasingly pressing and urgent way. Think, for example, of the growth of competition, of the evolution of medical knowledge and of technologies successfully applicable to health-care, of the increasing attention to quality (AA.VV., 2000).

Indeed, thence springs the need to *measure* HCO performances (in order to *improve* radically and constantly); it is only with a most complete and exhaustive view on performances that HCOs can in fact be led to goals that are now as ambitious as necessary and really undeferrable.

The approach currently employed in measuring health-care systems' performances cannot be considered but a "first step" towards the solution of the problem; and this for many reasons.

First of all, it should be kept in mind that the introduction of "managerial" performance measurement systems (PMS) into Italian HCOs is rather recent; thus, currently employed systems are likely to lack the "maturity" needed to represent a proper point of reference for the continuous improvement of organizational performances.

Besides, it should be remembered that the logic underlying performance measurement systems (PMS) in HCOs has been very often borrowed from experiences accomplished in other organizational contexts. Thus, one should avoid the risk of employing measurement systems that are in fact "indifferent" to the many-folded peculiarities of HCOs and make it peerless (such as, just to name a few, the difficulties faced in defining the "product" of health-care services precisely and in standardizing corresponding production processes and the roles of professionals involved in service supply). PM in HCOs must therefore emphasize (rather than neglect or, even worse, flatten) such peculiarities.

Finally, one should not ignore the substantial *new deal* that many companies, beyond the health-care context, are by now foretasting while designing and implementing PMS for their own performances. For ten years now many traditional paradigms of the traditional approach to the so-called *PM* have been wholly or partially "rephrased."

2. PERFORMANCE MEASUREMENT: A "PARADIGM SHIFT"?

PMS have played an absolutely relevant role in the history of modern enterprise, proving to be essential instruments for those companies having to reach excellent performances in conditions of complexity, scarce resources, environmental dynamism. It is besides noteworthy that only the existence of reliable PMS has, in fact, enabled the de-centralization of decision making and responsibility in complex organizations.

Since the end of the 1980s, nonetheless, many scholars and businessmen have begun expressing some perplexities about the effectiveness of the "orthodox" approach to PM. Indeed, some have questioned the actual capability of PMS to promptly provide useful information for both leading managerial processes (Johnson & Kaplan, 1987) and guiding people's actions (Lynch-Cross, 1991), even to the extent of considering their employment self-defeating (Dixon, Nanni & Vollmann, 1990). As Atkinson et al. (1997) emphasize, the "moral" that has to be duly drawn from these critical remarks is that PMS, in their traditional configuration, have "measured too much and, probably, wrong things".

Within the last decade, much has been done to examine, or even to overcome, some of these limits. Many new measurement tools have been proposed, discussed and set up "in the field". Although it can sound premature to state that an evolved approach to PM has been by now fully developed (and, thus, that it is easily embraceable), one cannot avoid admitting that nowadays effective "antidotes" are available to neutralize the most evident flaws in traditional PMS, such as: modest process orientation, basic monodimensionality and a tendency to favour an economic-financial view of performance, inward orientation, difficulties in linking operational objectives and strategic goals. A sort of *new deal* of PM has begun and provides the opportunity to increase and refine the capability of *doing better with less* and, in the long run, of competing successfully. Although they are approaching the issue of PM with some delay (and, rather, exactly for this reason), Italian HCOs seem to enjoy the best conditions to seize this opportunity in full.

3. THE BALANCED SCORECARD

Among the solutions proposed in the last years, the BSC seems to fully consistent with the evolved approach to PM and it is finding increasing diffusion outside the "health-care" world. The logic behind the BSC is that managers do not run companies trusting a single or a prevailing set of indicators (Kaplan & Norton, 1992). The complexity in business organizations requires managers to "read" and interpret performances employing several perspectives of analysis *simultaneously*.

Following these premises, the BSC proposes a multidimensional intepretation of corporate performances, using indicators of different kinds in a "balanced" way. These indicators are usually "drawn to" (Kaplan & Norton, 1996):

(a) the capacity of the organization to deliver the desired long-run economic performance (*financial perspective*);
(b) the customers' perception of corporate performances (*customer perspective*);
(c) the capacity to excel in carrying out *organizational processes* (*internal business perspective*);
(d) the capacity to improve performances constantly in a *continuous learning* process (*learning and growth perspective*).

The BSC tries to overcome some of the most evident pitfalls deriving from an orthodox approach to PM, as it:

(a) is a multidimensional system that can represent organizational performance according to several different perspectives of analysis;
(b) strikes a balance between leading and lagging performance indicators;
(c) offers a "strategic" vision of performance, explaining whether, to what extent and why strategies, once formulated, may even find effective accomplishment; in this way the BSC helps overcome existing barriers between strategy formulation and implementation;
(d) extends the PM process with a relevant outward orientation;
(e) becomes the unavoidable point of reference for all management processes. Offering an organic and exhaustive vision of organizational performance, the BSC "inspires" processes of planning and programming, goal setting, communication and rewarding (Kaplan – Norton, 2001); in other words, BSC-based measurement processes do not vanish in a sterile and useless representation but, rather, they become the "driver" of a performance-oriented management.

4. PM IN ITALIAN HEALTH-CARE INDUSTRY

The recent "history" of PMS in Italian HCOs can be usefully appraised referring to two elementary variables (Fig. 1):

- the *typology* of performance under investigation (what kind of performance is to be measured?);
- the *dimensions* towards which the performance measuring process is to be oriented (where to measure?).

Before the introduction of a "business" logic in Italian health-care, PMS were essentially aimed at containing the resources spent by health care system (*focus on expenditures,* stage 1). The traditional government accounting system allowed to verify to what extent expenditure budgets had been respected (or, most of the times, exceeded). No information was, on the other hand, available to describe how efficiently resources were employed and which results had been achieved by employing such resources.

With the introduction of financial accounting (Legislative Decrees 502/92 and 517/93) PMS have shifted their focus from expenditure to costs. The implementation of cost accounting systems shows "where" resources are consumed within the organization though omitting "how" and "why" (which results?) they are used. The PM process is substantially focused on costs control (*focus on costs,* stage 2).

Other instruments, such as standard cost accounting, budgeting, reporting, capital budgeting techniques and, above all, responsibility accounting, prompt a further shift to managerial responsibilities (*focus on responsibilities,* stage 3). Such PMSs highlight the performances of units which play an essential role in attaining organizational success. The chance to break down organizational goals into responsibility centers enables to fulfill a goal-focused management process whose emphasis remains nonetheless confined, in most cases, to its mere financial dimension.

Most Italian HCOs are now engaged in the attempted implementation of these "first-generation" PMS. At this point it is fundamental to cross-question:

(a) the limits of the current approach to PMS development for HCOs and the features of a reference model towards which to tend in the near future;
(b) the potential that some evolved or "second generation" instruments (the BSC in particular) might reveal when employed in health-care.

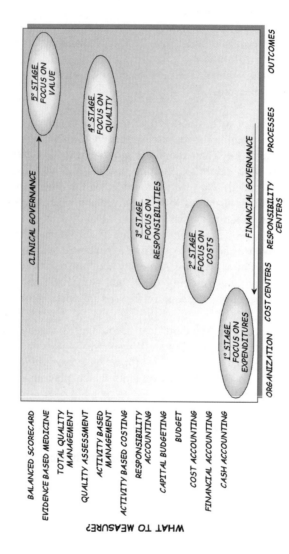

Fig. 1.

4.1. PM in Health Care: A Model-to-be ...

Many pitfalls of a traditional approach to PM may be found even in those PMS that are currently (and not effortlessly) being set up in the health-care industry. Above mentioned "first generation" systems do in fact show significant limits:

- being oriented mainly towards the financial dimension of performance, they do not highlight a series of phenomena that are absolutely relevant for HCO management (starting from health-care service "products" artfully quantified in terms of revenues); only the mere financial or "administrative" dimension of HCO performance is subject to systematic measurement. As already noted in other industries (Dixon et al., 1990), this monodimensional approach forces managers to run a "hidden HCO" in which phenomena such as clinical effectiveness and efficiency, supplied services quality, social effectiveness, acceptability of services provided and coherent use of available structures are in no way represented by "official" PMS;
- having their main focus on the vertical or hierarchical dimension of the organization, they hightlight (in full accordance with the controllability principle) the performances of operational units, directorates, etc. without emphasizing the results achieved while supplying health-care services which, in a teamwork logic, require the simultaneous engagement of different organizational units;
- they hardly succeed in giving a full image of the contribution granted by some staff areas (e.g. human resources, information systems, marketing, purchasing department, etc.) to HCO performance;
- being mainly inward oriented, they (in a "comparative" view of performance) provide little support to both competitive positioning and stakeholder relation management;
- by and large, they are employed by few actors within the organization and conceived more as a control means than as a tool for guiding and directing managerial actions. In HCOs, PMs seem to be mostly aimed at controlling achieved results and supplying corresponding rewards. In other words, measurements are intended to control and spur rather than to understand how performances can be improved and to motivate people that are in charge for achieving them.

The current approach to measurement in Italian HCOs can only be considered a "first step" towards more refined and evolved systems. There are in fact many performance dimensions that remain, so to say, "in the shade" and it is unthinkable to face the challenges impending on health-care management with such a limited vision of the phenomena that constitute some of its essential requirements.

One should tend, on the contrary, towards evolved PMS capable of *joining* the financial (inadequate on its own) and the clinical (insufficient on its own) dimensions of HCO performances. Pursuing an integrated approach to PM in HCOs means to embrace the logic underlying "second generation" systems, represented in Fig. 1, and intervene massively both on:

(a) the typology of the performances subject to measurement; it is necessary to enrich the information structure of the measurement system, accompanying traditional tools (financial accounting, management accounting, etc.) with other instruments capable of making such integrated vision of performance practicable and exploitable; and
(b) the perspectives towards which measuring processes have to be oriented, widening the investigation perspectives of PMS in order to evaluate the processes for delivering health-care services and thence generated outcome.

Extending the focus of PMS on processes means to give a decisive contribution in providing the information needed to effectively manage the quality of services (*focus on quality*, stage 4). Although in health-care this area has, until now, generally fallen under the exclusive and undisputed control of the professional autonomy of clinicians, one cannot underestimate the fact that, nowadays, instruments (e.g. *activity based costing, activity based management, total quality management*, etc.) are available that can reveal (and thus, let better manage) the process of health-care service delivery and its corresponding quality.

The perspective linked to developing PMS capable of orientating HCOs towards value (*focus on value*, stage 5) is likewise challenging. Once again, having at hand tools which are particularly fit for joining the financial to the clinical dimension of performance (*quality assessment, utilization review and management, evidence based medicine, benchmarking, BSC*, etc.) enables to evaluate the proper "product" of health-care assistance, both in terms of activity (DRGs) and of *outcome*.

4.2. A Potential Role for a "Health-Care" Balanced Scorecard

The attributes that make BSC employment in HCOs desirable are several. Its "natural" multidimensionality, its bent for joining *leading* and *lagging* indicators, its emphasis on the relations between performance and strategies, the flexibility shown in "conforming" to the peculiarities of different kinds of organizations, its attitude to become the main point of reference for managerial processes: these are the factors leading to consider the BSC one of the "evolved" measurement instruments that are most suitable to face and "metabolize" such a complex phenomenon as HCO performances.

It becomes hard, at this point, to imagine plausible motivations to deny the opportunity and the possibility of "gathering", within HCO BSCs, some definitely relevant dimensions of performance such as, among others, quality, clinical efficiency and effectiveness, social acceptability and so on.

The same logic underlying the BSC (e.g. PMS have to be developed along the perspectives and the key performance areas better reflecting the features of the organization and of the "journey" it intends to undertake) encourages its application in organizational contexts that are completely different from those it "was born" in.

On the other hand, "pioneer" health-care industry experiences do not lack, either. The BSC has been introduced as an experiment into some health-care structures (Gordon et al., 1998; Harber, 1998; Baker et al., 1999; Rimar & Garstka, 1999; Watchel et al., 1999; Curtright et al, 2000; Kaplan & Norton, 2001). The results of these experiences seem to be definitely positive. As shown in Fig. 2, both the performance areas more typically associated to health-care management (e.g. quality of services) and the indicators considered to be more apt to capture phenomena related to the former (e.g. sentinel indicators, result indicators, etc.) can be easily and adequately gathered within the BSC structure. Besides, the BSC seems to meet unexpected "approval" with professionals involved in its design and in its consequent implementation and use. In the case of the Sunnybrook Health Science Center in Toronto, in fact, interviewed people have decisively stated that the employment of the BSC has improved awareness of their own role in the organization, has contributed to make goals clearer and has provided basic feedback to evaluate achieved results; they have consequently declared (80% of the answers) their willingness to keep employing this instrument in the future (Rimar & Garstka, 1999).

The "lessons" learnt during these first experimentations have been numerous and encouraging as a whole:

- the employment of evolved measurement tools has been induced by the change of the environmental context such organizations have to live in; competition, scarce resources, evolution of demand, stakeholders' pressure, evolution of scientific knowledge and technologies, new organizational models – e.g. patient focused hospital – have caused the need for continuous improvement in organizational performances, thought to be hardly achievable by means of a traditional approach to PM;
- even in health-care (as in other contexts) the design and the implementation of the BSC takes time (2 years on average), resources and, above all, the engagement of those (the professionals) who shall then use it;

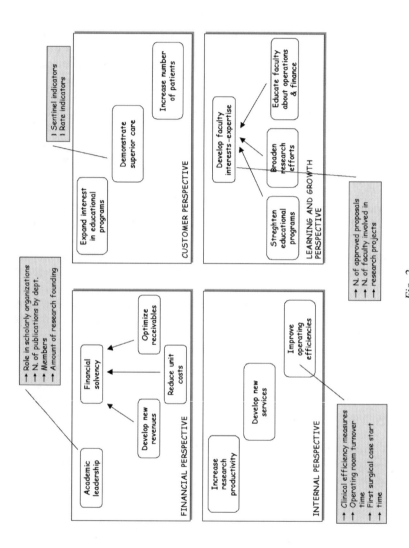

Fig. 2.

Source: Rimar & Garska, 1999.

- usually, most of the pieces of information needed to feed the BSC are already available; the role of the information system supporting the BSC remains nonetheless critical as it must integrate gathered information, keep it retrievable in time and it must be extremely pervasive, that is, capable of "showing much to many";
- once built and "running", the BSC becomes, indeed, the unavoidable point of reference for all decision-making processes (resource allocation, rewards, reengineering of processes and organizational structure, strategic planning, etc.);
- most important, the BSC can represent the ideal point of contact between the financial (or "administrative)" and the clinical dimensions in health care management, accepted as a means not to control but rather to guide medical workers' actions (Rimar & Garstka, 1999).

5. THE CASE OF THE S. CARLO BORROMEO HOSPITAL

The S. Carlo Borromeo Hospital (SCBH) lies north-west of Milan, next to one of the most crowded motorway junctions in Europe, in a 450 thousand dweller residential area. Yearly the hospital performs about 100,000 first-aid admissions, which place it among the first emergency structures in the region. Besides, it hospitalizes about 22,000 patients in 730 beds and carries out about 7,000 day-hospital admissions. The hospital also provides out-patient activities, both within its own structure and in separate clinics. SCBH employs about 2,000 people.

From an organizational point of view, SCBH is a public, multispecialized hospital consisting of medical and surgical wards (grouped according to a departmental logic), and of different specialties and services which ensure a complete diagnostic and therapeutic support.

5.1. Research Method

The use of case studies is generally recommended when researchers specifically address issues such as who made what decisions, why these decisions were made and how these decisions were implemented, evaluated and so on (Remenyi et al., 1998; Yin, 1994). Furthermore, case studies are acknowledged as a very effective method of recording innovative practice in accounting (Kaplan, 1983).

Given the issues addressed by the paper (how to face the typical problems arising in measuring performance in a hospital setting? what kind of "philosophy" and tools should lead and support an effective PM in hospitals?

could PM actually drive the implementation of hospital strategies, the evaluation of organizational units and teams, the incentive and compensation system? etc.), the experience of SCBH (actually the first reported experience of the of BSC in Italian HCOs) was very attractive.

The research evidence was collected by means of:

- the involvement of the researcher participating in the hospital's activities; the implementation of BSC in SCBH took eighteen months; the total time spent on the research site during the project was about 300 hours;
- the analysis of internal documents and archival records.

5.2. Why the Balanced Scorecard

The BSC was introduced into SCBH as management, planning and development system in 1999. The need to apply a performance-oriented and multidimensional management system was a "natural" choice for accomplishing the 1999–2001 three-year strategic plan. By mid-1998, in fact, the regional government asked public hospitals to formulate a three-year strategic plan to cut losses and break even by 2001. At the end of 1998 the financial "health" of SCBH was critical (a loss of about 25 million € compared by 105 billion of overall structure costs). Besides, the hospital's recovery plan was constrained by such regional rules as:

(a) a 4.6% year ceiling to DRG revenue increases;
(b) a 1% ceiling to personnel cost increases;
(c) some form of progressive lowering of reimbursements should outpatient treatments exceed given volume targets;
(d) the need to pursue a reduction in waiting lists;
(e) the need to reduce the reference population's hospitalization rate below 16%.

Basically, SCBH was expected to increase production (up to 4.6%) without increasing (if not reducing, actually) the number of admissions; this goal was achievable only by raising the "weight" of treated pathologies (that is, orientating the *case mix* towards pathologies characterized by a higher resource absorption) and completing a concomitant cutback in production costs (that is, intervening, above all, on personnel costs which amounted to about 70% of overall hospital costs).

Given such premises, the 1999–2001 Strategic Plan emphasized four highly-critical areas:

- re-definition of the mix of production activities, aimed at increasing DRG average weight;
- re-training of staff in order to adequately sustain the shift of production towards "heavier" pathologies;
- maintainance of the quality of services supplied to patients;
- substantial improvement in process efficiency.

The Strategic Plan formulated by the top management implied the achievement of yearly intermediate goals in all identified critical areas, tracing, in fact, a path which had to be consistent with the above mentioned principle of *doing (much) better with (much) less*. However, how was this strategic plan to be accomplished? how could "conceived" strategies be turned into practice? above all, how could people be "mobilized" towards the achievement of such ambitious goals? how could "top floor" conceived strategies become also (and at last) the main point of reference for the action of the different organizational units?

Indeed, organizational conditions showed several management flaws which prompted perplexity about the effective possibility of "translating" such pre-defined strategies "into action":

- still-in-"embryo" PMS (financial accounting still in progress, no management accounting);
- staff demotivation and disillusionment;
- executives with limited managerial expertise;
- a history of "precarious" leadership (5 different general managers from 1994 to 1997), which had caused a substantial desuetude to any medium-long term strategic planning and, above all, had prompted the emergence of "areas of interest" and of power fragmentation phenomena.

At such point, it is easy to understand how all these elements exposed SCBH to the risk of having a Strategic Plan which was perfect "on paper" but that, in practice, whose destiny was to be confined to top management archives; a plan, that is, which was completely unfit to modify behaviors and actions of people working within the organization.

The decision to provide the hospital with an "evolved" measurement system, capable of "getting" the hospital toward its own strategic goals, comes exactly from such motivations. In particular, choosing the BSC appeared to be definitely effective from different points of view.

First of all, BSC multidimensionality is fundamental to govern such an extremely complex phenomenon as HCO performance. The definition of a goal-achieving strategy is complex in a HCO context in which economic, ethical, moral and political interests interact. When, after defining the strategy, the need emerges to govern its implementation in a complex[1] production context, as the health-care industry, traditional programming and control systems reveal their whole limits. What manager would, in fact, be happy with a HCO (in particular if it were a public institution) able to reach even brilliant financial results to the detriment of supplied treatment quality or adequacy, patient satisfaction, ethics, staff motivation? On the other hand, even a public HCO cannot sustain *unlimited costs* for treatment quality and adequacy, for customer satisfaction, for employee motivation. Thence, a system is needed which can wholly and simultaneously represent, like the BSC, all the critical dimensions necessary to estimate the *value* of HCO performances.

The second reason favoring BSC adoption is connected to its capability of "hooking" strategies to individual goals pertaining to single operation units. At this point of its history, in fact, SCBH needed to emphasize the principle that hospital results were progressively built up thanks to the (at last measurable and, thus, visible) contribution of the different actors in the organization. In this sense, the BSC had all the features to highlight the efforts made by the individuals (in charge for the responsibility centers) for the "cause" (strategic goals), becoming a very effective tool to communicate strategies and to make them clear and visible by the whole organization.

Last, but likewise essential for choosing the BSC, is its success among health-care professionals workers. The possibility (better, the need) to customize and to design the BSC with professionals involved in the different processes (whether in health-care or not) has led the top management to consider this instrument potentially immune from (or less sensitive to) the numberless "rejection" crises that other more traditional PMS have undergone in health-care.

The BSC was chosen in the attempt of providing the hospital with an evolved measurement system capable of: (a) leading SBCH toward value generation; (b) qualifying as a widely-used work tool; and (c) integrate both the "administrative" and the clinical dimension of organizational performances.

5.3. The Balanced Scorecard Implementation

The BSC began to be introduced in the first half of 1999 and has been developed in two basic steps:

- a *designing phase*, intended to define its logical (which perspectives, which performance areas, etc.) and information (which tools to manage information needed to feed the system?) structure;
- an *exploitation phase*, aimed at linking all the managerial processes on BSC (resource allocation, individual goal setting, reporting, compensation, etc.).

The BSC *design* (that is, the definition of its logical and information architecture) required the following "steps":

(a) formulating the strategy (*what kind of strategy do I have?*);
(b) defining the investigation perspectives on performance (*where shall I "see" the success of my strategy?*);
(c) identifying the key performance areas (KPA) (*what cannot I absolutely miss?*);
(d) finding the key performance indicators (KPI) (*how shall I measure my performance?*).

Formulating Corporate Strategy
The process leading to hospital Strategic Plan formulation was analyzed in the previous paragraph.

Defining performance perspectives of investigation This step in BSC design turned out to be peculiarly critical as it was aimed at choosing the dimensions along which (past, present and future) hospital performance had to be "read" in order to successfully implement its strategies In defining the BSC for SCBH, the following perspectives of investigation were finally selected: (a) *clinical processes* perspective; (b) *people* perspective; (c) *customer* perspective; and (d) *financial* perspective. These seemed to be the most relevant "points of view" to represent the extent to which the entity could realistically requalify its own activities towards "heavier" pathologies, could maintain its service quality levels, could retrain its professional resources and, lastly, could improve its financial situation.

Identifying key performance areas (KPA) Performance areas considered to be absolutely necessary to accomplish chosen strategies were then identified. So, for instance, the shift in the mix of clinical activities could not take place without a massive increase in *day surgery* activity.

Finding key performance indicators (KPI) Achieved results (or goals to be achieved) in the different key performance areas (KPA) had to be formulated employing one or more indicators (KPI) selected for its/their capability to describe the analyzed phenomenon/a. According to their typology (the BSC gathers indeed different kinds of indicators), such selected indicators had to be associated to the various perspectives of investigation (*clinical, customer*, etc.). So, for instance, an adequate increase in *day surgery* activity (KPA) can be "read" in terms of revenues, of treated cases, of average revenue per case, of *day surgery* activity percentage on overall activity and so on.

5.4. The Balanced Scorecard as a Managerial Processes "Engine"

Once the designing step was completed, the BSC became the unavoidable point of reference for managerial processes at SCBH. In particular, the BSC "led" the following processes:

- strategy formulation and communication;
- budgeting and resource allocation;
- reporting;
- pay.

The Process of Strategies Formulation and Communication
As already noted, the BSC played a basic role in the corporate strategy formulation process. In fact, it turned out to be precious "litmus paper" to focus the SCBH overall strategic plan and to highlight key performance areas. Having to adapt, somehow, to the (if you want) rigorous methodology "imposed" by the BSC, top management often felt compelled to cross-question its own decisions, to figure out new alternatives, to collect further evaluation elements, etc., till the chosen strategic "route" became compatible with exogenous constraints and with stakeholder expectations. In other words, the BSC revealed to be a proper tool for supporting strategic planning, leading the hospital to formulate *better* strategies.

Equally precious was the BSC's contribution to strategy communication. For the first time in the history of the SCBH, the Strategic Plan was presented to operational units' heads and then to all hospital staff. Besides, the possibility of breaking corporate strategies down into several investigation dimensions and to carry out a detailed analysis of the effects expected from the chosen courses of action (which impact do they have on the different KPA) allowed the presentation of a Strategic Plan which was very "close" to the sensibility of medical and non-medical professionals. The BSC played a decisive role in triggering a communication and goal-sharing process no longer deferrable in such a highly demotivated and disillusioned organizational context as the SCBH.

The Budgeting and Resource Allocation Process
The BSC incisively oriented even processes for budget formulation, for the definition of single responsibility centers' goals and for the consequent resource allocation. The budgeting process developed in 10 weeks and involved about

150 people (top management, controllers, directorates and operational units' heads and their staff). The "philosophy" of the BSC diffusely permeated all steps leading to hospital budget definition:

(a) *formulating guidelines*: in this step the BSC enabled to effectively inform all actors involved in the process about: (1) the KPAs the hospital had decided to "aim at" to accomplish its strategy successfully; (2) the corresponding goals to be achieved by the whole hospital and how "far" these goals were from the current situation; and (3) organisational units' heads were furthermore asked to define their future role in contributing to the accomplishment of BSC organizational goals;

(b) *arranging proposals*: according to a bottom up approach, a budget form was distributed to all the responsibility centers, which were then prompted (given strategic goals formalized in the BSC) to specify:

- *responsibility centres' mission*: which role would each organizational unit play in the pursuit of hospital strategic goals?
- *goals to be achieved*: in which KPA would the organizational unit directly contribute to improve hospital performance? on which KPA would it be likely to share goals with other organization units involved in the same processes? which goals could be defined within the different (financial, clinical processes, customer, people) BSC perspectives?
- *actions to be carried out*: how (that is, by which plan of action and resources) could these goals be reached?
- *support required from other organization units*: what kind of coordination should be established with other corporate organizational units?

(c) *consolidating proposals*: the BSC enabled to consolidate these proposals in connection to defined perspectives of investigation and KPA; it was thus possible to:

- assess the hospital's ability to reach the results (financial and non-financial) required by the Strategical Plan (at least, in terms of "good intentions" by organizational units' heads);[2]
- highlight particularly critical performance areas (KPA);
- clearly determine the impact that the accomplishment of definite goals by operational units would generate in the units supporting their activity;[3]

(d) *approving proposals and budget*: after consolidating proposals and verifying their consistency with Strategic Plan goals, the process of proposals (first) and (then) budget approval began; even in this step, BSC contribution seemed wholly relevant:

- on the one hand, it allowed to shift proposal investigation emphasis from "political" elements (hardly quantifiable) to more objective criteria, such as the value of the results "promised" by each responsibilty center (all of them measured by BSC gathered KPI) and the resources required to reach them;
- on the other hand, the overall survey on feasible hospital performance provided the top management with tools and information needed to understand proposals' value and meaning in order to lead therewith connected decision-making processes.

Experience gained at the SCBH confirms that the use of the BSC overturns many of the paradigms of an "orthodox" budgeting process, as it would be defined, in Italian health-care at least.

Firstly, employing the *BSC* allowed to adopt a *bottom up* approach which was in many ways "revolutionary". It does not sound demagogic to state that the budget was actually defined by those in charge for working, then, in accordance to it. Organizational units' heads personally determined their own goals following their bent for contributing, more or less incisively, to corporate strategy success. On the other hand, the controller or, in some cases, the top management intervened only in case of evident incompatibility between proposed and overall hospital goals.

The process for goal definition and resource allocation was furthermore "led" by the multidimensional view of performances to be achieved. In practice, physicians and paramedical personnel were enabled to work on typologies of goals which were very "close" to their own sensibility and cultural background. Generally, the definition of goals and plans of action started with the definition of typical *clinical processes perspective* goals (DRG average weight, turnover rate, quality indicators, etc.) in order to determine their impact on other BSC dimensions. The model enabled to highlight the effects of clinical activity programming ("primum movens") onto the other KPA of the single operational unit (horizontal vision: what is the impact of a 1% average weight increase on the revenues of my unit?) and onto hospital KPA (vertical vision: what is the impact of the 1% average weight increase of my unit on hospital revenues?) *in real time*. The BSC defined budget was perceived more as a tool for rationalizing and guiding one's own job rather than as another, umpteenth (and onerous!) administrative task.

Employing the BSC positively influenced coordination among different organizational units too. Formulating goals which were "close" to operation activities and processes sensibly increased the awareness that cherishing a "monadic" vision of responsibility centers was definitely self-defeating as, especially in HCOs, "teamwork" is no doubt more precious than "running one's own race". Employing the BSC offered thus a precious contribution as:

- it made it easier to "perceive" consequences brought along by the actions proposed by single organizational units onto other units' or overall hospital performances;
- it dampened latent unrest in relations among organization units of different kind (e.g. between hospitalization directorate and diagnostic services), confirming the adequacy of (or rather, the need for) measuring achieved performance according to goals perceived in terms of shared, rather than individual, responsibility. In order to spur collaboration between clinical and service units, for instance, general medicine units' goals regarding average length of stay (notably influenced by the turnaround time performed by diagnostic services) have been shared between all the units involved in the process of delivering services; similarly, to reduce conflict caused by extreme competition among units belonging to the same directorate, individual goals (e.g. day surgery activity carried out by single operational units) were associated to other directorate-wide goals (e.g. day surgery activity carried out by all operational units belonging to the same directorate).

The emphasis granted by the BSC on hospital strategies and on the "strong" link that must bind strategies and performances also triggered a process of role differentiation among responsibility centers. The criticality shown by some KPA automatically determined, in fact, some sort of "discrimination" among organizational units that, necessarily, can affect these areas to largely different extents. This spread the awareness that organizational units do not have the same "weight" and that the reasons for such different "weights" are not political but rather stem from the different contribution offered to corporate strategy success. Such "meritocratic" awareness was the essential requirement to trigger compensation processes capable of overturning the traditional indiscriminate resources distribution.

Lastly, one should not forget how the BSC enabled to "draw" hospital strategies "closer" to goals pertaining to single organizational units (in previous experiences at the SCBH, such strategies had been completely inexistent or, at best, wholly unevident), becoming a tool which was essentially aimed at guiding managerial activity rather than controlling it.

The reporting process

As one can easily infer, the BSC became the reference tool for guiding the managerial control process, both as far as whole hospital and single operational units were concerned.

Even in this case many "rules of the game" were to be redefined. In the past, the controller used to send monthly reports to all responsibility centers displaying both synthetical activity data (number of discharges, average length of stay, case mix, number of surgical operations, DRG turnover, etc.) and special "warnings" identifying non-optimal activities (one-day hospitalizations, cases excedding DRG length-of-stay thresholds, cases with critical DRGs, etc.). Such information, nonetheless, was only marginally used to "guide" the hospital or the organizational units, both because it was considered to be completely neutral and "loose" from strategies and because rewards and pay systems made little reference to performance.

The BSC gave the chance to offer a complete and exhaustive representation of how hospital strategies were actually accomplished (and who accomplished them). Thanks to its multidimensionality, in fact, the BSC enabled to carry out an undoubtedly more refined investigation of achieved performances, highlighting reached results according to different perspectives (*financial, clinical processes, customer, people*) and to different KPA.

All actors involved in the budgeting process were given the chance to understand: (a) the extent to which their own actions were actually orienting performance towards predefined goals; (b) the extent to which predefined goals had been reached; (c) the forecast considering adopted pace; and (d) how and where should one act to improve performance. At last, thanks to the BSC, hospital performance had become an "issue" for many and not only for the few belonging to the top management.

Compensation and incentives

This was the area in which the employment of the BSC influenced managerial processes most incisively.

In the past, merit-based incentives were distributed indiscriminately, spreading great demotivation to doing more and better among the staff (in particular, among the most capable and those operating under the highest pressure). Such indiscriminate reward system (that had consolidated over the years) had turned incentives into a sort of "granted salary supplement", independent of one's commitment and hard work. In addition, this indiscriminate reward increased along the hierarchical management ladder while efforts and responsibilities did not lacking a corresponding responsible attitude. This clearly showed how the process was becoming even self-defeating: it was discouraging rather than encouraging, demotivating and responsibility-relieving rather than motivating and responsibility-spreading. Besides, resources absorbed by such reward mechanism (a fund amounting to several million €) were making it even harder to improve the hospital's financial conditions.

The BSC contributed to decisively change such state of things. At last, the chance to evaluate performances achieved by the hospital as a whole and different organizational units and, above all, the chance to assess the latter's contribution to the goals behind hospital strategy allowed to steer the rewarding process towards increased rationality and towards a "meritocratic" logic (incentives to those more actively "helping" the hospital in drawing closer to its own strategic goals).

5.5. Achieved Results

Since its introduction in 1999, the BSC has become an integral part in the management of the SCBH. Results of such experience can be read according to complementary dimensions.

On the one hand, the introduction of the BSC had a major impact on hospital performance. In programming and budgeting, for example, the BSC's strict logic, "compelling" to orientate all actions and allocated resources towards strategic goal achievement, enabled the identification of a series of costs and activities that were completely "out of control". It is besides noteworthy that, similarly to the old managerial saying, *you get what you measure*, BSC triggered measuring processes determined substantial improvement of hospital performance evaluated in terms of:

- DRG revenues net increase amounting to about 4.1 million € (from 53 to 57.1 million); out-patient activity recovery amounting to about € 9 million (from 7.2 to 16.4 million);
- concomitant achievement of predefined goals in terms of DRG average weight (from 1.04 to 1.07) and number of admissions (from 22,982 to 20,135);
- overall increase in day hospital admissions amounting to 4,933 (from 7,823 to 12,816);
- overall improvement of quality indicators;
- waiting lists cutback within regional limits (from 45 to 95% in service typologies).

On the other hand, the BSC deeply influenced organizational mechanisms, qualifying as a proper factor of change as far as managerial culture and processes were concerned. Results are hardly quantifiable but, in the author's opinion, they are undoubtedly more relevant than achieved performances in terms of revenues, DGR average weight, etc. The BSC was the trigger of a process of deep change in hospital culture as:

- it revealed to be a wholly effective communication tool; the possibility of "exhibiting" not only hospital strategies but also corresponding instrumental plans of action was exploited within the organization and to improve the fame of the SCBH in the eyes of its several stakeholders;
- among professionals, it promoted a proper change in their way of thinking influencing (for better or worse) hospital performance; responsibility centers' heads (professionals of medical and administrative sectors) involved in guided BSC measuring processes demonstrated to be willing to "take on" a managerial role (which had been, until then, rather alien to their own background) that prompted them to: (1) take on precise responsibilities in terms of achieved (in the clinical sector and not) management results and no longer in terms of carried-out activities; (2) extend their ability in long-term strategic analysis; (3) acquire a corporate vision of one's own working attitude and share the shift from an employee-focused to a customer-focused hospital; and (4) understand how, in a complex structure, performances do not depend only on excellence by single professionals or "solos" but rather (and, maybe, above all) on their bent for coordination and "teamwork";
- it increased staff motivation, providing the chance to get to know hospital strategies, to actively contribute to formulate plans of action to accomplish them, to evaluate achieved results thanks to their own initiatives; in particular, the BSC could overturn the traditional indiscriminate reward logic, prompting people to work more and better;
- it provided an "organic" view of performance, overcoming the traditional antinomy between administrative and clinical results; the possibility of evaluating performances according to several perspectives of analysis decisively contributed to "by-pass" much criticism, typically coming from medical professionals, about employing an "orthodox" measuring system (it does not account for HCO peculiarities, it only "sees" the economic side of management, it does not consider service quality, etc.) becoming, on the contrary, a particularly esteemed work-tool by medical professionals themselves.

6. CONCLUSIONS

In the author's opinion, the SCBH experience leaves two important "legacies."

Firstly, it confirms the adequacy of an evolved approach to PM in HCOs. Performance can, or rather must, be measured differently from how it was measured in the past. Improvements in such complex organizations' performances can hardly be pursued without clearly and exhaustively appraising the phenomena determining them, without "mobilizing" and properly coordinating the efforts of people that can achieve them, without overcoming the traditional borders dividing administrative and clinical visions of the same issue. Tools now exist to overcome the limits of traditional approaches and finalize PM to a value-oriented management in HCOs (and, as shown above, they seem to work effectively!).

Besides, if PM is carried out by means of evolved and integrated systems, it proves not to be sterile and pointless. On the contrary, it becomes an absolutely fundamental "lever" to trigger and sustain the process of change that HCOs are compelled to face when asked to do increasingly *better with less*. In the SCBH experience, the BSC played a basic role in formulating hospital strategies; it provided evaluation elements needed to change the organization in terms of structure, roles and responsibilities; it provided a basis for the development of managerial culture; it gave the chance to cross-question and, then, to refound consolidated operating mechanisms (e.g. incentives, resource allocation) on different bases; it changed the way decisions were made and the way the corporation was "led", introducing, indeed, a new managerial style.

NOTES

1. In hospitalization activity 492 complex production lines (DRG) are identified; each of them is determined by the interaction of several thousand other "simple" production lines that are the therapeutic and diagnostic services defined by the International Classification of Diseases (ICD IX Edition Clinical Modifications). Such data allow to evaluate the dimensions of so-called "complexity". For instance, a simple production line ranges from simple blood taking, to the accomplishment of a nuclear magnetic resonance to a surgical liver or heart transplant operation with a likewise huge variability of human, cultural, technological and financial resources absorption.

2. It is interesting to note how, in the first experience employing the *balanced scorecard* to support budgeting processes (1999), the whole value of goals proposed (and, thus, declared to be achievable) by responsibility centres' heads was higher than those expected by the hospital Strategic Plan. In this case the strategic planning process had underestimated the potentialities of the structure . . . the BSC took them "back to light".

3. The consolidation of proposals made by hospitalization directorates generated, in fact, the need for diagnostic services and, following, corresponding goal-proposals. Similarly, though with different KPI, the need for technical-administrative support was being generated.

ACKNOWLEDGMENTS

I would like to thank Dr. Carlo Montaperto, S. Carlo Hospital's controller, for his support and his comments.

REFERENCES

AA.VV. (2000). *Healthcast 2010.* PriceWaterhouseCoopers.

Atkinson, A. A., Waterhouse, J. H., & Wells, R. B. (1997). A stakeholder approach to strategic performance measurement. *Sloan Management Review, spring,* 25–37.

Baker, G. R. (1999). Hospital Report '99. A Balanced Scorecard for Ontario acute care hospitals. Ontario Hospital Association.

Castaneda-Mendez, K., Mangan, K., & Lavery, A. M. (1998). The role and the application of the Balanced Scorecard in healthcare quality management. *Journal of Healthcare Quality, 20*(1), 19–31.

Chow, C. W., Ganulin, D., Haddad, K., & Williamson, J. (1998). The Balanced Scorecard: a potent tool for energizing and focusing healthcare organization management. *Journal of Healthcare Management, 43*(3), 263–280.

Curtwright, J. W., Stolp-Smith, S. C., & Edell, E. S. (2000). Strategic performance management: development of a performance measurement system at the Mayo Clinic. *Journal of Healthcare Management, 45*(1), 58–68.

Dixon, J. R., Nanni, A. J., & Vollmann, T. E. (1990). *The new performance challenge.* Irwin.

Gordon, D., Carter, M., Kunov, H., Dolan, A., & Chapman, F. (1998). A strategic information system to facilitate the use of performance indicators in hospitals. *Health Services Management Research, II,* 80–91.

Harber, B. W. (1998). The balanced scorecard solution at Peel Memorial Hospital. *Hospital Quarterly, 1*(4), 59–63.

Johnson, H. T., & Kaplan, R. S. (1987). *Relevance lost. The rise and fall of management accounting.* Harvard Business School Press.

Kaplan, R. S., & Norton, D. P. (1992). The Balanced Scorecard: measures that drive performance. *Harvard Business Review, January–February,* 71–79.

Kaplan, R. S. (1983). Measuring manufacturing performance: a new challenge for managerial accounting, *The Accounting Review, October,* 686–705.

Kaplan, R. S., & Norton, D. P. (1996). *The Balanced Scorecard.* Harvard Business School Press.

Kaplan, R. S., & Norton D. P. (2001). *The strategy focused organization,.* Harvard Business School Press.

Lynch, R. L., & Cross, K. F. (1991). *Measure up! Yardstick for continous improvement,* Blackwell

MacDonald M. (1998). Using the Balanced Scorecard to align strategy and performance in long-term care. *Healthcare Management Forum, 3,* 33–38.

MacStravic, S. (1999). A really Balanced Scorecard. *Health Forum Journal, 42*(3), 64–67.

Pink, G. H., McKillop, I., Schraa, E. G., Preyra, C., Montgomery, C., & Baker, G. R. (2001). Creating a Balanced Scorecard for a hospital system. *Journal of Health Care Finance, 27*(3), 1–20.

Remenyi, D., & Wiliams, B., & Money, A., & Swartz, E. (1998). *Doing research in business and management. An introduction to process and method.* Sage Publications.

Rimar, S., & Garstka, S. (1999). The "balanced scorecard": development and implementation in an academic clinical department. *Academic Medicine, 74*(2), 114–122.

Sahney, V. K. (1998). Balanced Scorecard as a framework for driving performance in managed care organizations. *Managed Care Quartely, 6*(2), 1–8.

Santiago, J. M. (1999). Use of the Balanced Scorecard to improve the quality of behavioral health care, *Psychiatric Services, 50*(12), 1571–1576.

Wachtel, T. L., Hartford, C. E., & Hughes, J. A. (1999). Building a balanced scorecard for a burn center. *Burns*, *25*(5), 431–437.

Yin, R. K. (1994). *Case study research. Design and methods*. Sage Publications.

Zeltman, W., Blazer, D., Gower, M., Bumgarner, P., & Cancilla, L. (1999). Issues for academic health centers to consider before implementing a Balanced Scorecard effort. *Academic Management*, *45*(1), 1269–1277.

BALANCED SCORECARDS IN HEALTHCARE: EXPERIENCES FROM TRIALS WITH BALANCED SCORECARDS IN FIVE COUNTY COUNCILS

Lars-Göran Aidemark

ABSTRACT

This study discusses Balanced Scorecards (BSC) and the management processes in medical care organizations. The report presents and analyses the experiences of 74 county council employees in five county councils during trials of BSC over the last two years. The study shows that Balanced Scorecards are a very popular and practical measuring instrument both in healthcare and healthcare administration. However,the participants in the survey make one thing very clear. They wish to have a means for measurement, but not a measurement system for administrative regulation of activities. The study also gives the preconditions for a hypothesis about the relationship between measurement and goal congruence in the health care organization.

Performance Measurement and Management Control, Volume 12, pages 235–270.

INTRODUCTION

The medical care sector in Sweden has, during recent decades, struggled with financial problems. To keep the use of resources with budget frameworks, county councils (principal providers of health care) have introduced a whole string of financial control reforms. Budget responsibility, the internal market, purchaser-providermodel, increased competition and privatization have been tried in a number of regions. From a financial perspective, these reforms have all attempted to increase administrative influence over activities that have traditionally been dominated by medical and healthcare professionals.

Focusing on the acute financial difficulties and emphasizing budget restrictions have caused new problems for the county councils. The more long-term aspects of the healthcare organizations have been put to one side. Many are aware of this and the county councils have been searching for a new planning and follow-up system. They are looking for a control system that balances short-term financial restrictions with long-term needs such as personnel development recruitment and advancement of the organization.

Balanced Scorecards (BSC) have been introduced as a suitable management system for county councils and the medical sector. Co-workers have been inspired by seminars, conferences and courses to modernize their management system with the help of Balanced Scorecards. BSC has become the main course on the consultants menu of reform and not without the support of the academic world.

BSC is a model for strategic control of organizations. It was created to solve the problems of running large American corporations which had lost their competitiveness during the 1970s and 1980s (Kaplan & Norton, 1992). BSC was meant to be a fit inheritor of the short-term financial control systems that had lost their relevance (Johnson & Kaplan, 1987). The model is based upon the terms "balance" and "measurement." The latter point is made clear by the founders, Kaplan and Norton: *"If you can't measure it, you can't manage it"* (Kaplan & Norton, 1996b, p. 21). The term balance is exemplified by four desirable balances: (1) between sort- and long-term goals, (2) between financial and non-financial measures, (3) between indicators of activities and results as well as (4) the balance between the internal and external perspectives of the organization. Strategies of the organization are followed-up by measuring from four different perspectives: customers, processes, development and finance. The thought is that if the first three perspectives develop as desired, then long term financial success should result. The four perspectives are linked in a hierarchical cause-effect chain. Learning and development shall strengthen the competence of the employees. This is thought to support the realization and development of internal processes, which in turn leads to better customer relations. Increased loyalty from the customers shall result in financial success (Kaplan & Norton, 1992, 1993, 1996a, b). Kaplan and Norton (1996b, chap. 8) point out quite clearly that the priorities between the four perspectives must be different in a public, regulated operation than in a profit-making company. In the public sector, the essential driving force is that the citizens (voters) get a maximum return on their taxes. However, this does not affect the basic premise. When BSC is introduced, the operations will be regulated with the help of an administrative management system that is built on measurement.

Several organizational studies indicate however that it is anything other than easy to affect the activities of a medical care organization with administrative structures. The institutional perspective in organizational theory hardly gives financial management any reform potential at all. The financial management routines are ceremonies that can exist in organizations through being loosely coupled to the activities. They are based on myths and are developed in the organization for reasons of legitimacy (Meyer & Rowan, 1977). Kouzes and Mico (1979) see administration and activities as two domains with problems of integration as a result of great differences in success factors, structures and operational forms. Ouchi (1979) maintains that it is neither possible nor suitable for an administrative unit to try to regulate the work that is carried out in a hospital with the help of measuring results or behavior. The immediate risk is that management by measurement will lead to an undesirable adaptation of behavior in the organization to the closely measurable. Mintzberg (1983) suggests financial frameworks and legislation as possible management methods. Other control mechanisms can, according to Mintzberg, destroy the delicate relation between the administrator and the professional and transfer responsibility for service to the administrative structure.

There is an organizational defense mechanism that reacts to changes that break down the established organizational logic in medical care (Gustavsson, 1988). The plans to introduce new leadership structures simply do not work. Old patterns are hard to eradicate (Borum & Bentsen, 1999). Planned leadership systems are redefined by existing organizational contexts (Bentsen, 2000). The reformers hardly make an impression on those responsible for the activities. Reform remains simply talk (Rombach, 1986; Brunsson, 1990a). The possibilities to realize the ambitions of BSC against this background are limited.

Coombs (1987) however saw a tendency for the development of a mutual interest between administrators and groups of doctors in a study at a Swedish hospital. Convergence occurred mainly by doctors learning from arguments about financial rationality and attempting to mirror the connection between activities and use of resources. He realized that the heads of the clinics at the hospital showed attitudes that meant that they were willing to take part in development, even of new accounting solutions. Coombs maintains that this change will strengthen the possibilities for the heads of the clinics to act as "advocates" for the particular unit in question (cp. Wildavsky, 1975). However, the financial management reforms at the beginning of the 1990s were introduced mainly to support budget reductions and many county councils made impressive savings (Svalander & Åhgren, 1995; Aidemark, 1998). The question is; how will medical care organizations position themselves towards a new reform and a new system of management?

A preliminary interview study indicates that the introduction of BSC could very well find support among medical professionals (Aidemark, 2001). Those who took the initiative in the reform within the county council studied gave BSC a function that made it attractive for the operations and they met both support and enthusiasm from politicians, administrators and medical professionals. In connection with the reforms, there are those who act as translators. This means that the spread of ideas changes character during the process (Czarniawska & Seven, 1996). It is an open question as to what importance BSC has gained in the medical care organization. This must be studied empirically. Against this background the question is: *"What importance does BSC have in the medical care organization?"*

This study discusses BSC and the management processes in medical care organizations. The report presents and analyses the experiences in five county councils during trials of BSC over the last two years.[1] *The* aim is to understand the importance that BSC has in a medical care organization. Considering the nature of the empirical study and that the use of BSC is only just beginning, the conclusions will be of a somewhat speculative character. But with the support of a comprehensive study and the consequent questionnaire survey, certain conclusions can be drawn, even if at the moment they are somewhat hypothetical.

The study shows that Balanced Scorecards are a very popular and practical measuring instrument both in healthcare and healthcare administration. The investigation indicates that both an expressed ambition to complement traditional financial accounting and a wide-scale acceptance in personnel groups are needed if a county council shall succeed with BSC that is worthy of the name. However the participants in the questionnaire survey make one thing very clear. They want to have a means for measuring, but not a measuring system for comparing between clinics, hospitals or county councils. Comparative figures would disregard the special character of each unit and emphasize the general measurements. This means that BSC as a management system is applicable at clinic level. Inside the clinic it can be used both to measure how goals are reached and for meaningful comparisons over time. BSC can reduce the uncertainty that medical professionals are forced to work under and measure target fulfillment. Further, the respondents in the survey underlined that BSC has led to a better dialogue between the clinic leadership and hospital management.

The study also gives the preconditions for an interesting hypothesis about the relationship between measurement and goal congruence. The point of Balanced Scorecards in medical care organizations should, in that case, be something other than the traditional form. In these health care organizations measurement is not a way to supervise goal congruence. The Scorecard is a language in a dialogue that leads to co-operation and an increased agreement on the goals of the operation. Measurements are not derived from common goals, i.e. "top-down regulation", measurements contribute to common operational goals, "bottom-up."

From this point this report will be organized in the following way. Under the heading "Method", the survey is described in three parts. In the first, "Starting points", an overview of the interview survey, which is the basis for the study, is presented. In the second part, "The hypothetical pattern of explanation" the terms and contexts used in the survey are developed. Under the heading "Realization and revision of the model" I account for the practical side of the questionnaire study. Thereafter follows a presentation of "Results" and an "Analysis" of those results. The report concludes with a summary of the study.

METHOD

During the autumn of 1999, an in-depth study was carried out at Jönkping County Council, one of the first county councils that had commenced trials of Balanced Scorecards. The study gave surprising results. All the partners in the medical organization considered BSC to be an excellent and long-awaited remedy (Aidemark, 2001). An overall pattern of explanation, based on a theoretical perspective developed by Ouchi (1979, 1980) and inspired by the pilot study mentioned made this popularity more understandable. The pattern had two basic components. The study partly indicated that BSC, which was drawn-up with support from medical professionals, could lead to reduced uncertainty in reaching the goals of the medical organization. Dialogue and co-operation could replace directives and conflicts. Partly it arose that the multiple measurements created a clearer follow-up procedure for the organization and a basis for learning.

In the study presented, the abduction (overall pattern of explanation based on an empirical study and inspired by theory) was tested in a number of areas with the aid of a questionnaire to the administrators and medical professionals who actively took part in trials of BSC in five county councils.

Starting Points

Measuring performance and resource consumption is not the only possibility for the leadership of an organization to regulate the development of activities[2] *"Organizations stay tied together by means of controls in the form of incentives and measurement"* (Weick, 1995, p. 3). Ouchi (1980) states that goal congruence (mutual agreement about goals) and performance measurement are two independent mechanisms which can improve effectiveness in organizations. Each organization has to strike a balance between the two. He also underlines that certain organizations are not at all dependent on measuring to achieve goals (e.g. clan leadership – organizations dominated by professionals). In a profit-making company, operating under market conditions, conflicts of aims between the leadership and employees can lead to measurement being the only available instrument of control. On the contrary, in a professional organization a concentration around the goals of the organization can be an alternative strategy. Each administrative hierarchy can strive for the most cost-effective combination of these management forms. There is an unanswered question as to whether measurement and mutual agreement about goals are two independent or contextualised dimensions in the organization's management system. In reality, it is not illogical to think that measurement, with the aid of BSC, can contribute to dialogue and co-operation and, in the longer term, mutual agreement about the goals of the organization. If the measurement system is developed with the support of professionals, perhaps it can function as a system for following-up and learning as well as leading to increased mutual agreement about the goals of the organization.

In the earlier interview study (Aidemark, 2001), representatives of the leaderships of the county council, the hospital, clinics and development department considered that BSC was a very practical planning and follow-up system, almost as if designed for today's Swedish medical care organizations. One advantage of BSC was that it complemented the traditional one-dimensional financial follow-up system. Further, the interviewees realized that BSC had a potential to communicate the complex work that was carried out in the organization to the administrative and political leadership. Further, they contended that BSC stimulated a dialogue about visions and strategies at several levels in the organization. The four perspectives of BSC created new frameworks for discussion and co-operation in clinics, hospitals and the organization as a whole. Through dialogue and co-operation, BSC could reduce uncertainty about the goals of the organization.

It was surprising that the measurements within the four perspectives of BSC, which can be used for evaluating performance, appeared attractive in an organization traditionally characterized by professional dominance (cp. Ouchi, 1980, p. 135). The interviewees underlined that it was natural that measurement in itself is a generally accepted part of a scientifically-based activity, under the pre-condition that these measurements are experienced as meaningful (Aidemark, 2001, p. 30). Another explanation was that BSC, in this introduction phase, could not be said at all to contribute to increased administrative control of the organization. Within BSC, emphasis is placed on patients, medical processes and learning amongst the personnel. Because the medical professionals define what should be measured within the organization and the assign the targets for the measurement, they also control what is considered to be meaningful. Introduction of BSC came about from this viewpoint more as a confirmation of professional dominance rather than an increased administrative influence over activities. Perhaps it is, as Ouchi proposes, that the professionally dominated organization does not need measurement to function. But the interview investigation implied that medical care organizations can use measurement to reduce existing conflicts about goals (compare Ouchi, 1980, p. 135).

This clear-cut positive reaction to BSC is built upon two further pre-conditions. The first was formed in a realistic trial at clinic level. BSC was formed from the "bottom-up." The second is that the interviewees interpreted the term balance in a new way. In this organization, balance meant that between the four perspectives, that is to say the balance between workers, processes, patients and money. In the BSC that Kaplan and Norton created, the thought is that there should be a hierarchy of perspectives and a cause-effect relation. Nørreklit (2000) points out that this cause-effect relation is problematic. It is, for example, not so that high customer loyalty necessarily leads to financial success for the company. It is also not self-evident that growing financial resources always leads to increased patient satisfaction in medical care. Even if the latter is more likely than the former. Through giving the term balance a new meaning, the medical care organization avoided a problem. However, the eventual connection between visions and goals and measurement in the four perspectives becomes more a question about mutual agreement than the cause-effect relation.

Through reinterpreting the original model (Czarniawska & Seven, 1996; Røvik, 1998) a meaning shift occurs in the rationality, construction and function of the BSC model. Balance means balance between the four perspectives. Goals and measurements are shaped from the "bottom-up" and measurements become attractive as they can be used in a dialogue which aims at co-operation and participation.

But there is every reason to look upon this interpretation of what BSC means in the medical care organization with one reservation. This mix of control mechanisms (professional and administrative influence over activities) is by no means a stable mix (Brunsson, 1990b). There is a transitional form that contains contradictions. The professionals who were interviewed were completely aware that a developed BSC should be able to be used by an administrative hierarchy to regulate the activities from the top down. Detailed performance targets and a developed measurement system at the process level, which were formed by the professionals for leading the work of the clinic and for encouraging co-operation and dialogue in the organization, could be a system for judging future performance and for setting performance related pay. The control system in a professional organization is clearly a difficult area. The interview study concluded with the question as to how BSC will be shaped as a management and control instrument, top-down, and if so will end as a "story of failure" (Lapsley, 1993, p. 387). Or if it should be a measuring instrument for following-up and learning and which stimulates a dialogue about patients, processes, co-workers and finances. An instrument of measurement which reduces the conflicts concerning goals which have grown during the 1990s in medical care organizations.

The Hypothetical Pattern of Explanation

Alvesson and Sköldberg (1994, p. 42) write about the abductive method (my translation):

> This involves that an (often surprising) single case can be interpreted with a hypothetical overall pattern, which, if it were correct, explains the case in question The interpretation needs then to be strengthened through new observations (new cases).

Ouchi (1979, 1980) can support the shaping of such a pattern. Ouchi (1980) considers the transactional cost approach as providing a conceptual scheme that is capable of predicting suitable management forms based on effectiveness. The approach has the ability to identify those circumstances that create costs for management control: goal incongruence and ambiguous performance. He frames the transactional cost problem thus:

> in order to mediate transactions efficiently, any organizational form must reduce either the ambiguity of performance evaluation or the goal incongruence between parties (Ouchi, 1980, p. 135).

Ouchi (1979, 1980) systematized the basic conditions which different forms of management demand regarding information and rules for social contacts. Also,

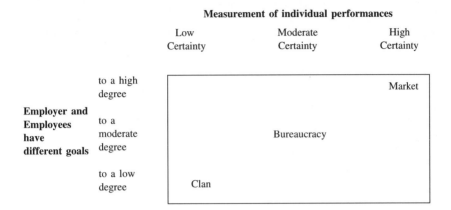

Fig. 1. Goal Conflicts and Preconditions for Various Management Forms
(a summary of Ouchi's discussion, 1980, p. 135).

he discussed the causes of- and pre-conditions for the transformation between various management forms. It is goal incongruence that creates the problem. The possibilities to bridge goal conflicts, or measure individual performances, are decisive for which management form is suitable. Three basic forms of management matched with the basic problem that the management should remove to be able to show what is needed for the management form to be suitable.

The market can tolerate a high degree of goal incongruence if it makes individual performances clear. Bureaucracy can be effective despite both goal incongruence and uncertainty of behavior being relatively high. The clan (professional dominance) is a social form that succeeds as high goal congruence can tolerate great indistinctness in individual performances.

According to the earlier interview survey, BSC was given the characteristic of being able to contribute to increased goal congruence. Several informants maintained that this was the most attractive characteristic of the new measurement system. In a summary description of what were thought to be the most praiseworthy characteristics (cp. Aidemark, 2001, p. 14) the possibility arose of BSC creating, amongst other things, a widened dialogue and more co-operation. BSC was further considered to be a good means by which behavior and results could be clarified through measurement and lead to learning and development of the activities.

With the starting point in the frame of reference presented above, the following overall pattern (hypothesis) can be suggested. *BSC gives better*

LARS-GÖRAN AIDEMARK

Table 1. Explanatory Model, Terms and Connections.

Characteristic	Dimensions	Indicators	Statements [a]
BSC provides an effective management system in medical care	BSC creates improved pre-conditions for for *measurement* of activities	BSC is a good means *following-up* performance of activities	5, 10, 20, 21, 22, 32
		BSC can be used for meaningful *comparisons* in the activities	11, 14, 17, 18, 33
(reduces goal incongruence and improves measurement)	BSC creates improved preconditions for increased *goal-congruence*	Leads to *dialogue* between parties in the organization	12, 2, 3
		Leads to *discussion* on direction	4, 9
		Is a language for *communication*	6, 8
		Promotes *co-opera*tion	1, 15
		Promotes *participation*	13, 19

[a] This column includes the statements which are left after factor analysis (see Appendix A) and statements taken out which showed themselves to be ambiguous or unclear so that they did not comprise variables in the respective dimesion (factor).

possibilities for measurement of behavior and results in medical care and stimulates increased goal congruence. Also, it is naturally interesting to test whether there is a connection between these characteristics.

The matrix below clarifies how the overall pattern has been put together in the frame of reference developed above. The indicators have been inspired by the previously collected empirical material and operationalised with the aid of the questionnaires. At this stage of the study I can only assume that the indicators are indicators of the actual dimensions.

Table 2. Statements on the Formulation and Use of BSC.

Formulation and use of BSC	Statements
Practical usability of BSC	24, 25, 26, 27, 29 (reversed scale)
BSC as a strategic management system	7, 31, 34, 37, 40, 43
BSC and detailed measures and goals	36, 39, 42, 45
BSC and the term balance	46, 47, 48, 49

The questionnaire included both closed and open questions around the design of BSC and questions to the respondents about their experiences from the trials about the practical aspects of BSC. Also there were open questions about the motives behind the trials, their form and leadership. The ambitions are to test whether these background relationships have importance for the characteristics that the respondents attribute to BSC.

Realization and Revision of the Model

The questionnaire was distributed mainly to the respondents through contacts in the respective county council. The Swedish Federation of County Councils has, during recent years, organized a network of representatives from county councils who have carried out trials of BSC. These contacts delivered the questionnaires to people within their own organizations (hospital/administration) who had actively participated in the trials. The respondents then sent the completed questionnaires directly to me. The contacts sent in a list of those personnel categories that had been asked to fill out the questionnaire.[3]

During the reading of the questionnaires, those forms, which had no clear indication of how long the respondent had worked with BSC, were omitted. For practical reasons (calculating indices) the questionnaires which did not contains responses to the first 49 responses were also omitted. Of the 196 questionnaires that were distributed to the contacts, 118 were reported as delivered to the respondents and 96 returned. Seventy-four were answered in sufficient detail to be included in the collected database. As the questionnaire promised anonymity, neither the hospital, the administration nor the county council or region will be identified this report, even if many of the respondents have volunteered this information.[4] The study is, in other words, a presentation and analysis of viewpoints from people with experience from working with BSC and who are interested enough in sharing these experiences with others that they spent time and care to answer the very comprehensive questionnaire. The questionnaire answers were recorded in Excel and statistically analyzed using SPSS.

With the aid of factor analysis (see Appendix A) I have tested whether the answers to the questionnaire form the dimensions that the model was based upon. The question is if the empirical material confirms that the indicators in the model are indicators in a common dimension. This analysis makes it clear if any of the questions lack clarity or are simply understood by the respondents in a way that the question-setter had not envisaged. With the factor analysis as the starting point certain questions have been excluded.

The investigation asked questions concerning whether BSC was a suitable instrument for measuring operational performances. In the initial investigation two characteristics had come to the fore from the interviews. BSC was seen to be an excellent instrument as it gave co-workers the possibility to follow-up changes in their own organization over time. The administrative side brought forward the possibility to compare between clinics, hospitals and different county councils. Measurements to be able to make such comparisons got no support at all from the medical professionals. They considered that there was not one single instance where it was possible to compare the same speciality at two different hospitals. Despite this, I have included, hypothetically, these two designs for measurement as indicators of the ability of BSC to function as a measurement system in medical care organizations. The indicator "BSC is a good means for operational measurements" was tested with the aid of six statements, while the indicator "BSC can be used for meaningful comparisons in the organization" was tested with the aid of five statements. Factor analysis indicated that these indicators are not seen by the respondents as a characteristic. [5] This means that those who agree with the statement that BSC can function well as an instrument of operational measurement, perhaps have a completely different view when it comes to using BSC for comparisons between different parts of the organization. The indicators can consequently not be summarized by a common index but will be treated as two separate characteristics. It will be interesting to investigate if the differences between different categories of respondents discussed above are confirmed in the investigation. It should be noted that the theoretical pattern which is used to understand what BSC means in a medical care organization, discusses the balance between the dimensions of "goal congruence" and "measurement of individual performance." In this case the measurement of performance will only in exceptional cases be able to be linked to individuals. Performances will encompass a group of workers, a department, a clinic, and so on.

The responses to the respective statements were quantified (4, 3, 2, 1) depending on if the respondent agreed to a very high degree, a high degree, a low degree or a very low degree. Two indices were calculated for each of the respondents, one a figure of the responses to the statements that belong to the dimension/indicator and the other a weighted figure. In the latter every answer is weighted with a factor which has been calculated in the factor analysis. These index variables were then used for relation analysis and analysis of eventual differences between categories of respondents. The non-weighted index variables were divided into groups. These grouped index variables give a more easily understandable picture as to what degree the questionnaire responses agreed with the statements about BSC (see Appendix B).

Factor analysis confers to a great extent that the statements that were designed to indicate various experiences, which can be connected to BSC, also statistically represented explanatory factors. With support in the frequency tables and chi-two tests, the eventual statistically significant tendencies are discussed that is to say if there is unanimity amongst the respondents above what might be expected by chance. The relations which are hypothetically discussed in the overall pattern are tested with the aid of, for example, Spearman rank correlation and the differences between categories of respondents with the aid of cross-tabulation and the Mann-Whitney test.

THE RESULTS

Introduction

Seventy-four people took part in the survey. Of these, 48 are doctors or nurses with experience of the trials in core medical activities or medical service activities. Twenty-six had experience of BSC in their roles as administrators. People with genuine experience answered the questionnaire. On average they have more than 2 years experience from the trials of BSC.

The questionnaire included open questions about how the BSC trials had been initiated, justified and organized. According to the respondents, the actual trials were *a leadership project*. Almost all the responses pointed out

Table 3. The Respondents Position and Experience of BSC, Measured in Months.

Category	Number	Average experience, months	Standard deviation
Doctors, Nurses	48	25.0	13.6
Administrators	26	23.8	10.4
Totals	74	24.2	11.5

Table 4. The Organization of and Motive for the BSC Trials.

Category	Organization		Motive	
	Run e.g. by the leadership	Widespread roots in personnel groups	Complement Financial	Introduce a control system
Doctors, Nurses	29	18	17	26
Administrators	12	12	11	14
Totals	41	30	28	40

the organization's leadership, the hospital's leadership or the hospital directors as the initiators of the trials. On the other hand, there are differences both regarding motive for and form of the trials. Forty of those who answered the questionnaire thought that the most important motive for the trials was the ambition to introduce a better management system. In 26 cases the answer was instead the need to form a more complete follow-up system as the cause behind the trials. The project was also mainly understood in two different ways, either as a project that was run by the leaders or leadership group ("top-down regulated)", or as a project with widespread roots in personnel groups ("democratic)". A number of the doctors and nurses who took part in the survey consider that "their" trials were organized "top-down regulated" and that they were designed to introduce a new control system in medical care.

Even if everyone did not answer these open questions so clearly that they could be categorized above, it is naturally interesting to study how the motive behind and the organization of the trials affected opinions about BSC in the organization.

The results from the survey are accounted for under seven headings (see factor analysis in Appendix A). The three introductory sections show how the respondents understand "their" BSC regarding "practical usability", "overall form" and "detailed goals and measures." The following two sections summarize how the participants in the survey aligned themselves with the statements about BSC as a "means for measurement" and "means for comparison." After this follows the account of how the respondents look upon the statement that BSC can lead to "increased mutual agreement on the goals of the organization" and the five indicators which according to the survey model formed this characteristic. Finally, the question of whether BSC leads to balance is taken up.

BSC is Practical

An overwhelming majority see BSC as a new and practically usable means in the organization. It is better than the old follow-up system and it is here to stay. BSC is rather not so demanding of resources that one might not use it for that reason. The index variables which have been designed to summarize the respondent's views on this question (cp. Appendix B) show that 69 of 74 agree to a high- or very degree (χ^2 (1 N = 74) = 55.35, $p. < 0.01$). There are no differences between professional categories on this point (respondent groups, see Table 3). But there are significant differences between those who see their trials as "top-down regulated" and those that experience it as having widespread roots amongst the personnel. In the latter group, the enthusiasm for BSC is even more noticeable (The Mann-Whitney test showed significant differences between the groups, $p < 0.05$). There are also strong indications that those who worked with the trials that they see as having grown out of a need for a broader follow-up are more positive to BSC as a practical means than those who saw BSC as a management form.

Even if there are differences between the questionnaire answers there is an overall tendency that the introduction of BSC is seen as a realizable project and that the project in any case should not need to be interrupted for practical reasons.

Overall Form of BSC

In the trials, BSC was formed with the aid of the four perspectives that were part of the original model and were presented by way of introduction (see p. 1). Sixty-four of seventy-four agree to a high or very high degree with the statement that their BSC was formed with overall goals and measures. There are no significant differences between different categories of respondents or between trials with different forms or trials that were started for different reasons.

The Form of BSC, Detailed Goals and Measures
Within Four Perspectives

Two-thirds of respondents state that they have worked with a BSC that included a patient perspective with detailed goals and measures. But for each and every of the other three perspectives, there are never more than 50% of respondents who declare that the respective perspective was developed so well that they agree to a high or very high degree with the statement that BSC contains detailed goals and measures.

Regarding the process perspective, it is especially heads of clinics and representatives of departments who are of the opinion that their BSC lacks detailed means that can be used to measure how the goals for the organization are reached. This is also a question of experience. The longer the experience that respondents have with BSC at clinic level, the more often they agree to a low degree or very low degree with the statement that their BSC includes a process perspective with detailed goals and measures which show how goal achievement should be measured. There are also strong indications that the motives for, and the organization of, the various BSC projects have importance for how BSC takes form. Those that believe that their trials were organized with widespread roots in personnel groups, concur to a higher degree than in the "top-down regulated" project, in that the process perspective has detailed goals and measures for measuring goal achievement. According to the respondents, the projects which were started, to complement the traditional financial follow-up procedures with measurement in several areas, the financial perspective as well as the process perspective often had more detailed contents of goals and measures. This is in relation to the trials that were considered for introduction with the aim of creating a better management control system. (The Mann-Whitney test showed significant differences between the groups in both cases, $p < 0.05$).

If the observations are correct then it means that the BSC projects which have been introduced with the aim of complementing traditional financial measurements, or with widespread roots in the personnel groups, also have been formed in a more complete way regarding goals and measurement in the process perspective. The investigation also shows strong indications of a similar relation between the learning perspective and the form of the trials.

BSC is a Good Means for Measuring in the Organization

General

A convincing majority of those who took part in the questionnaire agree to a high- or very high degree that BSC is an excellent means for measuring what occurs in the organization (χ^2 (1, N = 74) = 19.51 $p < 0.01$; Appendix B shows how the index variables have been summarized and grouped). On this point, there are no significant differences between the categories of respondents or between trials with different forms or that were started for different reasons. There is, however, a statistically significant correlation (on the 5% level) between this index variable (irrespective of how it is measured, summed up, grouped or weighted) and the form of BSC. This means that those who consider their BSC as being formed according to the original model (with detailed goals and measures in four perspectives) also agree to a higher degree than others with the statement that BSC is a good means for measuring in the organization. Perhaps it might be seen to be self-evident that a more comprehensive measuring system is also more practical. In professional organizations this appreciation of nuanced measuring possibilities is worth underlining against the background of the expectations presented in the introduction and based upon Ouchi's theoretical reasoning.

Subsidiary Questions

There are three special statements that have a decisive influence on the total picture of BSC as a means for measurement: (1) Our Balanced Scorecard is an excellent means for measuring to what degree we reach our stated goals; (2) Our Balanced Scorecard gives the possibility for meaningful comparisons over time in our own organization; and (3) Our Balanced Scorecard offers a structure for following-up on quality assurance in our organization. There is a significant majority that agree to a high- or very high degree with all these statements (for statement 20: χ^2 (1, N = 74) = 45.46 $p < 0.01$); for statement 10: χ^2 (1, N = 74) = 48.65 $p < 0.01$); for statement 5: χ^2 (1, N = 74) = 31.14 $p < 0.01$).

But there are statistically assured differences in attitude to the statement that "BSC is an excellent means for measuring to what degree we reach our stated goals." The respondents who see themselves as active in trials with widespread roots in personnel groups agree to a higher degree with this statement than those who look upon their project as "top-down regulated" (Mann-Whitney shows a significant connection, $p < 0.01$). There are also strong indications that heads of clinics and departmental representatives on one side and other respondents on the other emphasize BSC as an instrument for following-up on quality to differing degrees. The representatives of clinic leaderships underline this function of BSC more than others.

BSC can be used for Meaningful Comparisons in the Organization
A significant majority feel that BSC can not be used for meaningful comparisons between different areas of the medical care organization (Appendix B shows how the index variable has been summed and grouped). They agree to a low- or very low degree with the statement that BSC gives the possibility for comparisons between departments, clinics, hospitals or county councils (χ^2 (1, N = 74) = 4.38 $p < 0.05$).

There are no significant differences between the different categories of respondents or between trials with different forms or trials that were started for different reasons regarding opinions about BSC as a means for making comparisons. There is, however, a significant correlation between the index variable "BSC gives the possibility for meaningful comparisons" and the index variables which are thought to show how BSC is formed (as a "strategic management system" and "detailed measurement system" respectively). Those who agree with the statement that their BSC was formed as a "strategic management system" and "contains detailed goals and measures" respectively also believe, more than others that BSC gives the possibility to make comparisons. In the same way, there is a strong correlation between the index variables that test whether BSC leads to "balance" (as the concept is described by Kaplan & Norton, 1996b, p. 10) and the index variable "BSC stimulates increased mutual agreement on goals and the indicator" "BSC gives the possibility for meaningful comparisons" respectively (Spearman correlation coefficients = 0.239 respectively, 0.461 and $p < 0.05$ respectively < 0.01). But note that despite these connections, the majority of respondents think that BSC does not give the possibility for meaningful comparisons between different clinical areas in medical care. Attitudes towards the possibility to use BSC for comparisons is quite plain. A clear majority agree only to a low- or very low degree with the statements of this indicator.

BSC Leads to Increased Mutual Agreement on the Goals of the Organization (Goal Congruence)

General

A majority of respondents with experience from the trials agree to a high- or very high degree with the statement that BSC leads to increased mutual agreement on goals (χ^2 (1, N = 74) = 4,38 $p < 0.05$); how the index groups have been summarized and grouped is shown in Appendix B). Certainly, enthusiasm is greater on this point amongst administrators than amongst medical professionals and greater in projects with widespread roots than in those which are experienced as "top-down regulated." However the differences are not so great as to be statistically significant.

One factor, which may explain the differences between the different respondents is "time." There is a relation between the length of experience, measured in months, and the weighted and summed index variable "goal congruence." The longer the respondents have worked with BSC, the more they experience that BSC stimulates increased mutual agreement on goals (Spearman correlation coefficients are 0.262 and p < 0.05).

There is also a significant correlation (on the 1% level) between the view of BSC as an instrument of measurement and the experience of to what degree BSC leads to increased mutual agreement on goals (Fig. 2). The correlation is undiminished for all 9 of the comparisons which were made between the index variable "aid to measurement " (weighted, summed and grouped) and the index variable "goal congruence" (weighted, summed and grouped). In Fig. 2. boundaries have been placed between "agree to a high degree" and "agree to a low degree" for the respectively summed index variables. In the top right part of the figure are those who agree to a high- or very high degree to several of the statements which are included in the indicator/dimension (Spearman correlation coefficients are 0.398 and $p < 0.01$).

The analysis shows that in a trial where BSC was formed according to the original model, it is thought that BSC can also contribute to dialogue, co-operation, discussion, communication and participation, that is to say those indicators that are part of the "increased goal congruence" dimension. This can naturally be expressed that those who have a positive attitude to BSC as an instrument of measurement also believe that BSC can increase mutual agreement on the goals of the organization.

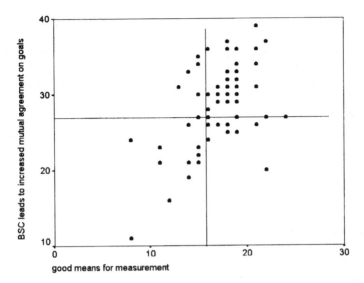

Fig. 2. A Significant Relation Between the Ability of BSC to Promote Goal Congruence and to Function as a Good Means for Measurement in the Organization.

The index variable /dimension "increased goal congruence" is the sum of the respondents agreements with 11 statements. These 11 statements are discussed below under the 5 indicators that were taken to contribute to increased mutual agreement on goals: dialogue, discussion, communication, co-operation and participation.

BSC Stimulates Dialogue
Several respondents agree to a high degree or very high degree with the statement that BSC stimulates a dialogue on the direction of the organization. This is true as much between clinic leadership and co-workers in the clinics (χ^2 (1, N = 74) = 21.63, $p < 0.01$) as between the clinic leadership and hospital leadership (χ^2 (1, N = 74) = 12.16, $p < 0.01$). On the other hand, there is divergent appreciation about whether BSC stimulates dialogue around the future direction of the organization. Half of the respondents agree to a high- or very high degree with the statement that such is the case (statement 3).

There are no significant differences between the various categories of espondents regarding these questions about whether BSC leads to better dialogue. Neither the differences in motive for, nor the form of, the trials leads to significant differences between the respondents. Perhaps because there is a positive feeling about BSC. Those that, for example, consider BSC to be an excellent tool for measuring and comparison, also mean that BSC stimulates dialogue. There is a strong indication of a relation between the attitude towards the statement "Our BSC stimulates a dialogue between the clinic leadership and the hospital's administrative leadership about the direction of the organization" and the length of experience from the trials at a clinic level, measured in months. The longer the experience of the respondents, the stronger they agreed with the statement.

BSC Stimulates Discussion
According to the questionnaire responses, BSC stimulates the clinic and hospital leaderships to discuss visions of the future direction of the organization. Fifty-two of 74 respondents agree to a high- or very high degree with statement 4 (χ^2 (1, N = 74) = 12.16, $p < 0.01$). On the other hand, there is no agreement regarding the statement that BSC stimulates strategic discussion between the medical care personnel about the future form of the organization.

BSC is a Language for Communication
Several respondents gave BSC characteristics that could facilitate communication in the organization. BSC was thought of as a new language (χ^2 (1, N = 74) = 9.14, $p < 0.01$) which is pedagogical and easy to understand (χ^2 (1, N = 74) = 15.62, $p < 0.01$).

BSC Promotes Co-operation
Several respondents agree to a high- or very high degree with the statement that BSC leads to increased co-operation between co-workers in the clinics or equivalent organizational levels in other areas than in the hospitals (χ^2 (1, N = 74) = 10.60, $p < 0.01$). Conversely, a statistically significant number state that this is not valid for co-operation between co-workers in different clinics within the hospital (χ^2 (1, N = 74) = 9.14, $p < 0.01$). The result is wholly in line with the respondents clear opinion that BSC can be used to advantage within the clinic for following-up one's own work and for learning, but not for comparisons between clinics.

There are strong tendencies for differences between, on the one side, doctors and nurses and administrators on the other, regarding the view of whether BSC leads to co-operation within the clinic. Almost all the administrators in the survey have a positive view on this question. For doctors and nurses the picture is not so clear, even if the majority agree to a high- or very high degree with the statement that BSC leads to increased co-operation within the clinic. These

Table 5. BSC Leads to Co-operation Between Co-workers Within the Clinic, by Work Category.

	Doctors, nurses	Administrators	Total
To a very low degree	3	1	4
To a low degree		3	19
To a high degree	16	19	44
To a very high degree	25	3	7
	4		
Total	48	26	74

differences, however, do not exist when it comes to the attitude as to whether BSC leads to co-operation between co-workers at different clinics.

If we compare the two groups, heads of clinics and departmental representatives with each other, these differences are even more obvious. Certainly, 56% of heads at the clinic level (heads of clinics and departmental representatives) agree to a high- or very high degree that BSC promotes co-operation within the clinic. However amongst other respondents the respective figure is 82% who agree to a high degree or very high degree. This means statistically significant differences (The Mann-Whitney test shows $p < 0.05$). The form of the trials is thought to have importance on this point (but not the reason for the trials). There is a clear tendency in the questionnaire responses which shows that wide support amongst personnel groups promotes co-operation within the clinic.

If we study only the doctors and nurses the picture is a little different in the BSC projects with widespread roots than in the "top-down regulated." In the former, 72% consider that BSC promotes co-operation in the clinic, whereas the corresponding figure in the "top-down regulated" is 52%. Even "time" has an importance. There is a significant relation between the length of experience and attitude towards "BSC promotes co-operation in the clinic." The longer the experience, the more positive the view (Spearman correlation coefficients $= 0.242$ and $p < 0.05$). Regarding consideration of the statement that BSC leads to co-operation between clinics, the negative attitude is not changed with the length of experience of BSC.

Further, there is a significant correlation (at the 5% level) between the respective co-operation variable and the index variable which indicates that BSC is a good "means for measurement", "can be used for meaningful comparisons", respectively "leads to "balance." Measurement and co-operation are not seen as contradictory phenomenon, quite the contrary in fact.

BSC promotes participation
Experience from the trials of BSC regarding the indicator "participation" also
point to BSC having its most important function within the clinic. A clear
majority 49 of 74, agree to a high- or a very high degree with the statement
that BSC leads to co-workers feeling an increased participation in the development of the clinic (χ^2 (1, N = 74) = 7.74, $p < 0.05$). An even more emphatic
majority, 53 of 74, underline that that this does not mean participation in the
organization's (the county council's) mission in general (χ^2 (1, N = 74) = 13.84,
$p < 0.01$).
    On this point, there are no significant differences between the various work
categories or positions. Conversely, there is a clear tendency that the form of
the trials has an importance. Those respondents that experience their work
as being in trials with widespread roots have a more positive view to the
statement that BSC leads to participation within the clinic than those who saw
their trials as "top-down regulated."

BSC leads to balance
Balance is an attractive state of affairs. It is a trend word that is hard to
question. The thought with BSC in its original form was to create long-term
financial success by replacing short-term financial measures with a strategic
management system that creates balance between four different perspectives.
BSC seeks balance: (1) between short- and long-term goals, (2) between
financial and non-financial measures, (3) between indicators of activities as well
as results, and (4) between an internal and an external perspective that the
organization has. These are ambitions that stand out as difficult to reach and
the participants in the studied trials thought that the goals had not yet been
reached. A majority of respondents consider that the trials have not been
successful in forming BSC so that it led to balance regarding points 1, 3 or 4
above. Conversely a significant number agree to a high- or very high degree
with the statement that BSC led to a balance between financial and non-
financial measurements (χ^2 (1, N = 74) = 4.38, $p < 0.05$).
    There are clear indications of differences between doctors and nurses on the
one side and administrators on the other. The latter consider that the trials have
achieved a balance to a greater extent than the former group. This is in regard
to considering each of the four balances. The differences between these groups
are statistically significant regarding attitude towards whether BSC has led to
balances between short and long-term goals and if BSC has led to balance
between the internal and external perspectives. We can also note certain
differences between those who have short or longer experience of BSC
respectively. The longer the experience one has at the clinic and departmental

levels, the more doubtful one becomes to BSC leading to a balance between financial and non-financial measures ($p < 0.05$).

ANALYSIS

County councils and medical care organizations need a new planning and follow-up system. In their study of the privatization of St. Görans hospital in Stockholm, Öhrming and Sverke (2001, p. 11) write (my translation):

> above the process character of the organization vague conceptions can be identified among the actors in healthcare about a common mission, unclear relations between goals and measurement and weak follow-up of results.

This is nothing new. Culyer et al. (1992) also saw a problem, as there was no method in the Swedish medical care system that was a force for higher effectiveness or generated such information that meant that it was possible to come to judgements about effectiveness and productivity.

The BSC that was formed with detailed goals and measures within four perspectives: customers, processes, development and financial, is seen in the study as a more practical planning and follow-up system than those which had been tried earlier. BSC contributes to reduced uncertainty about goals as well as performance.

The use of a number of perspectives can, to a certain degree, explain the enthusiasm that greeted BSC in county councils in general and medical care in particular. BSC is a planning and follow-up system that focuses on the problem of balancing the in- and outflow of resources within the organization and the problem of optimizing resource allocation from an internal perspective (cp. Vickers, 1965). Naturally, the medical care organization must accept the financial pre-conditions. The balancing problem concerns to bring resource consumption in line with supply of resources. This however is only a part of a complex web of problems that decision-makers need to consider. Vickers (1956, p. 224) writes:

> The cost-counting voice of budgetary judgement should never be silenced; yet it should never be mistaken for the voice of policy making, for it is concerned only with the conditions, not the criteria of success.

There remains to optimize the use of resources within the framework that the balancing decisions have set. If there are competing demands for scarce resources, this means that the optimization of resources becomes an allocation decision. Therefore, the task is to ensure that the long-term negative effects need to be minimized. In medical care, allocation decisions are even more difficult as not even short-term negative effects are acceptable.

In medical care, the politicians and administrators have focused on the balancing problem many times (Gustavsson, 1988). They are the controllers of the organization, but abdicate optimization decisions, at least in acute financial crises (Aidemark, 1998). The optimization that is needed, within the budget framework, is given to the professionals. This can, in itself, be seen as wise. The optimization decisions are delegated to co-workers who share the overall operational goals and also have the knowledge about how they can be realized. But in an ever more restrictive financial climate it may be impossible to avoid long-term negative effects. During the 1990s the mass media have, time and again, reflected upon the difficulties of getting adequate resources to solve short-term allocation problems. Acute care is one area that highlights this difficulty. A continuous discussion about priorities is needed where the politicians are given the possibility to participate.

BSC gives new possibilities for discussions about the use of resources from an optimization perspective, i.e. in relation to priorities that are medically-motivated or decided by politicians. This gives the organization the possibility to promote the complex work that is carried out in medical care and can be a basis for dialogue and co-operation. BSC can also be seen as an alternative to the logic of the market, e.g. the internal market system, regarding solving optimization problems in medical care. BSC can be an alternative to deciding resource allocation with the aid of supply and demand.

The participants in the questionnaire, however, make one thing clear. They want a means for measuring, but not a measuring system for control. An overwhelming majority see BSC as a possibility to follow-up work within a clinic (or equivalent). This means that they want to be able to measure how far they have achieved the goals that have been set and compare performance with previous measurements. Heads of clinics and departmental representatives emphasize, however, the roll that BSC can play in the continuous quality work that is carried out in medical care. Conversely, enthusiasm for measurement is completely flattened when measurements should be used for comparisons at different levels in the organization. Comparisons are otherwise a very practical method for setting out role models and formulating criteria for behavior and results. The research results from an experimental trial (Lipe et al., 2000) show that there is an obvious risk that when evaluating. The leadership of the organization will only use those measurements that are common for many units within the organization. This evaluation means that the special characteristics of different areas of the organization will be toned down and the measurements that make different units comparable brought to the fore (Lipe et al., 2000). At the same time, this will lead to a situation where the judgement criteria are placed outside the control of the clinic. Comparisons become a way to regulate through measurement. This investigation indicates that BSC, as implemented in these medical care organizations, has a new meaning. It is no longer a strategic management system built upon measurements which are derived from overall visions and strategies (cp. Czarniawka & Sevon, 1996).

The introduction of BSC has not meant that the traditional organizational logic of the medical care sector has been replaced by an administrative management system. But the survey underlines that BSC has an importance for regulating activities. Evaluation through measurement is not the only way to regulate development of an organization. In each organization there are different management forms. Ouchi (1979) describes three different ways for the organization to handle the problem of evaluation and regulation: market, bureaucracy and professional dominance. The market measures and rewards individual contributions. Bureaucracy relies upon a combination of close evaluation and social acceptance of common goals. The professionally dominated organization relies upon a relatively comprehensive socialization process (*ibid.*, p. 833). Ouchi arranges the management forms in further dimensions: social preconditions for co-operation and need for information.

These dimensions describe the preconditions for each respective management form. Each management form implies that the members respect the basic norms for mutual co-operation (Gouldner, 1960). The professionally dominated organization also accepts the legitimacy of professional authority and long-standing social agreements as to what is suitable behavior. The professionals socialize over long periods of education and in medical care organizations. Professional dominance is not a "deficient" management form in relation to the market or bureaucracy.

> Now, it is commonly supposed that such rituals which characterize not only research laboratories but also hospitals, schools, government agencies and investment banks, constitute quaint but essentially useless and perhaps even harmful practice. But if it is not possible to measure either behavior or output and it is therefore not possible to "rationally" evaluate the work of the organization, what alternative is there but to carefully select workers so that you can be assured of having an able and committed set of people, and then engaging in rituals and ceremonies which serve the purpose of rewarding those who display the underlying attitudes and values which are likely to lead to organizational success (Ouchi, 1979, p. 844).

According to Ouchi (1979, 1980) it is goal incongruence that creates management problems. The possibilities to bridge goal conflicts, or measure individual performances is decisive for which management form is suitable. The professionally dominated organization is really the organizational form that requires least surveillance by measurement. There will be a high degree of

mutual agreement about goals and shared values and co-workers striving to
fulfil the goals of the organization.

But in Swedish medical care conflicts over goals have grown during the
1990s in the shadow of increasing financial difficulties. This has, in line
the reasoning above, led to a management problem for the political and
administrative domain of the medical care organizations. This management
problem has found a solution in more bureaucratic (regular financial
follow-up) or more market-oriented (responsibility for results, market
conditions, competition, privatization) principles. The rational application of
bureaucracy or the market presupposes measurement. In the survey that preceded
this questionnaire, a number of the interviewees explained that the attraction of
BSC was that it gave possibilities for dialogue and discussion that led to
co-operation and participation. In Ouchi's terms BSC creates a platform for
increased goal congruence and more possibilities for mutual agreement on the
goals of the organization.

The respondents in the study confirmed that BSC has led to a wider dialogue
and discussion on the activities within the clinic. Therefore BSC is seen as a
language which is easy to understand and can be used for communication within
the organization. Further, BSC has led to a more intensive dialogue between
the clinic and the hospital leadership. In the latter case this characteristic is
emphasized more by those who have a longer experience of BSC at clinic level
than those with shorter experience. The study also shows that BSC promotes
co-operation between co-workers in the clinic and participation in the
development work of the clinic. But this co-operation and participation stops
at the clinic doors. It is valid neither for co-operation with others outside the
clinic nor participation in the general mission of the county council.

The conclusion is that BSC can function as a management system above all
at clinic level. Here it consists of both an attractive instrument of measurement
and a way for the clinic leadership to increase mutual agreement around the
goals of the clinic. Through dialogue and discussion BSC leads, according to
the study, to better co-operation and increased participation at the clinic. BSC
stand out in this way as a means for co-workers. It can reduce the uncertainty
which the medical professionals are forced to work under. Through dialogue
and co-operation, BSC reduces the problems that depend upon an ambiguous
and difficult working situation. Through measurement BSC reduces the uncertainty which comes from insufficient information (cp. Öhrming & Sverke, 2001,
chap. 2). BSC can also be the clinic leadership's tool to handle its double role.
This role being, partly to fight for sufficient resources for their organization,
partly as a guardian of resources so that the budget frameworks at the clinic
or department are complied with (cp. Wildavsky, 1975).

In summary, this means that the introduction of BSC in county councils and medical care organizations is a practically achievable project. This change of meaning, which we could detect, means at the same time that the reformers are avoiding two difficult problems. First, they are avoiding the problem to break down the overarching vision of health care (good health care on equal terms for every citizen) into goals on the four perspectives. Second, the definition of balance leads to them avoiding another difficult problem. When balance means that between the four perspectives, they do not need to try to construct a logical cause-effect relation between the perspectives.

According to the survey, the trials of Balanced Scorecard have been started at the initiative of the respective organization's leadership. But the project has been justified and organized in various ways. The respondents have either characterized "their" trial as controlled by the leadership group ("top-down regulated") or described it as having a widespread roots in the personnel groups ("democratic"). The participants in the survey have further been able to be categorized according to how they reported that the trials were justified. These groupings have helped to show some effects, which depend upon the motive and organizing of the projects.

The motive for the BSC trials has an importance. The respondents experience in every case differences depending on if they consider themselves taking part in a project that aims at complementing the existing financial measurements or if they see the trials as a control project.

The survey points towards widespread roots in the personnel groups contributing to trials where a number of characteristics of BSC are developed and/or valued to a greater extent than in the projects that lack these roots.

On several points, we have underlined differences between the trials which, according to the respondents, aimed at complementing financial accounting and those that were introduced to be a new control system for the activities. The

Table 6. Experiences from the Trials with the Aim of Complementing Financial Follow-up Procedures.

Characteristic	Experienced in "complementary project" in relation to "control project"	P <
Significant Relations		
Form of process perspective	More complete	0.01
Form of financial perspective	More complete	0.04
Strong indications of relations		
Practical usability	More positive attitude	0.08

Table 7. The Effect of Trials with a Widespread Roots
in Personnel Groups.

Characteristic	Experienced in project with widespread roots in personnel groups in relation to the project run by the leadership	$P <$
Significant Relations		
BSC as a measurement instrument	More positive attitude to BSC as a instrument to measure target fulfillment	0.01
Practical Usability	More positive attitude	0.05
Strong Indications of Relations		
BSC and co-operation within the clinic	More positive attitude to the statement that BSC lead to more co-operation within the clinic	0.06
Form of process perspective	More complete	0.06
Form of learning and development perspective	More complete	0.08
BSC and participation in the development of the clinic	More positive attitude to the statement that BSC leads to increased participation in the development of the clinic	0.09
BSC and balance	More positive attitude to the statement that BSC leads to balance	
	• between long- and short-term objectives	0.08
	• between indicators of action and outcome	0.07
	• between an internal and a external perspective of organizational performance	0.08

ambition to complement the traditional financial measurements with the aid of BSC has shaped a planning and follow-up system that is more complete and more widely appreciated as a functional aid.

Finally, we can draw the conclusion that the study provides a base for a hypothesis that gives an interesting starting point for continued research. Analysis shows a significant relation between measurement and goal congruence ($p < 0.01$). This means that those respondents who regard BSC to be an attractive measurement instrument also consider that BSC leads to increased mutual agreement on the goals of the organization. There is, however, an unanswered question as to whether measurement leads to goal congruence.

It may be so that a high level of mutual agreement on goals also leads to a positive attitude to measurement or that other common forces form both these characteristics.

CONCLUSIONS

Balanced Scorecards stand out in the study as a very popular and practical instrument of measurement for medical care organizations. After the revisions of the model which took place during the trials. Measurement is seen as an attractive means both for hospitals and for their administration.

The survey points towards the need both for an expressed ambition to complement the traditional financial accounting and a wide rooting in personnel groups for a county council to succeed in forming a BSC that lives up to the name.

Enthusiasm for BSC as a planning and follow-up system has partly been explained by BSC giving new possibilities to focus both on the problems of balance and optimization in medical care. BSC draws attention to both the problem of keeping within the budgetary framework and the question as to how resources are used. However the participants in the survey make one thing very clear. They wish to have a means for measurement, but not a measurement system for administrative regulation of activities.

The study points towards BSC as a management system useful above all at clinic level. Within the clinic it may be used both for measuring how goals are achieved and for meaningful comparisons. Follow-ups with the aid of BSC can reduce the uncertainty which medical professionals are forced to work under. BSC can even function as a leadership system for the heads of clinics. Through dialogue and discussion BSC leads to better co-operation and increased participation and thereby greater mutual agreement around the goals of the clinic. Further, the respondents in the survey underline that BSC has led to an altogether better dialogue between the clinic leadership and hospital leadership.

The study also gives a basis for a hypothesis on the relationship between measurement and goal congruence. The point of Balanced Scorecard in medical care organizations is that it should avoid traditional forms and stand on its own as an innovation. It is not so that the measurement should lead to common goals, i.e. "top-down", but measurement contributes to common operational goals, i.e. "bottom-up." Measurement does not become a way to supervise goal congruence. BSC is a language in a dialogue that leads to co-operation and increased mutual agreement on the goals of the organization.

NOTES

1. The respondents have on average 24 months experience from work with Balanced Scorecards, 25% have more than 3 years experience.

2. In research about accounting and information systems from a leadership perspective, the agent theory can also be used to identify the combination of contract and information systems which maximize the principal's benefit function. This considers that the agent has a self-interest. The agent can, for example, be offered part of the result that his/her efforts lead to (the sharing rule).

3. A further 42 questionnaires were sent to respondents in one county council according to a given list of names. The answers to these questionnaires were not included when it was shown that the development work had not yet resulted in BSC being used in operation. Some respondents (10) returned unanswered questionnaires and gave lack of time as the reason for not filling them out.

4. Questionnaires have come in from 9 hospitals and 5 administrations in 5 county councils/regions.

5. Statement 10 was moved with the support of factor analysis from "meaningful comparisons" to "operational measurements."

REFERENCES

Aidemark, L.-G. (2001). The meaning of Balanced Scorecards in the Health Care Organization. *Financial Accountability and Management, 17*(1), 23–40.

Aidemark, L-G. (1998). *Vårdens ekonomi i förändring. En studie av ekonomistyrning i Landstinget Kronoberg* (Health care economy in transition. A study of responsibility accounting in the Kronoberg county council). (Swedish). Göteborg: BAS.

Alvesson, M., & Sköldberg, K. (1994). *Tolkning och Reflektion* (Interpretation and reflection). (Swedish). Lund: Studentlitteratur.

Bentsen, E. Z. (2000). *Sygehusledelse i Danmark – Trojkamodellens opståen, spredning og funktion* (Hospital management in Denmark – The rise, popularity and function of the Troika model). (Danish). Copenhagen: Institut for Organisation og Arbejdssociologi.

Borum, F., & Bentsen E. Z. (1999). At skabe ledelse – Rikshospitalets import af centerstrukturen (To create management – The National Hospital importing the center structure). (Danish). In: E. Z. Bentsen, F. Borum, G. Erlingsdóttir & K. Sahlin-Andersson (Eds), *Når styrningsambitioner møder praksis – den svære omstilling af sygehus- og sundhedsvæsenet i Danmark og Sverige* (pp. 243–264). Copenhagen: Munksgaard.

Brunsson, N. (1990a). Individualitet och rationalitet som reforminnehåll (Individuality and rationality in reforms). (Swedish). In: N. Brunsson & J. P. Olsen (Eds), *Makten att reformera* (pp. 86–117). Stockholm: Carlssons.

Brunsson, N. (1990b). Reformer som rutin (Reforms as routine). (Swedish). In: N. Brunsson & J. P. Olsen (Eds), *Makten att reformera* (pp. 27–43). Stockholm: Carlssons.

Coombs, R. W. (1987). Accounting for control of doctors: Management information systems in Hospitals. *Accounting, Organizations and Society, 12*(4), 389–404.

Culyer, A. J., Evans, R. G., Schulenburg, J-M., Graf, V. D., van de Ven, W. P. M. M., & Weisbrod, B. A. (1992). *Svensk Sjukvård – bäst i världen?* (Swedish health care – best in the world?). (Swedish). Stockholm: SNS.

Czarniawska, B., & Sevon, G. (1996). *Translating Organizational Change.* Berlin: de Gruyter.

Gouldner, A. W. (1960). The Norm of Reciprocity: A Preliminary Statement. *American Sociological Review, 25*(2), 161–178.

Gustavsson, R. (1988). *Traditionernas ok* (The yoke of tradition). (Swedish). Solna: Esselte Studium.

Johnson, H. T., & Kaplan, R. (1987). *Relevance Lost – On the Rise and Fall of Management Accounting.* Boston, MA: Harvard Business School Press.

Kaplan, R., & Norton, D. (1992). The Balanced Scorecard – Measures That Drive Performance. *Harvard Business Review*, (January–February), 71–79.

Kaplan, R., & Norton, D. (1993). Putting the Balanced Scorecard to work. *Harvard Business Review*, (September–October), 134–142.

Kaplan, R., & Norton, D. (1996a). Using the balanced scorecard as a strategic management System. *Harvard, Business Review, 74*(1), 75–84.

Kaplan, R., & Norton, D. (1996b). *The Balanced Scorecard – Translating strategy into action.* Boston, MA: Harvard Business School Press.

Kouzes, J., & Mico, P. (1979). Domain Theory: An Introduction to Organizational Behavior in Human Service Organizations. *Applied Behavioral Science, 15*(4), 449–469.

Lapsley, I. (1993). Markets, Hierarchies and the Regulation of the National Health Service. *Accounting and Business Research, 23*(91A), 384–394.

Lipe, M. G., & Salterio, S. E. (2000). The Balanced Scorecard: Judgmental Effects of Common and Unique Performance Measures. *The Accounting Review, 75*(3), 283–298.

Meyer, J. W., & Rowan, B. (1977). Institutionalized Organizations: Formal Structure as Myth and Cermony. *American Journal of Sociology, 83*(2), 340–363.

Mintzberg, H. (1983). *Structure in Fives: Designing Effective Organizations.* New Jersey: Prentice-Hall.

Nørreklit, H. (2000). The balance on the balanced scorecard – a critical analysis of some of its assumptions. *Management Accounting Research, 11*, 65–88.

Ouchi, W. (1979). A Conceptual Framwork for Design of Organizational Control Mechanisms. *Management Science, 25*(9), 833–848.

Ouchi, W. (1980). Markets, Bureaucracies and Clans. *Administrative Science Quarterly, 25*(March), 129–141.

Rombach, B. (1986). *Rationalisering eller Prat* (Rationalization or talk). (Swedish). Lund: Doxa.

Røvik, K. A. (1998). *Moderne Organisasjoner. Trender i organisasjonstenkningen vedtusenårsskiftet* (Modern organizations. Trends in organization thinking at the millennial change). (Norwegian). Bergen-Sandvika: Fagbokforlaget.

Svalander, P-A., & Åhgren, B. (1995). *Vad skall man kalla det som händer i Mora? – och andra frågor om styrmodeller.* (What do you call things happening at Mora? – and other questions about models of control). (Swedish). Stockholm: Landstingsförbundet.

Weick, K. (1995). *Sensemaking in Organizations.* London: Sage.

Vickers, G. (1965). *The Art of Judgement A Study of Policy Making.* London: Sage, 1995.

Wildavsky, A. (1975). *Budgeting: a comparative theory of budgetary processes.* Boston: Little, Brown & Co.

Öhrming, J., & Sverke, M. (2001). *Bolagiseringen av S:t Görans Sjukhus – en proaktiv organisering* (St Göran Hospital going private – a proactive organizing). (Swedish). Lund: Studentlitteratur.

APPENDIX A

Of the 12 statements that were formulated to test if BSC leads to increased goal congruence, 11 formed a factor (Factor loading greater than 0.3). Question 16 was, according to the analysis, multidimensional and was omitted from further treatment. Statements 4 and 15 had factor loading over 3 in the "hypothesized" factor. They were loaded somewhat higher in other factors. They were allowed to remain as indicators of the intended characteristic. I regard the questions as interesting and important for the respective indicators as they indicate references to the terms "co-operation" and "discussion." These indicators would otherwise only have been estimated with the help of one question each (factor 1 in the factor analysis on the next page).

Eleven statements were formulated to test whether BSC was regarded as a means for measurement. The statements concerned partly measuring to form a basis for comparisons and partly for measurements of work performed within a certain organization. The factor analysis made clear that they were questions about two different characteristics. Factor 3 in the factor analysis on the next page shows which statements are included in the characteristic "aid to measurement" (6 statements). Factor 2 shows the statements that are included in the factor "comparisons" (5 statements).

In the questionnaire 26 statements were formulated regarding the form and practical use of BSC. The factor analysis was designed according to the model (see Table 2). Five statements on usability constituted one factor (factor 5 in the factor analysis) after 3 multi-dimensional statements were omitted (statements 23, 28 and 30). Four statements were omitted when it was shown that they did not provide the survey with any meaningful information. The nuance difference between the questions 36, 38, 41, 44 and 36, 39, 42, 45 was not really noticed by the respondents and the former set were omitted from treatment. After that, the remaining 14 statements made 3 different factors. One factor concerned the term balance and whether the respondents considered that their BSC led to the balances that Kaplan and Norton (1996b) saw as worth striving for in the organization (factor 7 in the factor analysis). Six statements can with the support of the factor analysis be handled as an indicator as to whether BSC is formed as an instrument of strategic leadership or not (factor 4 in the factor analysis on the next page). The remaining four statements formed an indicator as to whether the respondents considered that the BSC that that they were commenting upon also included detailed goals and measures within the four perspectives that were included in the original form of BSC (factor 6 in the factor analysis on the next page). These four factors were handled in the same way as the characteristic "goal congruence." The index was partly constructed with factor weightings and partly with summed questionnaire responses within the respective factor to a variable, which was then divided into groups. (see further Appendix B).

Above all, the factor analysis has been used to test that the formulated statements are practical as test questions for the intended characteristic. Factor

Table A1. Rotated Factor Matrix.

	1	2	3	4	5	6	7
F.2	**0.723**	0.152	0.134		0.204		0.152
F13	**0.600**		0.249	0.191		0.173	0.263
F1	**0.583**	0.163					0.273
F8	**0.579**	0.165	0.122		0.394	0.193	
F9	**0.547**	0.236	0.222		0.134	0.280	−0.198
F19	**0.518**	0.297				0.105	0.225
F12	**0.511**	0.204	0.178			0.249	
F3	**0.494**	0.274	0.257	−0.152		0.189	
F6	**0.467**	−0.139	0.194		0.298		0.148
F24	0.437			0.317	**0.379**	−0.268	
F17	0.232	**0.825**	−0.125	0.231	−0.115		0.175
F14	0.213	**0.747**	0.207				0.159
F18		**0.642**		0.112		0.172	
F11	0.139	**0.455**	0.327		0.106		
F15	**0.404**	0.426		0.117		0.245	0.128
F22	0.237		**0.746**	0.253		0.121	0.135
F21			**0.690**		0.235		
F32	0.299	0.234	**0.509**	0.223	0.149	0.228	0.113
F20	0.290		**0.498**		0.295		0.372
F10	0.220	0.158	**0.490**	0.272		−0.154	0.181
F5	0.236		**0.435**	0.376	0.155	−0.120	0.203
F4	**0.343**	0.170	0.349	0.240		0.273	
F40	−0.105		0.193	**0.781**			0.102
F37				**0.625**	−0.134	0.282	
F43	0.159	0.127		**0.555**	0.223	0.207	
F34		0.182	0.114	**0.517**	0.273	0.156	
F7	0.410	0.323		**0.460**	0.194	0.200	0.130
F31			0.370	**0.415**	0.194	0.232	
F27	0.144			0.225	**0.729**		0.126
F29	0.106	0.122	0.201		**0.652**	0.219	0.192
F26	0.482		0.157		**0.646**		
F25		−0.282	0.115	0.125	**0.494**	−0.107	0.114
F33		**0.478**		0.259	**0.486**		
F36	0.212	0.155			0.117	**0.749**	0.164
F39	0.155			0.193	−0.182	**0.703**	0.221
F42	0.164	0.150		0.309		**0.699**	0.124
F45	0.329	0.132		0.258		**0.509**	
F49	0.142	0.116	0.163	0.187	0.239	**0.135**	0.697
F46	0.396					0.168	**0.688**
F48	0.114		0.437		0.109		**0.673**
F47		0.201	0.183		0.205	0.127	**0.581**

Note: Extraction Method: Principal Axis Factoring. Rotation Method: Varimax with Kaiser Noramlization. Rotation converged in 13 iterations.

analysis has not been used as a statistical method to reduce the number of indicators. The analysis was carried out in a number of stages. First, it was carried out without a given number of desired factors. In the second stage, factors were chosen with eigenvalue > -1 (10 factors). But as a number of factors only consisted of one statement, the number of factors was reduced in further stages until every factor contained more than one statement. The final run presented the rotating factor analysis as it is shown on the following page. The seventh factor has an Eigenvalue of 1.5 and together the factors explain 62% of the variances in the empirical material.

APPENDIX B

The boundaries have been chosen in the following way. If, for example, more than half of the questions have been answered with "agree to a high degree" (3) and another 2 are answered "agree to a low degree" (2) this will give the sum of 13 to the respondent in question and the value 3 to the index variable. Further, a variable was calculated which was weighted with the respective factor (see factor analysis in Appendix A). In the relation analysis, the weighted-, summed- and grouped variables were all tested. The frequency tables show the grouped variables.

Table B1. BSC is Practical, Sum of Five Statements.

	1	2	3	4
Boundaries	< = 7	8–12	13–17	> = 18
Number	0	5	38	31

Table B2. BSC is a Good Means for Measuring in the Organization, Sum of Four Statements.

	1	2	3	4
Boundaries	< = 9	10–15	16–21	> = 22
Number	2	16	51	5

Note: Constructed as Table B1 above.

Table B3. BSC can be Used for Meaningful Comparisons in the Organization, Sum of Five Statements.

	1	2	3	4
Boundaries	< = 7	8−12	13−17	> = 18
Number	6	40	26	2

Note: Constructed as Table B1.

Table B4. Form of BSC, Overall Strategic Management Structure, Sum of Six Statements.

	1	2	3	4
Boundaries	< = 9	10−15	16−21	> = 22
Number	0	10	54	10

Note: Constructed as Table B1.

Table B5. Form of BSC, Detailed Goals and Measures, Sum of Three Statements.

	1	2	3	4
Boundaries	< = 7	8−10	11−13	> = 14
Number	9	27	35	3

Note: Constructed as Table B1.

Table B6. Goal Congruence, Sum of Eleven Statements.

	1	2	3	4
Boundaries	< = 16	17−27	28−38	> = 39
Number	2	26	45	1

Note: Constructed as Table B1.

Table B7.   BSC Leads to Balance, Sum of Four Statements.

	1	2	3	4
Boundaries	< = 7	8 – 10	11 – 13	> = 14
Number	6	37	26	5

Note: Constructed as Table B1.

PART IV:
PERFORMANCE MEASUREMENT AND REPORTING

THE DESIGN OF PERFORMANCE MEASUREMENT SYSTEMS FOR INTERNET "PURE PLAYS": IS A NEW PARADIGM REALLY NEEDED?

Paolo Maccarrone

ABSTRACT

This paper shows the early results of a research project aimed at analysing the peculiarities of performance measurement systems for Internet "pure plays" (i.e. Internet based new ventures), and focuses in particular on transaction based business models (e-commerce firms). The critical review of literature, supported by a case study of a on line insurance company, shows that the "revolution" in performance measurement approaches claimed by some literature is rather an adaptation and integration of existing models, which depends heavily on the kind of firm, its specific business model, the kind of product/service sold, and the competitive context.

INTRODUCTION

The tremendous impact of Internet on firms and on the industrial structure has been so far analysed under different perspectives. However, the great majority of contributions focus on:

Performance Measurement and Management Control, Volume 12, pages 273–297.

- Alternative methodologies for evaluating e-commerce ventures, especially start-ups (e-finance);
- Strategies of Internet companies, the new opportunities for value creation in the marketspace and the emergence of new/alternative business models (e-commerce strategy);
- The innovative marketing techniques and approaches enabled by Internet (e-marketing);
- The operational aspects linked to particular business models (i.e, distribution for e-tailing firms), and the opportunities of Internet for supply-chain management.

Instead, little attention has been given to the relationships between this new technology and the most advanced management control theories. In particular, this research issue can be seen under two different perspectives:

- The impact of Internet on management control activities (i.e. the use of Internet-based applications in day-by-day management control activities, and their integration with existing information systems based on other technologies – as in the case of most integrated – ERP – systems);
- The peculiarities of management control approaches for e-commerce firms (and, in general, for Internet-based companies). Indeed, according to the (still poor) literature on this topic, new metrics seem to be needed to support the (supposed) new economics that characterise the Internet-based firms.

With regard to the first point, it must be underlined that Internet does not seem to have the same disruptive impact on management accounting and control activities, as it had on other functional areas. In particular, the most relevant effects concern:

- The digitalisation of accounting-related business processes, in particular those linked to the passive/active cycle: supply chain management is greatly improved by Internet technology, as proved by the accelerated growth of "extended" ERP systems (based to a great extent on TCP/IP protocols and web technology). All related business processes (order fulfilment, accounting entries, etc.) can benefit of this closer link between the different firms positioned along a *filiere*;
- The development of complementary or ancillary systems, such as competitive intelligence systems or customer relationship management (CRM) systems. Although these cannot be considered properly part of management control systems, nevertheless their output can be used to improve the effectiveness of some typical planning and control activities, as the definition of budget targets, performance benchmarking with competitors, the development of

integrated performance measurement systems (with particular regard to non financial indicators in the customer relationship area), etc;
- The reporting activity: indeed, Internet (and in particular Intranet) enables a much more effective (and efficient) flow of management information inside the organisation, across organisational hierarchical levels and functional areas, as well the customisation of reports and a much higher interactivity.

But, although these kinds of effects must not be disregarded, anyway the overall impact of Internet on management accounting and control is not as revolutionary as it seems for other functional areas (like marketing, for example).

But the relationship between Internet and management accounting can be seen also under a different perspective, aimed at analysing the peculiarities of management accounting for Internet based companies. This paper focuses on this second point: it illustrates the first results of a research project, which has been designed with the aim to understand the real existence of a "new" paradigm of performance measurement and control activities in the new economy era. Some of the most important questions addressed are:

- Are the economics of Internet pure plays really different?
- Which are the new performance measures needed to track the successful implementation of an "e-commerce" strategy?
- Is the importance of non-financial measures higher than in the "old economy" world?
- Can a model of the evolution of performance measurement and control systems be identified, according to the different phases of the life-cycle of an Internet based firm?
- What the impact on "traditional" budgeting and control activities?

The paper is structured in four sections:

- The first illustrates the main kinds of "basic" Internet based business models: this phase is of a fundamental importance, since Internet pure plays can be reconducted to one of these business models, or to a combination of two or more of them;
- The second section resumes the main literature concerning the economics of Internet based companies, with particular regard to B2C initiatives, and the consequences on value drivers and performance measures;
- The third section presents some considerations on a possible "model" of a performance measurement system for Internet B2C pure plays;
- Finally, the last one illustrates a case study, concerning the performance measurement system of an Internet insurance company operating in Italy.

THE NEW ECONOMY FIRMS AND THE EMERGING BUSINESS MODELS

The diffusion of Internet has led to a huge number of new ventures. These Internet based firms (or "pure plays") have been characterised (at least at the beginning of this "new deal") by a great heterogeneity, which, in turn, has raised the need for some conceptualisation. Indeed, several attempts of "classification" of Internet business models have been proposed in the last two-three years: but, at a thorough analysis, most of them are quite incomplete or inconsistent, since the concept itself of "business model" differs from author to author, as well as the dimensions used for classification. For example, Michael Rappa (2000) identifies the following forms of business models:

- Brokerage
- Advertising
- Infomediary
- Merchant
- Manufacturer
- Affiliate
- Community
- Subscription
- Utility

According to Rappa, these models can be implemented in a variety of ways. Brokerage models, for example, include a variety of "elementary" configurations, all regarding the figure of brokers, i.e. market makers: for example, buy/sell fulfilment models, buyer aggregators, market exchange models, but also distributors, virtual malls, auction brokers, reverse auctions, "metamediaries". Advertising models include generalised portals, personalised portals, specialised portals, "pay for attention" based models, incentives-based marketing models, bargain discounters.

Moreover, any given firm may combine different models as part of its web business model: for example, many e-tailers try also to build a sense of "community" (this is especially true for specialised vendors), which, in turn, can lead to substantial revenues from advertising.

Anyway, although very exhaustive, this classification does not seem very robust, since the dimensions used for the identification of the typologies of business models are not clear: some of them seem to derive from the analysis of the value chain (merchant, manufacturer), while some seem to be linked to the revenue model (i.e. the main font of revenues: advertising, subscription), and some others to the content of the site (community, utility). As a matter of fact, the definition itself of business model given by Rappa is quite vague: "in the most basic sense, a business model is the method of doing business by which a company can sustain itself – that is, generate revenue. The business model spells-out how a company makes money by specifying where it is positioned in the value chain".

In this sense, more robust appears the definition proposed by Timmers (1998): "a business model defines the architecture of the product/service and of related information flows: this architecture includes the description of the actors involved, of their role and of their potential benefits, and the definition of consequent sources of revenue". The author then illustrates a classification of business models based on two dimensions: the number of actors involved and the "scope" of the business model, i.e. its extension along the value chain. But the choice of these two dimensions of classification, especially if compared with the quite rigorous description of business model, does not seem fully adequate and consistent. Hence, also in the case of Timmers the typologies of business models identified is not fully satisfactory; his taxonomy includes the following categories:

- E-shop
- E-procurement
- E-auction
- E-mall
- Third party market place
- Virtual communities
- Value chain service providers
- Value chain integrators
- Collaborations platform
- Information brokerage
- Trust services

Several other classifications have been proposed in the last years (see, for example, Bloch, Pigneur & Segev, 1996; Hutchinson, 1997; Bambury, 1998; Rangone, 2000). Each of them presents some interesting feature, but nevertheless they seem to fail in capturing the inherent complexity of the Internet world in a globally consistent model.

The Proposed Taxonomy

A correct classification of business models must be based on the impact on the value chain, on the kind of impact on internal processes, and on the relationships between the different actors across the chain.

An exhaustive and rigorous taxonomy of the different kinds of actors that operate with (or through) Internet is illustrated in Fig. 1 (Chiesa & Noci, 2001): as can be observed, there are several businesses fostered by Internet, which are very different in nature: most of them are technology providers, in the wider sense of the term (like ISPs, hardware and software vendors, etc.), or business complementary service providers (like e-business consultants, venture capitalists, etc). They can all included in the wide category of "Internet enablers".

Our attention, however, focuses on the upper level (the end users). At this level we can identify two fundamental typologies of business models, which, in ultimate analysis, can be reconducted to the classical dichotomy between market and hierarchy for the government of transactions:

(a) Market-based business models: these business models are characterised by the introduction of a new actor within the value chain (an intermediary): hence, this is the area of the "e-business new ventures", or "dot coms", but also of the Internet based projects of incumbents ("dot corp").

   According to the position occupied by this new economic entity along the chain, we can talk of "B2C" or "B2B" models. In some cases, the new or modified value chain can substitute the "old" one, in other cases there can be the contemporary presence of both models. Some examples:

   • B2B models: there can all be reconducted to the general category of "marketplaces", and include buyer/seller aggregators, demand/supply optimisers, B2B auctions or reverse auctions, etc. What differentiates the different specific models is the (main) objective for which the intermediary has been introduced (economies of scale, demand optimisation, higher competition between sellers or buyers), and the market functioning rules, which means the kind of relationships (one to one, one to many, many to many), and the way in which they are managed (pricing rules, for example);
   • B2C models: these can be classified according to the kind of good that is provided to the final customer :

     • Product/service (or transaction) based business models: these are the classical "e-commerce" business models. In this case, the customer pays for a physical or digital product or service. This category includes e-tailers, virtual malls, e-finance services, but also the so-called "bit vendor", i.e. who sells a digital product/service (Napster is probably the most famous example). All these business models have modified the existing value chains, eliminating or putting themselves in competition with existing distributors;

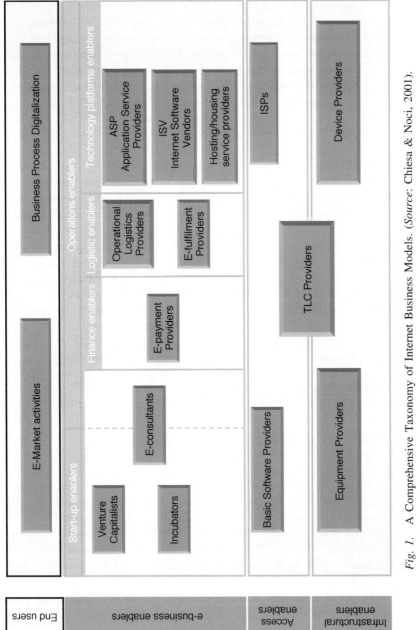

Fig. 1. A Comprehensive Taxonomy of Internet Business Models. (*Source:* Chiesa & Noci, 2001).

- "Attention-based" business models: in this case, the final customer (the user) usually gets information from the web site: information about other sites (as for search agents), news, information about personal interests/hobbies (cultural events, music, sports, etc.), information about other products/services, etc. This category comprises all the content based models (like on line media), portals, virtual communities, etc. According to the main source of revenues, they can be also classified as advertising or subscription based models (the first being largely the most important one, often the only one admitted);

(b) "Internal" business models: these are not "market making" models, and are substantially linked to the digitalisation of inter or intra-firm processes. A classical example of this category of Internet business models is the so-called e-procurement. E-procurement, at least in its traditional meaning, cannot be considered a real "business model", since it does not lead to the development of new, market based way of managing transactions. It simply consists in the digitalisation of the information flow between a firm and its suppliers: this kind of functionalities were already performed using other technologies, in particular EDI. In this sense, Internet enables a much more flexible interface, besides lower costs of data transmission. The same can be said for a lot of other intra or inter-firm applications.

Given the inherent differences of strategies, economic fundamentals and organisational configurations underlying each business model, the analysis must necessarily focus on a selected typology: this paper, in particular, will examine the peculiarities of B2C "pure plays", with particular regard to pure plays.

THE "NEW" ECONOMICS OF B2C

If the objective is to design a performance measurement system of a firm, including both financial and non financial metrics, one of the first steps consist in the analysis of its business processes, and of the underlying economics. With regard to this point, in the last two years there has been a quite contrasted debate about the supposed "new economics" of Internet companies: the reason for this "call" for new approaches must be searched in the supposed inadequacy of existing financial models in explaining new economy firms' market values. As a matter of fact, this gap between the value resulting from the application of "traditional" valuation models and the correspondent market values can be explained in different ways (Porter, 2001):

- The undoubtful inadequacy of some financial approaches (such as those based on multiples of firm economic and assets values);
- The need to adapt and tune the financial models based on value creation (discounted cash flows) to the characteristics of new economy firms;
- The high degree of environmental turbulence and the dynamic context, which, in turn, makes predictions extremely unreliable, thus hampering the application of cash flow based models;
- The over-estimation of market values of all new economy firms in 1999–2000, due to the general and unjustified euphoria about the Internet phenomenon.

Anyway, this debate and the consequent search for new valuation approaches has raised some interesting questions on the economics of Internet pure plays.

In particular, Keen (1999) was one of the first authors who tried to conceptualise the first findings emerging from the experience of business consultants dealing with IPOs and the management of Internet start-ups. According to Keen, three are the main peculiarities of Internet B2C pure plays:

(a) the customer acquisition cost: in the words of Keen, "the pace of electronic commerce profitability rests on the costs of customer acquisition [. . .] Many companies have greatly underestimated both the importance of customer acquisition costs in the basics of e-commerce strategy and its scale. The demise of large scale initiatives in online malls and sites carrying a major retail or media brand is largely explained by the fact that the brand did not transfer from off to on line".

(b) The repetition of business: given the high costs of customer acquisition, the only way to make the business profitable is to build a lasting relationship. Given the reduced number of transactions that can be generated for each kind of product sold, this "exploitment" of the customer must be obtained through new offers, cross-selling and other marketing techniques. Moreover, given the high percentage of fixed costs, the incremental margin for each new transaction is usually very high.

On the base of these considerations, Keen identifies some key indicators; according to the author, if correctly combined, these figures can represent a sort of *tableau de bord*, which can help managers in assessing the value of their e-commerce firm. In his words, to be useful to managers these indicators must: (a) make sense to them, (b) indicate value payoff, not some vague concept like "productivity", (c) be comparable with other firms, (4) provide meaningful comparison across time, and (5) help guide future prioritisation and planning. Three main categories of measures are identified, namely:

(a) customer relationship indicators: this category includes measures linked to the "long term relationship" concept. The main four are the following:

- repeat business in dollars per customer: its a percentage of repeated sales per each customer, measured on a appropriate time interval;
- customer retention rate: this is correlated to the previous index, but, according to Keen, needs separate tracking, since it is a key indicator of relationship versus transaction effectiveness;
- revenue growth rate per established customer, which measures the customer relationship intensity. Also this indicator implies the definition of the time span: this can vary from firm to firm, according to the specific nature of the business and its implicit dynamic (for example, for book e-tailers should be longer than for e-finance companies);
- net cash flow value for customer transaction: this figure is linked to the financial theory, and the measurement of firm value. It takes into account the fact that several B2C companies are characterised by negative net working capital, which means that they are financed by customers and then can create value investing free cash flows.

(b) operational efficiencies: this category comprises all the indicators apt at measuring the impact of Internet on the cost structure of the firm. The overall objective is to understand if e-commerce (and Internet, more in general) leads to value creation through changes in the firm's cost structure. For example:

- customer service cost effectiveness: it is the cost per unit of customer activity (purchase volumes, revenues). This indicator is aimed at measuring the impact of Internet on internal activities (for example, cost savings deriving from the use of web for customer care or order management activities);
- total relationship cost per customer: this figure bundle all costs, including investments in infrastructures and acquisition costs. This indicator must be compared with the "repeat business", to understand the value creation of each customer;
- revenue per employee: it is the fundamental measure of productivity (given the substitution of labour factor with technology);
- profit per employee: complementary to the previous one. Although not relevant in the short term, this figure is important to track progress and to compare the firm's e-commerce value generation with non e-commerce business.

(c) balance sheet strength: this category includes measures linked to EVA and shareholder value (for example, working capital per unit of revenue).

Although very interesting under different point of views, nevertheless the work of Keen seems still quite destructured. The set of measures appears quite heterogeneous, since typical profit oriented indicators are mixed with financial oriented parameters, and the consistency of the underlying theoretical approach is weak.

Moreover, some measures seems to be very important for e-commerce ventures, while other are more relevant in case of internal Internet projects of incumbents (it is the case of some efficiency related measures).

Quite strangely, few contributions have followed this "seminal" work of Keen. The most relevant and famous is perhaps the "e-performance scorecard", elaborated by McKinsey & Company (Agrawal et al., 2001). The e-performance scorecard expresses two key dimensions of e-business: the efficiency of costs (for example, the cost of acquiring visitors to a site and of maintaining active customers) and the effectiveness of a site's operations (such as conversion rates, the rate at which the number of customers increases, and customer gross margins).

The e-performance scorecard comprises 21 indicators, which measure performance statically (at one point in time) and dynamically (over a period of time). The indicators are grouped into three categories (attraction, conversion, and retention), as illustrated in Fig. 2. An overall performance is calculated, as weighted average of the 21 indicators: both individual companies and the e-business sector as a whole can be rated, and the results plotted on a continuum, from best to worst.

At a careful analysis, the e-performance scorecard shows a very poor relationship with the more famous balanced scorecard (Kaplan & Norton, 1992, 1993). Instead of the four areas of the balanced scorecard, we find three areas, all "customer-centric": indeed, almost all the measures are linked to the number of customers, or to the single customer, or to some related parameter (like the number of transactions). Also in this case what emerges is a customer relationship model: beside the problem of "holding" the acquired customer (the retention rate identified by Keen), two other macro-phases are identified, which come before retention: the attraction of the potential visitor, and the conversion of the visitor in a customer. Efficiency measures are taken into consideration only in an implicit way (through the customer operating income, for example), while innovation and financial measures are almost completely neglected.

Moreover, it is not clear how the weights of the different figures are determined, if they are fixed for all firms, whatever the sector or the specific business model adopted. It is quite unclear also how the comparison between different firms or e-business areas can be conducted.

ATTRACTION
- Visitor base
- Visitor acquisition cost
- Visitor advertising revenue

CONVERSION
- Customer base
- Customer acquisition cost
- Customer conversion rate
- Number of transactions per customer
- Revenue per transaction
- Revenue per customer
- Customer gross income
- Customer maintenance cost
- Customer operating income
- Customer churn rate
- Customer operating income before marketing spending

RETENTION
- Repeat-customer base
- Repeat-customer acquisition cost
- Repeat-customer conversion rate
- Number of transactions per repeat customer
- Revenue per repeat customer
- Repeat-customer churn rate

Fig. 2. The E-Performance Scorecard.

TOWARDS A "MODEL" OF A PERFORMANCE MEASUREMENT SYSTEM FOR INTERNET PURE PLAYS

The analysis of the relatively poor literature on the subject leads to the following considerations:

- the authors seem to be worried by the need to justify the bad economic results of almost all the B2C companies: hence, they tend to abandon short term profit related measures, substituting them with customer (long term) oriented measures;
- traditional, periodical measures of profitability (such as net operating profit, ROI) are replaced with a cross-periodical orientation. The visitor/customer is placed at the centre of the scene, and three fundamental phases are identified in his relationship with the Internet company: attraction of the potential customer to the site, his conversion in a real customer, and his retention for a period as long as possible.

The underlying assumption is quite simple: given the huge amount of start-up costs (due to technology infrastructures and marketing costs), short term profitability cannot obviously be achieved. But, since the great part of these initial costs must be considered as investments (i.e. *una tantum* costs, that should not be repeated), it is of fundamental importance to allocate them to the largest base of customers (another implicit assumption here is that marginal profitability – gross margin – for each transaction generated by customers is positive). Moreover, an high retention rate is very important to avoid the risk of "duplicating" the initial large amounts spent in mass-marketing (the higher the retention rate, the lower the marketing costs – customer acquisition costs – in the following years).

Is it a new paradigm? Are these characteristics of e-business so much different from those of the "traditional" economy? Are we really talking of "new economics" of e-business? The answer is quite obvious: all start-up firms have troubles with profitability, especially in B2C sector, where they generally need to invest a lot on marketing to build a brand and a customer basis. Even assuming that the transitory in the case of Internet companies is longer (which, for instance, has never been demonstrated), this nevertheless does not allow firms to talk only in terms of revenues and customers, and to disregard the analysis of the drivers of profitability, and the evolution of the economics over time.

Moreover, the "customer relationship model" is not a real novelty. Indeed, according to the value based approach all management decisions must be aimed

at maximising the value of the firm, calculated as sum of the discounted
predicted cash flows (Copeland et al., 1990; Young, 2001; Knight, 1998):

$$V(0) = \sum_{t=0}^{+\infty} \frac{CF(t)}{(1+k)^t}, \text{ or } V(0) = \sum_{t=0}^{T} \frac{CF(t)}{(1+k)^t} + \frac{V(T)}{(1+k)^T}$$

*where: V (0) is the economic value of the firm calculated at the time
"0", and CF(t) are the cash flows at the time t, V (T) the terminal value
(an estimation of the value generated after the period T).*

Following this approach, the firm can be seen as the result of a portfolio of
long-term projects, each of them bearing its contribution to the overall value
of the firm. This is a clear long-term oriented approach: all performance
measures are inter-periodical in nature, and there is no mention of short term
profitability figures, like operating profit or ROI. The underlying assumption is
that short-term profitability is not an objective that must be pursued: it must
be "sacrificed" to achieve long-term performance and to maximise the firm's
value. Of course, top management cannot really ignore short term economic
results, given the legal value of the balance sheet and the "psychological" impact
that these kind of figures have on stockholders, stakeholders and, for quoted
companies, on financial markets (which seems a contradiction, given the origin
of this management approach). In this sense, it can be said that these figures
represent a constraint that the management must take into consideration in the
elaboration of strategies aimed at the maximisation of value creation.

According to this perspective, if we think to each customer as an investment
project, we can measure the value of the firm as the sum of the value created
by the firm's customers along its life cycle. Anyway, in the implementation of
this conceptual approach some pitfalls must be carefully avoided:

- first of all, the dimension and the timing of all the investments needed to
  support the customer during his relationship with the firm must be carefully
  predicted, in order to assess the real value generated by customers correctly.[1]
  Too often this aspect have been overlooked in evaluating the potential value
  of e-business ventures. Amazon represents also in this case an emblematic
  example: the investments in fulfilment infrastructures (warehouses and logistics), as well as in front-office activities (call centers, etc.) has been by far
  underestimated, both in the elaboration of business plans and in subsequent
  strategic decisions (like price entry levels), and the consequences on firm's
  profitability have been dramatic. The correct dimensioning of investments is

fundamental to allocate them to the customer basis, to calculate the real customer profitability (or value created along his life cycle);

- secondly, much attention must be put on the evolution of the structure of operating costs, in order to calculate the marginal profitability for each transaction (this is particularly important in the case of e-commerce initiatives, of course), and, then, the operating net cash flow;
- thirdly, the indirect effects of the customer base on the amount of revenues that can be generated by advertising must not be overestimated. One of the fundamental assumptions of most B2C Internet plays (in particular for those adopting an "attention based" business model) is that, at least above a given least bound, the number of visitors/customers has a more-than-proportional effect on advertising revenues (i.e. selling banners spaces and hosting other advertising tools on the site). But, if we look at the estimates about the number of firms operating on the Internet in the future years, and we sum the predictions in revenues from advertising and in marketing expenses of all the business plans of Internet start-ups, it is easy to see that those predictions are quite inconsistent (also taking into account the possibility of a "massive" shifting of advertising from traditional media to the Internet – which, for instance, is unlikely to happen, at the moment).

But there is another, more relevant critical point that should be addressed: if we analyse more carefully this theoretical apparatus, it appears still quite a technicality, and the link with the firm's strategy quite missing. In other words, performance measures like "customer conversion rate", "customer gross income", "retention rate" represent already the result of the success of the firm's strategy. If the firm is not able to attract the customer with effective marketing campaigns, the visitor base will be poor; if the site is not able to persuade the visitor of the value of the offer, and of its superiority, compared with that of competitors, the conversion rate will be very low. Similarly, if the fulfilment process of an e-tailer has not been carefully designed, or if the price of the product has been wrongly cut (as for many e-tailers in the first wave of Internet economy), the gross margin will be too low to balance marketing expenses (if not negative itself).

Hence, these measures can be considered as generic or "first level" indicators: if we share the "customer-oriented" approach, it is quite evident to desume that, if the firm is able to keep under control and constantly improve these figures, it will generate brilliant economic and financial results. But then the key point is how to meet the target values of those indicators: how to reach satisfactory conversion rates? How to generate a sufficient amount of cross selling? This is not automatic: other indicators are required, aimed at controlling the implementation of the firm's competitive strategy and the achievement of the competitive advantages that can lead to the growth of the customer base and to its long-term retention.

In other terms, "retention rate" or "conversion rate" are the result of the quality of an e-commerce pure player strategy, and of the way in which business processes are designed and managed. Hence, other measures are needed, aimed at identifying the critical success factors, and, then, at monitoring the performance of internal processes and of actions/plans/projects that the company has undertaken to implement that strategy. The identification of these indicators is strictly linked to the marketing mix and to the competitive strategy of each firm (Kaplan & Norton, 1996, 2000). For example, to increase and maintain a high attraction rate, the quality of marketing campaigns is of fundamental importance. Hence, the key indicators apt at assessing the effectiveness of marketing initiatives should be carefully identified and included in the performance measurement system. Similarly, to retain customers (repeat customer conversion and churn rate indicators), it is important to understand which are the key success factors and the related "customer oriented" performance measures: price? Delivery time? Quality of products/services sold? Reliability of transaction systems? Once identified the key aspects, the related measures and the related processes that contribute to that measures must be carefully monitored.

The evolution of competition is another often overlooked aspect: almost all the business plans of Internet start-ups does not pay the necessary attention to the analysis of the competitors, especially in prospective terms. In a "sector" which is generally characterised by very low entry barriers, it is very dangerous to make economic and financial forecasts without taking into account the risk of new competitors, since the pressures deriving from an increasing competition might have dramatic effects on the number of customers, or on the margins per customer. A well designed performance measurement system should include some kind of indicators aimed at monitoring the creation of entry barriers and/or the level of competition.

More in general, poor attention is generally given by Internet start-ups to the measures related to the state of resources (the "learning and growth perspective", in the Kaplan's "balanced scorecard language"). If this can be justified in the very first stages of the life of the new venture, a too strict customer orientation might be very myopic in the middle-long term, since it could undermine the sources of competitive advantage of the firm.

Of course, a PMS is dynamic in nature: the content and the relative weight of each indicator is supposed to change according to the evolution of strategic priorities. For example, the emphasis on attraction and conversion of potential customers, which are key aspects of a start-up (as the e-performance scorecard shows), should be subsequently balanced with other strategically relevant issues in the subsequent phases of the life cycle of the firm.

THE CASE OF LLOYD 1885 – GENIALLOYD

Lloyd 1885 is the most important on-line insurance company operating in Italy. It belongs to the RAS group, which, in turn, is part of the Allianz group. The RAS group has implemented an Internet strategy based on three different strategic projects, each of them characterised by an independent web site:

- *www.ras.it* (recently renamed *www.rasbank.it*), which is dedicated to:
  - Intranet/Extranet applications for supply chain management (on line link between corporate management, inspectors and local agencies);
  - Customer care services: in particular, customers can get information about the current state of the "off line" products subscribed with RAS (insurance policies, investment funds, etc), through an Extranet gateway;
  - On-line banking services: account checking, on line trading, buy/sell of investment funds, etc.;
- *www.genialloyd.it:*, the web site of Lloyd 1885, an independent company that offers a complete set of insurance personal products;
- *www.genialpoint.it:* a car vertical portal characterised by advanced services (demand/offer matching, consulting services on financing opportunities and insurance policies, etc.).

In particular, in 1997 Lloyd 1885 was the first company to launch the direct (phone) selling of insurance products in the private segment in Italy. Nowadays it operates through two different channels: telephone and Internet, with the brand "Genialloyd". Its mission is to offer insurance solutions though direct channels in the "personal lines" segment. The value proposition declared by Genialloyd top management can be summarised in the following sentence: "a competitive offer (in terms of prices and service levels), tailored to the profile of each customer, and characterised by a new kind of relationship between the customer and the insurance company".

The company's yearly turnover has been of 47.6 million € in 2000, while in 2001 the expected revenues are about 76–77 million €. The number of delivered policies was about 128,000 in 2000, while in 2001 it should reach about 200,000.

The Direct Insurance Market

The market of direct insurance has known a rapid growth in the last years, and in the majority of European countries the direct insurance companies have reached a significant market share in the private segment, with particular regard to the car segment. The operational configurations can be quite different from country to country, according to the local laws. They are generally characterised by significant competitive advantages, with respect to traditional companies: moreover, these advantage has been increased by the diffusion of Internet technologies. In particular, the fundamental competitive advantage of Internet based companies rests on costs structure: while in a traditional insurance company marketing, selling, administration and general costs have an incidence on sales that varies from 26 to 32%, an Internet based company can cut them to 13–16% (what's more, calculated on discounted prices).

This has a very important competitive impact: recent studies show that the Italian insurance demand is characterised by a high degree of price elasticity. This means that the behaviour of the "average" Italian customer is influenced to a certain extent by the price of the policies (maybe due also to the oligopolistic characteristics of the sector, and the suspect of collusive practices between the main companies). In particular, with a price reduction of 12–15% the percentage of customers that are willing to change their supplier is about 20%. Moreover, if the price cut is about 18–20%, this percentage raises to about 40% (see Fig. 3).

The potential market of direct selling in Italy is then impressive, also due to the particular structure of the distribution channel, constituted mostly by "traditional" agencies, which counted for over 97% of the total market in 2000 (see Fig. 4).

The Strategy

In order to emphasise the inherent cost advantages of the Internet channel, great attention has been given to the identification of the target customers. As for the great majority of Internet B2C companies, also the customers of direct insurance companies have some common peculiarities: in particular, an analysis conducted in the first stages of the life of the Internet channel showed that the first customers of Genialloyd could be classified as "innovation sensitive", "technology confident, "self-makers", as well as "trend setters". Interesting to say, these variables were quite different from those that described customers of the telephone channel: indeed, this was preferred by "price sensitive", "service

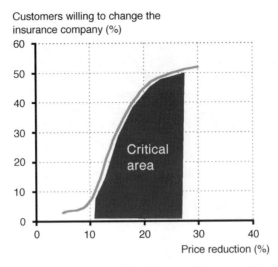

Fig. 3. The Price Sensitiveness of the Average Customer of Insurance
Companies in Italy.

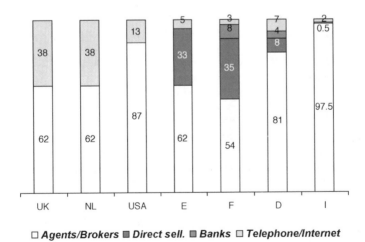

□ *Agents/Brokers* ■ *Direct sell.* ■ *Banks* □ *Telephone/Internet*

Fig. 4. The Structure of Distribution in the Insurance Sector in USA and in the
Main European Countries.

sensitive", "time saver" and "exploratory" customers. This had important reper-
cussions on the marketing strategy: the potential customer base of Internet
companies was concentrated in the big cities, and was generally characterised
by a high educational level and a professional activity, while clients of the
telephone channel were diffused all over the country, and belonged to nearly
all social classes. Anyway, with the massive diffusion of Internet this distinction
has become less shaped, and the potential market of an Internet insurance
company now is constituted by both males and females, of nearly every age,
living both in towns and in villages, belonging to almost all social classes.

In particular, with regard to the car insurance line, the potential market has
been analysed to identify clusters characterised by different risk levels (in terms
of number and typology of accidents, but also of risk of frauds): relevant
describing variables turned out to be sex, age, the kind of profession, the living
area (southern regions are notoriously characterised by a higher "propensity to
fraud"), and other less relevant parameters. The marketing efforts are then aimed
at capturing the low risk segments, and particular attention is paid also by the
commercial units in evaluating and selecting the requests coming from Internet
and call centers. The strategy is of course based on the reduction of average
premium prices (in the selected segments) with respect to "traditional" companies, given the inherent cost structure advantages illustrated in the previous
paragraph (while on the contrary prohibitive premiums are proposed to
"undesired" customers – i.e. people belonging to segments characterised by high
risk or, anyway, negative cost/premium payoff). Nevertheless, to contrast the
increasing competition on Internet, great attention is given also to the service
level, and, in general, to the customer satisfaction, through:

• the absolute respect of the conditions declared in the policy contracts;
• the continuous reduction of response times;
• the offer of customised products.

According to the company top management, this can be obtained through the
total involvement of all the organisational structure, from back-office to call
centers, the adoption of continuous improvement policies, a great attention on
innovation, and the adoption of well-designed performance measurement
systems.

Performance Measurement and Management Control in Genialloyd

The main peculiarities that characterise Lloyd 1885 and its underlying business
model can be resumed in the following points:

- highly innovative and rapidly growing company;
- very large potential market;
- a very delicate structure of the economics, due to the reduced margins generated by the main business (as a consequence also of the marketing mix and of the penetration strategy adopted);
- nearly absence of "buffers" in the operations;
- use of highly sophisticated techniques for product cost estimation (*ex ante*), but possibility of calculating the actual margin for each kind of policy only *ex post*, due to the inherent characteristics of the "product" sold and the inversion of the cycle (typical of insurance companies);
- high degree of automation and digitalisation of internal processes ("paperless company");
- continuous redesign of the business system to achieve simultaneously higher efficiency and higher effectiveness (service level).

These peculiarities of Genialloyd's strategy, structure and of the underlying economics have a strong influence also on the features of the management control system, which is characterised:

- by a marked orientation towards operational and business process (non financial) indicators (rather than "classical" management accounting measures); and, at the same time,
- by a highly strategic role (i.e. it is designed to support strategic control and strategic re-orientation).

At the moment, the integrated performance measurement system of Lloyd 1885 includes the indicators illustrated in Fig. 5. As can be noticed, the set of figures comprises both financial and non-financial measures, but the latter are predominant. It is possible to recognise some of the typical "customer oriented" measures (like the new customers acquisition cost), together with more "classical" figures (as for "operators productivity").

Besides being a typical "integrated" set of both financial and non financial measures, Genialloyd's PMS represents also a balanced mix of "old" and "new" economy indicators: the excessive customer-centric vision of some "new economy" models that have been illustrated in the previous sections seem not to have contaminated the top management of this company.

Nevertheless, at a thorough analysis the structure of the PMS shows some "weakness" or critical point. In particular:

- some indicators can be classified as "outcome" indicators (for example, customer retention rate, or conversion rate), since they represent the result of the quality of Genialloyd strategy and/or of operational performances,

• New customer acquisition cost	• Policy average premium
• New vs. renewed policies ratio	• Phone call average length
• Customer retention rate	• Operators productivity
• % Internet vs. call center customers	• Throughput time of the main
• Call Center and Internet service level	operational processes
• Conversion rates	• Frequency of accidents for each type of policy
• Number of quotations/offers/sold policies for each cluster of customers (both via CC and Web)	• Loss ratio
• Cross selling rate	• Cost ratio
	• Company internal climate

Fig. 5.   The Key Performance Indicators in Genialloyd.

while others are typical process performance measures (phone call length, throughput times);

• some measures are very aggregated (as for "call center service level" or "internal climate"), while others are very punctual ("phone calls average length"). Some indicators (or, better, key areas) are also difficult to operationalise (it is not clear how the "internal climate" can be measured, for example);

• some indicators are related to the implementation of particular strategies: for example, the Internet vs. call centers customers ratio, which reflects the attempt of maximising the number of policies subscribed via Internet, since this reduces the cost of customer acquisition – in a "horizontal" view – and the commercial/customer care costs – in a "traditional" or cost centres view. The same can be said for the "cross selling ratio", which monitors one of the "must" of e-commerce (the use of the Internet contact for cross selling). Other indicators are more "operational" in nature, and does not reflect particular strategic objectives;

• there's too little emphasis on financial measures (the economics!).

Some of the addressed issues can be solved through a more articulated a robust structure of the system, which is still in embryonic stage. Moreover, we should not forget the extremely dynamic and hardly predictable environmental context, as confirmed also by the words of the company's CEO: "we measure all the measurable, but rarely at the maximum degree of analyticity. We take rapid decisions on expected (quantitative) results; then we measure actual results, and take other decisions trying to improve our predictive ability, according to a classical cybernetic cycle where the learning capacity is the real critical success factor".

Anyway, in the "rationalisation" of the performance measurement system the following points should be taken into consideration:

- value drivers (the effect, the outcome measures, like conversion or retention rates) should be kept separate from operational (process) performance measures (the causes);
- moreover, performance measures should be linked to the business strategy (the strategic positioning) or to particular strategic priorities, according to a structured and logical scheme, aimed at showing in an explicit form the links between the different kinds of performance measures;
- accounting measures should complement the quantitative, non financial information: for example: the retention rate should be analysed jointly with the profitability of the different categories of customers: what's worth keeping segments of customers who turn out to be not (or not enough) profitable, at an economic analysis?

CONCLUSIONS

In this paper the peculiarities of performance measurement for B2C pure plays (or "dot coms") have been examined, with particular regard to e-commerce ("transaction based") companies. The critical review of literature and the results of the case study that has been illustrated seem to confirm that it is not correct to talk of a "revolution" in the economics of e-commerce ventures, since the underlying business models are quite similar to those of the "old" economy. Instead, a reinforcing of the long term orientation and of "cross-periodical" measures of profitability seems to emerge, coherently with some recent trends in the management control literature. Of course, the use of web site as "front end" contact channel with customers has an impact on cost structures and on key success factors. The need of adaptation of existing performance measurement systems approach depends heavily on the kind of firm (i.e. on its underlying specific business model), and on the sources of strategic advantage, with regard to "traditional" (or alternative) competitors.

NOTE

1. The correct estimation of the investments made for each customer is linked to the problem of bundling/unbundling of projects.

296 PAOLO MACCARRONE

ACKNOWLEDGMENT

The author is thankful to Alessandro Santoliquido, CEO of RAS 1885 – Genialloyd, for his collaboration in the development of the case study.

REFERENCES

Agrawal, V., Arjona, L. D., & Lemmens, R. (2001). E-performance: The path to rational exuberance. *The McKinsey Quarterly, 1*, 31–43.

Albrinck, J., Irwin, G., Neilson, G., & Sasina, D. (2000). From bricks to clicks: the four stages of e-volution. *Business & Strategy, 20*.

Bambury, P. (1998). A taxonomy of Internet commerce. *First Monday*, http://www.firstmonday.dk/issues/issue3_10/bambury

Bakos, Y., & Brynjolfsson, E. (1999). Bundling information goods: pricing, profits and efficiency. *Management Science, 45*(12).

Barsh, J., Crawford, B., & Grosso, C. (2000). How e-tailing can rise from the ashes. *The McKinsey Quarterly, 3*, 98–109.

Bloch M., Pigneur, Y., & Segev, A. (1996). On the road of electronic commerce – a business value framework, gaining competitive advantage and some reserach issues. http://haas.berkeley.edu/~citm/road-ec/ec.htm

Chiesa, V., & Noci, G. (2001). From euphoria to rationalisation (original title: "Dall'euforia alla razionalizzazione"). *IlSole24Ore,* 28th March.

Copeland, T., Koller, T., & Murrin, J. (1990). *Valuation.* New York: John Wiley and Sons.

De Haas, M., & Kleingeld, A. (1999). Multilevel design of performance measurement system: enhancing strategic dialogue throughout the organisation. *Management Accounting Research. 10*.

Drucker, P. (1998). The Information Executives truly need. *Harvard Business Review on Measuring Corporate Performance*. Boston: Harvard Business School Press.

Feeny, D. (2001). Making Business Sense of the E-Opportunity. *Sloan Management Review. Winter*, 41–51.

Kaplan, S., & Sawhney, M. (2000). E-Hubs: The New B2B Marketplaces. *Harvard Business Review, May–June*, 97–103.

Kaplan, R. S., & Norton, D. P. (1992). The Balanced Scorecard: Measures that Drive Performance. *Harvard Business Review, January–February*.

Kaplan, R. S., & Norton, D. P. (1993). Putting the Balanced Scorecard to Work. *Harvard Business Review, September–October*.

Kaplan, R. S., & Norton, D. P. (1996). Using the Balanced Scorecard as A Strategic Management System. *Harvard Business Review, January–February*, 75–85.

Kaplan, R. S., & Norton, D. P. (2000). *The Strategy Focused Organisation: How Balanced Scorecard Companies Thrive in the New Business Environment*. Boston: Harvard Business School Press.

Kearney, A. T. (Eds) (2000). *E-Business Performance*. A.T. Kearney Report.

Keen, P. (1999). New Sources and Measures of Value for eCommerce. Accenture Internal Report.

Keen, P. (1999). The New Economics of eCommerce Value Generation. Accenture Internal Report.

Knight, J. A. (1998). *Value based management. Developing a systematic approach to creating shareholder value*. New York: McGraw Hill.

Hagel, J., & Singer, M. (2000). Unbundling the corporation. *The McKinsey Quarterly, 3,* 148–161.
Gulati, R., & Garino, J. (2000). Get the right mix of bricks and clicks. *Harvard Business Review,* *May–June,* 107–114.
Young, S. D. (2001). *EVA and value-based management.* New York: McGraw Hill.
Maisel, L. S. (1992). Performance Measurement: The Balanced Scorecard Approach. *Journal of Cost Management, Summer.*
Porter, M. E. (2001). Strategy and the Internet. *Harvard Business Review, March,* 63–78.
Rayport, J. F. (1999). The truth about Internet business models. *Business & Strategy, 16.*
Rangone, A. (2000). The S4C model. *Politecnico di Milano Internal Research Report.*
Rappa, M. (2000). Business Models on the Web. http://ecommerce.ncsu.edu/business_models.html
Rayport, J. R., & Sviokla, J. J. (1996). Exploiting the virtual value chain. *The McKinsey Quarterly,* *1,* 20–37
Skirme, D. J., & Amidon, D. M. (1998). New mesaures for success. *Journal of Business Strategy,* *January–February.*
Timmers, P. (1998). Business models for electronic markets. *Electronic Markets, 8*(2).
Venkatraman, N., & Henderson, J. (1998). Real strategies for virtual organising. *Sloan Management Review, 40*(1, Fall).

THE DICHOTOMY BETWEEN INTERNAL AND EXTERNAL SOCIAL PERFORMANCE MEASURES

John Innes and Gweneth Norris

ABSTRACT

With the growth in research into social reporting, the focus has been over-whelmingly on the external reporting of social performance measures. In contrast, this case study explores the internally reported social performance measures and social information needs of managers in an organisation that published an external social report with more than 100 performance targets for community involvement, customers, employees, environment and suppliers. The corporate culture had a major influence on its social performance via clan control and employees' self-control. However, the external publication of detailed social performance targets does not imply similar detailed internal reporting of social performance.

INTRODUCTION

The international company in this case study is a retail organisation which emphasised social and environmental performance as well as the needs of stakeholders such as customers, employees, shareholders and suppliers. Its published social report (issued three years before this research project began) had more than 100 performance targets for community involvement, customers, employees, environment and suppliers.

Performance Measurement and Management Control, Volume 12, pages 299–312.

Existing social reporting theories identified by Gray et al. (1996) such as stakeholder theory, legitimacy theory and political economy theory all have an external reporting emphasis as do the corporate social performance models of Carroll (1979), Wartick and Cochran (1985) and Wood (1991). Carroll (1979) developed the first corporate social performance model and his ideas were later developed by Wartick and Cochran (1985) and Wood (1991). Probably the most influential corporate social performance model is that of Wood (1991) who added an action component to Carroll's model. Wood (1991, p. 693) defined corporate social performance as:

> a business organisation's configuration of principles of social responsibility, process of social responsiveness, and policies, programmes and observable outcomes as they relate to the firm's societal relationships.

There is a large literature on social reporting (such as Tinker, 1985; Parker, 1986; Puxty, 1986; Gray et al., 1988; Guthrie & Parker, 1990; Tinker et al., 1991; Gray et al., 1995; Matthews, 1997; Adams et al., 1998; Underman, 2000) and environmental reporting (such as Gray & Laughlin, 1991; Harte & Owen, 1991; Roberts, 1991; Cooper, 1992; Bebbington, 1994; Adams et al., 1995; Gray et al., 1995; Lehman, 1995, 1999; Deegan & Gordon, 1996; Owen et al., 1997; Parker, 1997; Neu, 1998; Milne & Adler, 1999). Gray (2000) gives an overview of both historical and current developments in social and environmental auditing and reporting. It is now fairly generally accepted that organisations have responsibilities to other stakeholder groups in addition to shareholders (Clarkson, 1995; Donaldson, 1995).

With this growth in research on social and environmental reporting, the focus has been overwhelmingly on the external reporting of performance measures. However, other research studies (such as Burns et al., 1996) have shown that managers react to and are influenced by such external reporting. Wood (1991, p. 699) has argued that an organisation's social objectives are not met by:

> some abstract organizational actor; they are met by individual human actors who constantly make decisions and choices, some big and some small, some minor and others of great consequence.

This research project attempted to begin to fill the gap in knowledge relating to the social performance measures and social information needs of managers in organisations that publish social reports.

METHODOLOGY AND METHOD

This case study was conducted using the Strauss and Corbin (1990, 1998) grounded theory approach with its open and axial coding of the data. Strauss and Corbin (1998, p. 101) defined open coding as:

The analytic process through which concepts are identified and their properties and dimensions are discovered in data.

Axial coding tries to identify the relationship between the open codes before substantive hypotheses are developed.

In contrast to Glaser (1992), Strauss and Corbin identify the general topic area to be investigated before entering the research site. In this case the topic was social performance measures. Parker and Roffey (1997) compare and contrast the Glaser (1992) and Strauss and Corbin (1990) approaches to grounded theory and another difference is that Strauss and Corbin consider that knowledge of the literature is a useful source of information for any case study. Strauss and Corbin consider that the literature can help to improve the 'theoretical sensitivity' of the researcher. However, the essence of grounded theory is that the theory or hypotheses are grounded in the data. As Dey (1993) suggests, it is important that researchers do not have an empty mind but keep an open mind during the case study.

During this case study open-ended questions were asked to facilitate discussion during the interviews with the interviewees being encouraged to talk. Nineteen interviews were conducted with both accountants and managers and the interviews varied in length from one to three hours with more than 30 hours of interviews in total. Approximately two weeks were spent at the research site. All interviews were recorded and some notes were also taken during the interviews. These interviews were later transcribed. In addition to these interviews and observation during the case study, copies of many documents were obtained including both external and internal reports.

CASE STUDY

The international retail company studied has a turnover exceeding £500 million and over 1,500 stores in over 40 countries. The mission statement of the company emphasises social and environmental performance as well as the needs of stakeholders such as customers, employees, shareholders and suppliers. In addition the mission statement states that this company wishes to contribute to local, national, and international communities in which it trades with a code of conduct to ensure fairness and honesty.

External Social Performance Measures

Given its mission statement, it is not surprising that this company had published an audited social report three years before this research project began. This social report has been widely distributed and includes various sections including community involvement, customers, employees, environment, shareholders and suppliers. The company had also set itself social performance targets five years before this research project began and the social report issued three years before this research project began includes both:

(1) past achievements against social performance targets
(2) future social performance targets.

There is a great range of social performance targets in this public social report and a selection from these performance targets is given in Appendix A. The company still intended to publish another social report but none had been issued during the past three years. This very detailed social report was issued three years earlier and the research question was what social performance measures are reported internally to managers to enable them to monitor progress against these published targets.

Internal Social Performance Measures and Management Control

Historically the internal social performance measures were very much less developed in this company than the externally reported social performance measures. As one interviewee stated:

> My perspective is that in the past in this company, social reporting was an event unto itself, and it was important to get all this information out there in voluminous detail but in reality it had very little to do with the business at all.

However, this did not mean that the interviewees did not care about the company's social performance – indeed the exact opposite was the case, with all our interviewees expressing strong interest in the social performance of the company. This was not achieved by imposed formal controls or by internal social performance measures but instead by employees' self-control via the culture and values of the company. For example, the same interviewee quoted above in this paragraph also stated:

> The values of this company are so integral to the brand in terms of its reason for being, its purpose, that you know we understand the need to bring, as we say, the values closer to the operating side of the business.

All 19 interviewees mentioned the importance of the values of the organisation to day-to-day decision-making. Indeed, the only topic mentioned by all 19 interviewees was the values of the organisation. Self-control by individuals rather than imposed management controls was closely related to these values. This self-control was within the context of the culture or values of the company as evidenced by the following quotes from eight different interviewees:

The company has a very high set of principles.

The company's core values are paramount to everything we do.

It is ingrained in the culture of the business that people would not even think about contravening our social values.

At each level of this company, people actively practise what they preach.

Social and commercial decisions are interlinked.

We, our values and who we are, drive a lot of our activity as well.

People follow the culture and are culturally motivated.

There are a significant number of things we do because we believe these to be the right things to do and we don't specifically look at the impact on the bottom line.

The culture and core values of the company had remained very much the same since its early days. More than 10 of the 19 interviewees identified the social values of the company as including the following:

(1) concern for the individual (15 interviewees)
(2) concern for the company's effect on society (15 interviewees)
(3) community service (14 interviewees)
(4) concern for the environment (14 interviewees)
(5) ethical approach to business (12 interviewees)
(6) concern for policies of suppliers (11 interviewees)

The company influenced the social values process in three main ways. Firstly, the values of the company were given in various documents (including the mission statement). Secondly, the recruitment and induction process reinforced the social values. Thirdly, the performance measurement system had a relatively minor influence on the social values process. In terms of monthly reporting there was also a Values Report from a cross-functional group which went to the top-level executive committee and it highlighted actual or potential problems relating to the values of the company which needed top management's attention.

The recruitment process was critical to maintaining and developing the values of the company, with emphasis placed on the values of the individual being consistent with those of the business. For example, one manager stated:

Part of the reason why people work at this company is because they feel they want to because of its values.

Another interviewee claimed:

> For a recent senior appointment, one candidate had the required skills and probably was
> the best candidate but that vital piece regarding values and interest in community activities
> was missing so that person was not appointed.

Similarly, the induction process emphasised the company's values including working on a community project within the first six months. These recruitment and induction procedures were similar to Ouchi's (1979) clan control.

Historically the internal performance measurement system had been relatively weak in relation to the social values of the company. For example a senior manager admitted:

> At present there is not a clear link between our mission statement and our internal perfor-
> mance measurement system and we are trying to move towards a more holistic way of
> looking at performance.

Very recently a new set of corporate targets was established and at the presentation to the executive committee someone asked 'where are our values targets?' It was therefore agreed to add three further targets:

(1) 100% staff participation in community involvement schemes.
(2) £x million purchases from suppliers from disadvantaged communities in the developing countries.
(3) Develop smaller suppliers so that they are not dependent only on this company.

To date the social objectives of the organisation have not been reflected in its formal, internal performance measurement system. Furthermore, the remuneration of top management was based solely on financial performance and was not related to social performance. However, given the values of the organisation it was recognised that this needed to change. One accountant argued in relation to the basis of remuneration for top management:

> I certainly believe that unless the basis of remuneration changes, and we include social
> performance then, we're not really marrying up performance against our mission, so we're
> not there yet.

It is always difficult to compare the culture and values of different organisations but one feature of this case was the number of interviewees who, without being asked, made comparisons with previous large company employers. For example, three different managers made the following comments:

> My previous employer had a very strong external ethical face but from the inside it was a
> very different story. This company probably has a less strong ethical face than my previous
> employer but inside this company is much more ethical than my previous employer.

> Here it's the first time that I've learnt about true representation and genuine consultation.

> The main difference from my previous employer is that this company is a business that it is absolutely committed socially and environmentally.

Such evidence suggested that employees perceived this company as being relatively highly committed environmentally, ethically and socially.

Although the internal social performance measures were not well developed within this company, it did systematically monitor the performance of its suppliers. It did so in the following four main ways:

(1) visits to suppliers' factories
(2) social audit of major suppliers by an independent party
(3) supply chain integrity programme
(4) suppliers' signed declaration.

All these methods of monitoring suppliers basically covered the same issues. This company was concerned about the social performance not only of its own direct suppliers but also of its suppliers' suppliers. Nevertheless, it was obviously more difficult for it to monitor its suppliers' suppliers, so it relied on a signed declaration from its own suppliers for that purpose.

The social performance measures for the suppliers included the following requirements in relation to the employees of suppliers:

(1) employees have proper written contracts
(2) employees are paid proper rates of pay and are given at least one day off in seven and holidays
(3) employees are paid for overtime worked
(4) employees have reasonable working conditions
(5) factories have proper licences from the government
(6) occupational health and safety guidelines are followed
(7) adequate grievance and disciplinary procedures exist
(8) there is a minimum age for employees
(9) workers are not bonded to the company (e.g. by debt)
(10) workers are free to leave the company after working due notice
(11) there are no prison workers
(12) employees are allowed to join a formal trade union or association of their choice.

There were similar detailed performance measurements in relation to the impact of suppliers on the environment.

CONCLUSIONS

This case study centres on an international retail company whose mission state-ment emphasised social and environmental performance as well as the needs of stakeholders such as customers, employees, shareholders and suppliers. This company had published, three years before this research project began, a very extensive range of social performance targets covering community involvement, customers, employees, environment and suppliers. However, the information concerning achievements reported in this public social report had generally been collected on a one-off basis. In contrast to the externally published social perfor-mance measures, there were few internally reported measures of social performance. Generally the interviewees considered the external publication of social performance measures as being a separate event and 'in reality it had very little to do with the business at all'. For example, although the published social performance targets included more than 20 measures relating to customers, 13 of the 19 interviewees never mentioned customers during their interviews. Indeed the area within the business with the most explicit social performance measures related to control of suppliers. This led to the first substantive hypothesis:

H_1: The fact that an organisation has published social performance measures does not imply that it reports regularly similar internal social performance measures.

Although this company had relatively few internally reported social performance measures monitored on a regular basis, this did not signify disinterest in the company's social performance. Indeed the opposite was the case, with all 19 interviewees expressing a passionate interest about the company's social performance. Obviously the interviewees may not be representative of all the company's employees (15 of the 19 interviewees were selected by the company and the researchers selected the remaining four interviewees). Although there were few internal social performance measures (other than in the areas of suppliers and, to a much lesser extent, community involvement) to influence behaviour, the culture and values of the company had a major influence on the company's social performance. Therefore the second substantive hypothesis is:

H_2: The culture and values of an organisation are more important influences on social performance than is the internal performance measurement system.

Although the formal performance measures were relatively ineffective controls over social performance, the values of the company were a significant control mechanism. Such values were applied in a similar way to the clan control of Ouchi (1979) with a great deal of emphasis on the recruitment of individuals with values consistent with the values of the company. There was also a very thorough induction process which included, for example, working on a community project. In addition to this clan control, self-control by employees was also an important element in relation to the social performance of this company. This led to the third substantive hypothesis:

H_3: Clan control and self-control by individual employees are the most important determinants of social performance.

In this company the internal social performance measures concentrated on the suppliers, and in particular on the suppliers' treatment of their employees and on the suppliers' impact on the environment. There were detailed social performance measures in these two areas in relation to suppliers but only one specific social performance measure in relation to community service. Similarly the controls on the suppliers (such as visits, social audits, supply chain integrity programme and signed declarations by suppliers) were relatively extensive whereas the formal controls in relation to other internal aspects of social performance were almost non-existent. The fourth substantive hypothesis is therefore:

H_4: There are more internal social performance measures and management controls related to suppliers than to other internal aspects of organisational social performance.

In grounded theory terms, the above four hypotheses are substantive hypotheses because they are derived from only one case study. Future research would involve more case studies in the areas of corporate social performance and management control so that further substantive hypotheses can be derived from each case and then a cross-case analysis can be conducted to determine the formal hypotheses for further testing.

This case study has shown that a very detailed published social report does not mean that there is a similar detailed internal reporting of social performance. Almost all the interviewees in this case stated without any prompting that the company needed to improve the social information reported to managers. Similarly several interviewees stated that both the remuneration system and the internal performance measurement system needed to be expanded to take the various aspects of social performance into account. To date there has been a significant number of research studies into published social reporting but this case study reveals the need for more research into both the internal reporting of social performance and the social information requirements of managers. This is important because the social performance of organisations ultimately depends on the operating decisions of their managers.

ACKNOWLEDGMENTS

We are grateful to the Chartered Institute of Management Accountants for funding the research on which this paper is based and we also wish to thank all the interviewees for all their time and assistance. We are also grateful for the constructive comments of colleagues at the University of Dundee and of participants at the Workshop on Performance Measurement and Management Control in Nice in October 2001.

REFERENCES

Adams, C. A., Hill, W. Y., & Roberts, C. B. (1995). *Environmental, Employee and Ethical Reporting in Europe*, ACCA Research Report No. 41, London.

Adams, C. A., Hill, W. Y., & Roberts, C. B. (1998). Corporate Social Reporting Practices in Western Europe: Legitimating Corporate Behaviour? *British Accounting Review*, *30*(1), 1–21.

Bebbington, J., Gray, R. H., Thompson, I., & Walters, D. (1994). Accountants' Attitudes and Environmentally-sensitive Accounting. *Accounting and Business Research*, *24*(94), 109–120.

Burns, J., Joseph, N., Lewis, L., Scapens, R., Southworth, A., & Turley, S. (1996). *External Reporting and Management Decisions: A Study of their Interrelationship in U.K. Companies*. London: CIMA.

Carroll, A. B. (Ed.) (1979). *Managing Corporate Social Responsibility*. New York: Little Brown.

Clarkson, M. B. E. (1995). A Stakeholder Framework for Analyzing and Evaluating Corporate Social Performance. *Academy of Management Review*, *20*(1), 92–117.

Cooper, C. (1992). The Non and Nom of Accounting for (M) other Nature. *Accounting, Auditing and Accountability Journal*, *5*(3), 16–39.

Deegan, C., & Gordon, B. (1996). A Study of the Environmental Disclosure Practices of Australian Corporations. *Accounting and Business Research*, *26*(3), 187–199.

Dey, I. (1993). *Qualitative Data Analysis: A User-friendly Guide for Social Scientists*. London: Routledge.

Donaldson, T., & Preston, L. E. (1995). The Stakeholder Theory of the Corporation: Concepts, Evidence and Implications. *Academy of Management Review*, *20*(1), 65–91.

Glaser, B. G. (1992). *Basics of Grounded Theory Analysis*. Mill Valley: Sociology Press.

Gray, R. H. (2000). Current Developments and Trends in Social and Environmental Auditing, Reporting and Attestation: A Review and Comment. *International Journal of Auditing*, *4*(3), 247–268.

Gray, R. H., Kouhy, R., & Lavers, S. (1995). Corporate Social and Environmental Reporting: A Review of the Literature and a Longitudinal Study of U.K. Disclosure. *Accounting, Auditing and Accountability Journal*, *8*(2), 47–77.

Gray, R. H., & Laughlin, R. (1991). Editorial: The Coming of the Green and the Challenge of Environmentalism. *Accounting, Auditing and Accountability Journal*, *4*(1), 5–8.

Gray, R. H., Owen, D. L., & Adams, C. (1996). *Accounting and Accountability: Changes and Challenges in Corporate Social and Environmental Reporting*. London: Prentice-Hall.

Gray, R. H., Owen, D. L., & Maunders, K. T. (1988). Corporate Social Reporting: Emerging Trends in Accountability and the Social Contract. *Accounting, Auditing and Accountability Journal*, *1*(1), 6–20.

Guthrie, J., & Parker, L. D. (1990). Corporate Social Disclosure Practice: An International Perspective. *Advances in Public Interest Accounting, 3*, 159–177.

Harte, G., & Owen, D. (1991). Environmental Disclosure in the Annual Reports of British Companies: A Research Note. *Accounting, Auditing and Accountability Journal, 4*(3), 51–61.

Lehman, G. (1995). A Legitimate Concern for Environmental Accounting. *Critical Perspectives on Accounting, 6*(6), 393–412.

Lehman, G. (1999). Disclosing New Worlds: A Role for Social and Environmental Accounting and Auditing. *Accounting, Organizations and Society, 24*(3), 217–242.

Matthews. M. R. (1997). Twenty-Five Years of Social and Environmental Accounting Research: Is There a Silver Jubilee to Celebrate? *Accounting, Auditing and Accountability Journal, 10*(4), 481–531.

Milne, M. J., & Adler, R. W. (1999). Exploring the Reliability of Social and Environmental Disclosures Content Analysis. *Accounting, Auditing and Accountability Journal, 12*(2), 237–256.

Neu, D., Warsome, H., & Pedwell, K. (1998). Managing Public Impressions: Environmental Disclosures in Annual Reports. *Accounting, Organizations and Society, 23*, 265–283.

Ouchi, W. G. (1979). A Conceptual Framework for the Design of Organizational Control Mechanisms' *Management Science, 25*, 833–845.

Owen, D., Gray, R. H., & Bebbington, J. (1997). Green Accounting: Cosmetic Irrelevance or Radical Agenda for Change?' *Asia-Pacific Journal of Accounting, 4*, 175–199.

Parker, L. D. (1986). External Social Accounting: Adventures in a Maleficent World. *Advances in Public Interest Accounting, 3*, 23–35.

Parker, L. D. (1997). Accounting for Environmental Strategy: Cost Management, Control and Performance Evaluation. *Asia-Pacific Accounting Review, 4*(2, 45–175.

Parker, L. D., & Roffey, B. H. (1997). Methodological Themes: Back to the Drawing Board: Revisiting Grounded Theory and the Everyday Accountant's and Manager's Reality. *Accounting, Auditing and Accountability Journal, 10*(2), 212–247.

Puxty, A. G. (1986). Social Accounting as Immanent Legitimisation: A Critique of a Technicist Ideology. *Advances in Public Accounting, 1*, 95–111.

Roberts, C. B. (1991). Environmental Disclosures: A Note on Reporting Practices in Mainland Europe. *Accounting, Auditing and Accountability Journal, 4*(3), 62–71.

Strauss, A., & Corbin, J. (1990). *Basics of Qualitative Research: Grounded Theory Procedures and Techniques.* Newbury Park: Sage.

Strauss, A., & Corbin, J. (1998). *Basics of Qualitative Research: Techniques and Procedures for Developing Grounded Theory.* Thousand Oaks: Sage.

Tinker, T. (1985), *Paper Prophets: A Social Critique of Accounting*, Eastbourne: Holt, Reinhart and Winstgon.

Tinker, T., Lehman, C., & Neimark, M. (1991). Falling Down the Hole in the Middle of the Road: Political Quietism in Corporate Social Reporting. *Accounting, Auditing and Accountability Journal, 4*(2), 28–54.

Underman, J. (2000). Methodological Issues; Reflecting on Quantification in Corporate Social Reporting Content Analysis. *Accounting, Auditing and Accountability Journal, 13*(5), 667–680.

Wartick, S. L., & Cochran, P. L. (1985). The Evaluation of the Corporate Social Performance Model. *The Academy of Management Review, 10*(4), 758–769.

Wood, D. J. (1991). Corporate Social Performance Revisited. *Academy of Management Review, 16*(4), 691–718.

APPENDIX A

Published Social Performance Targets

The company published an audited social report three years before this research project began and this report included a range of social performance targets and a selection from these targets are given in this Appendix.

(a) Community Involvement

There were more than 20 performance targets including the following:

(1) establish a process of monitoring levels of community involvement at store level
(2) set an annual budget for local community regeneration initiatives
(3) conduct annual survey of local opinions in specified areas
(4) work with managers to integrate community involvement activities into personal development plans
(5) share best practices in local community initiatives in different countries
(6) support initiatives such as work experience, teacher placements, and school visits
(7) support an annual community arts event in each market
(8) run a specific environmental campaign each year
(9) develop key performance indicators for community involvement.

(b) Customers

There were more than 20 performance targets including the following:

(1) agree an action plan for ongoing dialogue with customers
(2) launch a comprehensive set of instore materials explaining company's approach to business, its products and its values
(3) increase the amount of refills of refillable products sold to 5% of customer transactions
(4) increase recovery of recyclable plastic to 10% of plastic used
(5) ensure that 60% of customers do not take a plastic carrier bag
(6) provide information to customers on any genetically modified ingredients.

(c) Employees

There were more than 50 performance targets including the following:

(1) increase percentage of women in senior management positions

(2) employ more people from ethnic minority backgrounds

(3) educate all levels of staff about the issue of harassment in the workplace

(4) encourage staff and managers to consider flexible working practices

(5) organise first internal careers fair

(6) provide information to help employees make informed choices about their pensions

(7) achieve the Investors in People certification

(8) provide guidelines and training for managers on their responsibilities for communication

(9) participate in external assessment of organisation's health and safety management procedures.

(d) Environment

There were more than 10 environmental targets including the following:

(1) audit all sites to EMAS standards

(2) reduce average energy use per shop to 35,000 KWH per annum

(3) eliminate or compensate for distribution fleet's CO_2 emissions through tree planting and other initiatives

(4) reduce export freight going by air to no more than 2.5% of total export freight

(5) reduce annual stock disposals to less than 2% of the cost of ex-warehouse sales

(6) begin an environmental full cost accounting system.

(e) Suppliers

There were more than 20 performance targets including the following:

(1) organise regular suppliers' days to exchange information and ensure continuity of buying contracts

(2) provide special support for smaller suppliers both on business and value-related issues

(3) establish evaluation panels and supplier ratings for new and existing suppliers

(4) introduce a code of conduct for buyers to ensure probity at all times

(5) improve speed of payment to suppliers

(6) double the number of suppliers with a 3-star rating or higher under the supplier environmental rating scheme

(7) improve forecasting systems to better inform our suppliers and establish appropriate performance indicators to track forecasting accuracy

(8) develop key performance indicator model to assess the social impact of the trading links.

PART V:
DRIVERS OF PERFORMANCE, RISK AND FINANCIAL ANALYSIS

DRIVERS OF THE PERFORMANCE OF CHINESE INVESTMENT FUNDS – AN EMPIRICAL STUDY INVOLVING FOURTEEN CHINESE INVESTMENT FUNDS AND THIRTY AMERICAN MUTUAL FUNDS

X. Q. Cao and J. Bilderbeek

ABSTRACT

In this article, we explore from a managerial perspective what drives the performance of Chinese investment funds. A questionnaire survey and regression analysis on Chinese and American investment funds reveals that no matter how different investment funds are with regard to their internal and external environments, management and government policies are the most important driving forces of the performance of Chinese investment funds.

INTRODUCTION

As the economic reform in China progresses, new financial instruments are promoted to channel additional funds to further aid economic development. With

Performance Measurement and Management Control, Volume 12, pages 315–339.
ISBN: 0-7623-0867-2

the support of the Chinese government, the booming investment funds attract a lot of attention from individual and institutional investors. The proliferation of investment funds and their unique natures, such as the economics of scale and diversification, have made them a bright spot in the Chinese financial market. Millions of investors have favored this new type of investment and injected large amounts of funds. Their expectations are also high; that is, the returns, after costs and taxes, should be commensurate with the risks they bear. Do Chinese fund managers satisfy investors in delivering the expected rate of returns and if not, why not? Why are some fund managers more successful than others? Further, what are the driving forces behind the performance of Chinese investment funds? These questions have been lingering in the minds of many investment professionals; however, little work has been done in this area.

Since the inception of the first new securities investment fund[1] in March 1998, most such funds have exhibited reasonable performance. However, a significant portion of their performances is attributed to favorable government policies (Chen, 1999; Dai, 2000). Further, these funds are vulnerable to the highly volatile Chinese stock markets. Their performances fluctuate alongside the indices. Fund managers and the management of these investment funds are striving to determine the drivers of their performances as well as effective and efficient measures to control them.

Motivated by this strong demand, we have carried out empirical research by sending questionnaires to Chinese and American investment funds in the hope of identifying the driving forces behind the performance of Chinese investment funds. This was done for two reasons: firstly, the new securities investment funds in China have only had two and a half years' history since their birth, insufficient time to gather sufficient data for a statistical analysis that would identify the drivers of performance. A questionnaire survey is an acceptable substitute for gaining firsthand insights. Secondly, as an emerging financial instrument in a socialist market economic environment, a comparison with the world's leading mutual fund industry (American mutual funds) is expected to provide more representative and persuasive insights into understanding the success of Chinese investment funds. Using this approach, we are able to gain insights into the views of fund managers from both countries. Both Chinese and American fund managers see management as the most important factor that drives their funds' performance. In terms of external factors, government policy is almost as important as the market situation in determining the performance of Chinese investment funds, whereas the market situation[2] dominates in American, according to the results of the survey.

To enhance the evidence found in the questionnaire survey, we conducted multiple regression analyses between the funds' performance, and internal and external factors. It was found that management and the market situation have a positive relationship with the performance of American mutual funds. However, the same relationship has not been statistically proven for Chinese investment funds. By comparing and analyzing the answers to the questionnaire and the results of the regression analyses, we can assess the results of our study and try to bring it to the attention of Chinese investment professionals. We hope our preliminary study will provide guidelines for Chinese fund managers and enable them to draw inspiration from the experiences of American fund managers. An interesting avenue for further research would be to investigate recommendations for effective and efficient measures to control the performance of Chinese investment funds.

In this paper, we describe how the study was conceived and carried out, its major findings, and discuss the implications of these findings for Chinese investment funds that pursue excellence. The layout of the article is as follows: in the next section, we review western and Chinese literature on performance drivers of investment funds; then we set out our research proposition and research questions; followed by the methodology of the study and design of the questionnaire. Next, we describe the major findings; and then conclude the paper with a discussion and conclusions on the implications of these findings.

LITERATURE REVIEW

Studies on the drivers of investment funds' performance can be mainly grouped into two areas. The first concentrates on analyzing performance attributions of internal factors such as fund managers' market timing ability and stock selection ability. The second area of research focuses on examining the impact of external factors, such as stock market and other economic factors on portfolio performance. Fama (1972), however, suggested that the performance of a portfolio is determined by both internal and external factors. He attributed a portfolio's performance to two factors: the return from security selection (internal factor) and the return from bearing the risk (external factor).

Market timing ability is the ability of a fund manager to produce superior return distributions by forecasting overall market movements. The stock selection ability is the ability to produce more favorable return distributions based on superior information about individual stocks. Studies in this area include Kon (1979), Grant (1977), Daniel (1997) and Otten (2000). However, they did not identify the causes (drivers) of superior or inferior ability; is it due to management talent, staff quality, or something else?

Studies on internal performance drivers are rather limited. Treynor (1965) studied the effect of management on the rate of return on investments. He pointed out the implications of a characteristic line for management control, and stated that no matter how widely the rate of return for a fund may fluctuate; management performance is unchanged so long as the actual rate of return continues to lie on the characteristic line. Chan et al. (1999) provided an exploratory investigation into the investment styles of mutual funds and the forces that may drive managers to change styles. Chevalier and Ellison (1999) explored the differences in the behaviors and performances of mutual fund managers. They found that younger managers achieve much higher returns than older managers, and that managers who attended colleges with higher average SAT (Scholastic Achievement Test) scores earn much higher returns than do managers from less selective institutions. In a further similar study (1999), they used data on mutual fund managers to examine whether career concerns cause younger managers to behave differently to older ones. Another empirical study (Ambachtsheer et al., 1997) was based on questionnaire data from 80 pension funds and 50 senior pension fund executives. The authors found that of the three organization design elements – governance, planning and management, operations – good governance matters the most.

From the second group of studies that examine the external forces on a fund's performance, the most representative one is the Capital Asset Pricing Model (CAPM) proposed by Sharpe. It argues that the return of a portfolio is determined by its exposure to the market or its systematic risk (Sharpe, 1964). Ross (1976), however, attempted to demonstrate that a portfolio's return could be attributed to several macro economic factors such as interest rate, inflation rate and oil prices and hence developed Arbitrage Pricing Theory (APT). Proponents of multi-factor models (Fama, 1993, 1996; Chan, 1996; Carhart, 1997) developed similar hypotheses for a portfolio's performance. Fama (1993) added size and book to market next to a market proxy as two additional risk factors that could explain fund performance. Carhart (1997) extended the Fama model by adding a fourth factor that captures the Jegadeesh (1993) momentum anomaly. Chevalier (1997) studied the shape of the flow-performance relationship, which creates incentives for fund managers to increase or decrease the risk of the fund depending on the fund's year-to-date return. He found that mutual fund managers do alter their portfolio risk between September and December in a manner consistent with these risk incentives.

Having reviewed western studies, only a handful of publications can be found that address the performance drivers of Chinese investment funds. Lu (1999) discussed several factors that Chinese fund managers ought to consider in order to improve their performance, such as management, staff quality and R&D. Li (1998) briefly addressed the importance of management to fund management companies in China, and another paper written by the research center of

GuangFa Securities (2000) stated that the quality of fund managers are the key to the success of Chinese investment funds. However, these studies are far from in-depth or sufficient in scope. We believe that our study will help fill this gap by providing an in-depth empirical analysis of the performance drivers of funds, that is, tracing the impact of key success drivers such as management, organizational structures and staff quality on performance.

PROPOSITION AND RESEARCH QUESTIONS

Pozen (1998) describes the performance of investment funds as "Given the dual characteristics of investment opportunities and normal preferences of their clients, money managers should try to construct portfolios with the highest return for any given risk level or, in other words, the lowest risk for any given return". In order to attract and retain investors investing in mutual funds, fund managers must keep monitoring their performance on a daily basis to ensure everything is on track. Because there are several participants in the investment fund industry, such as investors, sponsors and custodians, our research is conducted at the level of fund management company. In other words, we intend to provide an exploratory investigation into performance drivers from a management perspective and not from the investors' perspective.

The findings documented in the literature lead us naturally to propose a tentative managerial framework of possible drivers of investment funds' performance. Within this framework, a coherent set of internal and external factors such as management, staff quality, organizational structure, market situation and government policy, influence the overall performance. In other words, performance is a function of this coherent set of factors. This proposition can be presented as follows:

Investment fund performance

$= \mathbf{f}$ **(internal factors, external factors, ε)**
$= \mathbf{f}$ **(management, staff quality, organizational structure, market situation, government policy, ε)**

This proposition can be broken down into several research questions:

Research question 1. What are the main drivers of the performance of investment funds (internal factors and/or external factors)?

Research question 2. What are the major internal factors that influence the performance of investment funds?

Research question 3. What are the major external factors that influence the performance of investment funds?

Organizational theories argue that an organization is an open system affected both by its external and internal environments (Gordon, 1990). In the case of investment funds, the internal factors are those factors that influence the performance decision-making process (e.g. management, staff quality, organizational structure.). External factors are factors that influence the environment of investment funds (market situation, government policy, science and technology development, etc.).

In order to answer the research questions and to reveal the driving forces behind Chinese investment funds' performance and to prove the proposition as set out earlier, a questionnaire was used as a means to discover what creates success in investment funds. To further test the proposition, multiple regression analyses were also conducted. We believe that the study helps understand these issues. The subjects of our study are Chinese securities investment funds that were established after March 1998, and American domestic hybrid funds that were ranked as four or five stars by Morningstar[3]. It is believed that the results of the investigation are both representative and persuasive and will provide valuable insights into understanding the driving forces of the performance of Chinese investment funds, that is, the ingredients of their success.

RESEARCH METHOD

Between the end of June and the end of October 2000 identical questionnaires were sent to both Chinese and American fund managers. The reason for choosing American mutual funds is because they are the leaders in the investment fund industry in terms of market capitalization and numbers of funds under management. Chinese investment funds are limited in number, short of history and have evolved from a closed and developing capital market characterized by small capitalization and high volatility (Cao, 2001). Through comparison, we are able to identify which drivers of Chinese investment funds are common with American mutual funds, and which drivers are unique. So the results are assumed to be more inspirational and persuasive to gain a better understanding of the drivers of Chinese investment funds' performance.

Because all the new securities investment funds in China are domestic hybrid funds, the chosen American counterparts are all the four and five stars domestic hybrid funds to increase comparability. There are two reasons to choose only four and five stars funds, one is because not all the funds have detailed information for contact which hindered us to send questionnaires; second, an investigation of performance drivers of these top funds is expected to provide positive guidelines from which Chinese investment funds can draw inspiration.

At the end of May 2000, there were 67 American domestic hybrid funds ranked with four or five stars by Morningstar, belonging to 43 fund management companies. Since some funds were managed by the same fund managers, we decided to send out the questionnaires based on the numbers of fund managers and not on the numbers of funds. The answers are assumed to be the same for those funds managed by the same fund managers. The actual operational populations in the survey are sixty funds managed by twenty-four fund managers, of which twelve fund managers (representing thirty funds) provided answers – a response rate of 50%.

As of July 2000, there were ten fund management companies in China under which 28 investment funds were managed. All of these 28 investment funds are closed-end funds with a maturity of fifteen years. They are so-called "new" type securities investment funds as opposed to "old" funds set up before November 1997 (see Appendix).

The questionnaires were sent to all ten fund management companies of which nine responded. The questionnaires were answered by fourteen fund managers, covering fourteen funds, again an effective response rate of 50%.

The questionnaire was laid out in the following way: in the first part we collected basic information such as age, education level and investment style. In the second part we asked fund managers to identify the main determinants of fund performance, whether it is internal or external factors. Then we went on to ask fund managers to identify the main internal as well as external drivers. Finally we invited them to indicate what are the major barriers to good performance and suggestions to improve the performance.

Following the questionnaire survey, we ran multiple regression analyses to search for statistically significant relationships between fund performance and the drivers.

We used the Sharpe ratio to represent the performance of funds (regressand). The Sharpe ratio is essentially the excess return adjusted by the portfolio's total risk. The reason for choosing the Sharpe ratio is not only because it is one of the most widely applied performance indicators both by academics and practitioners all over the world, but also because this indicator is suitable for use with Chinese investment funds (Cao, 2001). Cao stated that the Sharpe ratio is preferable to the Treynor ratio as it is immune to the criticism of using the standard deviation as a measure of risk and does not rely on the validity of the Capital Asset Pricing Model (CAPM) or the identification of a market model

322 X. Q. CAO AND J. BILDERBEEK

or APT (Sharpe, 1998). The independent variables (regressors) are the internal and external factors found from the questionnaire survey.

RESULTS (MAIN FINDINGS)

Regarding research question 1, all of the Chinese respondents chose internal factors as the main determinants of a fund's performance. Among the American respondents, 90% chose internal factors as the main determinant, while the other 10% tended to believe that performance is determined by external factors. With regard to research questions 2 and 3, we asked fund managers to prioritise factors we provided by ordering the three they considered most important. The results are presented in Table 1. The numbers in the parentheses are the total scores each factor received. We assigned a score of 4 to the factor ranked as the most important, 3 to the second ranked factor, a score of 2 to the third ranked factor and a score of 1 to factors that were not ranked; then we summed these scores together to get the overall importance of each factor.

At first glance we see that Chinese fund managers chose 'management' as the most important factor with a score of 42, followed by 'organizational structure', 'staff quality', 'research' and 'risk management'. By the Americans,

Table 1. Comparison of Internal and External Factors between Chinese and American Fund Managers.

	Chinese Fund Managers	American Fund Managers
Main internal drivers	1. Management (42)[a]	1. Management (99)
	2. Staff quality (36)	2. Research (81)
	3. Organisation[b] (27)	3. Staff quality (59)
	4. Research (25)	4. Organisation (44)
	5. Risk manag. (23)	5. Risk manag. (43)
Main external drivers	1. Govern. (44)	1. Market (102)
	2. Market (43)	2. Science (56)
	3. Bankin. (23)	3. Bankin. (51)
	4. Customer (19)	4. Govern. (46)
	5. Science (18)	5. Customer (41)
	6. Sponso. (17)	6. Culture (37)
	7. Others (17)	7. Sponso. (35)

[a] The figures in the parenthesis are the scores for each factor.
[b] Hereafter we abbreviate "organizational structure" to "Organization", "Risk management" to "Risk manag.", "Government policy" to "Govern.", "Market situation" to "Market", "Science and technology development" to "Science", "Relationship with sponsors" to "Sponso." And "Banking" to "Bankin."

'management' was also ranked as the most important factor; with a score of 99, followed by 'research', 'staff quality', 'organisational structure' and 'risk management'. However, such intuitive feeling can sometimes be misleading, and we conducted further cluster analysis in order to obtain more robust ranking results and to determine the most important factor driving the performance of investment funds. By using a four-cluster solution, it was found that management is the most important factor in determining the performance of investment funds. The second most important factor is organizational structure according to Chinese fund managers and research according to American fund managers. Both Chinese and American fund managers chose staff quality as the third most important factor. The fourth most important factor includes research and risk management according to Chinese fund managers and risk management and organisational structure according to American fund managers. The new grouping is represented in Table 2.

Although according to the opinions of most fund managers, fund performance is less affected by external factors than internal factors, their indirect influences on the external environment of mutual funds should not be ignored. The ranking of these external factors is also shown in Table 1. 'Market situation' represents the condition of the securities market in general, and it received a total score of 102 from American fund managers, and was seen as far more important than the other factors. In comparison government policy was ranked as the most important factor in determining the performance of Chinese investment funds. It received a score of 44 and was closely followed by the market situation with 43. The third to seventh most important factors received much lower scores. A five-cluster solution approach provides further clarity of the actual grouping and is shown in Table 3.

To see whether the differences in the opinions on these internal and external factors between the Chinese and the American fund managers are statistically significant or not, we used a nonparametric technique, the Mann-Whitney test. The results are presented in Table 4 for internal factors and in Table 5 for external factors.

Table 2.   Cluster Analyses of Internal Factors.

Clusters	Chinese investment funds	American mutual funds
1	Management	Management
2	Organization	Research
3	Staff quality	Staff quality
4	Research, risk manag.	Risk manag., Organisation

Table 3. Cluster Analyses of External Factors.

Clusters	Chinese investment funds	American mutual funds
1	Govern.	Market
2	Market	Science
3	Bankin.	Bankin.
4	Customer	Customer
5	Science, Sponso., and Others	Govern.

Table 4. Mann-Whitney Test for Sharpe Ratio and Internal Factors Between Chinese and American Investment Funds.

	Mann-Whiteney U	Z-score	Asymp. Sig. (2-tailed)
Sharpe	169,00	−1,03	0,30
Management	179,00	−0,86	0,39
Staff quality	146,50	−0,17	0,09+
Organization	184,00	−0,81	0,41
Risk manag.	169,00	−1,19	0,23
Research	118,50	−2,58	0,01*

$+ p < 0.10$
$* p < 0.05$

Table 5. Mann-Whitney Test for Sharpe Ratios and External Factors Between Chinese and American Investment Funds.

	Mann-Whitney U	Z-score	Asymp. Sig. (2-tailed)
Sharpe	169,00	−1,03	0,30
Market	144,50	−1,82	0,07+
Science	144,00	−1,85	0,07+
Bankin.	205,00	−0,15	0,88
Govern.	62,00	−3,95	0,00***
Customer	196,50	−0,54	0,59
Culture	175,00	−1,60	0,11
Sponso.	195,00	−1,46	0,68
Others	201,00	−0,41	0,14

$+ P < 0.10$
$*** P < 0.001$

From Table 4, we can see that the difference in opinions on research is significant at the 5% level and for staff quality is significant at the 10% level. Opinions on management, organizational structure and risk management are not significantly different which indicates similar views on these factors. From Table 5, we can see that the difference in opinions on government policy is significant at the 1% level, and on market situation and on science and technology development are significant at the 10% level. Opinions on other factors can be considered as similar.

To investigate further the opinions on management, we inspected the whole portfolio management process and found that most of the fund managers (85.7% Chinese and 83.3% American fund managers) are in favour of an active management style.

The average education level of the Chinese fund managers is quite high, over 55% of them have a Masters or Ph.D. degree. They are very young (average age 29.7) compared with other industries. For the data collected, there is no clear correlation between the investment styles of the funds and the ages of fund managers and their education level. However, there is a relationship between investment style and the fund managers' views of market efficiency and their investment strategies. The majority of Chinese fund managers of aggressive growth, growth, growth and income growth funds tend to believe that the capital market is only weak form efficient, or even inefficient, and therefore their investment strategies are asset allocation and market timing. Fund managers of balanced funds tended to believe the market was efficient, and therefore the investment strategy is indexing.

On the American side, the average age (43.8) of American fund managers is much higher than that of Chinese fund managers. There is no clear difference between the education levels of Chinese and American fund managers. Nor is there any clear relationship between the style of investment funds and the age and education level of American fund managers. The majority (two-thirds) of the fund managers believe the market is semi-strong form efficient. This is in line with research findings by many academics (e.g. Fama et al., 1969; Fama, 1991). However, their corresponding investment strategies seem inconsistent with their views on market efficiency; 83.3% of them are in favour of an active management style.

In terms of research activities, both Chinese and American fund managers concentrate on fundamental analysis.

As another driver of performance, organisational structure seems also to have impact on performance. All the Chinese fund managers were in favour of the existing investment committee whereas only 50% of the American fund managers favoured this type of organisational structure; the others recommended less layers in the investment decision-making process thereby streamlining the function of fund managers.

With regard to risk management, we observed from the questionnaire that, apart from diversification, there are no measures that allow Chinese fund managers to control risk, such as the derivatives that are normally adopted by American mutual funds.

To further corroborate the findings we obtained from the survey, we went on to conduct multiple regression analysis in the hope of finding a statistically significant relationship between the internal and external factors and the performance of the new Chinese securities investment funds. The data consists of answers on 14 funds; the reason for choosing funds, instead of fund management companies, is because we can assign to each fund its risk-adjusted return, whereas with a company this cannot be done. The performance of these funds is measured using the risk-adjusted return (Sharpe ratio) from the period January 1st to November 24th 2000.[4] This period includes the majority of funds allowing us to regress fund performance against the internal and external variables. Further, in this period, the distribution of the Sharpe ratios is near normal, unlike in other periods, which in turn means they are the most accurate ones (Cao, 2001).

The descriptive statistics of the internal and external factors as well as the Sharpe ratios are shown in Table 6 and Table 7. From the tables, the Sharpe ratios of the Chinese investment funds range from a low of 0.27 to a high of 0.42 with an average of 0.33. The size of these funds range from 0.5 to 2 billion Yuan.[5]

The regression analyses show that no relationship is found between fund performance (Sharpe ratio) and the internal and external factors since t and F

Table 6.   Descriptive Statistics and Correlations of Sharpe Ratio and Internal Factors of Chinese Investment Funds.[a]

Variable	Mean	s.d.	1	2	3	4	5
1. Sharpe	0.33	0.04					
2. Management	3.00	1.11	−0.00				
3. Staff quality	2.57	1.16	0.18	−0.36			
4. Organization	1.85	1.30	−0.46	−0.22	−0.25		
5. Risk manag.	1.64	0.84	−0.00	−0.41	−0.33	−0.12	
6. Research	1.93	0.99	0.40	−0.07	−0.16	−0.67**	0.15

[a] n=14
** Correlation is significant at $p < 0.01$ level (2-tailed)

values are low. There are several possible reasons why a relationship cannot be found or identified. First, the time interval of the Sharpe ratios is rather short. Although the period we chose includes the most funds, the time span is only ten months despite the fact that Sharpe ratios are the most significant ones compared with other periods. Second, the sample size is too small. There are only 14 funds participating in our questionnaire survey.

To further investigate whether the conclusion drawn by the regression analysis is unique to Chinese investment funds or has generality, we conducted the same analyses for the American funds. Sharpe ratios were obtained from Morningstar.com and they represent three years' trailing records through to December 2000. The descriptive statistics of these internal factors and Sharpe ratios are shown in Table 8.

As can be seen from the table, the Sharpe ratios of these thirty funds range from a high of 0.63 to a low of –0.27 with a mean of 0.22. The sample was comprised of funds with assets under management ranging from 13 million US$ to 12,038 million US$.

A positive relationship is found between Sharpe ratio and management as shown in Fig. 1. The coefficient of management has a t value of 2.66 and a F value of 7.06 at the 5% level, which indicates a statistically significant positive relationship with the investment fund's performance. The R Square is 0.21, which indicates that management explains 21% of the variations in performance of these American domestic hybrid funds. This finding supports the results of the questionnaire.

Table 7. Descriptive Statistics and Correlations of Sharpe Ratio and External Factors of Chinese Investment Funds.[a]

Variable	Mean	s.d.	1	2	3	4	5	6	7	8
1. Sharpe	0.33	0.04								
2. Market	3.07	0.73	–0.32							
3. Govern.	3.14	1.16	0.02	–0.28						
4. Bankin.	1.64	0.93	–0.11	–0.19	0.19					
5. Science	1.28	0.47	–0.37	0.16	0.34	–0.45				
6. Sponso.	1.21	0.80	0.02	–0.42	–0.53	–0.19	–0.18			
7. Customer	1.35	0.84	0.37	–0.05	–0.13	–0.12	–0.29	–0.12		
8. Others	1.21	0.57	0.11	–0.40	–0.39	–0.28	–0.24	0.89	–0.17	
9. Culture	1.00	0.00	b	b	b	b	b	b	b	b

[a] $N = 14$
[b] Cannot be computed because the variable is constant
** Correlation is significant at $p < 0.01$ (2-tailed)

Table 8. Descriptive Statistics and Correlations of Sharpe Ratio and Internal Factors of American Mutual Funds.[a]

Variable	Mean	s.d.	1	2	3	4	5
1. Sharpe	0.22	0.24					
2. Management	3.27	0.98	0.45*				
3. Research	2.77	0.86	0.08	−0.42*			
4. Staff	1.97	1.06	−0.08	−0.09	−0.35		
5. Organization	1.47	0.94	−0.39*	−0.63[c]	0.18	−0.40*	
6. Risk Manag.	1.37	0.72	−0.16	0.19	−0.47**	−0.21	−0.11

[a] N = 30
* Correlation is significant at $P < 0.05$ level (2-tailed)
** Correlation is significant at $P < 0.01$ level (2-tailed)

Sharpe = −0.14 + 0.11 * Management + ε
$\quad$ **(−0.99)** $\quad$ **(2.66)**

$R^2 = 0.21$ $\qquad\qquad$ **F = 7.06**

Fig, 1. Management as One of the Performance Drivers of American Mutual Fund.

Objectively speaking, there is still room to enhance the reliability of this finding as it is limited by several reasons. Firstly, the sample size is still not that large (N = 30) although it is a significant improvement on the Chinese investment funds (N = 14). Secondly, the Sharpe ratios could be obtained for an even longer observation interval (e.g. five years or ten years). Since not all the funds have a detailed history of more than five years, so we were forced to choose three years in which all the funds had a track record. Thirdly, other variables that may drive performance have not been identified. Nevertheless, there is an important message: good management leads to good performance. More importantly, it provides clues for Chinese investment funds that are in search of performance drivers.

The unexplained element of performance prompts us to consider the relationship between the Sharpe ratio and external factors using a similar analysis. The Sharpe ratios had been regressed against the external factors and the descriptive statistics of the external factors are summarised in Table 9.

A relationship is observed between the Sharpe ratio and the market situation, which is summarized in Fig. 2.

Table 9. Descriptive Statistics and Correlations of Sharpe Ratio and External Factors of American Mutual Funds.[a]

Variable	Mean	s.d.	1	2	3	4	5	6	7	8
1. Sharpe	0.22	0.24								
2. Market	3.43	0.82	0.36*							
3. Science	1.87	1.00	0.02	0.19						
4. Bankin.	1.70	0.95	0.19	0.39*	−0.22					
5. Govern.	1.53	0.63	−0.02	0.21	0.23	−0.07				
6. Customer	1.37	0.96	−0.08	−0.12	−0.34	−0.18	0.00			
7. Culture	1.27	0.69	−0.24	0.03	−0.09	−0.19	−0.10	−0.15		
8. Others	1.17	0.59	0.07	−0.01	−0.25	−0.21	−0.25	0.01	0.31	
9. Sponso.	1.00	0.00	[b]	[b]	[b]	[b]	[b]	[b]	[b]	[b]

[a] N = 30
[b] Cannot be computed because the variable is constant
* Correlation is significant at $P < 0.05$ level

Sharpe = −0.15 + 0.11 * Market + ε
    (−0.81)   (2.01)

R² = 0.13   F=4.29

Fig. 2. The Market Situation as One of the Performance Drivers of American Mutual Funds.

The value of R Square indicates that about 13% of the variation in funds' performance among the observations can be explained by one of the external factors, the securities market situation. Despite the fact that 83.3% of the American fund managers considered internal factors to be the main determinant of their funds' performance, their performance is significantly also influenced by external factors as we anticipated. We can at least perceive that both internal and external factors exert influence on funds' performance as discovered by Fama (1972).

To prove it statistically, we added the market as another driver, alongside the five internal factors, to the regression model (see Fig. 3), and the result is encouraging, the market and management together account for 33% of the variations in funds' performance as indicated by R square. This is a relatively low R square when compared with what is commonly found in time-series work, but R square values tend to be low in cross-section studies (Mirer, 1983). The F value of this model is 6.55 and is significant at the 5% level. To see

Sharpe = –0.49 + 0.11 * Management + 0.10 * Market + ε
               (–2.4)   (2.8)   (2.2)

$R^2 = 0.33$ $F = 6.55$

Fig. 3.   Management and Market as Two of the Performance Drivers of
American Mutual Funds.

whether there is any collinearity among these factors, we studied the tolerance
statistic (it was 1) and the condition index. Apparently, no multi-collinearity is
present.

Our research questions are thus answered, and our overall findings appear to
support the proposition set out at the beginning of the paper albeit with some
modifications, that is, management and market situation are added to the model
as two statistically significant variables in determining American mutual funds'
performance whereas staff quality, organisational structure etc. (see Table 1)
are now excluded. The empirically improved proposition for drivers of the
performance of American investment funds is:

Investment fund performance = f (management, market, ε)

DISCUSSION AND CONCLUSIONS

The summaries of the questionnaire and regression analyses presented above
paint a clear picture for Chinese investment funds that wish to pursue excellence.
The analysis highlights the current thinking of Chinese fund managers and
indicates what they can learn from American mutual funds as the development
of Chinese investment funds progresses. These findings deserve both practical
and academic attention since they have implications for improving the performance of Chinese investment funds. Our proposed performance driver model
is remarkably simple, and its interpretation is therefore straightforward. A
discussion on, and summary of, these findings are highlighted below:

Management

Among the various internal factors that influence the performance of investment
funds, both Chinese and American fund managers selected management as
the most prominent factor. The reason for this can be explained by the importance and implications attached to management as essentials in the success of

investment funds. Bilderbeek (1980) described the ultimate managerial function as "to let achieve systems consisting of human talents and material means, those goals which are determining their societal raison d'être". The implication of this definition is that an essential function and purpose of having managers in an organisation is to ensure that all the activities undertaken contribute towards the attainment of the overall aims or objectives.

In the context of investment funds, the implication on management is two fold. One relates to personnel management and the other to portfolio management. Personnel management involves leadership, decision-making and motivation, etc., which covers the management of the portfolio managers themselves by the top management (such as board or the investment committee) in order to reach goal congruency. A team of fund managers, each concerned with their own specialist activities, need to act together in a managerial role to co-ordinate the results of their work into a coherent set of outcomes. The style adopted by top management exerts substantial influence over the whole control process of the investment funds. Moreover, management style is influenced by the manager's background and personality (Anthony, 1998).

Portfolio management is the process by which money is managed (Sharpe, 1998). It involves the whole process of dealing with securities including setting investment policies, security analysis, portfolio construction, portfolio revision, and performance evaluation. From the survey, the majority of fund managers prefer active management; which can be interpreted as a strategy that seeks to change investment proportions and/or assets in the belief that profits can be made (Jones, 1994). It seems that the majority of fund managers do not act as if they believe the securities market to be efficient. It is a paradox that American fund managers adopt an active management style while still believing that the stock market is semi-strong form efficient. This phenomenon deserves further research.

Other Internal Factors

Alongside management, other drivers identified from the questionnaire should be kept in mind although no statistically significant relationship was found between them and the performance. There are two possible explanations. Firstly, because of the limitations of regression analysis as discussed before, especially with a small sample size, statistically significant relationships could still exist. An insignificant coefficient of a variable does not necessarily mean it has no importance (Mirer, 1983). Secondly, internal drivers such as staff quality, research, and organisational structure can be interpreted as a set of underlying elements of management. Management provides the foundations for performance, which leads to improved staff quality, research activity, organisational structure, etc.

Although these factors may not influence performance directly, they are derived from the quality of management which performance does depend on.

In identifying the second most important driver from the cluster analysis, the Chinese fund managers chose organizational structure whereas the American fund managers chose research. The reason that Chinese fund managers chose organisational structure is because of the perceived importance of an investment committee. Most of them support the existence of an investment committee despite the fact that many American investment funds retrench their organisational structure in a more efficient way. Such American funds usually employ only a few security analysts as the fund managers also act as analysts. Furthermore, their decision-making process is streamlined by avoiding an investment committee, and by giving fund managers considerable discretion to research securities and to construct portfolios. The organisational structure plays a minor role in this rather efficient market. Given the fact that Chinese investment funds are at an early stage of development, investment committee play important and critical roles in the decision-making process unlike in many American mutual funds.

Staff quality can be interpreted as fund managers' investment experiences, professional ethics, etc. Since a manager's own abilities and attitudes are perhaps the most important factors affecting his decision-making. This is not only true for American mutual funds, but also for Chinese investment funds. As we have found from the survey, Chinese fund managers are relatively young and their education level is quite high. However, since Chinese investment funds have grown out of a socialist market economic environment with less than ten years history, fund managers have little experience to draw on, insufficient historical data to support decision-making, and few lessons to learn from. There is a strong need for qualified fund managers who deeply understand the implications of Modern Portfolio Theory (MPT) and other investment principles. A variety of techniques and computer software to assess and control the performance of investment funds that are available in developed countries are not obtainable in China. Fund managers are confronted with great challenges in trying to employ Modern Portfolio Theory both theoretically and empirically to guide their investment strategies and decision-making. American mutual funds are much more mature and well developed, and their focus has shifted more to the research side including fundamental analysis. They also emphasise the quality of their fund managers, since they are the engineers of investment management. Although research was not chosen as the second most important factor by Chinese fund managers, we expect that as investment funds develop, the market matures, and efficiency increases, more attention will be gradually placed on the research side in China.

Risk management has different implications for Chinese investment funds and for American mutual funds. For American mutual funds, risk management is an inseparable element of portfolio management and there are various techniques that can be applied. In China, because of the different nature and implications of the risks involved (Cao, 2001) and the lack of adequate methods to control risk, risk management has not yet received sufficient attention by policy makers and fund managers, and therefore needs to be encouraged.

External Drivers

A final and interesting point is that although the majority of fund managers tend to believe that performance is determined by internal factors, statistics show that external factors do indeed influence overall performance. Funds are not immune to their external environment. With Chinese investment funds, government policy is an important external factor. It is apparent that despite the importance of the market situation, the impact of government policy on the performance of Chinese investment funds is substantial and therefore should not be overlooked. This is very much a Chinese characteristic; it is commonplace in China for the market to be overridden by government policies (Bo, 1999). Both government policies and market situation play substantial roles in influencing fund managers' decisions and their success.

CONCLUSIONS

It is likely that the different opinions on the various factors found in the survey occur for two reasons. Firstly, the circumstances are different. Chinese investment funds come into being and developed in a so-called socialist market economic environment, while American mutual funds are backed by a well-developed market economy. The transition of the economic system in China is less transparent, and will influence the operation and performance of Chinese investment funds. Unlike their American counterparts, the Chinese stock market is strongly characterised by a policy-driven mechanism; the objective of a market-driven mechanism is still a very long way off. Secondly, because of this system difference, and the brief history of fund development, strong management, high quality fund managers and centralised organisational structure are essentials in order to strengthen the performance of Chinese investment funds.

The similarities and differences between internal and external drivers identified by Chinese and American fund managers have profound implications for Chinese fund managers in pursuit of excellence. As an emerging financial instrument in a young capital market, Chinese investment funds have a long and challenging way to go. Despite the differences in the two countries systems, patterns of economy, nature of the stock markets and the stage of fund development, the road to success is paved by the same material; that is, effective and efficient management. External factors such as government policy and the situation of the securities market affect the performance of Chinese investment funds to some extent. It should be noted that progress in the development of Chinese investment funds is dynamic. As the market becomes more mature and efficient, the various mechanisms will improve, and become more perfect, the gap between Chinese and American mutual funds will be narrowed and may eventually vanish.

ACKNOWLEDGMENTS

The authors would like to thank all the Chinese and American fund managers who participated in the questionnaire survey for their sincere support and valuable insights. Without their enthusiastic involvement, this paper would have never come into being. We are also grateful for the helpful comments from Beate van der Heijden, Fons Quix, Frans Houwling, Marc Wouters, Rien Steen, Roel Schuring and Sander van Triest.

NOTES

1. On November 14, 1997, the Chinese Securities Regulatory Commission (CSRC) promulgated "The Interim Measures for the Management of Securities Investment Funds". Investment funds established before this date are considered to be "old" funds, and after this date "new" funds.
2. Market situation refers to the condition of the securities market in general.
3. The definition of star rating can be found at http://www.Morningstar.com.
4. The performance evaluation of these Chinese investment funds is contained in working paper by Cao (2001). The Sharpe ratios are the most reliable in this period because their distributions are near normal as requested by the model.
5. 1 US$ = 8.3 Yuan.

REFERENCES

Anthony, R. N., & Govinarajan, V. (1998). *Management Control Systems*. U.S.A.: McGraw-Hill.
Ambachtsheer, K. P. A., & Scheibelhut T. (1997). *Good Governance Matters Most*. The Netherlands: KPA Advisory Services Ltd.
Bilderbeek, J. (1980). Financiering in het Kubische Stelsel. Inauguration paper. The Netherlands: Enschede.

Bo, T. (1999). *The Adaptability analysis of Investment Theories and Strategies.* Beijing, P.R.China: Economy and Management Press.

Cao, X., & Bilderbeek, J. (2001). Performance measurement of Chinese investment funds. *Investment and Securities, 8,* 119–128.

Cao, X., & Esman, M. (2001). Evaluating the Performance of Chinese Investment Funds. Working paper. The Netherlands: Enschede.

Carhart, M. M. (1997). On Persistence in Mutual Fund Performance. *Journal of Finance, 52,* 57–82.

Chan, L., Chen, H., & Lakonishok, J. (1999). On Mutual Fund Investment Styles. Working paper, U.S.A.

Chan, L., Jegadeesh, N., & Lakonishok, J. (1996). Momentum Strategies. *Journal of Finance, 52,* 1681–1714.

Chen, J. (1999). Influences of New IPO Strategies on the Performance of Chinese Investment Funds. http://www.cs.co.cn/enp/fund/yanjiu86.htm

Chevalier, J., & Ellison, G. (1999). Are Some Mutual Funds Managers Better than Others? Cross-sectional Patterns in Behaviour and Performance. *Journal of Finance, 3,* 875–899.

Chevalier, J., & Ellison, G. (1999). Career Concerns of Mutual Fund managers. *Quarterly Journal of Economics, 114*(2) ,389–432.

Chevalier, J., & Ellison, G. (1997). Risk Taking by Mutual Funds as a Response to Incentives. *Journal of Politics Economics, 105*(6) 1167–1200.

Dai, Z. (2000). Re-discussion of IPO Contribution to the Performance of Chinese Investment Funds. http://www.cs.com.cn/enp/fund/yanjiu100.htm

Daniel, K., Grinblatt, M., Titman, S., & Wermers, R. (1997). Measuring Mutual Fund Performance with Characteristic-based Benchmark. *Journal of Finance, 3,* 1035–1058.

Fama, E. F., Fisher, L., Jensen, M. C., & Roll, R. (1969). The Adjustment of Stock Prices to New Information. *International Economic Review, 10,* 1–21.

Fama, E. F. (1972). Components of Investment Performance. *Journal of Finance, 3,* 551–567.

Fama, E. F. (1991). Efficient Capital Markets: II. *Journal of Finance, 46,* 1575–1617.

Fama, E. F., & French, K. R. (1993). Common Risk Factors in the Returns on Stocks and Bonds. *Journal of Financial Economics, 33,* 3–56.

Fama, E. F., & French, K. R. (1996). Multifactor Explanations of Asset Pricing Anomalies. *Journal of Finance, 51,* 55–84.

Gordon, J. R., Mondy, R. W., Sharplin, A., & Premeaux, S. R. (1990). *Management and Organisational Behaviour.* U.S.A.: Allyn and Bacon.

Grant, D. (1977). Portfolio Performance and the "Cost" of Timing Decisions. *Journal of Finance, 3,* 837–846.

Jegadeesh, N., & Titman, S. (1993). Returns to Buying Winners and Selling Losers: Implications for Stock Market Efficiency. *Journal of Finance, 48,* 65–91.

Jones, C. P. (1994). *Investments.* U.S.A.: John Wiley & Sons, Inc.

GuangFa Securities (1999). Research Centre of GuanFa Securities. Excellent Fund Managers are the Soul of Chinese Investment Funds. http://www.securitiestimes.com.cn/199907/13/ztyi.

Li, J. (1998). A Brief Discussion on Management of Fund Management Companies in China. http://www.cs.com.cn/enp/fund/yanjiu36.htm

Lu, Y. (1999). An Idea about How to Improve the Performance of Chinese Investment Funds. http://www.cs.com.cn/enp/fund/yanjiu75.htm

Otten, R. (2000). Ranking German Mutual Funds: The LIFE-index. Working paper. Maastricht, The Netherlands: Maastricht University.

Mirer, T. W. (1983). *Economic Statistics and Econometrics.* U.S.A.: Macmillan Publishing Co., Inc.

Pozen, R. C. (1998). *The Mutual Fund Business*. London, England: The MIT Press.
Ross, S. A. (1976). The Arbitrage Theory of Capital Asset Pricing. *The Journal of Economic Theory*, *13*, 343–362.
Sharpe, W. F. (1964). Capital Asset Prices: A Theory of Market Equilibrium Under Conditions of Risk. *Journal of Finance*, *19*, 425–442.
Sharpe, W. F. (1998). *Investments*. U.S.A.: Prentice-Hall International Inc.
Kon, S. J., & Jen, F. C. (1979). The Investment Performance of Mutual Funds: An Empirical Investigation of Timing, Selectivity, and Market Efficiency. *Journal of Business*, *2*, 263–289.
Treynor, J. L. (1965). How to Rate Management of Investment Funds. *Harvard Business Review*, *1*, 63–75.

APPENDIX

Overview of Chinese Securities Investment Funds.

Fund Management Companies	Name of Fund (Code)	Inception (Date)	Scale (Yuan)	Custodian
China Southern Fund Management Co., Ltd	Kaiyuan (4688)	March 27th 1998	2 Billion	Industrial and Commercial Bank of China
	Tianyuan (4698)	August 25th 1999	3 billion	Industrial and Commercial Bank of China
	Jinyuan (500010)	March 28th 2000	0.5 billion	Industrial and Commercial Bank of China
China Guotai Fund Management Co., Ltd	Jintai (500001)	March 27th 1998	2.0 billion	Industrial and Commercial Bank of China
	Jinxin (500011)	October 10th 1999	3 billion	China Construction Bank
	Zhujiang (4703)	April, 26th 2000	0.5 billion	China Construction Bank
Huaxia Fund Management Co., Ltd	Xinhua (500008)	April 28th. 1998	2.0 billion	China Construction Bank
	Xinhe (500018)	July 14th 1999	3.0 billion	China Construction Bank
	Xinke (4708)	April 8th 2000	0.5 billion	China Construction Bank

APPENDIX Continued.

Fund Management Companies	Name of Fund (Code)	Inception (Date)	Scale (Yuan)	Custodian
	Anxin (500003)	June 22nd 1998	2.0 billion	Industrial and Commercial Bank of China
Huaan Fund Management Co., Ltd	Anshun (500009)	June 15th 1999	3.0 billion	Bank of Communications
	Yuyang (500006)	July 25th 1998	2.0 billion	Agriculture Bank of China
	Yulong (4692)	June 15th 1999	3.0 billion	Agriculture Bank of China
Boshi Fund Management Co., Ltd	Yuyuan (500016)	November 12th 1999	1.5 billion	Industrial and Commercial Bank of China
	Yuze (4705)	March 27th 20000.	5 billion	Industrial and Commercial Bank of China
	Yuhua (4696)	November 10th 1999	0.5 billion	Transportation bank
	Puhui (4689)	June 1st 1999	2.0 billion	Bank of Communications
Penghua Fund Management Co., Ltd	Pufeng (4693)	July 14th 1999	3.0 billion	Industrial and Commercial Bank of China
Harvest Fund Management Co., Ltd	Taihe (500002)	April 8th 1999	2.0 billion	China Construction Bank

APPENDIX Continued.

Fund Management Companies	Name of Fund (Code)	Inception (Date)	Scale (Yuan)	Custodian
	Tongyi (4690)	April 8th 1999	2.0 billion	Industrial and Commercial Bank of China
Changsheng Fund Management Co., Ltd	Tongsheng (4699)	November 8th 1999	3.0 billion	Bank of China
	Tongzhi (4702)	March 8th 2000	0.5 billion	Bank of China
	Jinghong (4691)	May 4th 1999	2.0 billion	Bank of China
	Jingyang (500007)	November 12th 1999	1.0 billion	Agriculture Bank of China
Da Cheng Fund Management Co., Ltd	Jingho (4695)	November 12th 1999	1.0 billion	Agriculture Bank of China
	Jingfu (4701)	December 30th 1999	3.0 billion	Agriculture Bank of China
Fuguo Fund Management Co., Ltd	Hansheng (500005)	May 5th 1999	2.0 billion	Agriculture Bank of China
	Hanxing (500015)	December 30th 1999	3.0 billion	Bank of Communications

STRATEGY AND FINANCIAL RATIO PERFORMANCE

Mark L. Frigo, Belverd E. Needles, Jr.
and Marian Powers

ABSTRACT

This paper examines the connection between strategy, strategic performance drivers and financial ratios. We examine the strategy, strategic performance drivers and financial ratios of three companies: Dell Computer Corporation (Operational Excellence), Intel Corporation (Product Leadership), and Four Seasons Hotels and Resorts (Customer Intimacy). We also compare their performance with industry averages. The financial performance of Dell, Intel, and Four Seasons clearly reflects the expected performance characteristics of companies that emphasize value-creating strategies of operational excellence, product leadership, and customer intimacy, respectively. Our objective is to develop an approach that can be used for further study.

STRATEGY, VALUE CREATION AND PERFORMANCE MEASURES

How are strategy, value creation and performance measures interrelated? Porter (1996, p. 68) defines strategy as follows: "Strategy is the creation of a unique and valuable position, involving a different set of activities." Strategy is

Performance Measurement and Management Control, Volume 12, pages 341–359.
ISBN: 0-7623-0867-2

fundamentally about choice. Strategic choices relate to the value proposition and activities of an organization to establish sustainable competitive advantage. Strategic choices are fundamental to strategy as described by Porter (1996, p. 77): "Strategy renders choices about what not to do as important as choices about what to do. Indeed, setting limits is another function of leadership. Deciding which target group of customers, varieties, and needs that company should serve is fundamental to developing a strategy." Strategic choices will define the strategy and determine which performance measures as most relevant.

STRATEGY, MARKET LEADERSHIP, PERFORMANCE MEASURES AND VALUE CREATION

How does superior strategy translate to value creation? We selected the three companies representing three strategy categories based on the Discipline of Market Leadership (DML) (Treacy & Wiersema, 1995) as one level of strategy assessment and strategy classification:

(1) Operational Excellence: Dell Computer Corporation
(2) Product Leadership: Intel Corporation
(3) Customer Intimacy: Four Seasons Hotels.

If an organization is truly a "market leader", does financial performance follow? We examine the strategy of three companies using the DML concepts. We then use that strategy description to examine the strategic performance drivers that "fit" the strategy. The DML has been incorporated in the Balanced Scorecard customer value proposition by identifying basic requirements and differentiators for the three disciplines (Kaplan & Norton, *The Strategy-Focused Organization*, 2001, pp. 86–89). This provides part of a strategic foundation for examining the strategic performance measures of an organization. The Balanced Scorecard framework helps us to understand how the strategic non-financial performance measures lead to financial performance. In this study, we present cash financial ratio analysis for the companies that will include: Cash Flow Yield, Cash Return on Assets and Cash Return on Sales.

DISCIPLINE OF MARKET LEADERSHIP

Treacy and Wiersema's Discipline of Market Leadership is based on the premise that a company's focus on one of the three disciplines will be more likely to achieve market leadership. Although the premise of market leadership is focus on one of the three disciplines, we also considered how superior performers use other strategy tenets and activities to reinforce and leverage the primary strategy focus. Here we considered tenets of Return Driven Strategy (Frigo & Litman, 2001; Litman, 2001) that allowed us, for example, to examine how an innovation company would use operational excellence strategies and branding strategies to leverage the innovation strategy for maximum value creation.

Dell Computer Corporation (Treacy & Wiersema, 1995, pp. 36–37) represents a good example of operational excellence. Dell did this not by focusing on the product, but on the value chain, the delivery system, selling directly to the customer and building to order rather than to inventory. This provided a strong competitive advantage relative to inventory performance. Valuechain.dell.com is one of the steps that Dell has taken in moving toward virtual integration. Though the use of Dell's "hub" system and valuechain.dell.com, Dell has been able to reduce inventory holdings from 35 days in 1993 to 6 days in 1999. Dell's "hub" system involves having special storage facilities near its factories. Dell expects suppliers to constantly replenish the hubs and Dell pays for the products as it uses them. Dell's web site allows suppliers to have real-time information about inventory levels at each hub. Michael Dell envisions being able to measure inventory in hours rather than days. Although Dell focuses on operational excellence, it also excels in brand management and innovation that is consistent with its strategic focus.

Intel Corporation (Treacy & Wiersema, 1995, pp. 104–110, 120–121) represents a good example of the innovation discipline. In 1999, Intel invested $3.1 Billion in Research and Development focusing on pushing the edge of computing technology (1999 Annual Report). Intel leads the race to develop the fastest most reliable chips. Currently Intel's P4 chip is the fastest chip on the market. Other innovative chip designs include the 64 bit Merced chip that Intel has co-developed through a strategic partnership with Hewlett Packard as well as the StrongArm embedded processor that Intel developed through a strategic acquisition of Digital Equipment Corporation.

Since product innovation is so important; every aspect of the product design and prototyping phase impacts the end product. Improper chip design increases size and limits the processing power. To combat this, Intel has created a collaborative design process that allows both engineers and production managers to understand every aspect of the component design, feeding off each other to ensure a superior design. These innovative design teams allow Intel to design smaller faster more compact chips.

Although Intel focuses on innovation, it also performs certain aspects of operational excellence and customer intimacy that support and leverage its focus on innovation. In operational excellence one key to Intel's success is its ability to manufacture its chip designs by optimizing the manufacturing process, and then rolling out that process to Intel's other fabs in a process called "Copy Exact." Copy Exact is a major competitive advantage for Intel. Most of Intel's competitors continue to struggle with chip reproduction once their designs are finalized. Also, Intel strives for customer intimacy or branding to leverage it innovation. The Intel brand far surpasses any of their competitors for inspiring trust and confidence. Intel has successfully built the Intel brand through years of delivering the most innovative and reliable chips in the world. Intel successfully leveraged their power in the distribution channel to have the "Intel Inside" logo attached to all PC's containing their products. This amounts to a substantial number of "eyeballs" on the Intel logo everyday. Intel also spends heavily, promoting their products though television, print and Internet advertising. Intel in 1999 spent over $1.7 billion on adverting (1999 Annual Report). Here we see how the supporting operational excellence and branding strategies leverage the innovation discipline for value creation.

According to Treacy and Wiersema (1995, pp. 134–135) the Four Seasons focuses on customer intimacy. Although, the Four Seasons focuses on customer intimacy, it has also excelled in innovation. For example, the Four Seasons was the first hotel company to employ Concierges company-wide in North America. Also, Four Seasons was the first hotel company to provide complimentary newspapers with room service breakfast delivery in North America. In the area of operational excellence, the Four Seasons excels as evidenced by the many hotel and resort honors, including being rated by *Gourmet Magazine* survey of restaurants in North America.

STRATEGIC PERFORMANCE MEASURES

Treacy and Wiersema have suggested that organizations should align their performance measures with the specific type of customer value strategy the firm is focused on (see *CFO Magazine*, April 1995, "What Value-Driven CFO's Do"). Based on three disciplines of market leadership, each organization would focus on somewhat different performance measures. For example, a company focusing on operational excellence, such as Dell Computer, the company would focus on providing reliable products at the best price. This type of organization would focus on price and service performance with the goal of driving down the total delivered cost to the customer. This type of organization would focus on using activity based costing and other techniques. Dell Computer aggressively focuses its processes and performance measures on cost and price reduction ("Lean Machine: How Dell Fine-Tunes Its PC Pricing to Gain Edge in a Slow Market", *The Wall Street Journal*, June 8, 2001, p. 1). For a company focusing on a product leadership strategy, product quality rating and percent of financial performance as indicated by cash flow and the principal determinate of the difference between cash flow ratios and accounting income ratios. If cash flow yield exceeds 1.0 there will be a positive multiplier effect on cash flow performance. Conversely, if cash flow yield is less than 1.0 cash flow performance will suffer. Cash flow yield is also an indicator of a company's ability to manage its receivables, inventories, and payables. Relative decreases in receivables and inventories and increases in payables will enhance cash flow yield. Cash flow yield is an indicator of sustainable cash flow if one-time items such as gains and losses, write-downs, and other adjustments are not present.

Consideration of cash flow yield is also important because cash flow measures of profitability are superior to accounting income measures in comparing companies, especially those from different countries. There are at least three ways in which they are superior. First, cash flow measures tend to neutralize differences in accounting standards. For example, whereas the rules for revenue recognition may vary from country to country, the rules for recognition of cash transactions tend to be the same. Second, cash flow measures tend to nullify the effects of accounting choices. For instance, differences in depreciation methods or inventory valuation methods do not affect cash flows. Third, the effects of conservative income measurement methods prevalent in some countries are overcome. For instance, Sony Corporation, a company that falls in the innovator class, as does Intel, has traditionally reported a very low profit margin in the range of 1.0%. However, when analyzed on the basis of cash flow return on sales, its margins exceed 10.0%, placing it in an excellent range for its industry.

Cash flow yield measures for Dell, Intel, and Four Seasons, compared with the averages for the industry, are shown in Fig. 1. This figure shows that these companies display the characteristics we would expect based on the strategic approach of the company to excellence. For instance, Dell, which is known for operational excellence and efficiency, exceeds Intel and Four Seasons in all three years by a significant margin especially in 1999, and 2000. Its cash flow yield varies from 1.67 to 2.36 with an average of just over 2.0 over the three-year period. Further, Dell's performance on this dimension exceeds the industry average in all three years and the three-year industry average of 1.37 (Three-year industry averages are found in Appendix D) by a substantial margin. Intel's cash flow yield is somewhat lower (1.22 to 1.55 with an average of about 1.4), but still significantly above 1.0, and shows low volatility. The low point of 1.22 would have been about 1.5 if the one-time gain were eliminated. As an innovator, Intel's relatively high expenditures on research and development will depress cash flow yield in comparison to Dell, but its cash flow yield average comfortably exceeds the semi-conductor industry's three-year average of 1.17. Finally, Four Seasons cash flow yield is lower than either Dell or Intel with a

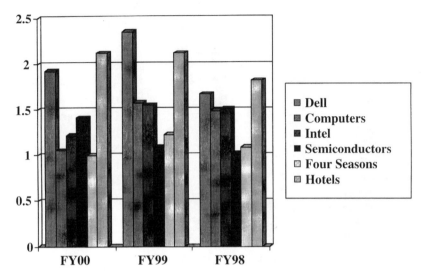

Fig. 1. Performance Driver: Cash Flow Yield.

range of 1.00 to 1.23. This lower cash flow yield for Four Seasons is expected because as a service business it does not have a high level of depreciation and has lower receivables and no inventories to manage. The fact that Four Season's cash flow yield averages about 1.1 or slightly above 1.0 calls into question Four Season's cash generating ability. This conclusion is further reinforced by the fact that its cash flow yield was significantly less than the industry average in all three years. Over the three-year period its cash flow generating ability was only about half the industry average of 2.02.

Two other drivers of financial performance are asset turnover and total debt to assets. Asset turnover is a measure of the ability of a company to use assets to drive revenues. Thus, it is a key factor in converting profit margin and cash return on sales to return on assets and cash flow return on assets. An asset turnover of greater than 1.0 will drive higher return on invested capital. Figure 2 compares the asset turnover for Dell, Intel, and Four seasons, compared with industry averages, for the three-year period. Dell's ability to utilize assets efficiently comes through in this analysis. Its asset turnover range of 2.56 to 3.27 with an average of 2.86 easily exceeds that of Intel and Four Seasons, and also that of the industry which is 1.37 for the three-year period. Dell achieves this efficiently through extreme use of just-in-time inventory management and good receivables management. Intel displays an asset turnover more in line with traditional manufacturers with a range of 0.71 to 1.01 with an average of 0.84

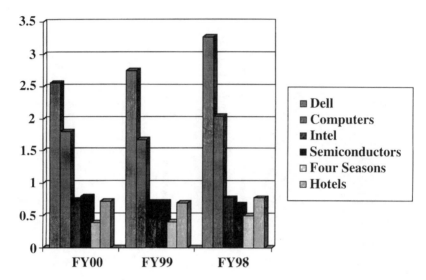

Fig. 2.   Performance Driver: Asset Turnover.

and is less than the industry average of 1.17. Intel's emphasis on innovation, as opposed to efficiency, would lead one to expect that it would not be a standout performer in this category. With an asset turnover significantly less than 1.00 (range 0.31 to 0.53 and an average of 0.47) and also less than the industry average of 0.73, Four Seasons' returns on invested capital is negatively impacted. This low asset turnover derives from the large capital investments relative to competitors that Four Seasons must make in hotel and resort properties to achieve its elite status. To overcome such a low asset turnover Four Seasons needs to charge premium prices to achieve high profit margins.

The second driver of profitability performance is the financial structure of the company as measured by the ratio of total debt to assets and is shown for the three companies in Fig. 3. The financial structure of a company is the major factor that converts return on assets and cash flow return on assets to return on equity and cash flow return on equity. It is not a result of the operating or value-creating strategy of the company but of its financing strategy. Thus, it is included here for completeness and is not directly related to the thesis of the paper relating financial performance and value-creating strategies. Although increasing amounts of debt in relation to asset will increase the returns on stockholders' equity, it also increases the riskiness of the business. Thus, higher returns are associated with higher risk to the owners. Further, the return on equity and cash flow return on equity must be interpreted

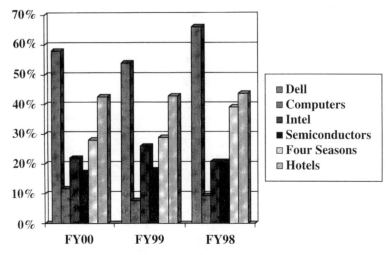

Fig. 3. Performance Driver: Debt/Total Assets.

with care because the denominator, stockholders' equity, is more subject to management manipulation than other denominators such as total assets. For instance, stock buyback plans by many companies in recent years have significantly lower the amount of stockholders' equity and improved profitability measures without necessarily improving the top line revenue and net income growth.

Dell has a consistently high level of debt in relation to assets ranging from 0.54 to 0.70 with an average of 0.62. This is much greater than the computer industry as a whole, which has a three-year average of only 9.48%. In contrast, Intel has a relatively low debt to asset ratio in the range 0.21 to 0.33 and an average of only 0.26, which is much lower than the industry average of 0.72. This is a fairly conservative level of debt and reflects Intel's history of profitability and enables it withstand the abrupt downturns that occur periodically in the semiconductor industry. Four Seasons has steadily decreased its debt in relation to assets over the three-year period reaching a low of 0.28 in 2000, down from a high of 0.39 in 1998 for a three-year average of 0.32. Four Seasons has less debt on average than the industry, which averages 0.43.

CASH FLOW AND PROFITABILITY PERFORMANCE

Turning now to the cash flow and profitability performance of the individual companies, the cash flow ratios for Dell are pictured as graphs in Fig. 4a

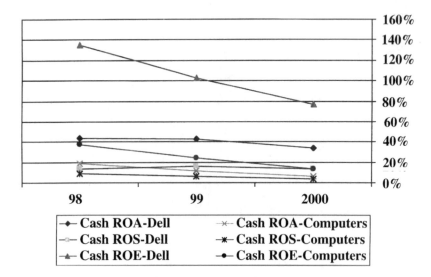

Fig. 4a.   Dell Cash Performance Measures.

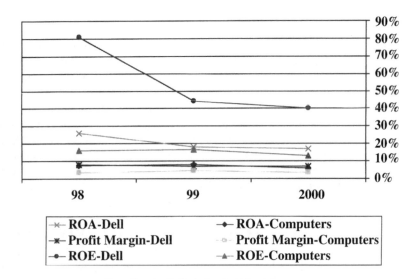

Fig. 4b.   Dell Cash Profitability Measures.

and the profitability ratios are shown in Fig. 4b. In both cases the ratios have been compared with the industry averages. Although there has been a slight downward trend in recent years, the advantage of Dell over its competitors as a highly efficient company can easily be seen in these charts. In Fig. 4a, Dell's strong cash flow yield pushes its cash flow ROS up to the range of 13 to 18%, compared with the industry average of just over 6%. Its robust asset turnover pushes cash flow ROA up to the 40% range, compared with the industry average of about 12%. Profit margins in the computer industry are constantly squeezed. In Fig. 4b, Dell has shown a steady profit margin of only 7 or 8%, about twice as much as the industry average of 4.0%. Low margins are typical of companies that are not product innovators and whose products are more of a commodity. These figures reflect Dell's highly efficient use of assets and support the hypothesis that the company's value-creation strategy is reflected in the company's financial performance. Dell's ROE measures have declined in recent years due to the downtrend in earnings and in debt but still remain at relatively high levels.

Intel's performance, in contrast to Dell, clearly reflects its position as a product innovation and brand leader, as shown in Figs 5a and 5b. Intel has robust cash return on sales of above 35% and a lower cash return on assets of about 28%, the latter due to a relatively low asset turnover. These figures exceed industry averages because of Intel's superior cash flow yield. Intel has very good profit margins ranging from 0.23 to 0.31 with an average 0.26. Intel's superb margins reflect its leadership as a product innovation and brand leader, but the margins have been dampened by low turnovers in recent years. Increases in assets may reflect acquisitions and investments for future performance but Intel is clearly not as efficient as Dell in the area of asset management. As a result, return on asset averaged 22% and cash return on assets 32%, the difference the result of a fairly strong cash flow yield. Overall, these figures support our thesis of the value-creating strategy chosen by Intel as being reflected in its financial performance. Return on equity and cash flow return on equity averaged 30 and 45%, respectively.

Four Seasons as a service company presents another view of above average financial performance, as shown in Figs 6a and 6b. With a cash flow yield that has been declining in recent years to 1.0 in 2000, the company with a cash return on sales of above 30% produces a cash flow ROA of only 0.11 to 0.16 (average 0.14). Further, It's profit margins are strong and similar to those Intel with profit margin in the range of 0.30. However, the need of Four Seasons to provide exceptional facilities for hotel and resort guests has led the company to make substantial investment in property and facilities. As a result its turnover ratios, as noted above, are very low and have dampened its margins to a return

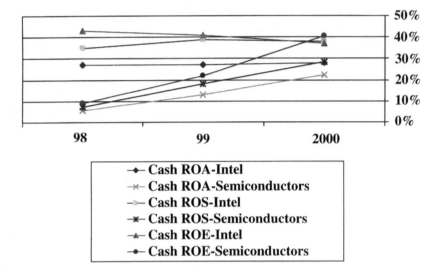

Fig. 5a.   Intel Cash Performance Measures.

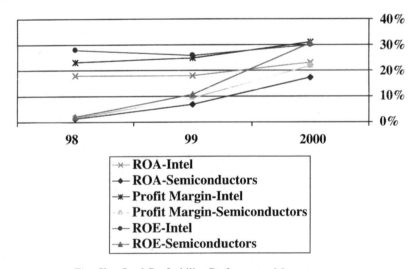

Fig. 5b.   Intel Profitability Performance Measures.

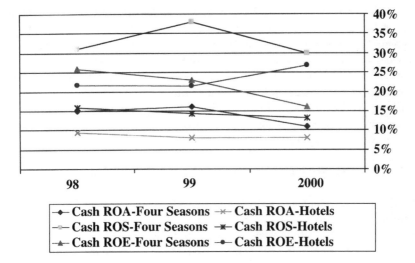

Fig. 6a. Four Seasons Cash Performance Measures.

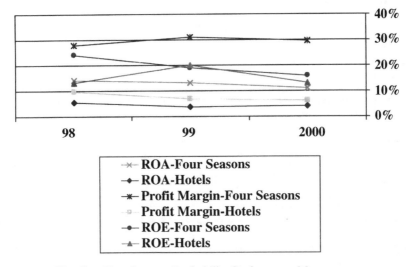

Fig. 6b. Four Seasons Profitability Performance Measures.

on assets to a range of only 0.11 to 0.14 with an average of 0.13. These figures reflect the fact that a company that emphasizes customer intimacy must produce high profit margins (presumably people will pay more for very high quality service) to offset the inefficiencies that are inherent in this type of business. The declining debt in relation to assets for Four Seasons has led to declining return on equity and cash flow return on equity over the five year. Four Seasons, in contrast to both Dell and Intel, appears to be a work in progress as to whether it can make the concept of superior customer intimacy produce superior performance over the long-term.

SUMMARY AND FUTURE RESEARCH

In summary, the financial performance of Dell, Intel, and Four Seasons clearly reflects the expected financial performance characteristics of companies that emphasize value-creating strategies of operational excellence, product leadership, and customer intimacy, respectively. These conclusions would seem to support further development of this approach of benchmarking financial performance to the strategy directions of the company. Further research would include identification of definitive criteria for choosing companies in each of the three strategic categories, pair comparisons with reference companies, refinement of ratio components, study strategic performance drivers' role in cash flow and profitability performance, and statistical analysis of differences in ratios among the three strategies.

REFERENCES

Epstein, M. J., & Birchard, B. (1999). *Counting What Counts: Turning Corporate Accountability to Competitive Advantage*. Reading, Mass.: Perseus Books.

Frigo, M., & Litman, J. (October 4–5, 2001). Strategy, Performance Measures and Value Creation: Research Study of "Great" Consumer Goods and Retail Companies Shows a Common. *Return Driven Strategy* Theme. *Proceedings of the European Institute for Advanced Studies in Management*. Brussels: EIASM.

Kaplan, R. S., & Norton, D. (2001). *The Strategy-Focused Organization: How Balanced Scorecard Companies Thrive in the New Business Environment*, Cambridge: Harvard Business School Press.

Litman, J. (Fall, 2001). Understand, Execute and Communicate Return Driven Strategy to Maximize Your Valuations. *Strategic Investor Relations* (pp. 21–26).

Porter, M. E. (November–December, 1996). What is Strategy? *Harvard Business Review*.

Treacy, M., & Wiersema, F. (1995a). *The Discipline of Market Leaders*. Reading, Mass.: Perseus Books.

Treacy, M., & Wiersema, F. (April, 1995b). What Value-Driven CFO's Do. *CFO Magazine*.

APPENDIX A

Dell Data

	FY00 2/2/01	FY99 1/28/00	FY98 1/29/99
Net cash provided (used) by Operating Activities	$4,195	$3,926	$2,436
Net Income	$2,177	$1,666	$1,460
Depreciation and amortization	$240	$156	$103
Tax benefits on employee stock plans	$929	$ 1,040	$444
Special Charges	$ 105	$0	$0
Gain on sale of investment	($307)	$0	$0
Purchased in-process R&D	$0	$ 194	$0
Other	$109	($24)	$11
Changes in operating working capital	$671	$812	$367
Changes in non-current assets and liabilities	$271	$82	$51
– **Net capital expenditures**	482	397	296
– **Dividends**	0	0	0
CASH FLOW RATIOS			
Free cash flows	**$3,713**	**$3,529**	**$2,140**
Net cash provided (used) by Operating Activities	$4,195	$3,926	$2,436
Net Income	$2,177	$1,666	$1,460
Cash Flow Yield	**1.93**	**2.36**	**1.67**
Net cash provided (used) by Operating Activities	$4,195	$3,926	$2,436
Net Sales	$31,888	$25,265	$18,243
Cash ROS	**13%**	**16%**	**13%**
Net cash provided (used) by Operating Activities	$4,195	$3,926	$2,436
Average Total Assets	$12,453	$9,174	$5,573
Cash ROA	**34%**	**43%**	**44%**
Net cash provided (used) by Operating Activities	$4,195	$3,926	$2,436
Average Stockholders' Equity	$5,465	$3,815	$1,807
Cash ROE	**77%**	**103%**	**135%**
ACCOUNTING INCOME RATIOS			
Net Income	$2,177	$1,666	$1,460
Net Sales	$31,888	$25,265	$18,243
Profit Margin	**7%**	**7%**	**8%**
Net Sales	$31,888	$25,265	$18 243
Average Total Assets	$12,453	$9,174	$5,573
Turnover	**2.56**	**2.75**	**3.27**

APPENDIX A (Continued).

Net Income	$2,177	$1,666	$1,460
Average Total Assets	$12,453	$9,174	$5,573
ROA	17%	18%	26%
Debt	$7,813	$6,163	$4,556
Total Assets	$13,435	$11,471	$6,877
Debt/Total Assets	58%	54%	66%
Net Income	$2,177	$ 1,666	$ 1,460
Average Stockholders' Equity	$5,465	$3,815	$1,807
ROE	40%	44%	81%

APPENDIX B

Intel Data

	FY00 12/30/00	FY99 12/25/99	FY98 12/26/98
Net cash provided (used) by Operating Activities	$12,827	$11,335	$9,191
Net Income	$10,535	$7,314	$6,068
Depreciation	$3,249	$3,186	$2,807
Amortization of goodwill and other costs	$1,586	$411	$0
Purchased in-process research and development	$109	$392	$165
Gains on investments, net	($3,759)	($883)	$0
Gain on assets contributed to Convera	($ 117)	$0	$0
Net loss on retirements of PPE	$ 139	$ 193	$282
Deferred taxes	($130)	($219)	$77
Chances in assets and liabilities			
Change in AR	($384)	$153	($38)
Change in Inventories	($731)	$ 169	$ 167
Change in AP	$978	$79	($180)
Accrued compensation and benefits	$231	$ 127	$ 17
Income taxes payable	($362)	$726	($211)
Tax benefits from employee stock plans	$887	$506	$415
Other	$596	($819)	($378)
– Net capital expenditures	$6,674	$5,450	$6,506
– Dividends	$470	$366	$217

APPENDIX B (Continued).

CASH FLOW RATIOS			
Free cash flows	$5,683	$5,519	$2,468
Net cash provided (used) by Operating Activities	$12,827	$11,335	$9,191
Net Income	$10,535	$7,314	$6,068
Cash Flow Yield	1.22	1.55	1.51
Net cash provided (used) by Operating Activities	$12,827	$11,335	$9,191
Net Sales	$33,726	$29,389	$26,273
Cash ROS	38%	39%	35%
Net cash provided (used) by Operating Activities	$12,827	$11,335	$9,191
Average Total Assets	$45,897	$41,394	$33,909
Cash ROA	28%	27%	27%
Net cash provided (used) by Operating Activities	$12,827	$11,335	$9,191
Average Stockholders' Equity	$34 929	$27.956	$21,336
Cash ROE	37%	41%	43%
ACCOUNTING INCOME RATIOS			
Net Income	$10,535	$7,314	$6,068
Net Sales	$33,726	$29,389	$26,273
Profit Margin	31.2%	24.9%	23.1%
Net Sales	$33,726	$29,389	$26,273
Average Total Assets	$45,897	$41,394	$33,909
Turnover	0.73	0.71	0.77
Net Income	$10,535	$7,314	$6,068
Average Total Assets	$45,897	$41,394	$33,909
ROA	23%	18%	18%
Debt	$10,623	$11,314	$8,094
Total Assets	$47,94	$43,84	$38,938
Debt/Total Assets	22%	26%	21%
Net Income	$10,53	$7,314	$6,068
Average Stockholders' Equity	$34,929	$27,956	$21,336
ROE	30%	26%	28%

APPENDIX C

Four Seasons Data

	FY00 12/31/00	FY99 12/31/99	FY98 12/31/98
Net cash provided (used) by Operating Activities	$102,633	$106,787	$75,798
Net Income	$103,074	$86,497	$69,702
– Net capital expenditures	$111,997	$102,858	$117,158
– Dividends	$3,579	$3,539	$3,502
CASH FLOW RATIOS			
Free cash flows	($12,943)	$390	($44,862)
Net cash provided (used) by Operating Activities	$102,633	$106,787	$75,798
Net Income	$103,074	$86,497	$69,702
Cash Flow Yield	1.00	1.23	1.09
Net cash provided (used) by Operating Activities	$102,633	$106,787	$75,798
Net Sales	$347,507	$277,548	$247,941
Cash ROS	30%	38%	31%
Net cash provided (used) by Operating Activities	$102,633	$106,787	$75,798
Average Total Assets	$908,268	$688,598	$499,134
Cash ROA	11%	16%	15%
Net cash provided (used) by Operating Activities	$102,633	$106,787	$75,798
Average Stockholders' Equity	$646,931	$458,050	$292,458
Cash ROE	16%	23%	26%
ACCOUNTING INCOME RATIOS			
Net Income	$ 103,074	$86,497	$69,702
Net Sales	$347,507	$277,548	$247,941
Profit Margin	29.7%	31.2%	28.1%
Net Sales	$347,507	$277,548	$247,941
Average Total Assets	$908,268	$688,598	$499,134
Turnover	0.38	0.40	0.50
Net Income	$103,074	$86,497	$69,702
Average Total Assets	$908,268	$688,598	$499,134
ROA	11%	13%	14%
Debt	$276,233	$244,442	$214,653
Total Assets	$984,397	$832,139	$545,056
Debt/Total Assets	28%	29%	39%
Net Income	$103,074	$86,497	$69?702
Average Stockholders' Equity	$646,931	$458,050	$292,458
ROE	16%	19%	24%

APPENDIX D

Industry Data

Ratios	Hotels				Computers				Semiconductors			
	Yearly Averages			Historical Averages	Yearly Averages			Historical Averages	Yearly Averages			Historical Averages
	2000	1999	1998		2000	1999	1998		2000	1999	1998	
Cash Flow Yield	2.12	2.12	1.82	**2.02**	1.05	1.58	1.49	**1.37**	1.41	1.09	1.02	**1.17**
Cash ROA	8.15%	8.11%	9.47%	**8.58%**	6.43%	11.65%	18.96%	**12.35%**	22.36%	13.05%	5.40%	**13.60%**
Cash ROS	13.16%	14.21%	15.83%	**14.40%**	3.81%	6.47%	8.59%	**6.29%**	28.27%	18.00%	7.50%	**17.93%**
Cash ROE	26.92%	21.54%	21.59%	**23.35%**	13.68%	24.44%	37.57%	**25.23%**	40.44%	21.81%	9.09%	**23.78%**
Profit Margin	6.14%	6.87%	9.52%	**7.51%**	3.72%	4.69%	3.63%	**4.01%**	21.60%	9.25%	1.60%	**10.82%**
Turnover	0.72	0.69	0.77	**0.73**	1.80	1.67	2.04	**1.84**	0.79	0.71	0.66	**0.72**
ROA	4.02%	3.92%	5.63%	**4.52%**	6.14%	7.92%	7.69%	**7.25%**	17.10%	6.81%	1.23%	**8.38%**
Debt/Total Assets	42.55%	42.74%	43.74%	**43.01%**	11.86%	7.84%	9.46%	**9.72%**	17.09%	18.07%	20.85%	**18.67%**
ROE	13.13%	10.87%	13.09%	**12.36%**	13.11%	18.49%	16.09%	**15.23%**	30.53%	10.86%	2.18%	**14.52%**

HOW DO VENTURE CAPITALISTS HANDLE RISK IN HIGH-TECHNOLOGY VENTURES?

Gavin C. Reid and Julia A. Smith

ABSTRACT

This article presents new empirical evidence, obtained by fieldwork methods, on the risk-handling practices of investors in the U.K. venture capital industry. Its focus is on high-technology firms and the techniques their venture capital backers use for risk management. The active areas of risk management were explored under the headings of risk premia, investment time horizons, and sensitivity analysis. Investors' attitudes to risk were found to imply a coherent 'high to low' risk spectrum. Those factors which may have an impact on risk were also systematically ranked. This, plus further qualitative evidence, supported our use of a decomposition of total risk into 'agency risk', 'business risk' and 'innovation risk'. These three risk classes displayed a ubiquitous capability for embracing most aspects of evidence that the field work produced.

Performance Measurement and Management Control, Volume 12, pages 361–379.
ISBN: 0-7623-0867-2

1. INTRODUCTION

This article reports upon a field work investigation (Sekaran, 1992, Ch. 4) into the risk appraisal methods used in investment contexts, when venture capitalists back high-technology new ventures. The main evidence is based on face-to-face interviews (Oppenheim, 1992, Ch. 6) with eighteen leading U.K. investors in the year 2001. Each investor participated in a semi-structured interview involving eight key issues: risk premia; investment time horizon; sensitivity analysis; expected values; predicted cash flows; financial modelling; decision making; and qualitative risk appraisal.

In this article our focus is on the first three of the above agenda items. Where appropriate, cross-reference is also made to other agenda items. The structure of this article is as follows. First, it provides relevant background about the U.K. venture capital industry. Second, it deals with general problems of risk appraisal in high-technology ventures. Third, it explains the fieldwork methodology adopted. Fourth, and finally, it presents and discusses new results, under the headings risk premia, investment time horizon and sensitivity analysis.

Our main finding is that actions taken by investors under the various agenda headings can all be viewed as risk management strategies. We argue that these can be broken down into three key components: 'agency risk', 'innovation risk', and 'business risk'. The terminology for these risk classes is suggestive of their meanings, which will be more fully treated below. Briefly, agency risk arises from inefficient contracting between the investor as principal and the investee as agent. Innovation risk arises because new technologies are not tried and tested, and both development costs and prospective revenue flows are uncertain, as well as the discovery process itself. Business risk arises because the business 'games' which rivals play with emerging technologies are hard to read, with unpredictable 'plays' being endemic. In moving to the adoption of these categories, we have been influenced by the work of Fiet (1995). However, unlike him, we feel these types of risk are best explored by face-to-face interviews, rather than indirectly.

We find that the three categories of risk which we identified (innovation, agency and business risk) have a pervasive influence on investor conduct towards high-technology ventures in the U.K. The form this influence took was traced by use of evidence under the agenda headings of risk premia, investment time horizon, and sensitivity analysis. It was found that the riskiness of investment types (e.g. seed, MBO etc) could be clearly ranked by investors. These rankings were found to be generally consistent with principles of financial economics. Investors were also asked what factors were most important to their risk appraisals, for given high technology investments. Of a wide range of possible factors, it was found that the most important to risk appraisal could be directly related to our categories of 'agency risk' and 'business risk'. Further, it was found that the time profiles of investments, and their sensitivity to changed assumptions, also could be approached using our three risk categories. Of these, 'innovation risk' was perceived by investors to be particularly high. This perceived high risk exposure engendered various forms of extreme adaptation by investors. These entailed actions like setting very high hurdle rates of return, and deploying radical stress tests of investment models.

2. THE U.K. VENTURE CAPITAL CONTEXT

The background to this empirical work is the U.K. venture capital market. Here, we use the term venture capital in its broad sense, which accords with European practice, VCR Guide (2000, p. 80). More narrowly, particularly in U.S. terminology, venture capital is that part of private equity that is used to finance the launch, early growth and expansion of entrepreneurial firms (Bygrave & Timmons, 1992). We adopt a broader definition, which includes MBO and MBI activity, for example (Wright & Robbie, 1999). Some ten years ago, when one of the authors was first engaged in the analysis of U.K. venture capital markets, it was said by many investors that they avoided investments at the 'leading edge' (Mitchell, Reid & Terry, 1992). They were too risky, and were referred to, in somewhat jocular terms, as the 'bleeding edge'.[1] This picture is now rapidly changing, and U.K. investors are increasingly willing to contemplate more risky investments by stage (e.g. start-up) and by sector (e.g. high-technology).

The U.K. venture capital industry is second only in importance to the USA, and currently is responsible for placing about one half, by value, of European venture capital investment. Almost one half of its investment is in venture capital financing for expansion, which is generally perceived to be a relatively low risk area of venture capital involvement. This perhaps explains the U.S. perception of the U.K. scene as being biased towards the provision of private equity. However, there has been a recent shift of interest in the U.K. to seed corn and start-up activity. Further, the technology field, previously starved of funds, is becoming quite vigorous. In 1999, over £1 billion was invested in U.K. high technology companies, and in that same year a similar amount was also raised, in the form of new funds, for future investment in such companies.

To get a contemporary sense of where the U.K. venture capital industry is now heading, the first step in our research was to engage in relatively unstructured, qualitative field work, Oppenheim (1992, Ch. 4). Here, the goal was simply to go into the field with an open mind, and to get a feel for what were now the main trends, the important issues, and the leading influences. At the earliest opportunity, we contacted two of the major figures in the U.K. venture capital industry: a Director with the 3i Group in London; and the new Chairman of the British Venture Capital Association (BVCA). The BVCA was founded in 1983, with 50 members, and now has over 120 members. BVCA members collectively account for almost all the venture capital finance provided in the U.K. 3i is Europe's leading venture company, having evolved from being the U.K.'s sole provider of venture capital funding (as the ICFC) during the period 1945–1980. It remains the dominant player in the U.K. industry, and currently has a total of over £2 billion in venture capital funds under management.

Meetings were held with senior personnel at 3i and the BVCA at their places of work. Our purpose was to exchange ideas, and to be receptive to suggested approaches that our research might usefully adopt. These initial meetings were helpful in 'setting the scene' concerning recent developments in U.K. venture capital markets. For example, if we are to compare the U.K. to the U.S., we should first be aware that investors' experience is obviously longer and deeper in the U.S. (Wilson, 1985). The Nasdaq, since its introduction as the world's first electronic stock market, has been at the forefront of innovation and is now the fastest growing major stock market in the world. It is home to over half of the companies traded on the primary U.S. markets. As a Director at 3i explained,[2] "Venture capital funds deliver very attractive returns – everyone wants to be in it. It's a matter of supply and demand, and the willingness of some people to take healthier views of risk. In the U.K., we are relatively young in investing in high-technology. The pricing of 3i deals has increased, and returns are coming down. U.S. funds, such as CISCO and Intel, are serious investors in technologies".

The Chairman of the BVCA referred to the history of venture capital investment in the U.K. He stated that, "Until recently, the U.K. venture capital scene has been directed predominantly towards buyouts, and to revitalising British industry. Now, however, about half of venture capital funding is in (predominantly) early stage technology. The venture capital industry in the U.K. is growing, partly due to Government encouragement, and partly because the internet breaks down big business – it has a beneficial effect on speed to market. It now knows no national boundaries. New types of venture capital are emerging e.g. incubators are having an impact, and this is due to personal wealth and international investors. The regulators want to ensure that venture capitalists adhere to the right professional standards."[3]

In the last decade, the U.K. venture capital scene has changed a lot, and now, instead of there being an aversion to technology involvement, between a third and a quarter of new fund allocation is to the technology sector. To illustrate, in the Cambridge area alone, there are over 1,500 young, small high-technology companies, all anxiously seeking to secure venture capital funding, with varying degrees of success. Corresponding to this new enthusiasm for involvement by venture capitalists in a more risky type of investment deal, has been a development in their methods and practice. The broader purpose of this article is to explore this development.

3. RISK IN HIGH TECHNOLOGY VENTURES

New high-technology ventures are troublesome business propositions. Certainly, they involve high 'business risks' (caused by an uncertain competitive environment) and high 'agency risks' (caused by incomplete alignment of investor and investee interests). They also, singularly, involve high 'innovation risk' (caused by ignorance of what value new technology can create, and when). The first two, to some extent, and the last, to an almost exclusive extent, are not amenable to standard methods of risk appraisal. These appeal to the so-called 'frequency limit principle',[4] which only holds under unchanged conditions. However, when one is dealing with essentially new events (of which an innovation is an example) the notion of frequency limit becomes irrelevant, as the essence of innovation is that conditions have changed. Thus in the case of true 'innovation risk', there is no statistical track record to which one can appeal for assessing the riskiness of completely new technologies. The computation of actuarial risk, based on mathematical expectations, defined on a probability density function, is therefore just not possible, as it is in Value at Risk (VaR) contexts (Webb, 1998).

Instead, subjective appraisal of risk is necessary. This may appeal to a variety of forms of evidence, like the best available yardstick comparisons (e.g. related technologies), or expert evaluations made by technology specialists (e.g. technology foresight consultants). Then, assigning new technologies to risk classes (e.g. high, medium, low) may be the best that can be done, though the subjective (rather than statistical) assigning of numerical probabilities, with the usual properties, is also possible.

In Murray and Lott (1995) it is suggested that U.K. investors are reluctant to back new technology-based firms. These authors believe that high-technology investments make more demands on risk management capabilities than other investments (see also Murray, 1995). As a consequence, higher (risk adjusted) IRR thresholds are set for investments in new technology projects, than for investments elsewhere. That is, a risk premium (RP) is set to compensate investors for bearing additional risk (Brigham, 1992, Ch.4). Thus hurdle rates of return as high as 40%, or even more, can be set. It seems U.K. investors use, at least, different (and perhaps more exacting) criteria in investment appraisal than do their U.S. counterparts. Such conduct is supported by the evidence that they allocate proportionally far less (perhaps as little as a third) venture capital finance to new technology-based firms, compared to U.S. investors.

4. RESEARCH METHODOLOGY

For the purposes of this article, the three initial stages of our research involved: (a) unstructured, preliminary, qualitative field work; (b) the determining of an appropriate sampling frame for selecting our sample of venture capitalists; and (c) the designing of an administered questionnaire schedule, suitable for face-to-face interviews with investors, based on the extant risk and venture capital literature. The final, and substantive stage of the research involved interviews with venture capitalists, in the field, working through the agenda of the questionnaire schedule, with one researcher as interviewer, and the other as rapporteur. A detailed consideration of how these stages were undertaken would be too extensive to report upon here, so the treatment below will be brief.

We derived early benefits from making our first approach to the institutions mentioned above, like the BVCA and 3i. The acceptance by institutions like the BVCA and 3i of the legitimacy of what we aimed to do, made them valuable 'high communicators' in the network of U.K. venture capitalists. In seeking 'ports of access' to the field, we also benefited from both our previous acquaintance with major players in the U.K. venture capital world, and our earlier success in making contact with targeted individuals and eliciting their co-operation. Investors were selected by constructing a list, based on data from the VCR Guide (2000), of those U.K. investors who were active in high-technology deals. We then selected a random sample from this list.

The instrument with which we investigated the risk handling of investors was, in a technical sense, an administered questionnaire of the semi-structured interview format. Use of this involved working through an eight point agenda, of which respondents (viz. the investors) had prior notice. Previous work on risk appraisal in a venture capital context (Fiet, 1995), using U.S. data, has used a postal questionnaire. Although this has convenience and economy to recommend it, our intention was that a custom designed questionnaire should be administered in face-to-face interviews with investors (and, at later point, investees).[5] It was felt that the use of face-to-face interviews has major advantages over the postal questionnaire method, see also Sapienza (1989). It avoids a variety of serious non-response biases, particularly on the venture capital side, and also facilitates a more ambitious and thorough investigation of how types of risk are handled.

In our instrumentation for analysing risk management, a considerably more refined approach is possible, compared to those available using postal surveys. Probably most important is the avoidance, wherever possible, of the more technical terms of risk analysis in the questionnaire itself, a weakness of previous work in this area. Such specialist terms (e.g. 'degree of risk aversion') have many ramifications, few, if any, of which are likely to be familiar to the respondent.[6] An appropriately designed instrument should seek to elicit data on the subject matter with no requirement that the respondent understands the disciplinary base of the investigation. On the other hand, one is frequently dealing with relatively sophisticated business personnel in interview contexts, many of whom are trained in economics, accountancy and cognate areas, so the depth of discussion can be quite considerable. Both concrete data on risk handling should be gathered, as well as attitudinal data. For example, one is interested in both concrete facts like 'which variables are used in sensitivity analysis?', and also in attitudinal variables like 'how important is staff morale to risk appraisal?'

A significant aspect of the novelty of such research work is embodied within the questionnaire design itself. Such work should be 'state of the art', in terms of reflecting the current literature, yet free of any assumption that the respondent is familiar with the terms of reference of the enquiry. With the exception of work by Ruhnka and Young (1991), little attention has been paid to the analysis of risk management in venture capital contexts, so there is not much to guide us in the explicit format of our instrumentation. This article aims to help to remedy this deficiency in the literature. Reid (1998) provides the base from which this further work is undertaken. In approaching the problem of designing new instrumentation, the authors were able to draw on considerable prior experience in prototyping, piloting and constructing successful administered and semi-structured interview schedules (Reid, 1993, 1998; Smith, 1997).

Also of relevance to instrument design is the distinction between 'hard' and 'soft' analysis.[7] Both types are relevant to our work. For example, we ask the investor what variables are used in the sensitivity analysis she applies to her model of the business. This is a type of 'hard' analysis. We also ask the investors how she goes about determining a 'reference point' or 'base case' of what she expects to happen. This is a type of 'soft' analysis. As in previous work by the authors on risk in the U.K. venture capital industry, we aim to combine such 'hard' and 'soft' analysis, see Reid, Terry and Smith (1997).

5. RESULTS

The instrument developed for gathering information from investors was a semi-structured questionnaire. This took investors through an agenda which covered: risk premia; investment time horizon; sensitivity analysis; expected values; predicting cash flows; financial modelling; decision making; and qualitative appraisal. Over eighty numerical responses, and over forty qualitative (text) responses were generated by every interview which used this instrument.

Given editorial space limitation on the length of our article, we have focused on the first three agenda headings, Risk Premia, Investment Time Horizon, and Sensitivity Analysis. As appropriate, though, we have also drawn on evidence appearing under later headings, when such cross-referencing makes analytical sense. This article therefore does not fully reflect the richness of the full evidence, but there are such notable features of the evidence gathered under the early agenda items, that they seem well worth reporting in their own right. As an overarching principle, we have tried, wherever possible, to refer to the general categories of 'agency risk', 'business risk' and 'innovation risk'.

5.1. Risk Premia.

A risk premium is defined in our schedule as the additional return which an investment must offer, to compensate investors for accepting the additional risk. A clear majority, 84% of the respondents, said that they did attach risk premia to their discount rates. However, when they did so, the cost of capital was not usually used as a reference point. Indeed, only 33% used the cost of capital as a reference point. On the face of it, this seems surprising. One might argue that investors might take the cost of capital as defining a minimum acceptable rate of return, in ideal conditions, on top of which one constructs a margin to reflect departures from the ideal. The reason for not proceeding in this way was interesting. It was common for investors to suggest that they ensured there was considerable 'head room' in the risk management plan. In effect, the margins set were high, reflecting ignorance of the future success of the technology, and high risk. Fine movements in the cost of capital had little leverage on this 'head room'.

The actual methods used in determining risk premia varied, but the following explanation is quite typical: "We do it on the basis of IRR calculations. Early-stage technology companies require a higher rate of return . . . you're looking at about 60% per annum. We double the IRR because we're in a high risk sector". This quote anticipates our analysis of the use of the idea of a risk class by investors. It also makes the point clearly that when the 'innovation risk' is high, and compounded with early stage involvement uncertainties, the required rates of return reflect very high risk premia.

In the interview schedule, risk classes were defined as categories of similar degrees of risk, into which projects can be grouped for effective risk management. Investors were asked if they recognised investment opportunities as lying in risk classes, and if they used such classes for setting risk premia. Nearly all investors (95%) identified their investments as lying in risk classes, so defined. A common response was "we would do it by stage of investment". Another was "we'd look at risks in specific areas – for example, technology, market and manager – people – risk". The last quote is particularly telling, making reference, in effect, to our chosen three risk categories viz. 'innovation risk', 'business risk', and 'agency risk'.

This way of proceeding is borne out by the responses to an additional, attitudinal question (see results in Fig. 1). This required investors to refer to their experience of the high technology area. It asked them to assess, on a six point Likert scale (Oppenheim, 1992, Ch. 11), from low = 0 to high = 5, how risky they thought certain investment types were. This scale was our principal device for converting attitude to risk into a numerical ranking. On our interview

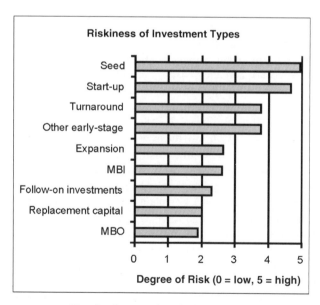

Fig. 1.   Investors' Attitudes to Risk.

schedule, these types were ordered as follows: seed, start-up, other early stage, expansion, MBO, MBI, turnaround, replacement, follow-on. Average scores, for the perceived risk of each investment type, are indicated by the length of the horizontal bars in Fig. 1. They indicate the average attitude to risk, across investment types, for our sample of investors.[8]

Seed-corn, start-up, and turnaround were ranked by investors as being the three most risky investment involvements, in that order. Why is this so? It is suggested by theories of venture capital investment (e.g. Chan, 1983; Chan et al., 1990) and of entrepreneurial firms (e.g. Jovanovic, 1982; Frank, 1988), both of which emphasise the importance of market experience. The entrepreneur learns to run her firm better by the hands-on experience of doing it, and her learning curve can be quite steep. In the start-up phase, the learning process has scarcely begun, and the 'raw' entrepreneur is least equipped to handle unexpected shocks to the firm. Further, the investor has little evidence to go on. This is true both of his evaluating the fitness of the entrepreneur as an owner-manager, and of his lack of experience in controlling the relationship in a way which aligns her interests with his own. Therefore agency risk is high. As a consequence, seed-corn and start-up are perceived to be especially risky. Turnaround also appears to be high in risk. This is because it is usually associated with poor performance of a firm early in its life-cycle. It therefore needs radical re-structuring in order to improve its performance.[9]

The converse side of the coin, is that the MBO is seen to be by far the safest investment type, involving, as it does, ample evidence of what the company can do, and who will run it. Logically, the MBI, which involves a bit more of a 'shot in the dark', in the sense of bringing in a new team, which may not be 'experience rated', is ranked as being more risky than the MBO. Follow-on investment had a mixed response. On average, it ended up having a fairly low perceived risk. But, as several investors observed, 'it all depends on the follow-on'. That is to say, follow-on is not intrinsically less risky than other investment types. It is more accurate to say that risky follow-on opportunities will tend to be rejected by investors. A similar remark was also made about replacement capital, which although being appraised as having relatively low risk (on average) was thought to be potentially highly risky, in certain critical replacement situations.

Following some discussion in the interviews about the risk-return relationship (not reported here), investors were then asked to rank the importance (on a six point scale of 0 = low to 5 = high) of any of many factors which had a potential impact on their appraisal of the riskiness of an investment opportunity. We listed fifteen such factors for them to consider. The list included: market opportunities, the global environment, the local environment, the quality of the proposal, the management model, the business model, the sales model, the scale of the business, and so on. They were presented in the above order in our interview schedule. The results from this part of our enquiry are given in Fig. 2. The length of a bar indicates the average, across of investors, of the perceived importance of these fifteen factors in risk appraisal. It will be noted that this rank order by importance is very different from the rank order of factors listed in our interview schedule.

We see from Fig. 2 that the management team was thought to be, on average, the most important factor (first ranked) to investors in their risk appraisal of an

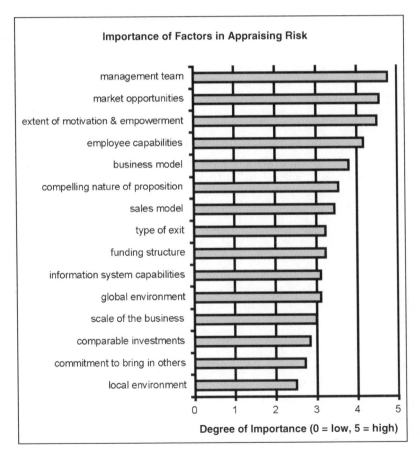

Fig. 2. Most Important Factors in Risk Appraisal.

investment opportunity. Other related factors of importance were: the extent of
motivation and empowerment (third) within the potential investee company;
and employee capabilities (fourth). This suggests that agency risk comes high
in the overall risk appraisal. Broadly speaking, agency risk arises from the
operation of superior/subordinate relations between people within a firm.
The management team drives the direction of the firm, but the success or
otherwise of their actions depends on their skills, in the face of incomplete
information and uncertainty, and on the compliance of the employees with
managers' wishes. Managers need to be able to disentangle chance variations
in pay-offs from variations due to employees' actions.

In turn, there is an agency relationship between the investor, as principal,
and the investee (owner-manager), as agent, involving similar forces (see Reid,
1996, 1998, 1999).[10] If the management in place in the investee firm were not
thought to be appropriate, then the investor would often reserve the right to
make changes as and when necessary, Chan et al. (1990). In the post-investment
phase, the prospect of moral hazard might arise in the relationship between
investor (as principal) and the investee (as agent). One way of attenuating
the effect, which arises from the desire of the investee to push all the risk on
to the investor, post-investment, is to extend the frequency and range of
information about investee activity that the investor requires, see Mitchell, Reid
and Terry (1995, 1997, 1999). Our evidence suggests intense post-investment
scrutiny to manage 'agency risk'. Under the interview agenda heading of
'predicting cash flow' 72% of investors said they modelled inter-relationships
between variables. Further, 95% then used these models for planning. As one
investor put it: "We do a lot of investment monitoring – especially about where
the funds are investing. We're always working with the managers very closely.
We measure profit against initial financial projections." Such models were used
by 83% of investors to estimate the future profitability of the firm; and of these,
all used it to influence the firm's long-run strategy. In pursuing the modelling
side, investor and investee often worked together. As another investor put it:
"The assumptions you input to produce the model are assumptions about how
the business will run. It's an interactive process." All this suggests an intense
desire to attenuate agency risk.

Also of note in Fig. 2 are the relatively high importance, for risk appraisal,
of factors like: market opportunities (second); the business model (fifth); the
quality of the proposal (sixth); and the sales model (seventh). All these factors
relate to 'business risk', which arises from the uncertainty of market opportunities, and, therefore from the uncertain future value of the business. Further
risk elements of this sort arise from the relatively untested ability of the investee
(as compared to rivals) to exploit these market opportunities, in the face of

competitive pressure. The business and sales models, and the quality of the proposal should help the investor to gauge how strong the investee firm will be when competing head-to-head with rivals. These factors, along with the analysis of market opportunities, will show how well adapted the investee firm will be to action-reaction effects, of an oligopolistic nature, in the market place.

In undertaking analysis which relates to the 'business risk', the use of 'sensitivity analysis', as dealt with third in our interview agenda, is also important. As one investor put it: "From market assessment you can work out what a reasonable revenue and cost line would be. Management as a whole does the market analysis and we take a top down approach. We tend to be quite rigorous in doing a careful analysis of the market." That is, the handling of 'business risk' involves an interaction between investee and investor, as in the handling of 'agency risk'. In a similar vein (as we discovered while posing questions under the 'cash flow' interview agenda heading) the desirability of having a positive interaction between investor and investee, in order to handle 'business risk' better, is well recognised. This is especialy so of downside risk. A typical investor's comment reflecting this is: "What you try and handle is your response to the 'catastrophic' things when they come up. There's a lot you can do to help the company cope with what might happen. You might put two non-executive directors on the Board instead of one, for example."

To conclude: that 'agency risk' (the management side) and 'business risk' (the market side) are important, is evident from the responses given in Fig. 2. It is also backed up by qualitative evidence. Typical of the comments made by investors was the following, which was also uttered when we were making enquiry under the 'cash flow' part of the interview agenda: "The key things for us are the management team and the market – hopefully a global market".

5.2. Investment Time Horizon

The section of the interview schedule (the second) that dealt with investment time horizon started with a definition. It defined the payback period as 'the length of time it takes to recover the initial cash outlay on an investment from its cash flow returns'. Just over half (53%) of investors said that they took account of payback periods in their investment decisions. On average, they would be looking for their investment to pay back within thirty-two to fifty-one months. Time horizons, which were generally thought to be important, tended to be mentioned in the context of stage and/or technology. One investor explained his long time horizon by saying he adopted it: "because it's early-stage and it often takes that long before it's successful and proving itself. Even if it floats, you're often locked in for one or two years". Another investor considered the issue of time horizon and technology together, explaining his approach by saying: "we expect money back in year 6, 7 or 8. If you had an early-stage technology company you could probably exit in a year to 18 months. But we believe that technology investments will have a longer time horizon and need more money – maybe two to three years to payback."

'Innovation risk' was often thought to be very high, cf. Murray and Lott (1995). Eighty four percent of investors said they would back off if the investment were perceived to be too risky or (usually an equivalent notion) too complex. Complexity was often interpreted as 'too novel a technology to be able to understand its potential'. As one investor put it, he backed off from an investment opportunity "when we can't comfortably model it, and get our heads round about where the business is going to go."

One method which investors used in dealing with high 'innovation risk' was to scrutinise the profile of returns, and modify investment conduct in the light of its shape. As one investor put it: "If we saw a return in 18–24 months we'd want to double or triple the investment. In 6 years we'd want 10 times – we have to see the capacity to multiply our investment." Further, if there were an element of investment 'lock-in' to the technology, a higher return would be expected. Reflecting this, another investor said: "If we're going to be in there for longer we'd be looking for a better multiple. From the outset, if you were expecting to be in there longer, you would be expecting a higher multiple." Under the seventh agenda heading of 'decision making' in the interview schedule, a related type of reference was made to timing issues. A rational way to handle 'technology risk', could be to defer investing, and to wait and see where the technology is going. Exemplifying this approach was the investor who said: "take the Internet – the people who held back and looked at the market will have made a sound decision." A similar comment by another investor, in the same context, was: "We might be looking at a possible invest-ment which we would put on hold until we'd had a peer review of the individual and the research he intends to use."[11]

5.3. Sensitivity Analysis

In the interviews with investors, the use of 'sensitivity analysis' was explored under our third agenda heading. It was defined by saying that it 'tests how a project's expected outcome (e.g. NPV, IRR) changes in response to changes in project variables (e.g. sales, price). It aims to identify the variables which have most effect on the expected outcome'. Our interest was in how models used to evaluate the potential value of risky high technology investments were subjected to tests of robustness. We found from our enquiries into modelling (the sixth agenda item) that 90% of investors constructed an explicit model of the firm, and this was generally spreadsheet-based. Essentially, we wanted to know how sensitive these models were: to the assumptions used; and to the values of key parameters. The initial question we asked investors was: how important is use of sensitivity analysis to the investment decision. Again, 'importance' was calibrated using a six point Likert scale (from $0 =$ irrelevant, $1 =$ unimportant to $5 =$ very important). The average value of responses to this question, across all investors, was 3.6. That is to say, sensitivity analysis was typically perceived to be important.

Investors were also asked how widely they let variables range in their sensitivity analyses. We found that such variables were allowed to range from between 15% to 50%, with an average range adopted of 34%.[12] In other words, quite severe tests of robustness were implied by the variations which investors typically imposed in their sensitivity analyses. This suggests a determination to 'flush out' vulnerability to risk factors. There was keen awareness that sensitivity analysis was necessary for checking the robustness of the models used. Thus one investor said: "We would look at reasonably wide variation. We know from experience that people don't always get their forecasts right." Elsewhere (in the part of the interview concerned with modelling) it was made clear that sensitivity analysis was put to other uses as well, of which scenario analysis was important. One investor suggested it was not that any faith was put in specific predictions from models, but rather that: "It's more the scenarios – how they would propose to do it. Then we tear it apart and propose a different model". In a similar, but less radical way, another investor said: "It's scenario-based. Maybe a downside case, and sometimes an upside case."

We also asked investors what variables they used in their sensitivity analyses. Here, to judge by our qualitative responses, choice of variables could vary widely. This seemed to depend on the type of market in which the investee firm was active, and on the 'technological intensity' of their firm. One brief reply, emphasising 'business risk' was from an investor who said: "Revenue – it's almost all top line. We sensitise and push it through. Time horizon. Costs are not normally the key driver as they tend to follow the revenue." Another investor gave a more detailed reply, emphasising 'innovation risk', when asked what variables were used in sensitivity analysis. This investor said that what counted was: "Whether or not the technology or drug either succeeds in getting to market or to the suitable stage at which we would exit. I guess the technology can either succeed 'to plan', take longer, or fail. The main sensitivity is: what would happen if it failed? We could factor it in, taking longer. If it hits problems and takes longer, it probably means it will need more money. Do you raise more money and dilute what you put in at the beginning?"

Finally, investors were asked if they constructed their sensitivity analyses around a 'reference point'. There was general assent to this, with 89% of investors saying that they performed the sensitivity analysis around a reference point, or 'base case'. However, the methods of constructing base cases were diverse, to judge by the qualitative evidence we gathered on this issue. They seemed to reflect different 'house styles' or 'investment philosophies'. This was partly dependent on the technology or the sector which the investor usually handled. One detailed response was as follows: "Base case? From market assessment, you can work out what a reasonable revenue and cost line would be. Management as a whole does the market analysis, and we take a top down approach. We tend to be quite rigorous in doing a careful analysis of the market. Early-stage, financial analysis is not the driver. The most crucial work we do is commercial analysis."

This quote emphasised the importance of managing both 'business risk' and 'agency risk'. Another quote, a reply by a different investor to the same enquiry, emphasised 'business risk' and 'innovation risk'. When asked what factors were taken into account in constructing the 'base case', he said: "Some of the issues we have discussed – the complexity of the technology, the extent to which we have a clear field through intellectual property, the extent to which other people have products which could compete. We wouldn't expect to get into areas where there was just an incremental improvement. We want a novel technology. There's a downside of getting that wrong. (Interviewer interjection, saying: "Do you refer here to a radical technological change?"). It's not a term we use, but we probably would, if we were economists." These nuggets of qualitative evidence display well how, in practice, all three categories of our categories of risk are managed, 'business risk', 'agency risk' and 'innovation risk'.

6. CONCLUSION

The purpose of this article has been to introduce new evidence on the risk appraisal of high technology new ventures in the U.K. Here, we focussed on the venture capital investor. The article developed the evidence under the headings of risk premia, investment time horizon, and sensitivity analysis. These headings corresponded to those used in a semi-structured interview, for face-to-face discussions with investors. The framework of our analysis involved a decomposition of total risk into 'business risk', 'agency risk' and 'innovation risk'. This framework was confronted with both quantitative and qualitative evidence. Quantitative evidence included the calibration of investors' attitudes to risk for various investment types, and measures of the key factors in investors' risk appraisal procedures. Qualitative evidence included responses by investors under specific agenda items, concerning matters like market assessment, technology appraisal, and robustness of models. We found that this framework adopted, of three risk classes, generally encompassed the evidence found under the main agenda heading.

ACKNOWLEDGMENTS

This research has enjoyed the support of the Research Foundation of the Chartered Institute of Management Accountants (CIMA), to whom grateful acknowledgement is made. This article was prepared for the Workshop on Performance Measurement and Management Control, EDHEC School of Management, Nice, October 2001. We are grateful to delegates attending that workshop for useful discussion of issues arising from our work, both during the presentation, and afterwards. We also are grateful to the British Academy for providing some sponsorship which helped the authors attend the meeting. Finally, we should thank the numerous investors, and related personnel in the U.K. venture capital industry, who so generously allocated some of their scarce time to discussions with us. The authors remain responsible for all the views expressed in this article, including any errors of omission or commission that it may contain.

NOTES

1. In the vivid picture drawn of the U.K. venture capital industry by Anthea Masey (1993, p. 11) in *The Adventurers*, this aversion to the 'white coated boffin with a bright idea' is palpable. It is said that finance for them is 'extremely hard to obtain and few venture capitalists specialise in this area, as many frustrated scientists can confirm'.
2. Meeting of 14 June 2000.
3. Meeting of 14 June 2000.
4. According to which, if event A occurs a times in n trials, then the probability of A, denoted P(A), is the limit of the ratio (a/n) as n tends to infinity. Trials must increase under unchanged conditions.
5. This further work is now ongoing, with support from the Carnegie Trust.
6. For example, informal discussion will often confuse relatively low risk aversion (compared to other investors) with risk loving behaviour. This does not mean that many investors have convex Friedman-Savage utility functions!
7. This distinction is also sometimes expressed as being between 'quantitative' and 'qualitative' analysis.
8. It will be noted that this average rank ordering differs in major ways from the ordering of investment types in the interview schedule.
9. The importance of learning in venture capital relations has also been emphasised by Gompers and Lerner (1999), with especial focus on the upstream investor.
10. See Schertler (2000) for a recent survey of issues of this sort.

11. In this context, it should be noted that investors often commissioned third party due diligence on the technology of an investee.

12. Typically, as measured from a base value. See below for how this was determined.

REFERENCES

Brigham, E. F. (1992). *Fundamentals of Financial Management* (6th ed.). Orlando, Fl: The Dryden Press.

Bygrave, W. D., & Timmons, J. (1992). *Venture Capital at the Crossroads*. Boston, Mass: Harvard Business School Press.

Chan, Y. -S. (1983). On the Positive Role of Financial Intermediation in the Allocation of Venture Capital in a Market with Imperfect Information. *The Journal of Finance, 38*(5), 1543–1568.

Chan, Y. -S., Siegel, D., & Thakor, A. V. (1990). Learning, Corporate Control and the Performance Requirements in Venture Capital Contracts. *International Economic Review, 31*(2), 1543–1581.

Fiet, J. O. (1995) Risk Avoidance Strategies in Venture Capital Markets. *Journal of Management Studies, 32*, 551–574.

Frank, M. Z. (1988). An intertemporal model of industry exit. *Quarterly Journal of Economics, 103*, 333–344.

Gompers, P., & Lerner, J. (1999). An analysis of compensation in U.S. venture capital partnerships. *Journal of Financial Economics, 51*(3), 3–44.

Jovanovic, B. (1982). Selection and Evolution of Industry. *Econometrica, 50*, 649–670.

Masey, A. (1993). *The Adventurers: A Year in the Life of a Venture Capital House*. London: BBC Books.

Mitchell, F., Reid, G. C., & Terry, N. G. (1992). Some agency aspects of venture capital investment behaviour. Working Paper. University of Edinburgh: Centre for Financial Markets Research.

Mitchell, F., Reid, G. C., & Terry, N. (1995). Post-Investment Demand for Accounting Information by Venture Capitalists. *Accounting and Business Research, 25*(99), 186–196.

Mitchell, F., Reid, G. C., & Terry, N. (1997). Venture Capital Supply and Accounting Information System Development. *Entrepreneurship Theory and Practice, Summer*, 45–62.

Mitchell, F., Reid, G. C., & Terry, N. (1999). Accounting information system development and the supply of venture capital. In: M. Wright & K. Robbie (Eds), *Management Buyouts and Venture Capital: Into the Next Millennium* (Chapter 12, pp. 263–279). Cheltenham, U.K.: Edward Elgar.

Murray, G. (1995). Managing investors' risk in venture capital-financed new technology-based firms. Article presented to the ESRC conference on Risk in Organisational Settings, The White House, London, mimeo.

Murray, G., & Lott, J. (1995). Have U.K. Venture Capitalists a Bias Against Investment in New Technology-Based Firms? *Research Policy, 24*, 283–299.

Oppenheim, A. N. (1992). *Questionnaire Design, Interviewing, and Attitude Measurement* (2nd ed.). London: Pinter.

Reid, G. C. (1993). *Small Business Enterprise*. London: Routledge.

Reid, G. C. (1996). Fast Growing Small Entrepreneurial Firms and their Venture Capital Backers: an Applied Principal-Agent Analysis. *Small Business Economics, 8*, 1–14.

Reid, G. C. (1998). *Venture Capital Investment: an Agency Analysis of Practice*. London: Routledge.

Reid, G. C. (1999). The Application of Principal-Agent Methods to Investor-Investee Relations in the U.K. Venture Capital Industry. *Venture Capital, 1*(4), 1–18.

Reid, G. C., Terry, N. G., & Smith, J. A. (1997). Risk Management in Venture Capital Investor-Investee Relations. *European Journal of Finance, 3*(1), 27–47.

Ruhnka, J. C., & Young, J. E. (1991). Some Hypotheses about Risk in Venture Capital Investing. *Journal of Business Venturing, 6*, 115–133.

Sapienza, H. J. (1989). Variations in venture capitalist-entrepreneur relations: antecedents and consequences. Unpublished doctoral dissertation, University of Maryland at College Park. UMI Dissertation Services, Ann Arbor, Michigan.

Schertler, A. (2000). Venture Capital Contracts: A Survey of the Recent Literature. Keil Working Paper, No. 1017.

Sekaran, U. (1992). *Research Methods for Business: a skill building approach* (2nd ed.). New York: Wiley.

Smith, J. A. (1997). Small business strategy: an empirical analysis of the experience of new Scottish firms. Unpublished doctoral dissertation, University of Abertay, Dundee, Economics Division.

VCR Guide (2000). *The Venture Capital Report Directory 2000/01: private equity and venture capital in the U.K. and Europe*. London: Financial Times/Prentice Hall (Pearson Education).

Webb, N. (1998). An introduction to the technology of risk. In: C. Alexander (Ed.) *Risk Management and Analysis* (Vol. 1): *Measuring and Modelling Financial Risk* (Chapter 6). New York: John Wiley.

Wilson, J. W. (1985). *The New Venturers: Inside the High-Stakes World of Venture Capital*. Reaing, MA: Addison-Wesley.

Wright, M., & Robbie, K. (Eds) (1999). *Management Buy-Outs and Venture Capital: into the next Millennium*. Cheltenham, U.K.: Edward Elgar.